Understanding the Poverty Impact of the Global Financial Crisis in Latin America and the Caribbean

DIRECTIONS IN DEVELOPMENT
Human Development

Understanding the Poverty Impact of the Global Financial Crisis in Latin America and the Caribbean

Margaret Grosh, Maurizio Bussolo, and Samuel Freije, Editors

THE WORLD BANK
Washington, D.C.

ISBN (paper): 978-1-4648-0241-6
ISBN (electronic): 978-1-4648-0243-0
DOI: 10.1596/978-1-4648-0241-6

Cover art: Alejandro Espinosa Mejía, Son Ideas Design Firm. Used with permission. Further permission required for reuse.
Cover design: Debra Naylor, Naylor Design, Inc.

Library of Congress Cataloging-in-Publication Data
Understanding the poverty impact of the global financial crisis in Latin America and the Caribbean / Margaret Grosh, Maurizio Bussolo, and Samuel Freije, editors.
    1 online resource. — (Directions in development)
    Includes bibliographical references.
ISBN 978-1-4648-0241-6 (alk.) — ISBN 978-1-4648-0243-0 (ebook)
    1. Poverty—Latin America. 2. Poverty—Caribbean Area. 3. Global Financial Crisis, 2008-2009.
4. Latin America—Economic conditions—21st century. 5. Caribbean Area—Economic conditions—21st century. I. Grosh, Margaret E. II. Bussolo, Maurizio, 1964- III. Freije, Samuel. IV. World Bank.
    HC130.P6
    339.4'6098090511—dc23   201402067

Contents

Boxes

Figures

Maps

Tables

Understanding the Poverty Impact of the Global Financial Crisis in Latin America and the Caribbean
http://dx.doi.org/10.1596/978-1-4648-0241-6

Foreword

Crisis and poverty have long been linked in Latin America and indeed around the world. Countries that are prone to macroeconomic and financial crises tend to be poorer, and crisis episodes produce significant spikes in poverty rates. This study adds to a venerable and rather gloomy tradition of work trying to parse the impacts and pathways that run from financial collapse in banking centers to poverty in the villages of Latin America.

The authors begin by documenting the effects of the 2008–09 global financial crisis on poverty in Latin America and the Caribbean. They sketch the story of the macro crisis, looking at growth, trade, monetary policy, and fiscal balances using national data for 28 countries. They then describe and decompose in detail the effects of the crisis on poverty, on the basis of data from comparable household budget surveys for Argentina, Brazil, Chile, Colombia, Costa Rica, the Dominican Republic, Ecuador, El Salvador, Mexico, Paraguay, Peru, and Uruguay; and labor force surveys for Argentina, Brazil, Chile, Colombia, Ecuador, Mexico, Peru, and Uruguay. Their study then moves to macro-micro modeling of crisis and no-crisis scenarios for Brazil and Mexico to isolate the impacts of the crisis from other contemporaneous changes. Finally, the authors bring to bear new data on social protection expenditures for Argentina, Brazil, Chile, Colombia, Ecuador, El Salvador, Honduras, Mexico, Peru, and Uruguay; and provide program-specific details of the social protection policy responses for these countries and more.

This examination of the recent crisis is enriched by the availability of a large amount of data from diverse sources: national accounts, household surveys, national budgets, and the administrators of social protection programs. These data provide an unusual and strong basis for understanding the impacts of the crisis, although they add some puzzles where the different perspectives do not fully align.

This study confirms and quantifies many of the sobering links between crisis and poverty, but it also shows how powerful good policy in stable times is in attenuating those links. It thus underscores the need for sound growth policies, good macro prudential care, fiscal balance, low debt, reasonably flexible exchange rates, and the like to help prevent and manage crises. It equally shows how effective social protection responses built on adequate existing programs can be.

This work is of interest throughout the region and beyond. With its rich, careful analysis, it will serve as a long-lived reference on the poverty consequences of economic downturns caused by external factors. Meanwhile, it reinforces two policy agendas currently at the forefront of the policy debate in the region: re-establishing and consolidating the macro fundamentals that helped the region weather the crisis and continuing to build social protection systems that not only enhance equality of opportunity but also increase resilience to shocks.

Augusto de la Torre
Chief Economist
Latin America and the Caribbean Region
The World Bank

Understanding the Poverty Impact of the Global Financial Crisis in Latin America and the Caribbean
http://dx.doi.org/10.1596/978-1-4648-0241-6

Acknowledgments

This study was produced as a regional study under the Chief Economist's Office in the Latin American and the Caribbean Vice Presidency of the World Bank. The study was co-led by Margaret Grosh, Human Development Department for Latin America and the Caribbean (LCSHD); Samuel Freije, Poverty and Gender Unit for Latin America and the Caribbean (LCSPP); and Maurizio Bussolo, Development Prospects Group (DECPG). They were aided by a core team composed of Anna Fruttero, Social Protection Unit for Latin America and the Caribbean (LCSHS); Rafael E. de Hoyos, Education Unit for Latin America and the Caribbean (LCSHE); and Cristina Savescu, DECPG.

We depended on a much larger team for the empirical analysis. Gabriel Facchini Palma produced most of the estimates for the chapters on poverty and labor. Andrés Casteñeda Aguilar, Maria Dávalos, Rebecca Fair, and Viviana San Felice, at the World Bank, assisted in earlier drafts. The computable general equilibrium models for chapter 5 were constructed by Peter Dixon, Maureen Rimmer, and George Verikios at Monash University, Canberra. Camilo Bohorquez helped with the data collection and analysis, and Israel Osorio-Rodarte carried out the microsimulations for chapter 5. Maria Laura Oliveri and then Paula Cerutti were the mavens of the social protection expenditure database and Claudia Rodriguez the maven of the ASPIRE database. Gabriel Barrientos, Lerick Kebeck, and Anna Mousakova assisted in the document formatting. Sabra Bissette Ledent edited the book.

Overall supervision was provided by Augusto de la Torre and the series managers—Tito Cordella, Francisco Ferreira, and Daniel Lederman—in their turns.

Helpful comments, peer review, or detailed inputs were provided by João Pedro Azevedo, Lucy Bassett, Louise Cord, Aline Coudouel, Theresa Jones, Silvana Kostenbaum, Mabel Martinez, Denis Medvedev, Edmundo Murrugarra, Mansoora Rashid, Gonzalo Reyes, Helena Ribe, Concepción Steta, Lucia Solbes, and Asha Williams; and by participants in a series of seminars in the LCSHD, LCSHS, and LCSPP units at the World Bank, and at the IZA Conference "The Effects of the Economic Crisis on the Labor Market, Unemployment and Income Distribution" held in Bonn, Germany, February 21–22, 2013. Peer reviewers at the concept note stage were Ravi Kanbur, Ambar Narayan, Sergio Schmukler, and Hassan Zaman. Peer reviewers for the draft study were David Coady, Phillippe Leite, Julian Messina, Ambar Narayan, and Ana Revenga.

In addition to funding from the Chief Economist's Office, the study received significant support from LCSHD, LCSPP, and DECPG units at the World Bank and a grant from the Bank-Netherlands Partnership Program.

About the Authors

Maurizio Bussolo is the lead economist in the Chief Economist's Office for Europe and Central Asia. He led operational teams in the aftermath of the 2008–09 crisis that were advising governments in Latin America and the Caribbean on reforms to shield the most vulnerable in the population. He previously worked at the Organisation for Economic Co-operation and Development, the Overseas Development Institute in London, Fedesarrollo, and Los Andes University in Colombia. He has extensively published in peer-reviewed journals on trade, growth, poverty, and income distribution. He holds a PhD in economics from the University of Warwick.

Peter Dixon is a professor at the Centre of Policy Studies, Victoria University, Melbourne. Dixon is known internationally for his work in computable general equilibrium modeling. He is the co-developer of the ORANI and MONASH models of the Australian economy and the USAGE model of the U.S. economy. He has published about 200 articles and eight books. A Distinguished Fellow of the Economic Society of Australia, he holds a BEc from Monash University and a PhD from Harvard University.

Samuel Freije is the lead economist for Colombia and Mexico in the Poverty Reduction and Economic Management Sector of the World Bank. He is co-author of *World Development Report 2013: Jobs*. He is also an associate editor of *Economia, Journal of the Latin American Economic Association*. Before joining the World Bank, Samuel was associate professor in the Department of Economics at Universidad de las Americas, Puebla (2003–08) and at the Instituto de Estudios Superiores de Administracion, IESA, in Caracas (2001–03). He holds a PhD in labor economics from Cornell University.

Anna Fruttero is a senior economist with the Social Protection team in the Latin America and the Caribbean Region at the World Bank. She has been leading implementation and technical support of Bank projects in Brazil and the Dominican Republic, as well as analytical research on social protection programs and poverty in the Latin America and the Caribbean region. Most recently, she has co-authored several reports and papers on Brazil, focusing on aging, chronic poverty, and the impact of the 2008–09 global financial crisis and food crisis on poverty. She holds a PhD in economics from New York University.

Margaret Grosh is the lead economist for the World Bank's Latin America and the Caribbean Human Development Department. She has written, lectured, and advised extensively on social assistance programs, especially on targeting and cash transfer programs, globally and for Latin America. She has extensive experience with social protection for responding to a crisis and for improving equality of opportunity. Previously, she has led the team for social assistance in the World Bank's global Social Protection Department and, before that, the Living Standard Measurement Study in the Research Department. She holds a PhD in economics from Cornell University.

Rafael E. de Hoyos is a senior economist in the education unit for Latin America and the Caribbean of the World Bank. Previously, he was the chief of advisers to the underminister of education in Mexico. Before joining the underministry, he worked in the Development Economics Vice Presidency at the World Bank (2006–08), at the Judge Business School at the University of Cambridge (2005–06), and as a consultant for the United Nations Economic Commission for Latin America and the Caribbean in Mexico and at the United Nations World Institute for Development Economics Research in Finland. He holds a PhD in economics from the University of Cambridge.

Maria Laura Oliveri is a research fellow in the Inter-American Development Bank's Labor Markets and Social Security Unit. She previously worked as a junior professional associate in the World Bank's Latin America and the Caribbean Human Development Department and has undertaken consultancies for the International Labour Organization and the Argentinean Ministries of Economy and Health. She has experience with microdata analysis and has performed analysis on social protection topics in the Latin America region. She holds a BA in economics from Universidad de Buenos Aires and is a MA candidate in economics from Universidad Nacional de La Plata.

Maureen Rimmer is a professor at the Centre of Policy Studies, Victoria University, Melbourne. She is the author and co-author of 55 articles in mathematics and economics journals and edited volumes. She specializes in model development and application and is an author of numerous consultancy reports. She is the co-developer of the MONASH model of the Australian economy and the USAGE model of the U.S. economy. She has a PhD in mathematics and a master's in economics from La Trobe University.

Cristina Savescu is an economist in the Economic Policy Unit for Latin America and the Caribbean of the World Bank. Previously, she was an economist in the Development Economics Vice Presidency of the World Bank (2005–13). Before joining the World Bank, she was an economist at Standard and Poor's DRI and

Global Insight (2000–05) and an adjunct professor at Suffolk University. She holds an MSc in international economics from Suffolk University.

George Verikios is a senior research fellow at the Centre of Policy Studies, Victoria University, Melbourne. His main research interest is the application of computable general equilibrium modeling techniques to quantitative policy analysis. He has been involved in research projects analyzing a diverse range of issues, including multilateral services trade liberalization, the effects on income distribution of reforming Australian infrastructure industries, the effects of influenza pandemic and epidemics, and the effects of improved health on labor supply in Australia. He is the author and co-author of 17 articles in economics journals. He holds a PhD from the University of Western Australia.

Abbreviations

AFC	Asignaciones Familiares Contributivas (Contributory Family Allowance, Argentina)
ALMP	active labor market policy
ANEFE	Acuerdo Nacional en Favor de la Economía Familiar y el Empleo (National Agreement in Support of Households and Employment, Mexico)
APS	Aporte Previsional Solidario (Solidarity Contribution, Chile)
AUH	Asignación Universal por Hijo (Universal Child Allowance, Argentina)
BaU	business as usual
BDH	Bono de Desarrollo Humano (Human Development Grant, Ecuador)
BPC	Benefício de Prestação Continuada (Continuous Benefit, Brazil)
BSP	Pensión Solidaria Basica (Basic Solidarity Pension, Chile)
CASEN	Encuesta de Caracterización Socioeconómica Nacional (National Socioeconomic Characteristics Survey, Chile)
CCT	conditional cash transfer
CEDLAS	Centro de Estudios Distributivos Laborales y Sociales (Center for Distributive, Labor, and Social Studies, Argentina)
CES	constant elasticity of substitution
CET	constant elasticity of transformation
CGE	computable general equilibrium (model)
CONEVAL	El Consejo Nacional de Evaluación de la Política de Desarrollo Social (National Council for the Evaluation of Social Development Policy, Mexico)
DECPG	Development Prospects Group (World Bank)
ECH	Encuesta Contínua de Hogares (Continuous Household Survey, Uruguay)
EHPM	Encuesta de Hogares de Propósitos Múltiples (Multipurpose Household Survey, Costa Rica, El Salvador)
ENAHO	Encuesta Nacional de Hogares (National Household Survey, Peru)

ENEMDU	Encuesta de Empleo, Desempleo y Subempleo (Employment, Unemployment, and Underemployment Survey, Ecuador)
ENE/NENE	Encuesta Nacional de Empleo y Nueva Encuesta Nacional de Empleo (National Labor Survey and New National Labor Survey, Chile)
ENFT	Encuesta Nacional de Fuerza de Trabajo (National Labor Force Survey, Dominican Republic)
ENIGH	Encuesta Nacional de Ingresos y Gastos de los Hogares (National Household Income and Expenditure Survey, Mexico)
ENOE	Encuesta Nacional de Ocupación y Empleo (National Employment and Occupation Survey, Mexico)
EPE	Encuesta Permanente de Empleo (Permanent Employment Survey, Peru)
EPH	Encuesta Permanente de Hogares (Permanent Household Survey, Paraguay)
EPH-C	Encuesta Permanente de Hogares-Contínua (Continuous National Household Survey, Argentina)
FHIS	Fondo Hondureño de Inversión Social (Honduran Social Investment Fund)
GDP	gross domestic product
GEIH	Gran Encuesta Integrada de Hogares (Integrated Household Survey, Colombia)
GIC	growth incidence curve
ILO	International Labour Organization
IMF	International Monetary Fund
IMSS	Instituto Mexicano del Seguro Social (Mexican Institute of Social Security)
INDEC	El Instituto Nacional de Estadística y Censos (National Institute of Statistics and Census, Argentina)
INEGI	Instituto Nacional de Estadística y Geografía (National Institute of Statistics and Geography, Mexico)
LABLAC	Labor Database for Latin America and the Caribbean
LAC	Latin America and the Caribbean
LAV	linking aggregate variable
LCSPP	Poverty and Gender Unit for Latin America and the Caribbean (World Bank)
LCU	local currency unit
LES	linear expenditure system
NRAF	Nuevo Régimen de Asignaciones Familiares (New Family Allowances Scheme, Nicaragua)
OECD	Organisation for Economic Co-operation and Development

PAAZAP	Programa de Apoyo Alimentario en Zonas de Atención Prioritaria (Program for Food Assistance in Priority Areas, Mexico)
PAL	Programa de Asistencia Alimentaria (Program for Nutritional Assistance, Mexico)
PATI	Programa de Apoyo Temporal al Ingreso (Temporary Income Support Program, El Salvador)
PBS	Pensión Básica Solidaria (Basic Solidarity Pension, Chile)
PEM	Programa de Empleo Mínimo (Minimum Employment Program, Chile)
PET	Programa de Empleo Temporal (Program for Temporary Employment, Mexico)
PICE	Programa para Impulsar el Crecimiento y el Empleo (Program to Boost Growth and Employment, Mexico)
PINE	Programa Integral de Nutricion Escolar (Integral Program for School Nutrition, Nicaragua)
PME	Pesquisa Mensual de Emprego (Monthly Employment Survey, Brazil)
PNAD	Pesquisa Nacional por Amostra de Domicílios (National Household Survey, Brazil)
POJH	Programa de Ocupación para Jefes de Hogar (Program for Jobs for Heads of Household, Chile)
PPP	purchasing power parity
REPRO	Programa de Recuperación Productiva (Productive Recovery Program, Argentina)
SEDLAC	Socio-Economic Database for Latin America and the Caribbean
SUF	Subsidio Único Familiar (Unified Family Subsidy, Chile)
TFP	total factor productivity
UC	unemployment compensation
UCT	unconditional cash transfer
UI	unemployment insurance
UISA	unemployment insurance savings account

CHAPTER 1

Overview

Margaret Grosh, Maurizio Bussolo, Samuel Freije, Anna Fruttero, Rafael de Hoyos, and Cristina Savescu

Any time there is an economic crisis, there is the very real potential that its consequences for human welfare will be severe. Thus when the developed world plunged into such a crisis in 2008 and growth rates in Latin America and the Caribbean (LAC) began to plummet, fears rose that the region would suffer rising unemployment, poverty, malnutrition, and infant mortality, among other things.

This study documents the effects of the 2008–09 global financial crisis on poverty in 12 countries in the LAC region,[1] and it comes away with six big-picture messages, each with much nuance and many caveats that are explained briefly in this overview and in more detail in the related chapters of the study. The messages are as follows:

1. *The effects of the global financial crisis on those living in poverty, while not as bad as feared initially, were not trivial: more than 3 million people fell into or remained mired in poverty in 2009 as a result of the crisis.* Part of the reason that poverty did not rise by as much as feared was that, although growth declined in almost all countries and indeed collapsed in some, it turned negative in only half of the LAC countries. Where growth continued, albeit slowly, one would not expect to see an outright increase in poverty. However, in countries with slower growth, we did see a decrease in the rate at which poverty fell. We estimated that because of the crisis an additional 3.2 million people were poor in 2009 compared with what was expected without the crisis. Of these, 2.5 million were Mexican because Mexico is both large and one of the countries most affected by the crisis.

2. *Changes in poverty are mostly explained by changes in labor incomes. In Mexico and Ecuador, the fall in earnings explains more than two-thirds of the increase in poverty, and in Colombia and Uruguay the rise in earnings explains more than half of the decline in poverty.* Changes in inequality account for between a tenth and a third of changes in poverty because during the crisis average earnings for the bottom quintile of the

distribution fell more than for other income groups, making changes in the earnings distribution very regressive. However, these unequal changes in labor incomes were partially offset by nonlabor earnings, including social transfers, in several countries. Social transfer programs such as Bono de Desarrollo Humano (Human Development Grant) in Ecuador, Oportunidades in Mexico, and the social pension in Uruguay helped those at the bottom of the distribution.

3. *Changes in labor incomes stem from a combination of changes in employment rates and real wages that varies by country and severity of the crisis. Mexico and Chile endured significant declines in both employment rates and real wages; in Argentina, Brazil, and Ecuador employment declined while wages rose; Colombia, Peru, and Uruguay experienced increases in both employment and wages.* For those countries seeing a decline in their gross employment rate (i.e., employment as a share of the working-age population), this decline is mostly explained by fewer youth with jobs, followed by fewer employed males aged 25–64. This result was partly, but not totally, offset by an increase in employment of females aged 25–64. This evolution of employment is mostly explained by changes in participation rates rather than changes in unemployment rates, which were consistent with the LAC countries' relatively low elasticity of unemployment to the gross domestic product (GDP). Interestingly, despite most countries experiencing a deceleration or outright decline in GDP per worker as measured in national accounts, monthly real earnings as reported in household surveys fell in 2009 only in Chile and Mexico, the countries with the deepest recessions. The short-term disconnect between GDP per worker and average earnings can be partly explained by methodological differences between macroeconomic aggregates and survey data, but it may also be the consequence of the observed larger impact of the crisis on capital returns than on labor incomes, particularly in those countries where the crisis was shallow and short-lived such as Colombia.

4. *An in-depth analysis of the impact of the crisis reveals different adjustment mechanisms but similar final incidence results for Brazil and Mexico.* The macro-micro modeling of the labor market adjustments in Brazil and Mexico indicates that the market adjustments in these countries depended on the type of shock, the institutional settings of product and factor markets, and agents' reactions to the shock. The trade shock decreased aggregate employment in both countries in roughly the same proportion (explaining between 40 percent and 50 percent of the total reduction in employment), and changes in public consumption were not very significant in either country. However, private consumption was more resilient in Brazil than in Mexico, while the relative reduction (i.e., with respect to a 1 percent reduction in GDP) in investment demand was much larger in Brazil. It is thus clear that the *shapes* of the shocks affecting Mexican and Brazilian labor markets were quite dissimilar. Other factors behind the labor market's adjustment—changes in wages, productivity, and labor

hoarding—were very different in Brazil and Mexico. Nonetheless, the distributional impact was similar—regressive overall, with the middle of the income distribution hit even a bit more than the poor.

5. *Countries were quite active in their social protection policy responses, largely taking advantage of programs built in precrisis years.* The expansion of conditional cash transfer (CCT) programs proved helpful in the crisis, perhaps surprisingly so because they were not tailored to a crisis response. This outcome stemmed from the widespread income reductions that affected the poor who were targeted by these programs. There were also many changes in labor market programs. Overall, the responses of the labor market programs were channeled in sensible directions, but in many countries they were too small or too late to help much in mitigating the effects of the global financial crisis. Providing protection for workers who lose employment is complex, and probably calls for a range of programs, each able to carry part of the load. Looking forward, more can be done to improve social protection in future crises in both social assistance and labor-related programs.

6. *Overall, the policy messages are that good policy helps attenuate the links between a global crisis and poverty in the LAC countries, and many of the important things need to be done ex ante.* The fundamentals of strong growth, low debt, good fiscal space, reasonably flexible exchange rates, and sound financial systems helped limit the impacts of the crisis in most countries and created space for fiscal stimulus, including increased social protection to mitigate social impacts.

Analytic Framework

A graphic illustration of the analytic framework adopted in this study is set out in figure 1.1, which measures poverty on the vertical axis and time on the horizontal axis. The first indications of the impact of the crisis are produced by tracking key indicators over time, making before and after comparisons. We undertook this exercise for a relatively large number of countries for the indicators poverty, inequality, and labor. The level of poverty before the crisis is defined by point A. After the crisis, the observed level of poverty is at point B, and thus the observed change in poverty is the distance A'B.

However, fully assessing the impact of the global financial crisis on LAC requires considering what might have happened had the crisis not occurred. What would have happened had growth continued on the positive trajectory of the early 2000s? Poverty could have declined, say to point D. What would have happened if the crisis had not been accompanied by any compensatory measures? Poverty could have been even higher, say at point E. And how does that compare with what in fact happened? The figure illustrates that the differences between E and D, or between B and D, need not be equal to the observed change in poverty A'B. This study provides estimates

Understanding the Poverty Impact of the Global Financial Crisis in Latin America and the Caribbean
http://dx.doi.org/10.1596/978-1-4648-0241-6

Figure 1.1 Assessing the Impact of the Global Financial Crisis on Poverty in Latin America and the Caribbean

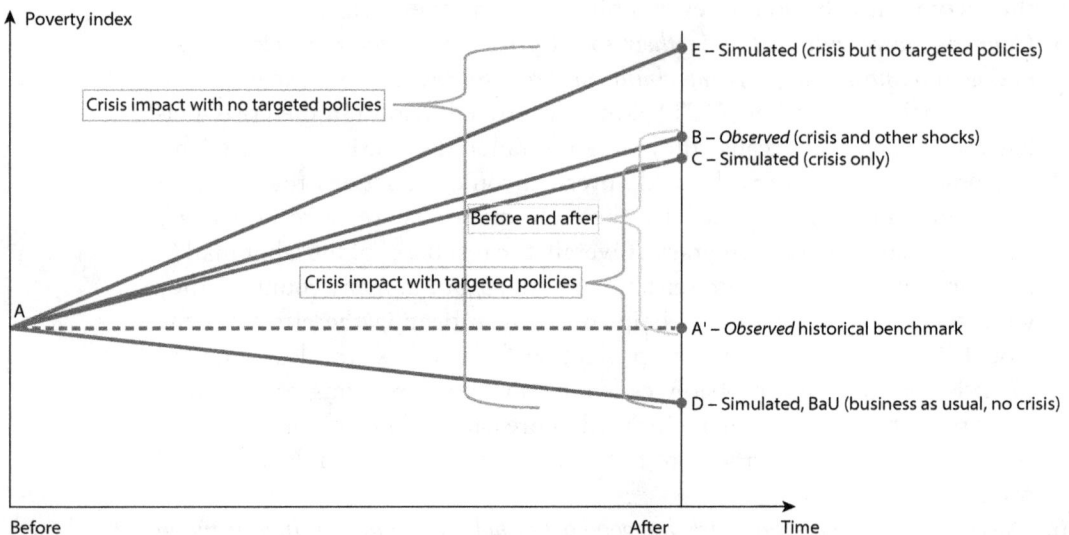

of CD and ED using counterfactual simulations of various levels of complexity and coverage.

This study adopts a fairly general and well-accepted conceptual framework for how shocks play through from the initial shock to macro outcomes and from labor and capital markets to households (see the graphic depiction of this framework in figure 1.2).[2] At the macro level, the size of the GDP reduction and the change in price level will depend on the magnitude of the initial shock and the structure of the economy. Moving from the macro to the "meso" level, the fall in aggregate output can be mapped in reductions of individual sectors and a related contraction of factor incomes. For simplicity's sake, the figure assumes that the economy has just two factors of production: capital and labor. A reduction in factor income can thus be the result of a fall in profits (or other capital rents) or a fall in the wage bill. The structure of the economy—in particular the degree of competition and the functioning of the labor markets—will determine the size of the final income contraction. For example, lower labor demand can be accommodated by reducing employment or reducing wages, or by a combination of the two adjustment mechanisms, or by shifting workers from formal (full-time, well-paid) jobs to informal (part-time, lower-paid) ones. Moving from the meso to the micro level, it is possible to map changes in welfare and poverty from the changes in real factor income and real public and private transfers. *Real* is used here to take into account the changes in the prices of the bundle of goods consumed by the household. The figure highlights only first-order effects, but feedback (second-order or general equilibrium) effects can be very important and need to be considered.

Figure 1.2 Conceptual Framework: Linking a Macroeconomic Shock to Its Microeconomic Impacts

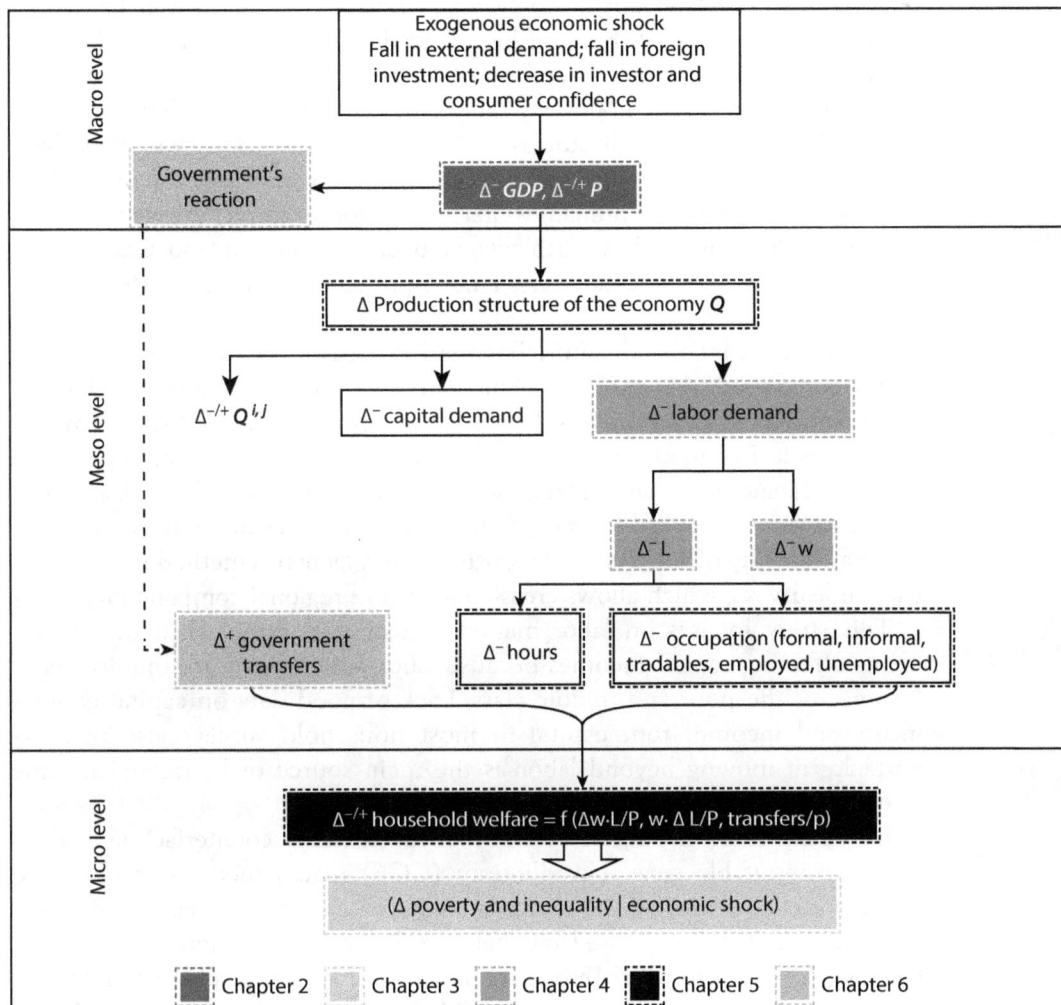

Macro level

Exogenous economic shock
Fall in external demand; fall in foreign investment; decrease in investor and consumer confidence

$\Delta^- GDP, \Delta^{-/+} P$

Government's reaction

Meso level

Δ Production structure of the economy Q

$\Delta^{-/+} Q^{i,j}$

Δ^- capital demand

Δ^- labor demand

$\Delta^- L$

$\Delta^- w$

Δ^+ government transfers

Δ^- hours

Δ^- occupation (formal, informal, tradables, employed, unemployed)

Micro level

$\Delta^{-/+}$ household welfare = f ($\Delta \cdot w \cdot L/P$, w $\cdot \Delta$ L/P, transfers/p)

(Δ poverty and inequality | economic shock)

Chapter 2   Chapter 3   Chapter 4   Chapter 5   Chapter 6

Applying the Framework to This Study

We begin by looking at the changes in growth in the LAC region, their heterogeneity across countries in the region, and some of the transmission channels that help account for that heterogeneity. This observation is carried out lightly, as context rather than deep diagnostics (see chapter 2).

For outcomes, we focus on various dimensions of employment, income, and poverty, examining these outcomes for as many countries as possible, although the number of countries and representativeness of the sample with respect to the region vary among dimensions. Ideally, we would observe a larger number of attributes of welfare, such as child nutrition, schooling, and use of health care. However, the data on these topics are not included in enough household surveys to allow much analysis, nor were administrative records available in a timely or

Understanding the Poverty Impact of the Global Financial Crisis in Latin America and the Caribbean
http://dx.doi.org/10.1596/978-1-4648-0241-6

comprehensive enough way. Instead, we rely on monetary measures of welfare such as poverty headcounts, income inequality indexes, and mean household incomes (see chapter 3). Because loss of income is often the first link in the causal chain that can lead to poorer nutrition, health, or education indicators, the magnitude of the change in poverty should indicate whether much deterioration in human development indicators is likely. Although the evidence on these later indicators is still scarce, it appears that where poverty increased the most, there were some impacts on human welfare—see, for example, Azevedo (2011) showing an increase in low birth weight babies in Mexico, and Chang et al. (2013) showing higher suicide rates among prime-age men across 18 countries in the Americas.

The poverty, inequality, and labor market statistics used in this study are from a comprehensive set of household and labor surveys collected and harmonized by a World Bank/Universidad de la Plata project. The statistics provided by its Socio-Economic Database for Latin America and the Caribbean (SEDLAC) and the Labor Database for Latin America and the Caribbean (LABLAC) are produced for most of the larger countries in the region as often as the availability of surveys permits, using a homogeneous method for all countries and surveys, which allows cross-country and regional comparability.[3]

This study focuses on labor market adjustments rather than the adjustments affecting capital incomes because labor adjustments are the drivers of income for the poor and middle class. Lack of good data on capital endowments and income from capital in most household surveys also presents obstacles in moving beyond labor as the main source of household income (see chapter 4).

For Mexico and Brazil, we construct a much richer counterfactual analysis pairing computable general equilibrium (CGE) macro modeling with micro simulations to understand the channels linking an exogenous financial crisis and household welfare, and, based on that, we discern the distributional impacts. Because such macro-micro modeling is a more complex and data-intensive exercise, we focus on just two countries, Mexico and Brazil. Mexico was selected because it was the largest country hard-hit by the crisis, accounting for 90 percent of the region's total loss of GDP. Mexico is contrasted with Brazil, also a large country, but one in which the crisis had a milder and different impact and one that has very different trade patterns (see chapter 5). The evidence presented in chapter 5 is the first attempt to quantify, in a formal way, the welfare effects of the financial crisis in Latin America using a framework like the one depicted in figure 1.2.

Moving back to the larger LAC region, chapter 6 describes the shape of the social protection sector prior to the crisis and the policy actions in the sector that provided the population with support around the time of the crisis. The chapter compiles comprehensive and comparable new data on social protection spending for the 2000s for 10 countries and uses official sources, academic literature, and the gray literature to illuminate specific programs and changes in them.

This study pulls together data from national accounts, household surveys, and administrative data, and yet shortcomings in the data limit our ability to understand the impact of the crisis and the best policy options in data-scarce countries. Fortunately, the data-richer countries are more populous, although even they lack some data that would have been desirable to more fully understand the crisis (see box 1.1).

Box 1.1 Data Shortcomings and Their Implications

It is possible to track poverty over a long time period using comparable, harmonized data from only 12 countries in the region. The most populous countries have data, but most of the Caribbean countries and several of the Central American countries greatly affected by the global financial crisis lack data. Specialized labor surveys are even less common in the region and especially in the most affected countries. In reading this study, it is important to keep these omissions in mind.

Data on social protection are scarce and fragmented. The household survey data in most countries are inadequate for making reliable and frequent estimates of the coverage or distribution of benefits from many social protection programs, even for flagship programs. Spending on social protection programs is spread throughout the budgets of many agencies across government. Because the spending of these agencies is not aggregated automatically or regularly, it is difficult to undertake a comprehensive review of efforts or trade-offs among them. Nor are administrative data on processes such as applications for social assistance or social insurance collected or reported in ways that proxy changes in welfare at the household level.

National accounts (macro) and household sample surveys (micro) do not agree on poverty levels or, more worrying, on changes in those levels. This is a well-known and documented issue (Bhalla 2002; Deaton 2003; Ravallion 2003, 2011; Robilliard and Robinson 2003; Szekely et al. 2004). In the current study, for two reasons the impact of the global financial crisis may be less severe when poverty is measured using the consumption aggregates from the household surveys than using the income or GDP macro aggregates. First, the crisis may have generated more informalization, which is not well captured by the national accounts. As a consequence, average income from the macro accounts would drop significantly, overstating the impact of the crisis, at least with respect to the change in average consumption measured from the microdata—this is the formalization issue raised by Deaton (2003). The second reason is that survey data seldom measure well the consumption (or incomes) of the richer groups of a population; for example, incomes from capital assets and financial investments are not well captured in a survey. In 1999 Szekely and Hilgert (1999) reported that in a number of Latin American surveys the incomes of the richest sampled individuals were never above the earnings expected for a typical manager as assessed by an international consulting firm. If the crisis affected mainly capital incomes, this will be recorded in the national accounts but not necessarily in the household surveys.

Messages

Message 1: The effects of the global financial crisis on those living in poverty, while not as bad as feared initially, were not trivial and especially of concern in the countries with the worst macro outcomes.

At the outset of the global financial crisis, there were significant concerns that the crisis would substantially increase poverty in the LAC countries.

Latin America has a long history of macro shocks, and their grave effects on poverty have been thoroughly reported and studied. As Lustig (2000) points out, countries in the region experienced more than 40 episodes of growth declines of 4 percentage points or more between 1980 and 1998. Several studies—for example, Lustig (2000); Fallon and Lucas (2002); Halac and Schmukler (2004); and Ferreira and Schady (2008)—confirm that these episodes had severe impacts on income and consumption as well as on other social welfare indicators such as nutrition, education, and health, particularly among the poor. Even financial assets and their returns were affected by the crises, and disproportionately more for those owned by the poor. These studies report that poverty rates rise suddenly with crises and take longer to decline, with the result that for several years poverty rates are much higher than in precrisis periods. Furthermore, crisis-related declines in nutrition, health, and education have consequences not only in the short term but, more important, also in the long term. These studies also highlight that, in most cases, fiscal policy in the region has not been countercyclical, which worsens the poverty and welfare impact of crises. They also highlight the need for more appropriate risk-mitigating mechanisms in terms of both social assistance and social insurance to cope with the repeated crises the region faces. The need for a cohesive and coherent risk-mitigating social policy for developing countries was cited earlier by Ferreira, Prennushi, and Ravallion (1999) and more recently by Kanbur (2010).

Thus as the global financial crisis detonated in the fall of 2008 and spread around the world, concern about how it would affect Latin American and Caribbean populations was high. Different studies warned about the serious impact of the crisis on developing countries, and on Latin America in particular, dismissing the idea that the emerging economies would decouple from the crisis in the developed world. In Latin America, a combination of declining exports because of the collapse of international trade, restricted access to international finance, and lower remittances were forecasted to produce a serious negative impact in most countries of the region—see, for example, World Bank (2009); Grifith-Jones and Ocampo (2009); and IMF (2009).

But this was not the "usual" crisis.

Marked improvements in macroeconomic and fiscal policy frameworks in conjunction with lower external vulnerability cushioned the external shock and allowed governments in the region to respond with countercyclical policies. Playing a crucial role were sounder monetary policy frameworks, including exchange rate flexibility and more independent central banks; better-regulated banking systems; significantly lower currency and rollover risks; deeper local currency debt markets; and lower net public sector borrowing requirements. Furthermore, improved current account balances and larger foreign exchange liquidity buffers also played a role in helping the region weather the 2008–09 crisis better than previous ones.

Countercyclical macroeconomic policies, especially monetary policy and in a few cases countercyclical fiscal policy, contributed to a quick and sharp recovery. The monetary stimulus was significant, with emerging countries in the region reducing policy rates by 360 basis points on average from August 2008 to October 2009, the largest reduction among developing regions. The fiscal response (as measured by the change in the primary deficit) was stronger than expected in view of past performances during other crises, and included refraining from slashing spending in response to the decline in revenues, allowing the automatic stabilizers to work, and introducing new discretionary spending or revenue measures (IMF 2010). The fiscal impulse varied across countries and depended crucially on the available fiscal space.

Despite a marked deterioration in economic activity, the LAC region did not experience a systemic financial crisis. This situation stood in sharp contrast with previous crises when currency mismatches and deficient regulatory frameworks lay the groundwork for and amplified the financial crisis. During 1994–98, for example, the region experienced 11 systemic banking crises,[4] a foreign currency debt crisis, and three currency crises. However, unlike the past, in the 2008–09 crisis there were no underlying systemic banking, foreign currency debt, or currency crises. Bank and corporate balance sheets were not severely impaired because of the absence of currency crises, and more generally because of lower financial and corporate sector vulnerabilities when compared with previous pre-crisis periods.

The global coordinated response to the crisis and the prompt provision of significant financing from international institutions limited the fall in output. Even in the highly vulnerable emerging economies, the initial fall in economic activity was less pronounced than in past crises (IMF 2010). The growth collapse was larger in financially integrated economies in the region.

Meanwhile, in part because there were no systemic banking crises, output began to recover more rapidly than in previous episodes and when compared with the middle-income country average, and the recovery was stronger. The stronger labor market performance reflected this resilience as well, with unemployment increasing far less than in previous crises. Furthermore, the real average wages remained constant or increased in some countries, and the trend of labor market formalization was not reversed in most countries.

Poverty reduction continued in many countries, but it slowed and reversed in the countries with the worst macro outcomes.

At the regional level—that is, in the 12 countries examined in this study, covering nearly 90 percent of the regional population—poverty decreased slightly, but at a slower pace than during the period that preceded the crisis. The average (nonweighted) moderate poverty headcount for the selected 12 countries in the region moved from 29.7 to 28.7 between 2008 and 2009, with an overall decrease of 1.0 percentage point. The analogous figures for extreme poverty were almost unchanged, falling from 15.0 in 2008 to 14.8 in 2009. These figures contrast with the average annual decline in moderate (extreme) poverty of 2.7 (2.1) percentage points between 2003 and 2008.[5]

Over the period 2008–09, poverty increased in most countries that experienced a sharp contraction in GDP per capita. In Costa Rica, Ecuador, El Salvador, and Mexico, moderate poverty (measured by US$4.00 per person per day) increased (see table 1.1).[6] In Costa Rica, El Salvador, Mexico, and Paraguay, extreme poverty (measured by $2.50 per person per day) increased. The Jamaican data are not harmonized with the other data, but according to the local poverty lines, poverty increased in that country, from 16.5 percent in 2008 to 17.6 percent in 2009. Chile was among the countries in recession in 2009. However, Chile's household survey was conducted only every three years, in 2006 and 2009. Moderate and extreme poverty declined over this whole period (GDP grew by 5.5 percent in 2007 and 3.3 percent in 2008, but fell by −1.0 percent in 2009). However, we do not know whether the decline was continuous or initially sharper and then attenuated by an increase in 2009.

Argentina, Brazil, and Peru experienced zero or slightly negative GDP per capita growth from 2008 to 2009, and yet poverty rates went down. In these three countries, national accounts figures show stagnant or negative growth, but the household surveys show continued income growth and declining poverty. In Paraguay, a severe recession of more than 5 percent decline in GDP per capita

Table 1.1 Changes in Poverty: Latin America and the Caribbean, 2008–09

Country	Moderate poverty ($4.00/person/day)		Extreme poverty ($2.50/person/day)	
	Change in headcount	Change in poverty gap	Change in headcount	Change in poverty gap
Argentina	−0.9	−0.2	−0.2	−0.1
Brazil	−1.6	−0.4	−0.6	0.0
Chile[a]	−4.0	−1.0	−1.0	−0.1
Colombia	−2.2	−2.0	−2.5	−1.7
Costa Rica	**0.7**	**0.4**	**0.5**	**0.5**
Dominican Republic	−3.2	−1.4	−2.0	−0.7
Ecuador	**0.5**	**0.1**	−0.2	0.0
El Salvador	**0.6**	**2.2**	**1.8**	**2.6**
Mexico[b]	**2.6**	**1.1**	**1.3**	**0.7**
Paraguay	−2.2	**0.6**	**1.1**	**1.1**
Peru	−1.2	−0.5	−0.4	−0.4
Uruguay	−2.0	−0.6	−0.6	−0.1

Sources: Socio-Economic Database for Latin America and the Caribbean (SEDLAC) harmonized data sets and La Encuesta Nacional de Ingresos y Gastos de los Hogares (ENIGH, National Household Income and Expenditure Survey), 2008 and 2010.
Note: Poverty increased in the countries highlighted.
a. Data refer to the period 2006–09.
b. Data refer to the period 2008–10.

contrasts with the mild decline of 0.2 percent in per capita household income as reported by the household survey. This mild reduction combined with a very regressive pattern explains higher poverty gaps and extreme poverty while moderate poverty went down. All these cases highlight the disconnect between macro- and microdata on incomes (as discussed in box 1.1). In effect, then, the changes in average income growth reported in the surveys do not coincide with the growth in GDP per capita in most countries in the sample.

Decomposing changes in total poverty by population group reveals that changes in the total are mostly explained by changes in the large population groups such as urban households or male-headed households (which usually have a lower incidence of poverty) than by changes in the smaller but sometimes initially poorer groups. For almost every country in the sample, moderate and extreme poverty rates are higher among rural households and households headed by females, unskilled workers, and workers in the informal sector or without jobs. However, these groups did not necessarily experience the largest poverty increases.

The crisis had a sizable hidden cost in terms of a lost opportunity for additional poverty reduction.

A simple counterfactual can be generated by using poverty growth elasticities, and it suggests a significant impact of the crisis: about 3.2 million people remained in poverty who, with continued growth, would have escaped it. This assumes no change in inequality and that countries had economic growth equal to the average growth of the last five years (i.e., 2003–08, a period known for accelerated poverty reduction in the region), giving a very simple estimate of the distance BD in figure 1.1. For Costa Rica, Ecuador, and Mexico, the simulations suggest that actual postcrisis poverty rates were more than 2.0 percentage points higher than they would have been had growth rates been maintained (see table 1.2). For Argentina, El Salvador, and Peru, the simulation suggests that the actual postcrisis poverty rates were between 1.0 and 2.0 percentage points higher than they would have been otherwise. For Chile, Panama, and Uruguay, the simulations suggest very little impact from the crisis—for example, actual poverty rates were no more than 0.5 percentage points higher than expected. Brazil, Colombia, and the Dominican Republic reduced poverty even more than predicted. For the region, the actual decline in moderate poverty of −1.0 percentage point (an unweighted average for the 12 countries in the sample) might have been nearly double that without the crisis, to −1.7. In population terms, moderate poverty in these 12 countries declined by 2.4 million people. Our simulation exercise, however, would have predicted a decline of 5.6 million. Thus because of the crisis about 3.2 million people remained in moderate poverty. Of them, 2.4 million were Mexican. The other large country, Brazil, had fewer people (300,000) in moderate poverty than would have been predicted in our elasticity-based simulation. A much smaller GDP decline and a different reaction of labor markets to the crisis, as explained later in this chapter, account for this contrast.

Understanding the Poverty Impact of the Global Financial Crisis in Latin America and the Caribbean
http://dx.doi.org/10.1596/978-1-4648-0241-6

Table 1.2 Moderate Poverty: Actual and Forecasted Population in Poverty: Latin America, 2009

	Poverty in 2008 (%)	Poverty in 2009 (%)	Forecast poverty in 2009 (%)	Number of poor in 2008 (millions)	Number of poor in 2009 (millions)	Actual change (millions)	Forecast number of poor in 2009 (millions)	Forecast change (millions)	Forecast "excess" poor (millions)
Argentina	17.3	16.4	14.7	6.85	6.57	−0.28	5.88	−0.97	0.69
Brazil	29.2	27.6	27.8	55.93	53.34	−2.59	53.63	−2.29	−0.30
Chile[a]	13.1	11.8	11.7	2.21	2.00	−0.21	1.98	−0.23	0.02
Colombia	44.8	42.6	43.3	20.17	19.45	−0.72	19.78	−0.39	−0.34
Costa Rica	18.9	19.6	17.3	0.86	0.90	0.04	0.80	−0.06	0.10
Dominican Republic	37.9	34.7	35.9	3.66	3.40	−0.26	3.52	−0.14	−0.12
Ecuador	37.1	37.6	35.5	5.21	5.36	0.15	5.07	−0.15	0.29
El Salvador	42.1	42.7	41.0	2.58	2.63	0.05	2.53	−0.05	0.10
Mexico[b]	27.5	28.8	26.5	30.42	32.27	1.84	29.74	−0.69	2.53
Paraguay	37.1	34.9	35.7	2.31	2.21	−0.10	2.26	−0.05	−0.05
Peru	36.9	35.7	34.6	10.50	10.27	−0.23	9.96	−0.54	0.31
Uruguay	14.0	12.0	11.9	0.47	0.40	−0.06	0.40	−0.07	0.00
Total				141.2	138.8	−2.4	135.5	−5.6	3.2

Sources: SEDLAC harmonized data sets and ENIGH, 2008 and 2010.

a. The poverty rate in Chile between 2008 and 2009 is derived from the average annual change from 2006 to 2009 surveys.

b. The poverty rate in Mexico between 2008 and 2009 is derived from the average annual change from 2008 to 2010 surveys.

Message 2: Changes in poverty are mostly explained by changes in labor incomes.

Changes stemming from labor incomes range from a large portion of the poverty reduction such as that in Colombia and Uruguay, to a large part of the increase in poverty rates in Mexico and Ecuador. In 10 out of the 12 countries, the changes in labor incomes go in the same direction as changes in poverty and account for the largest share of changes in moderate poverty (see table 1.3).

Observed average earnings for the bottom decile of the distribution fell more than for other income groups, making changes in the distribution of earnings very regressive.

In most of the countries in which poverty increased—such as El Salvador, Mexico, and Paraguay—labor incomes show a very regressive pattern, and nonlabor incomes have little or no compensatory role.[7] Figure 1.3 illustrates this pattern. It shows the rate of growth of total income by income decile, and its decomposition into labor income and nonlabor income. In almost every country under study, the labor income growth of the first, second, and, in some cases, third deciles of the population is smaller than the upper deciles of the distribution. In some countries such as Argentina, Brazil, and Chile, labor incomes also show a regressive pattern, but nonlabor incomes show a progressive pattern that helps offset the impact of the shock among the poorest sections of the population. And yet in other countries, such as Colombia and Ecuador, labor market performance was progressive, but with a fundamental difference. All groups experienced positive growth in Colombia, whereas in Ecuador all groups experienced a decline in income. In both of these countries, nonlabor incomes grew faster for the bottom deciles of the distribution, thereby inducing an accelerated poverty reduction in Colombia and a subdued moderate poverty increase in Ecuador.

This regressive pattern of changes in the earnings distribution led to changes in inequality, which explain between a tenth and a third of changes in poverty. A decomposition into growth and redistribution components (table 1.4) shows that in the majority of countries, growth is the dominant factor explaining changes in both moderate and extreme poverty. However, the redistribution component is particularly important in countries where poverty increased. In Paraguay, for example, the redistribution component explains almost 80 percent of the increase in extreme poverty. This is clearly due to the large drop in earnings among those in the first decile of the income distribution. Similarly, in Costa Rica, El Salvador, and Mexico increases in extreme poverty are explained, at least in part, by worsening income inequality.

Comparing the crisis case with a hypothetical scenario without it reveals that the middle class in both Mexico and Brazil was hit the hardest.

In macro-micro modeling, when all effects, wages, hours worked (in the case of Mexico), and unemployment rates are considered in order to compare them not with those of previous periods but with a counterfactual simulation, the effects

Understanding the Poverty Impact of the Global Financial Crisis in Latin America and the Caribbean
http://dx.doi.org/10.1596/978-1-4648-0241-6

Table 1.3 Decomposition of Poverty Changes, by Source of Income: Latin America, 2008–09
Percentage points

	Argentina	Brazil	Chile[a]	Colombia	Costa Rica	Dominican Republic	Ecuador	El Salvador	Mexico[b]	Paraguay	Peru	Uruguay
Moderate poverty ($4/person/day)												
Labor income	−0.1	−0.7	−2.2	−1.2	2.3	−1.8	0.7	3.5	1.6	−1.5	−1.3	−2.1
Nonlabor income	−0.4	−0.5	−1.4	−0.7	−0.4	−1.3	−0.3	1.0	1.0	−0.5	0.4	0.3
Rank correlation	−0.3	−0.4	−0.4	−0.3	−1.2	0.0	0.1	−3.9	0.0	−0.1	−0.3	−0.1
Total change 2008–09	−0.9	−1.6	−4.0	−2.2	0.7	−3.2	0.5	0.6	2.6	−2.2	−1.2	−2.0
Extreme poverty ($2.5/person/day)												
Labor income	0.4	−0.1	0.4	−1.4	1.9	−1.2	0.6	5.0	0.8	1.0	−1.2	−0.9
Nonlabor income	−0.2	−0.2	−0.8	−0.8	−0.2	−1.1	−0.4	1.3	0.5	0.1	0.4	0.3
Rank correlation	−0.3	−0.3	−0.6	−0.3	−1.1	0.3	−0.4	−4.6	0.0	0.0	0.4	0.1
Total change 2008–09	−0.2	−0.6	−1.0	−2.5	0.5	−2.0	−0.2	1.8	1.3	1.1	−0.4	−0.6

Sources: SEDLAC harmonized data sets and ENIGH, 2008 and 2010.
a. Data refer to the period 2006–09.
b. Data refer to the period 2008–10.

Figure 1.3 Growth Incidence Curve, by Income Source: Latin America and the Caribbean, 2008–09

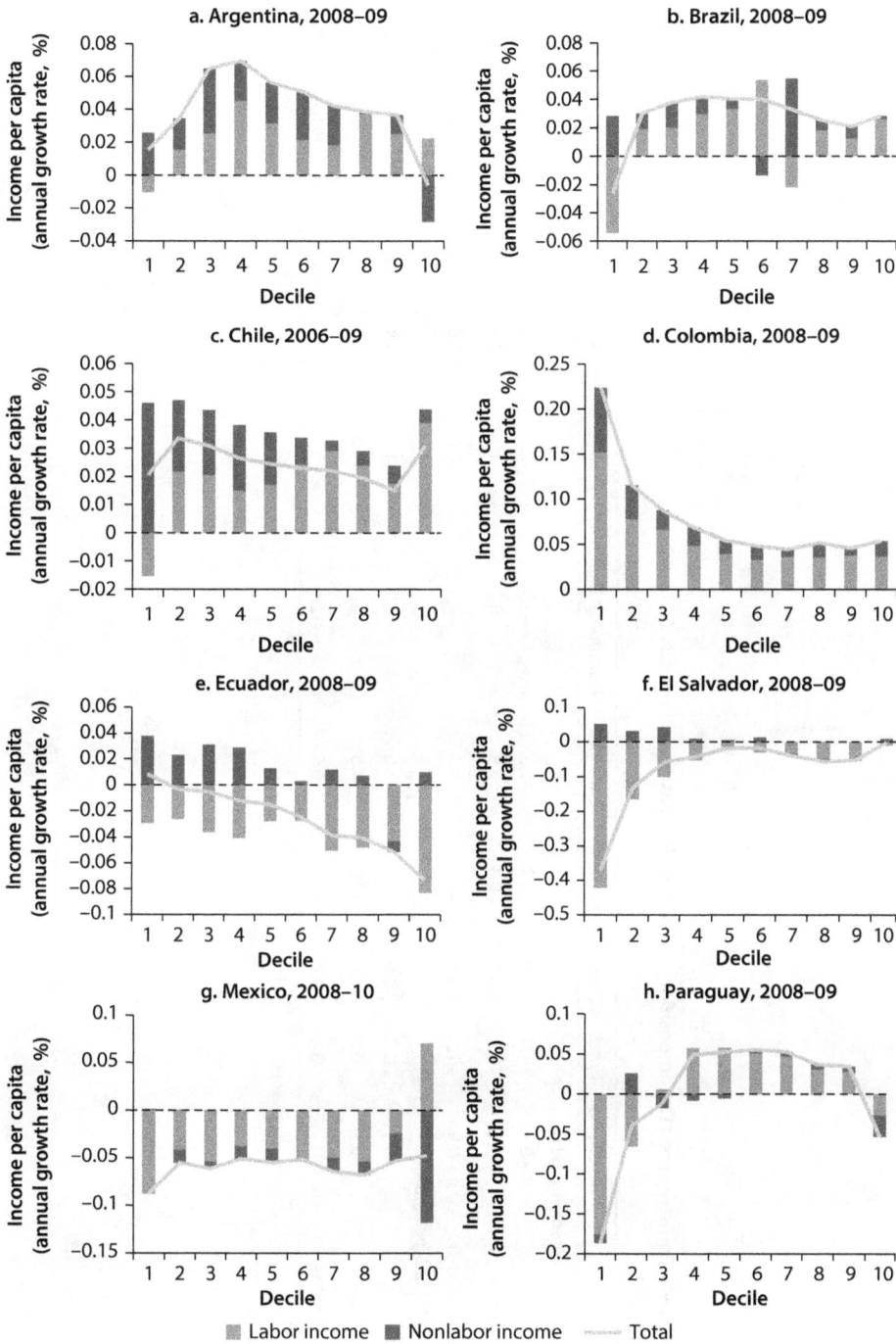

a. Argentina, 2008–09

b. Brazil, 2008–09

c. Chile, 2006–09

d. Colombia, 2008–09

e. Ecuador, 2008–09

f. El Salvador, 2008–09

g. Mexico, 2008–10

h. Paraguay, 2008–09

Labor income   Nonlabor income   Total

Sources: SEDLAC harmonized data sets and ENIGH, 2008 and 2010.

Understanding the Poverty Impact of the Global Financial Crisis in Latin America and the Caribbean
http://dx.doi.org/10.1596/978-1-4648-0241-6

Table 1.4 Growth Redistribution Decomposition of Poverty Changes: Latin America, 2008–09

Percentage points

	Argentina	Brazil	Chile[a]	Colombia	Costa Rica	Dominican Republic	Ecuador	El Salvador	Mexico[b]	Paraguay	Peru	Uruguay
Moderate poverty ($4/person/day)												
Growth	−0.7	−1.0	−3.2	−1.9	−2.2	−2.9	2.2	1.6	2.1	0.1	−1.2	−2.0
Redistribution	−0.2	−0.6	−0.8	−0.3	2.9	−0.2	−1.7	−1.0	0.5	−2.3	0.0	0.1
Total change 2008–09	−0.9	−1.6	−4.0	−2.2	0.7	−3.2	0.5	0.6	2.6	−2.2	−1.2	−2.0
Extreme poverty ($2.5/person/day)												
Growth	−0.3	−0.5	−1.0	−1.5	−1.0	−1.9	1.5	1.1	1.2	0.2	−0.9	−0.8
Redistribution	0.1	−0.2	0.0	−1.0	1.5	−0.2	−1.7	0.7	0.1	0.9	0.5	0.2
Total change 2008–09	−0.2	−0.6	−1.0	−2.5	0.5	−2.0	−0.2	1.8	1.3	1.1	−0.4	−0.6

Sources: SEDLAC harmonized data sets and ENIGH, 2008 and 2010.

a. Data refer to the period 2006–09.

b. Data refer to the period 2008–10.

of the crisis are shown to be regressive, but largest among households located in the middle part of the per capita household income distribution in both Mexico and Brazil (see figure 1.4). The average household in Mexico loses 8 percent of its income as a result of the crisis (comparing the incomes in a scenario without the crisis with the observed levels), with households located in the middle part of the income distribution losing more than 9 percent of their per capita household income as a result of the crisis. In Brazil, the effect is milder, with an average loss in income of 4 percent and close to 5 percent among households located around the 40th percentile of the income distribution.

Figure 1.4 Overall Distributional Effects of the Global Financial Crisis, Observed and Counterfactual Simulation

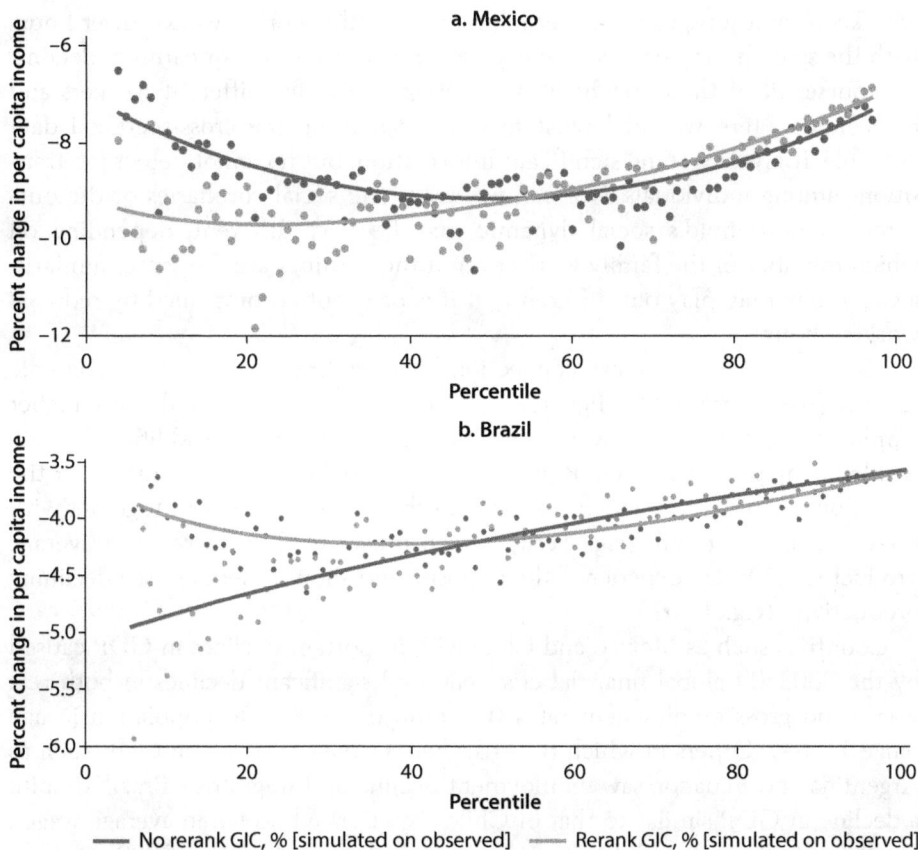

a. Mexico

b. Brazil

— No rerank GIC, % [simulated on observed]   ━ Rerank GIC, % [simulated on observed]

Source: World Bank data.
Note: A growth incidence curve (GIC) with no reranking (called in the literature an "anonymous" GIC) compares the income of individuals who are not necessarily in the same initial position. This GIC shows the difference between the initial income of those individuals who originally were in percentile *p* and the income of the individuals who are in the same percentile *p* in the terminal distribution. They are not necessarily the same individuals. A GIC with reranking (a nonanonymous GIC) allows for mobility and compares the initial and final incomes of the same individuals ordered according to the initial position in the distribution.

Understanding the Poverty Impact of the Global Financial Crisis in Latin America and the Caribbean
http://dx.doi.org/10.1596/978-1-4648-0241-6

For some households, the impact of the global financial crisis was so strong that their positions in the income distribution shifted (causing downward mobility). In Mexico, reductions in hours worked were enough to push some households originally located in the middle part of the distribution into lower income brackets. More important, in both Mexico and Brazil increases in unemployment shifted the position of households originally situated in the middle part of the income distribution toward the bottom percentiles.

Message 3. Changes in labor incomes stem from a combination of changes in employment rates and real wages that varies by country and severity of the crisis.

A recession can reduce a household's income in many ways. A worker may lose a job and remain unemployed, or the worker may lose a job and find a new one that pays less, or one member of the household may lose a job and another member of the household may find one but earns less. Even for those workers who keep their jobs, earnings per job may fall if the worker works fewer hours with the same hourly earnings, or because the hourly wages or earnings decline. Of course, all of these mechanisms come into play for different workers and households. Here we shed what light we can using the cross-sectional data available. It gives us some significant information, but it cannot detect job transitions among individuals. Nor can we assess the social corollaries of the outcome—a household's social dynamic may be very different, depending on which member of the family works even if the earnings are the same; similarly, a cut in pay may play out differently if it is or is not accompanied by reduced working hours.

There is a tenuous linear connection between employment and economic growth (see figure 1.5). Higher economic growth is associated with higher employment growth and lower unemployment, but how much additional or less employment per unit of GDP growth varies widely from one country to the next. Some countries experience almost no change in employment together with some economic growth (e.g., Peru), which must entail an increase in average productivity. Others experience the opposite and should therefore see declining productivity (e.g., Brazil).

Countries such as Mexico and Chile with important declines in GDP caused by the 2008–09 global financial crisis endured significant declines in both real wages and gross employment rates (the ratio of workers to population in age range 15–64). Others in which the crisis had a smaller impact on GDP, such as Argentina and Ecuador, saw employment decline and wages rise. Brazil, despite a decline in GDP similar to that of Chile, experienced no fall in average wages. Finally, countries that did not undergo a decline in GDP in 2009, such as Colombia and Uruguay, saw increases in both employment and wages.

The stylized picture of labor adjustment is that Latin American countries with declining gross employment rates, mostly caused by declining youth and prime-age male employment, partly offset them with a rise in prime-age

Figure 1.5 Gross Employment Rate and Growth: Latin America, 2009

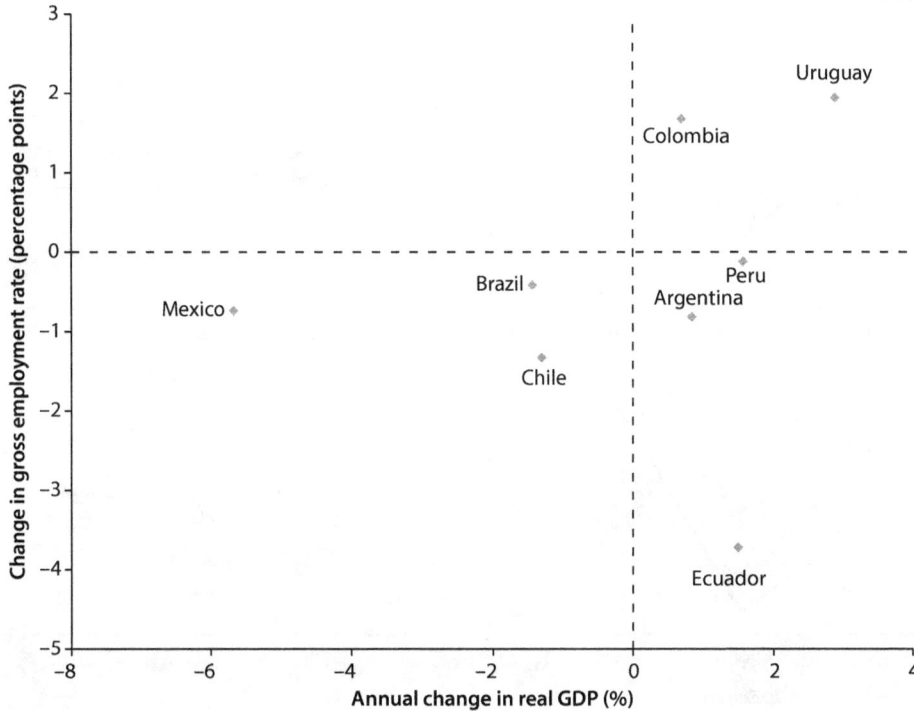

Sources: Labor Database for Latin America and the Caribbean (LABLAC) (Centro de Estudios Distributivos Laborales y Sociales [CEDLAS, Center for Distributive, Labor, and Social Studies] and World Bank) and International Monetary Fund, International Financial Statistics (database), various years; real GDP for Argentina: El Instituto Nacional de Estadística y Censos (INDEC, National Institute of Statistics and Census).
Note: Changes in the gross employment rates correspond to year-to-year differences in the gross employment rate rate for the third quarter of 2009 (except for Argentina where it corresponds to the fourth quarter of 2009). Changes in GDP growth correspond to the percentage change in yearly real GDP by the third quarter of 2009 (fourth quarter for Argentina).

female employment. Three main messages can be derived from figure 1.6, which illustrates these changes. First, in countries in which the gross employment rate declined, this decline was mostly caused by falling employment among youth. The exceptions were Chile and Mexico in 2009, where there was also a decline among prime-age males. In 2008 Peru underwent a decline in gross employment rates due to both youth and prime-age females.

Second, in Argentina, Brazil, and Mexico these declines are partly offset by the increase in employment rates among prime-age women. In Peru, prime-age females offset the decline in youth and prime-age male employment, so that 2009 was a year with no decline in its gross employment rates. Chile was again an exception because prime-age women showed no change in employment in 2009. In Ecuador, female employment reinforced the employment decline among males and youth.

Understanding the Poverty Impact of the Global Financial Crisis in Latin America and the Caribbean
http://dx.doi.org/10.1596/978-1-4648-0241-6

Figure 1.6 Decomposition of Changes in Gross Employment Rate: Latin America and the Caribbean, 2008–10

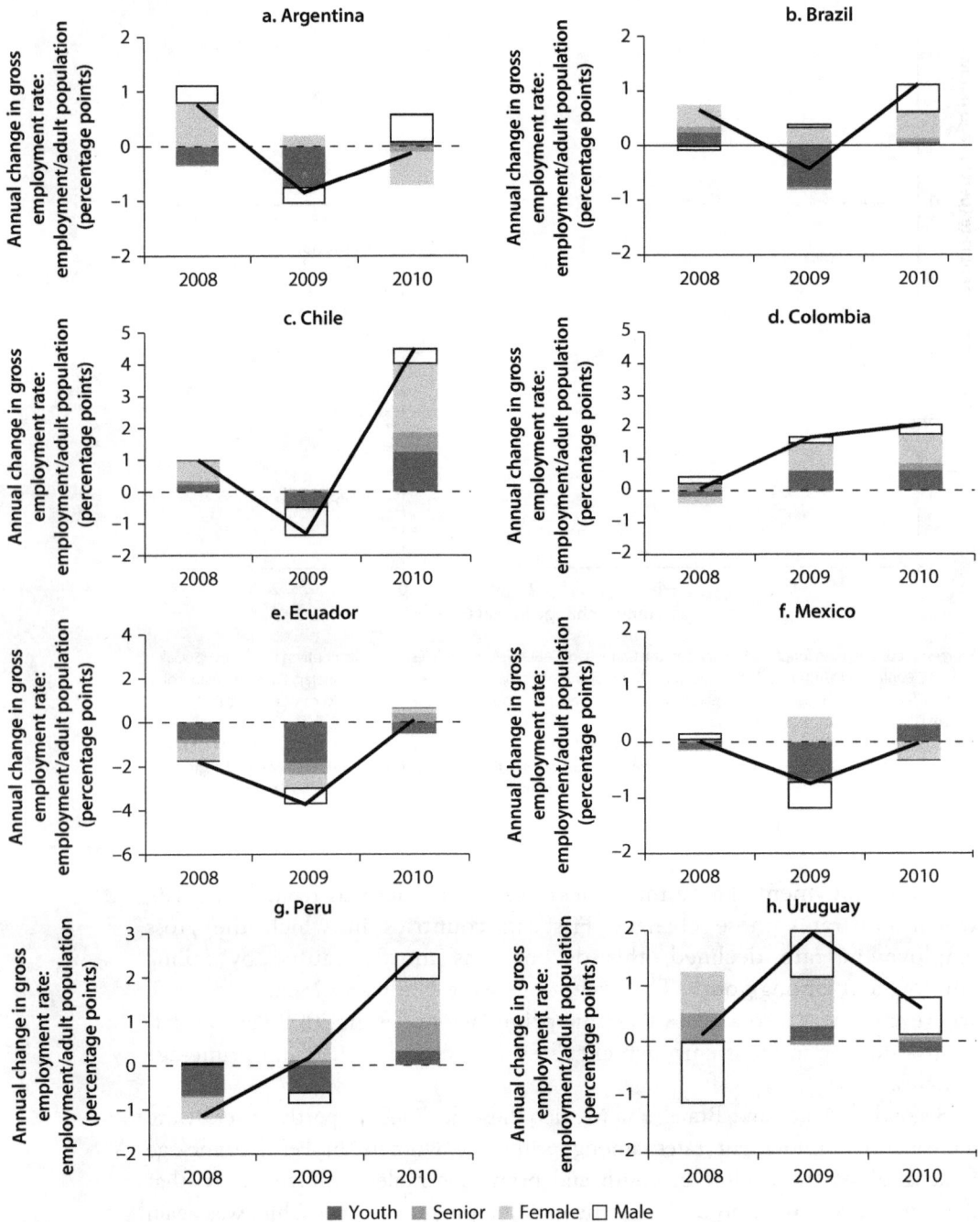

Youth ■   Senior ▓   Female ▒   Male ☐

Source: LABLAC (CEDLAS and World Bank).
Note: Graphs show the decomposition of the gross employment rate (i.e., the ratio of jobs to working-age population) by population group for the third quarter of each year (except for Argentina where it corresponds to the fourth quarter). For a description of the algebra of this decomposition, see chapter 4.

Third, countries that had positive growth in 2009 (i.e., Colombia and Uruguay) underwent no decline in employment for any group. On the contrary, the employment rates rose for youth and prime-age males and females.

These findings seem to indicate that in most LAC countries families compensated for the loss of employment among men and the young with the higher labor participation of women. Interestingly, the country with the most extensive and mature unemployment insurance (UI) system in the region, Chile, is the only country that saw no increase in female employment during the crisis.[8]

Overall, no country in the sample had a large decline in gross employment rates one year after the onset of the crisis. Among those that endured a decline in 2009, the gross employment rate fell less than or around 1 percentage point. Colombia and Uruguay saw their rates grow in 2009, and the deceleration in 2008—perhaps attributable to an early response to the crisis—was also below the 1 percentage point mark.

Increases in the unemployment rate were modest.

The 2008–09 global financial crisis resulted in relatively modest increases in the unemployment rate in most countries (in keeping with Latin America's past experience), unlike the sharply higher effects felt in Europe.[9] The Latin American countries are not usually characterized by large changes in the unemployment rate in response to changes in GDP growth. The unemployment rate in 2008–09 in the LAC countries was in keeping with predictions based on Okun's coefficient, a statistical measure of changes in the unemployment rate and changes in GDP growth. Relying on annual data and linear models, Okun's coefficients range from −0.017 in Peru to −0.40 in Colombia. These estimates are at the lower end of the range for developed countries. Recent estimates of Okun's coefficients for Organisation for Economic Co-operation and Development (OECD) countries range from around −0.10 in countries such as Japan and Austria, to −0.45 in Canada, the United States, and the United Kingdom, to −0.80 in Spain.

Unemployment was a bigger concern in Chile and Mexico, with increases on the order of 2 percentage points. Both countries underwent a very unusual output decline (more marked in Mexico) that drove the increase in unemployment, which was in line with their respective Okun coefficients. In Chile, the output changes were smaller than in Mexico, but the Okun coefficient was higher.

Although unemployment increased in the aftermath of the crisis in every country, in some countries the increase was small and short-lived (one or two quarters). Four quarters after the onset of the crisis, Brazil, Colombia, Peru, and Uruguay had the same or higher gross employment rates than before the crisis. By contrast, Argentina, Chile, Ecuador, and Mexico had not reached their precrisis gross employment rates eight quarters after the crisis.

Youth suffered the most from the impacts of the crisis on employment. Not only was youth unemployment chronically high in all LAC countries, but it also increased the most during the 2008–09 crisis. In fact, youth unemployment underwent the largest increase among all population groups. For example, in Mexico the youth unemployment rate rose by 3.4 percentage points, while prime-age adults (24–64) experienced an increase of 1.8 percentage points and seniors (65 years and over) a 1.1 percentage point increase. Similar trends were seen in Argentina, Brazil, Chile, Colombia, and Ecuador. Interestingly, in Peru and Uruguay, countries that experienced a decline in unemployment, youth unemployment also declined faster.

Although most countries had a deceleration or outright decline in GDP per worker as measured in national accounts, monthly real earnings as measured in household surveys fell only in the countries with the strongest recessions.
As a consequence of the crisis, all countries in this study saw their GDP per capita decline from the first quarter of 2009. This decline was very abrupt in some countries (Argentina, Brazil, and Mexico) and less so in others. The decline lasted one or two quarters in some countries (Argentina, Peru, and Uruguay) and longer in others (Brazil, Ecuador, and Mexico), where precrisis GDP per capita levels were not reached until seven or eight quarters after the crisis. The orange line in figure 1.7 shows this evolution of GDP per capita for the selected countries.

There is evidence of a disconnect between GDP per worker and earnings per worker, or between macro and survey data. During the recent crisis, the evolution of average earnings as reported by labor surveys did not necessarily follow changes in labor productivity as measured by the national accounts. In Argentina, Brazil, Ecuador, Peru, and Uruguay, average real earnings as reported in surveys increased despite declines in output per capita or in labor productivity during the initial quarters of the crisis. On the other hand, real earnings in Mexico declined despite the recovery of labor productivity beginning with the fifth quarter after the onset of the crisis. Finally, reported earnings in Colombia followed a similar trend to labor productivity because they declined during the initial quarters of the crisis and increased afterward. Data for Chile are incomplete, but they seem to indicate a decline and then a rise in real earnings that goes in the same direction as the decline in GDP per worker.

This disconnect may stem from misreporting or the fact that surveys capture only labor income whereas macroeconomic GDP figures capture all income. Misreporting of labor income can play a role in the differences, especially when there are high rates of informality and unemployment and short-term work is widespread. Moreover, it can be difficult to track exact wages over a long period of time. Overall, it is difficult to identify the causes of this divergence without further inquiry into the methods of national accounts and labor surveys in each country. In any case, we report these trends to highlight the need to recognize different trends in earnings and labor productivity during the recent crisis.

The short-term disconnect between GDP per capita, labor productivity, and average earnings can be explained in part by methodological differences between macroeconomic aggregates and survey data, but it may also be the consequence of the larger impact of the crisis on capital returns than on labor incomes. For the four countries with the available data, there is some evidence that the latter is the case. All countries saw the share of labor in total GDP rise in 2009 because workers' compensation was less affected by the crisis than other income. On the

Figure 1.7 Quarterly Trends in GDP Per Capita, GDP per Worker, and Average Earnings: Latin America and the Caribbean

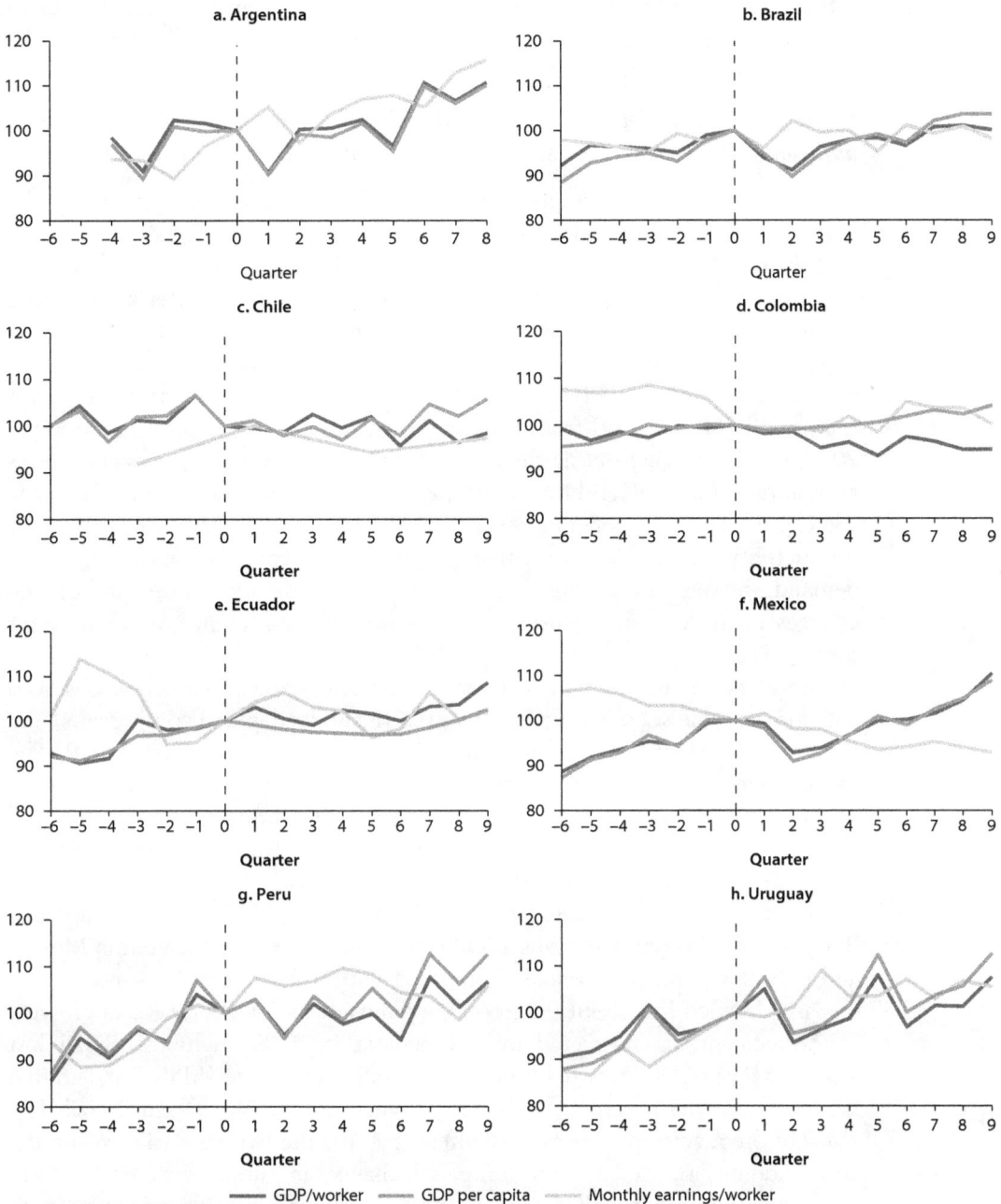

a. Argentina
b. Brazil
c. Chile
d. Colombia
e. Ecuador
f. Mexico
g. Peru
h. Uruguay

GDP/worker   GDP per capita   Monthly earnings/worker

Source: LABLAC (CEDLAS and World Bank).

Note: The x-axis refers to quarters after or before the quarter of reference (second quarter of 2008). On the y-axis, the index equals 100 at the third quarter of 2008 (except for Argentina where it corresponds to the fourth quarter of 2008). Chile's earnings data correspond to fourth quarter only of 2007, 2008, 2009, and 2010. All variables are defined in real terms using the implicit GDP deflator.

Understanding the Poverty Impact of the Global Financial Crisis in Latin America and the Caribbean
http://dx.doi.org/10.1596/978-1-4648-0241-6

other hand, the gross operating surplus (i.e., the contribution of capital from incorporated firms to value added) declined or decelerated in all countries in the subsample. The only common pattern across the four countries is that all of them show a decline in "mixed income." This can be interpreted as indicating that the informal sector was the one unequivocally affected by the crisis.

Message 4: An in-depth analysis of the impact of the crisis reveals different adjustment mechanisms but similar final incidence results for Brazil and Mexico.

For Brazil and Mexico, single-country CGE models were used to build the macro counterfactuals and to generate general equilibrium consistent variables, such as employment and wages by sector and skill level, which were then transferred to a microsimulation model to build micro counterfactuals. The business as usual (BaU) scenario (i.e., a hypothetical counterfactual representing what would have been the behavior of the Mexican and Brazilian economies without the global financial crisis of 2008–09) was built from trends for the period 2001–07 and from forecasts available in 2007 or early 2008 (IMF 2007, 2008). In constructing the BaU scenario, the CGE model uses exogenous growth rates for GDP and for the supply of primary factors (labor by skill type and capital) and thus generates endogenously the needed change in total factor productivity. In addition, to attain the expected evolution of the aggregate demand, the model estimates endogenous shifts in the export demand curves, changes in the current account balances, investor confidence, and consumer preferences.

The global financial crisis scenario is then simulated using actual observed data for the same set of macro variables (GDP and its demand components) and labor market variables (employment and wages by sector and skill level). The model generates endogenously changes in productivity, investor and consumer confidence, and trade flows, among other things. The differences in the levels of these variables between the counterfactual and the simulated crisis scenarios represent our measurement of the impact of the crisis.

The macroeconomic impact of the crisis was quite different in Mexico and Brazil. In macroeconomic terms, GDP contracted by about 6 percent in Mexico and only 0.3 percent in Brazil. Compared with a counterfactual—no crisis—scenario, Mexico lost about 9 percentage points of its GDP (instead of growing at 2.8 percent, it contracted by 6.2 percent in 2009), whereas Brazil lost 4 percentage points. The size of the macro shock was thus very different, and that is reflected in the much larger poverty increase in Mexico than in Brazil. The *shape* of the macro shock was also different across the two countries. When the crisis and no-crisis scenarios are compared, changes in public consumption were not very significant in either country (but private consumption was more resilient in Brazil than in Mexico); imports and exports dropped in both countries, and the relative reduction in investment demand (i.e., with respect to a 1 percent reduction in GDP) was much larger in Brazil.

A main difference in the labor market adjustments in the two countries is that Mexico experienced a widespread reduction in number of hours worked that did not occur in Brazil. For each percentage point reduction in GDP (when comparing the no-crisis scenario to the crisis scenario), employment contracted by 0.2 percent in both Mexico and Brazil. However, when employment is measured in number of hours worked and not in number of people employed, the picture that emerges is quite different. In Mexico, for the same 1 percent slowdown in GDP (the same "dose" of crisis), employment, as newly defined, contracts sixfold—that is, 1.2 percent instead of 0.2 percent. Clearly, working fewer hours had a negative effect on income, but this factor generally represented a transitory and less severe loss than the one associated with becoming unemployed.

Wages also adjusted differently: they were less flexible in Brazil than in Mexico. Earnings changes were progressive in Mexico, as skilled workers and those in the nontradable sectors—groups with higher labor incomes—experienced a drop in their wage premia. Brazil's skill premium increased slightly and generated some unequalizing pressures.

In Mexico, workers in both the tradable and nontradable sectors suffered, with workers in the tradable sectors suffering larger (hour) employment losses but less severe wage declines than workers in the nontradable sectors. These differential adjustments resulted in an increase in the tradable to nontradable sectoral wage premium. Similarly, unskilled workers were more likely to lose jobs than skilled ones, and the rise in the two unemployment rates reflected that difference. However, the skill wage premium was almost unaffected. A main adjustment channel of the Mexican labor market was factorial intensity. For both the tradable and nontradable sectors of the economy, the skilled to unskilled employment ratio increased by about 3 percent. In the no-crisis scenario, Mexico would normally have employed 1.02 (effective) skilled workers per each unskilled worker in the tradable sectors and 2.18 in the nontradable sectors. But because of the crisis, these ratios became 1.06 and 2.26. This change in the skill intensity of Mexican labor markets was enough to save about 1 million skilled jobs during the crisis.[10]

In Brazil, employment in the tradable sectors went down as well, and more severely for unskilled workers. The nontradable sectors reacted differently and registered a slight increase in employment that, however, benefitted only unskilled workers. This positive impact did not fully compensate for the job losses in the tradable sectors, which were large enough to amount to a collective loss of employment of about 1 percent for unskilled workers. The adjustment in the Brazilian labor markets appears to have been substituting unskilled employment for skilled employment in the nontradable sectors and the opposite in the tradable sectors. These quantity adjustments were accompanied by negligible changes in the skill and sectoral wage premia.

These cross-country differences in the labor market adjustment are the result of the type of shock that hit the countries, the institutional settings of their product and factor markets, and agents' reactions to the shock. A decomposition analysis (performed by using the CGE model in decomposition mode) can shed light on the contribution of these different mechanisms.

Message 5: Countries were quite active in their social protection policy responses, largely taking advantage of programs built in precrisis years but also making new starts that will serve in the future.

The LAC countries undertook a big secular expansion in social protection before the crisis, especially in social assistance.

Because data on social protection expenditures are not systematically available, the World Bank's LAC Social Protection team built a new data set that allows analysis of overall trends in and composition of spending on social protection in 10 countries in the LAC region: Argentina, Brazil, Chile, Colombia, Ecuador, El Salvador, Honduras, Mexico, Peru, and Uruguay (Cerutti et al. 2014). The harmonized data focus on social assistance and labor market programs. Data collection is directed at a core set of programs for which we tried to collect complete and comparable information. This is not a matter of principle but of practicality, and it implies that we were biasing downward our measurement of the efforts governments are making to provide a social floor for the poor by not counting housing assistance, price subsidies for food and energy, or subsidized access to health insurance.

Expenditures on social assistance programs increased significantly in the 2000s in the 10 LAC countries with new and comparable data. The average spending in the 10 countries for which we have data went from 0.4 percent of GDP in 2000 to 1.2 percent in 2010. Argentina's social assistance expenditures, for example, exhibited a sevenfold increase over that period, from 0.2 percent to 1.5 percent of GDP. In 2000 only 4 of the 10 countries in the data set—Brazil, Chile, Colombia, and Ecuador—were spending more than 0.4 percent of GDP on social assistance, whereas by 2010 all countries but Honduras were spending more (see figure 1.8).

Figure 1.8 Spending on Social Assistance as a Share of GDP for Selected Countries: Latin America and the Caribbean, 2000–10

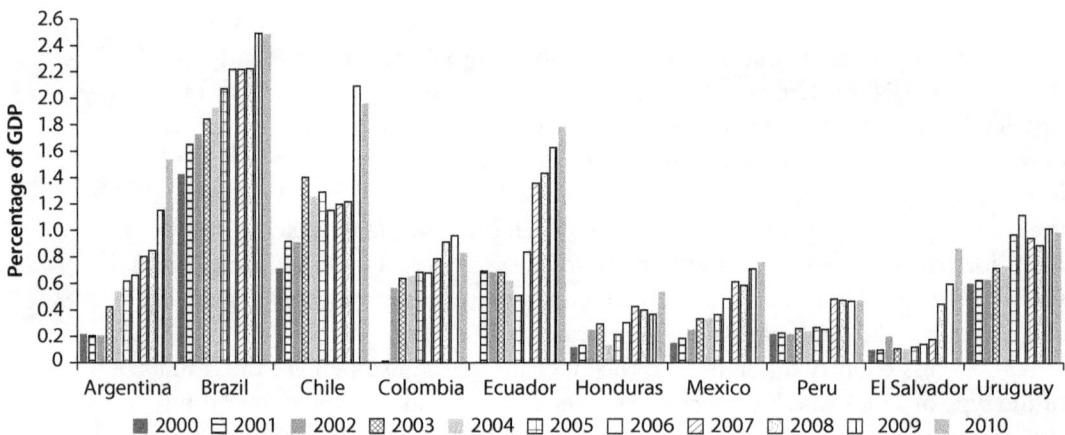

Source: Latin America and the Caribbean Social Protection (LAC SP) database, World Bank.
Note: This graph includes only expenditures by central governments.

The overall picture of social assistance in the LAC region is that most countries have a rich and diverse set of programs, but with a great deal of variation in the mix within each country. Latin America is rightly famous for the rise of the CCT program in the decade preceding the crisis. Perhaps less widely recognized but also important parts of the social assistance systems being built are the new social pensions in many countries and the child allowances in a few, the ongoing school feeding programs, and the still significant presence of in-kind food programs in several countries.

Expenditures on labor market programs—UI, employment services, training, wage subsidies, incentives for self-employment or direct public employment—are much lower. They are on the order of 1 percent of GDP only in Brazil and for selected years in Argentina; on the order of 0.3–0.5 percent of GDP in Colombia, Ecuador, and Uruguay; and still lower in the other five countries tracked in our data set (see figure 1.9). By way of comparison, the OECD average for UI alone is in the range of 0.7–1.0 percent of GDP, depending on the year, and active labor market programs ranged from 0.5 percent to 0.7 percent of GDP over the decade 2000–10 (OECD iLibrary). Active labor market policy (ALMP) spending in 10 Eastern and Central European countries was 0.5 percent of GDP in 2008 and 1.0 percent of GDP in 2010 (Kuddo 2012). Although expenditures on labor market programs are still low in the LAC countries, this has been a rather active area of social policy making over the last decade, especially in more recent years and in the higher-income countries.

There was an active social protection policy response to the crisis.

Beginning in 2008, a number of policy changes were implemented in the LAC region. The changes were somewhat more numerous in the countries more affected by the crisis and more heavily weighted to social assistance than to labor market programs. Policy responses were also apparent in some countries—such as the Dominican Republic and Argentina—that were not so deeply affected by this crisis but that had relatively recent scars from prior crises and would not have known at the outset of the global downturn how well their economies would fare.

Table 1.5 is a brief summary of policy actions taken after the crisis. This tally is of policy changes, thereby discounting the support to households that flowed from ongoing programs. For example, Ecuador did not change the design of its UI savings account after the crisis, but the number of beneficiaries doubled and expenditures nearly doubled.

Of the 26 countries listed in table 1.5, 19 expanded their cash transfer programs by increasing coverage (5 countries), benefit levels (3 countries), or both (11 countries). CCT programs were the workhorses of the social assistance response—every country that had a CCT program used it as a key part of the crisis response. Moreover, a number of social pensions programs were rolled out or expanded at about the same time as the crisis (although not necessarily because of it), as were reforms that expanded the noncontributory child allowances in the Southern Cone. Other cash transfers—the poverty-targeted

Figure 1.9 Spending on Labor Market Programs as a Share of GDP for Selected Countries: Latin America and the Caribbean, 2000–10

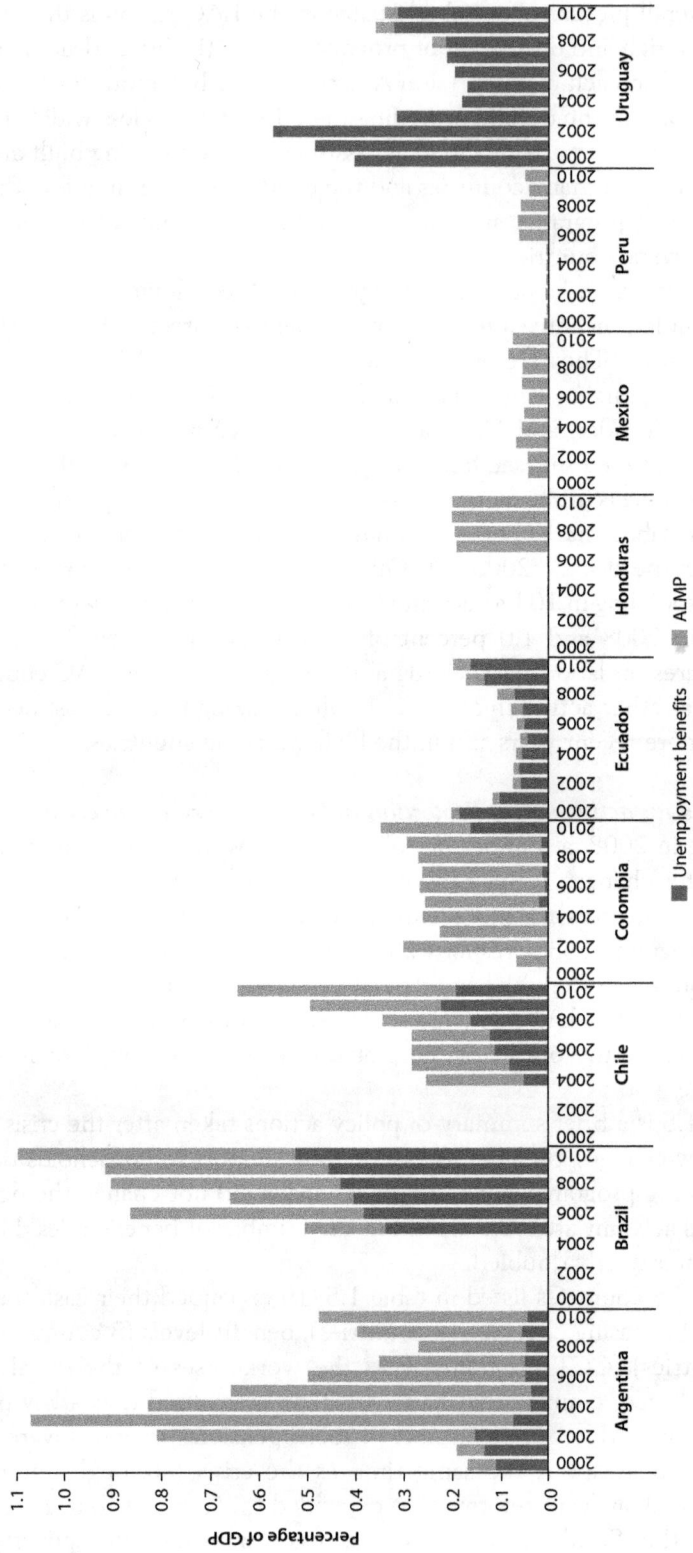

Source: Latin America and Caribbean Social Protection (LAC SP) database, World Bank.

Note: ALMP = active labor market policy.

Table 1.5 Social Protection Policy Responses to the 2008–09 Global Financial Crisis: Latin America and the Caribbean

Outcome	Country	Cash transfer response (conditional and unconditional)			Minimum wage	Labor market			
		Increased benefits	Increased coverage	Developed new program		Wage subsidies	UI/UISA	Training	Temporary employment
Strong (negative growth)	Antigua and Barbuda						X		
	Mexico	X	X		X		X	X	X
	Paraguay	X	X		X			X	X
	Venezuela, RB				X				
	El Salvador	X			X				X
	Jamaica	X	X		X			X	
	St. Vincent and the Grenadines	X							
	Honduras		X	X	X				
	Nicaragua				X				
	St. Lucia								X
	Chile	X	X	X	X	X	X	X	X
	Costa Rica		X		X			X	
	Dominica	X			X				
	Brazil	X	X		X		X		
Moderate (positive growth but significant deceleration)	Peru	X	X				X	X	X
	Panama		X	X					
	Argentina	X		X	X	X		X	
	Ecuador		X		X			X	
	Uruguay	X	X		X	X	X		
	Belize			X					
Low (positive growth with moderate deceleration)	Bolivia	X	X	X	X				
	Guatemala	X	X	X	X				
	Colombia	X	X		X	X		X	
	Dominican Republic	X	X		X				
	Guyana				X				
	Haiti				X				

Sources: ILO/World Bank 2014 and CEPAL 2010.

Note: Countries were ordered from more affected to least affected. UI/UISA = unemployment insurance/unemployment insurance savings account.

programs in the Caribbean and disability allowances in a handful of countries—
were also expanded.

Liberalization of UI requirements or expansion of labor market programs was
also a common response, but generally small in magnitude. Most of the largely
upper-middle-income countries that had UI or unemployment insurance savings
accounts (UISAs) liberalized their rules to extend somewhat benefits. Brazil, for
example, liberalized its UI benefits in a way that temporarily assisted only
217,000 additional job seekers against a backdrop of 7–8 million unemployed.
Chile carried out a more significant and permanent reform of its UISA program
in ways that would increase coverage, especially of contract workers, and yet the
share of unemployed benefitting fell temporarily, from 22 percent before the
crisis to 18 percent during the crisis. Some countries without full UI allowed
those who lost formal jobs to keep their health insurance for a few months, and
a few countries started new UI schemes. Mexico allowed unemployed workers
to make withdrawals from their pension funds. A few countries ran short-work
schemes, and some tried to improve their public employment services. Public
works programs were undertaken in some countries but were generally a small
part of the response.

Social protection expenditures partially offset the declines in labor income, although we can only partially quantify the effect.

Some governments took steps in sensible directions to improve social protection
during the crisis, but the extent of response in increased spending, in increased
number of beneficiaries, or in number of policy changes was only weakly related
to the extent of the macro impact and often too small. In Mexico, total spending
on labor market and social assistance programs increased by about the value of
the increase in the poverty deficit using the extreme poverty line. In Ecuador, the
increase in spending was about two-thirds the value of the extreme poverty line,
and in El Salvador a small fraction. Conversely, in Argentina, Brazil, and Chile
there were large increases in social assistance and labor market spending, though
not mostly crisis-related, and poverty did not increase with the crisis.

Rigorous impact evaluations of policy responses to the crisis will not be possible in most cases. However, most program responses seem to incorporate sensible design elements, and a good share were built on established mechanisms for
implementation. Therefore, it seems likely that the bulk of expenditure was
reasonably fruitful.

Government transfers partially offset declines in labor income and other
nonlabor income, especially for the poorer. This is well illustrated in Ecuador,
Mexico, and Uruguay, where public transfers are the largest component of
nonlabor income and thus define the compensatory role of nonlabor income
at the bottom of the distribution. Increases in public transfers were concentrated in the lower deciles and large enough to offset declines in other nonlabor income for the poorest decile, but could not match the much larger drops
in labor earnings. In Ecuador, the rise in transfers offset the fall in labor earnings. In Mexico, the rise in public transfers could barely compensate for the

Figure 1.10 Growth Incidence Curve, by Four Income Sources: Ecuador, El Salvador, Mexico, and Uruguay, 2008–09

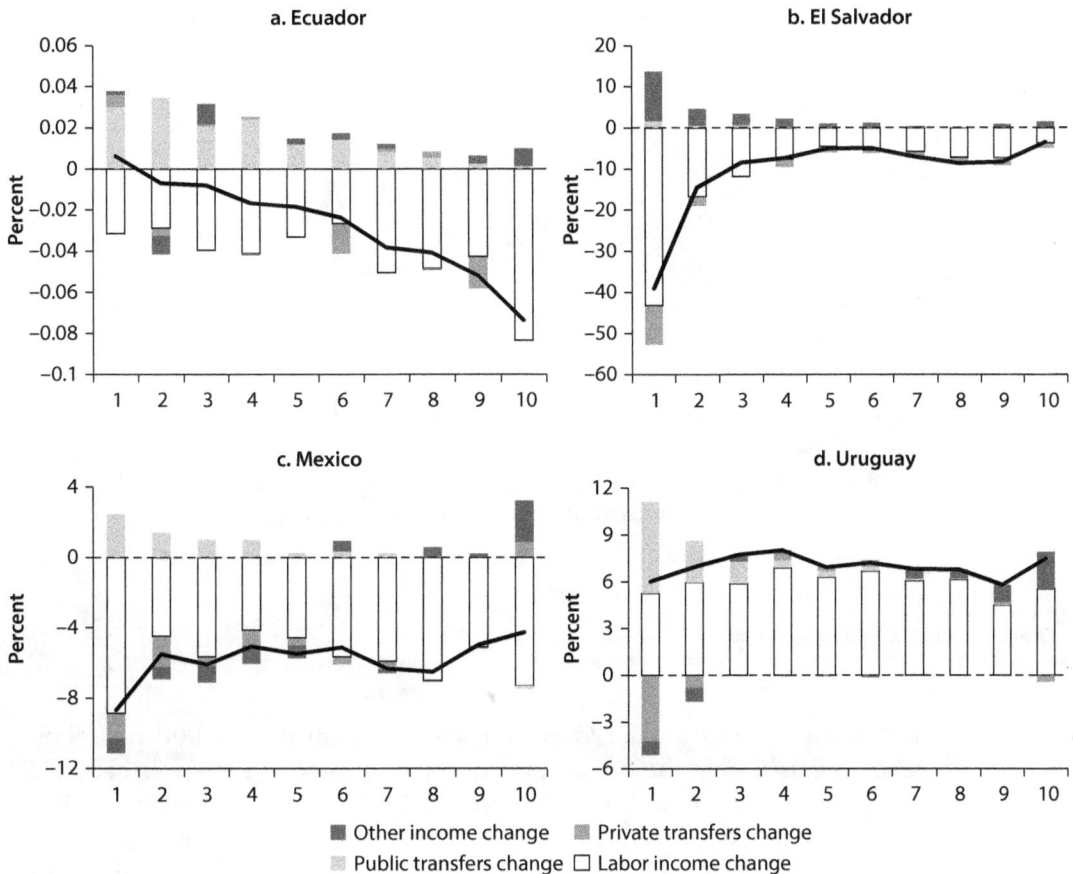

a. Ecuador

b. El Salvador

c. Mexico

d. Uruguay

■ Other income change   ▨ Private transfers change
▨ Public transfers change   □ Labor income change

Sources: SEDLAC harmonized data sets and ENIGH, 2008 and 2010.
Note: Data for Mexico are for 2008–10.

decline in remittances and other income received by those at the bottom of the distribution. Data in El Salvador show a change in public transfers too small to offset the very large declines in labor or other income for the poor (see figure 1.10).

Because the pain of the crisis was felt more through reductions in wages or hours than open unemployment, with the biggest reductions among the poorest, the existing poverty-targeted social assistance programs were more useful instruments of policy than might have been presumed. According to the macro-micro modeling, an estimated 42 million Mexicans earned about 8 percent less in 2009 because of the crisis, and about 750,000 workers lost their jobs and suffered far larger declines in income. Thus the ability to supplement the income of the households that were earning the least at the outset and could least afford to suffer the income drop was a very big part of an adequate crisis response. The simulations in figure 1.11[11] show the effects of the

Figure 1.11 Simulated Effects of Increased Coverage and Benefits for Mexico's Oportunidades Program

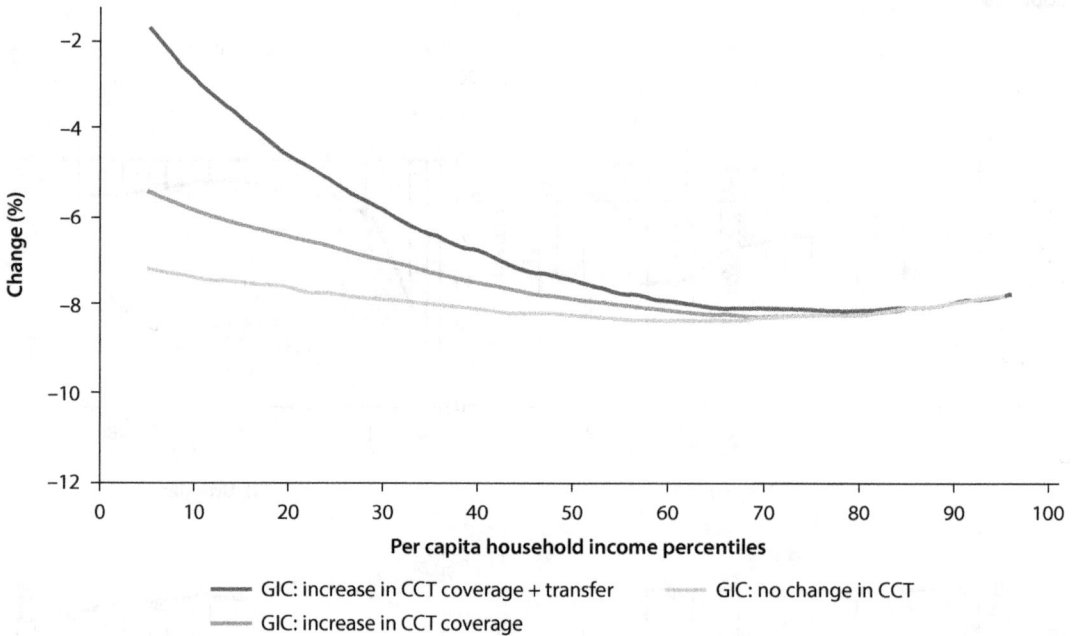

Source: La Encuesta Nacional de Ingresos y Gastos de los Hogares (ENIGH).
Note: Deciles from simulated income distribution. GIC = growth incidence curve; CCT = conditional cash transfer.

expanded coverage of the Oportunidades program by 750,000 households, assuming, first, that the increase in coverage all came in the lower half of the income distribution and is proportionate to the families already enrolled[12] and, second, that all recipients, old and new, received an increase in benefits of 120 pesos per two months. The orange line shows the effect of the increase in the coverage, and the blue line is the result of the combined policy change. Without the policy response, the income of those in the 20th percentile of the distribution would have fallen by just over 8 percent; after the change the drop was less than 6 percent. For those in the 10th percentile, the effect was even larger; their incomes fell not 8 percent but 3 percent. The expansion of Oportunidades was only a portion of the policy response in Mexico,[13] but we model it here in isolation partly for data reasons and partly to illustrate how the expansion of CCT programs may have played out in other countries.

A single instrument is not sufficient to provide social protection in a crisis, and even a thoughtfully balanced portfolio may fall short.
Households with workers who lost jobs suffered significant income losses, enough to prompt some observers to urge a social policy response. The macro-micro modeling for Mexico suggests that income losses were significant for job losers—on the order of 24 percent for skilled workers who lost their jobs and 37 percent for unskilled workers who lost their jobs, enough to tumble them down the income distribution. The simulations also suggest that two-thirds of

Figure 1.12 Distribution of Job Destruction Caused by the Global Financial Crisis, by Decile and Skill Level: Mexico

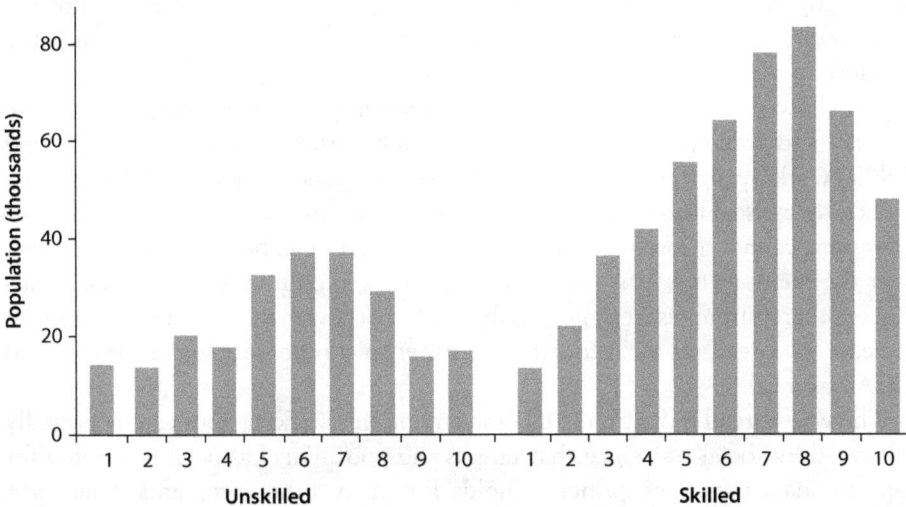

Source: ENIGH.
Note: Graph depicts simulation of job losses among unskilled workers (232,000) and skilled workers (507,000).

losses were concentrated among those who had more years of education and who were younger, and that job losses were spread across the income distribution, but peak in the sixth decile for unskilled workers and the eighth decile for skilled workers (see figure 1.12).

No single program will solve the full problem of income support for the unemployed, but a carefully devised set of programs may begin to weave together a safety net that can lessen the shocks to some if not all households.

UI can support those in the formal sector. In Mexico, the crisis propagated in large part in the manufactured tradable sectors, which are relatively formal. However, the coverage of UI will always be limited by the extent of the informal sector, which, overall, constituted 50 percent of the Mexican workforce in 2008.

UI savings accounts have the potential, though not a strong track record, of including voluntarily workers from the informal sector. Affiliating workers in the middle or top of the income spectrum and those among the more educated with UISA programs may be somewhat easier than affiliating poorer or less educated workers. In Mexico, it was possibly easier to affiliate groups that were hit the hardest by the crisis.

Employment in labor-intensive public works projects is another option for income support for the unemployed. This option has a track record of assisting those at the lower end of the earning and skills spectrum, often informal workers who are the people least likely to benefit from UI or UISA, making public works a good complement to UI and UISA programs.

A further option is to provide training, job search assistance, or employment support focused especially on youth, the cohort both most affected by the crisis and with the highest baseline rates of unemployment.

Even programs of income support for the unemployed and active labor market programs with incomplete coverage are valuable. They assist the covered portion of the population directly, reducing the welfare and human capital costs of the crisis. Indirectly, more extensive and successful labor programs may reduce the pressure to burden CCT programs with the need to deal with labor shocks. This would allow these programs to focus on their core mission of mitigating chronic poverty and fomenting equality of opportunity. Both UI/UISA programs and public works programs can be highly countercyclical, able to automatically reduce their fiscal burden when a crisis eases in a way that social assistance programming cannot. Moreover, UI and UISA programs can be largely self-financing over the medium run. It is important, especially in countries where social assistance programming is reaching high levels of coverage and benefits, not to increase the pressures for it to expand further to compensate for missing UI and UISA coverage.

The widespread reduction in income among the working poor can be partially mitigated by social assistance that targets the poor. This has been illustrated for Oportunidades, but the principle holds for many other programs. There are, however, limits to the mitigation that poverty-targeting programs, especially the region's CCTs, can provide, and the crisis outlined vividly the differences in programs geared toward providing equality of opportunity versus managing risk.

The region's CCTs do target the poor, and thus will help few households in the middle of the income distribution, although in Mexico it was those in the middle of the distribution that suffered the largest proportional income losses. The CCT programs of most countries serve only families with children, and in some countries operate in only defined geographic areas, usually favoring rural areas where chronic poverty is highest, but which may not have been the worst areas affected by the global financial crisis.

The region's poverty-targeting programs in general had targeting criteria that were too static to cater to those whose incomes fell. Rather, the programs' expansion served more to complete coverage among those more likely to be chronically poor.

Even where the CCTs do not suffer these limitations to a crisis response, to scale them up too far can be imprudent. For example, the coverage and benefit levels of Oportunidades were significant before the crisis.[14] To scale them up too far would increase questions of sustainability, labor disincentives, and balance among elements of social policy. Ecuador, Brazil, and Colombia also had programs that were quite large before the crisis.

Message 6: Overall, the policy messages are that good policy helps attenuate the links between the global crisis and poverty in the LAC region, and many of the important things need to be done ex ante.

The impacts of the global financial crisis on poverty were smaller than predicted at the outset of the crisis. A large part of the reason was that growth was so high before the crisis that there was significant room for deceleration before plunging into negative growth. Meanwhile, macro and fiscal fundamentals were stronger than in earlier crises, which meant that in most LAC countries internal weaknesses did not magnify the effects of external problems. Moreover, there was space for immediate policy actions, including the social protection responses, which were largely built on platforms developed before the crisis.

There are some actions that could be taken now that the recovery is well under way to strengthen the LAC region's position for the next downturn. These actions fall into two categories. The first includes rebuilding the buffers that allowed countercyclical policies to be implemented during the crisis. This entails fiscal consolidation while maintaining and possibly extending the social protection networks. Improvements in the efficiency of taxation (i.e., increases in revenues without increasing tax rates) should thus be part of the fiscal adjustment, especially for those countries with quite low ratios of tax revenues to GDP. The second category includes measures that would strengthen the resilience and sustainability of economic growth, for example, by maintaining sound macroeconomic and financial policies and intensifying efforts to raise productivity.

Social assistance programs for the chronically poor could be improved in some ways that would allow them to better serve their core goals of chronic poverty relief and yet enable them to also stand in for vulnerability reduction programs. The most important tweaks to these programs would be improving the match between their design and funding and establishing on-demand/open registries and more regular recertification of eligibility.

The LAC countries should press ahead in expanding coverage and improving the performance of labor market programs. Cost-effective active labor market programs can improve productivity and equity and have a place in both long-run and crisis agendas. Likewise, income supports for the unemployed have a place in these agendas.

There may be benefits from strengthening the coherence of and linkages within different parts of the social protection system. At the highest level, this will involve thinking about the mix of policies to balance the coverage among groups and risks—for example, addressing chronic poverty and inequality versus shorter-term risks to income (both cyclical and idiosyncratic) or, within the risk of unemployment, the relative roles of severance pay, UI, UISA, and public works. On a lower level, this will entail creating greater linkages between income support and active labor market policies.

Finally, data collection must be improved. Countries need basic poverty and labor data from household surveys to track trends in outcomes. These surveys should also provide information on the coverage, targeting, and adequacy of the larger social protection programs. Some countries have reached adequate levels of survey data, but many of the smaller economies have not, and even countries with good poverty tracking and large and stable social programs do not always reflect them well in their survey questionnaires. Administrative data should be brought together across agencies and levels of government to track the evolving size and shape of the social protection sector. And more real-time centralization of data on the use of health and education services, either for the population as a whole or for participants in CCT programs, could give early warning of human capital issues that may result from widespread income shocks.

Understanding the Poverty Impact of the Global Financial Crisis in Latin America and the Caribbean
http://dx.doi.org/10.1596/978-1-4648-0241-6

Notes

1. Conceptually, we consider the region to consist of all countries from Mexico south and all of the Caribbean Islands except Puerto Rico. However, practically, for most outcomes, we have data for only some of these countries. We define in each chapter, and sometimes for each table or concept, the list of countries covered. The 12 countries examined in the poverty chapter that is the heart of this study are Argentina, Brazil, Chile, Colombia, Costa Rica, the Dominican Republic, Ecuador, El Salvador, Mexico, Paraguay, Peru, and Uruguay (see chapter 3).

2. This conceptual framework is partially based on Ferreira, Prennushi, and Ravallion (1999); Dercon (2006); Bourguignon, Bussolo, and Pereira da Silva (2008); and Bussolo, de Hoyos, and Medvedev (2010).

3. For a description of the project and its databases, see http://sedlac.econo.unlp.edu.ar /eng/index.php. We have also benefitted from the inputs of the Group for Statistical Development of the Poverty and Gender Unit for Latin America at the World Bank and their recent publications on poverty during the crisis, *Did Latin America Learn to Shield Its Poor from Economic Shocks?* (World Bank 2010) and *On the Edge of Uncertainty: Poverty Reduction in Latin America and the Caribbean during the Great Recession and Beyond* (World Bank 2011).

4. Systemic banking crises occurred during 1994–98: in Bolivia, Brazil, Costa Rica, Haiti, Mexico, and República Bolivariana de Venezuela in 1994; in Argentina and Paraguay in 1995; in Jamaica in 1996; and in Colombia and Ecuador in 1998. Antigua and Barbuda suffered foreign currency debt crises in 1996, and Mexico, Suriname, and República Bolivariana de Venezuela experienced currency crises in 1994.

5. The 2003–08 time span refers to a weighted average of a larger set of countries (see World Bank 2011). The trends are not strictly comparable but still illustrative of the deceleration of poverty decline in the region.

6. All dollar amounts are U.S. dollars unless otherwise indicated.

7. Household surveys in the region fail to fully capture many sources of nonlabor income, particularly rents and other capital income. They are better at capturing sources of income that are important for the poor—that is, transfers and remittances. However, these sources of income are not collected equally in all countries. Figures showing growth incidence curves decomposed into labor and nonlabor incomes should be interpreted with these caveats in mind.

8. Ecuador, as mentioned earlier, is an outlier. There, prime-age women, as well as other groups, experienced a decline in employment despite economic growth.

9. We speak here of full, open unemployment. In Europe, some countries had job-sharing schemes that reduced hours of work significantly. Latin America had fewer and smaller formal job-sharing programs, but, at least in Mexico, the number of hours per worker was reduced, indicating that the total reduction in hours of work was larger than indicated by open unemployment alone.

10. In the no-crisis scenario, the employment of effective workers equals 13.6 million for unskilled and 23.5 million for skilled and an overall ratio of skilled per unskilled worker of 1.73. In the crisis scenario, this ratio increases to 1.81, and thus—assuming nothing happens to the level of employment of the unskilled—the number of employed skilled workers is estimated at 24.5 million (13.6 million × 1.81). The difference in employment for skilled workers between the two scenarios is equal to 1 million.

11. The difference between the green line and the orange line is a partial estimate of the concept D'C in figure 1.2.

12. In fact, the expansion was disproportionately targeted to urban areas and used a revised formula for the proxy means test, but the simpler simulation makes it more representative of how such expansions may work generally.

13. The policy responses included expansion of unconditional cash transfer programs, public works jobs, short-work schemes, continued access to health care for formal sector workers who lost their jobs, and the ability to withdraw funds from retirement benefits.

14. In the poorest decile, transfers accounted for about 40 percent of recipient household income in 2008. In 2010, as their autonomous income fell and transfers rose, the share was closer to 50 percent—levels high enough to raise concerns about labor market incentives.

References

Azevedo, João Pedro. 2011. "Business Cycles and Intergenerational Mobility: Evidence from the First Great Recession of the XXI Century." Presentation, World Bank, Washington, DC.

Bhalla, Surjit S. 2002. *Imagine There's No Country: Poverty, Inequality and Growth in the Era of Globalization*. Washington, DC: Institute for International Economics.

Bourgignon, François, Maurizio Bussolo, and Luiz Pereira da Silva. 2008. *The Impact of Macroeconomic Policies on Poverty and Income Distribution: Macro-Micro Evaluation Techniques and Tools*, edited by François Bourgignon, Maurizio Bussolo, and Luiz A. Pereira da Silva. Washington, DC: Palgrave and World Bank.

Bussolo, Maurizio, Rafael E. De Hoyos, and Denis Medvedev. 2010. "Economic Growth and Income Distribution: Linking Macro-Economic Models with Household Survey Data at the Global Level." *International Journal of Microsimulation* 3 (1): 92–103.

CEPAL (Comité de Economia y Política de América Latina). 2010. "La Reaccion de los gobiernos de las Américas frente a la crisis internacional: una presentación sentética de las medidas de política anunciadas hasta el 31 de diciembre de 2009." División de Desarrollo Económico, CEPAL, Santiago.

Cerutti, Paula, Anna Fruttero, Margaret Grosh, Silvana Kostenbaum, Maria Laura Oliveri, Claudia Rodriguez-Alas, and Victoria Strokova. 2014. *Social Assistance and Labor Market Programs in Latin America: Methodology and Key Findings from the Social Protection Database*. Social Protection and Labor Discussion Paper Series. World Bank, Washington, DC.

Chang, Shu-Sen Chang, David Stuckler, Paul Yip, and David Gunnell. 2013. "Impact of 2008 Global Economic Crisis on Suicide: Time Trend Study in 54 Countries." *British Medical Journal* 347: f5239.

Deaton, Angus. 2003. "How to Monitor Poverty for the Millennium Development Goals." *Journal of Human Development* 4 (3): 2003.

Dercon, Stefan. 2006. "Economic Reform, Growth and the Poor: Evidence from Rural Ethiopia." *Journal of Development Economics* 81 (1): 1–24.

Fallon, Peter R., and Robert E. B. Lucas. 2002. "The Impact of Financial Crises on Labor Markets, Household Incomes, and Poverty: A Review of Evidence." *World Bank Research Observer* 17 (1): 21–45.

Ferreira, Francisco H. G., Giovanna Prennushi, and Martin Ravallion. 1999. "Protecting the Poor from Macroeconomic Shocks." Policy Research Working Paper 2160, World Bank, Washington, DC.

Ferreira, Francisco H. G., and Norbert Schady. 2008. "Aggregate Economic Shocks, Child Schooling and Child Health." Policy Research Working Paper 4701, World Bank, Washington, DC.

Grifith-Jones, Stephanie, and Jose Antonio Ocampo. 2009. "The Financial Crisis and Its Impact on Developing Countries." Working Paper 53, International Policy Centre for Inclusive Growth, Brasilia.

Halac, Marina, and Sergio Schmukler. 2004. "Distributional Effects of Crises: The Financial Channel." *Economía* 5 (1): 1–67.

ILO/World Bank. 2014. *Inventory of Policy Responses to the Financial and Economic Crisis.* Joint Synthesis Report, World Bank, Washington, DC.

IMF (International Monetary Fund). 2007. *Mexico: 2007 Article IV Consultation—Staff Report; Staff Supplement; and Public Information Notice on the Executive Board Discussion for Mexico.* IMF Country Report 07/379, Washington, DC.

———. 2008. "Article IV Consultation with Brazil." Public Information Notice (PIN) 08/103, Washington, DC, IMF.

———. 2009. "Regional Economic Outlook: Western Hemisphere: Crisis Averted—What's Next?" *World Economic and Financial Surveys.* Washington, DC: IMF.

———. 2010. "How Did Emerging Markets Cope in the Crisis?" IMF Policy Paper, http://www.imf.org/external/pp/longres.aspx?gsa=true&id=4459.

Kanbur, Ravi. 2010. "Macro Crises and Targeting Transfers to the Poor." *Journal of Globalization and Development* 1 (1): article 9.

Kuddo, Arvo. 2012. "Public Employment Services and Activation Policies." Social Protection and Labor Discussion Paper 1215, World Bank, Washington, DC.

Lustig, Nora. 2000. "Crises and the Poor: Socially Responsible Macroeconomics." Working Paper 108, Poverty and Inequality Advisory Unit, Sustainable Development Department, Inter-American Development Bank, Washington, DC.

Ravallion, Martin. 2003. "Measuring Aggregate Welfare in Developing Countries: How Well Do National Accounts and Surveys Agree?" *Review of Economics and Statistics* 85 (3): 645–52.

———. 2011. "A Comparative Perspective on Poverty Reduction in Brazil, China and India." *World Bank Research Observer* 26 (1): 71–104.

Robilliard, Anne-Sophie, and Sherman Robinson. 2003. "Reconciling Household Surveys and National Accounts Data Using a Cross Entropy Estimation Method." *Review of Income and Wealth* 49 (3).

Szekely, Miguel, and Marianne Hilgert. 1999. "What's Behind the Inequality We Measure: An Investigation Using Latin American Data." Working Paper 340, Inter-American Development Bank, Washington, DC.

Szekely, Miguel, Nora Lustig, Martín Cumpa, and José Antonio Mejía. 2004. "Do We Know How Much Poverty There Is?" *Oxford Development Studies* 32 (4).

World Bank. 2009. *Global Economic Prospects: 2009.* Washington, DC: World Bank.

———. 2010. *Did Latin America Learn to Shield Its Poor from Economic Shocks?* Washington, DC: World Bank.

———. 2011. *On the Edge of Uncertainty: Poverty Reduction in Latin America and the Caribbean during the Great Recession and Beyond.* Washington, DC: World Bank.

Highlights of the Macro Effects of the 2008–09 Global Financial Crisis

Cristina Savescu

The global financial crisis that began to unfold in the second half of 2007 intensified in the fall of 2008 and quickly precipitated into a global economic crisis that affected virtually every country in the world. The bursting of the global financial bubble triggered by the collapse of the U.S. financial services house Lehman Brothers in September 2008 led initially to frozen credit markets, sharp capital flow reversals, tremendous losses in equity prices and market capitalization, and large currency movements. For example, by March 2009 the major stock markets had lost more than 40 percent of their value. Meanwhile, a staggering $31.6 trillion in market capitalization in 20 of the largest stock markets was wiped off the books between mid-May 2008 and March 2009. The financial volatility was accentuated by deleveraging worldwide. The financial crisis promptly triggered an economic crisis, and the global economy was thrust into the deepest recession since the Great Depression (Almunia et al. 2009). Difficulties in accessing capital and a sharp increase in the cost of capital, in conjunction with a spike in risk aversion by investors and consumers, resulted in delays and cutbacks in investments and a sharp contraction in demand for capital goods, durable goods, and finance-sensitive items such as electronics. The production of manufactured goods and exports of manufactured goods were particularly hard-hit.

The impact on global economic activity was severe. Global output, as measured by the gross domestic product (GDP), contracted 2.2 percent in 2009, the only global recession in at least five and a half decades. With the United States at the epicenter of the crisis, economic activity in high-income countries declined 3.5 percent, while growth in developing countries slowed markedly, to 1.9 percent from 5.8 percent the previous year. Output in the developing world contracted 1.6 percent if China and India are excluded. Among the developing regions, the Europe and Central Asia (ECA) region was by far the hardest hit by the global crisis, with GDP contracting 6.5 percent and two-thirds of countries recording a contraction in GDP. The Latin America and the Caribbean (LAC) region was the second-worst affected, with output declining 1.9 percent and one in two countries recording negative GDP growth (figure 2.1). By contrast, no countries in the Middle East and North Africa (MNA) or South Asia (SAR) regions recorded negative growth in 2009, and only one in five countries in Sub-Saharan Africa (SSA) saw GDP decline in 2009.

The collapse in growth, calculated as the difference in growth in 2009 relative to 2008 and arguably a better measure of the impact of the global crisis, was even larger. Growth collapsed by 10.5 percentage points in ECA, and 5.9 percentage points in Latin America and the Caribbean, compared with 3.6 percentage points in high-income countries. The impact on Sub-Saharan Africa was slightly less at 3.1 percentage points, while the less integrated economies of the MNA and South Asia saw growth decelerate 0.5 and 0.9 percentage points, respectively, between 2008 and 2009.

The most acute phase of the global economic crisis commenced in the last quarter of 2008 and lasted through the first quarter of 2009, slashing global industrial production by 7.4 percent (seasonally adjusted) in the fourth quarter of 2008 and by an additional 3.0 percent in the first quarter of 2009. Global trade was affected even more severely, with merchandise trade collapsing 11.6 percent and 5.8 percent in the two quarters, respectively (figures 2.2 and 2.3). Global GDP contracted an estimated 2.1 percent in the

Figure 2.1 Effects of the 2008–09 Global Financial Crisis, by GDP Growth, 2009

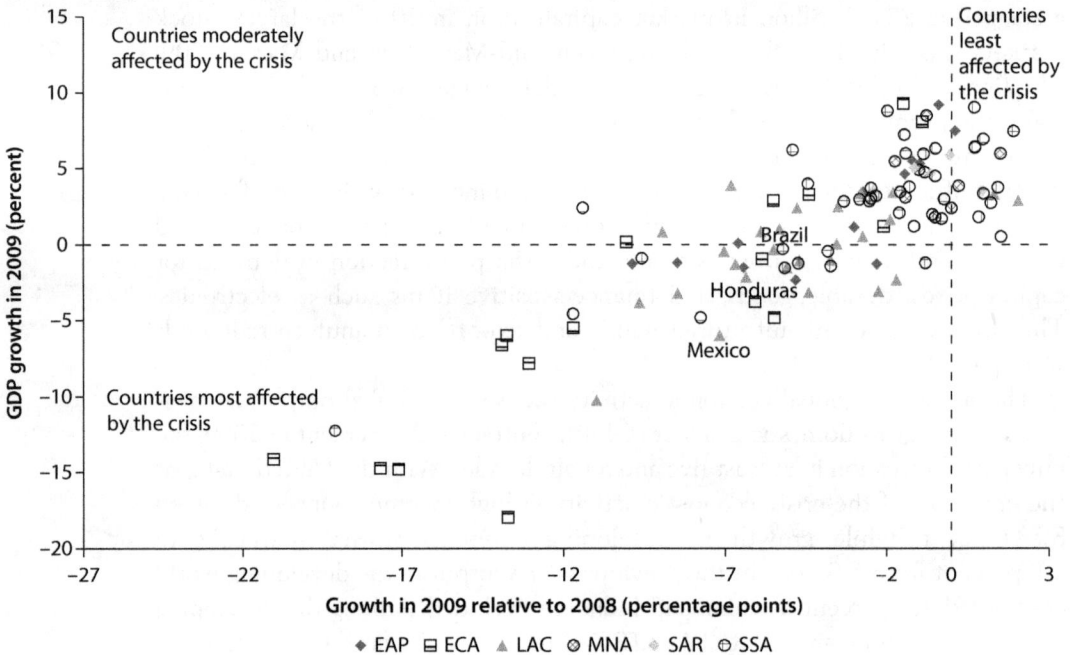

Source: World Bank.
Note: EAP = East Asia and Pacific; ECA = Europe and Central Asia; LAC = Latin America and the Caribbean; MNA = Middle East and North Africa; SAR = South Asia; and SSA = Sub-Saharan Africa.

Figure 2.2 World Industrial Production and Exports during the Global Financial Crisis, 2007–12

Percent growth, three-month moving average, seasonally adjusted annualized rate

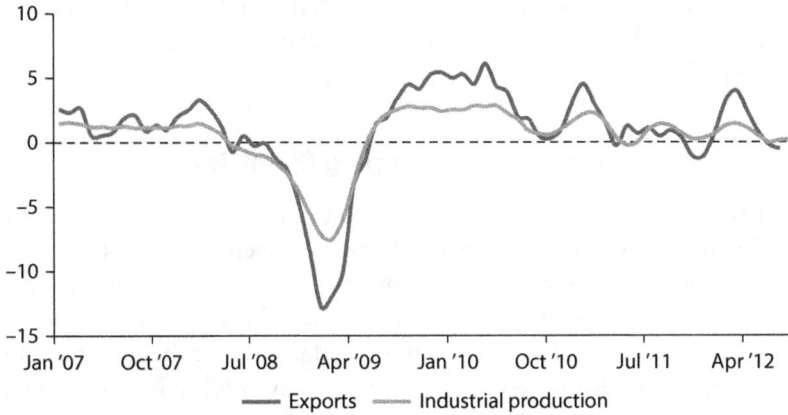

Exports ——— Industrial production ———

Sources: Thomson Datastream and World Bank.

Figure 2.3 Industrial Production during the Global Financial Crisis, 2007–12

Percent growth, three-month moving average, seasonally adjusted annualized rate

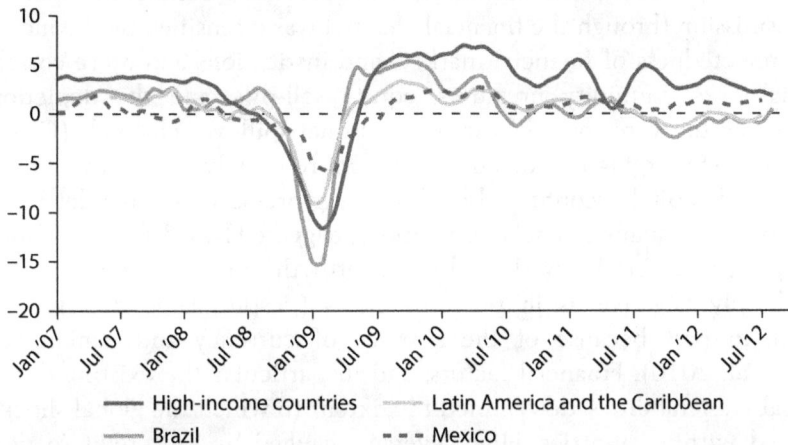

——— High-income countries ·········· Latin America and the Caribbean
——— Brazil   - - - Mexico

Sources: Thomson Datastream and World Bank.

fourth quarter of 2008 and an additional 2 percent in the first quarter of 2009, for a peak-to-trough contraction of 4.5 percent. Output in high-income countries contracted 5.2 percent peak to trough, and output in developing countries declined 3.1 percent. The tight linkages between the financial sector and the real economy created a negative feedback loop that resulted in historically sharp contractions in fixed investment (7.6 percent), industrial production (8.1 percent), and world trade (10.5 percent) in 2009.

Understanding the Poverty Impact of the Global Financial Crisis in Latin America and the Caribbean
http://dx.doi.org/10.1596/978-1-4648-0241-6

The collapse in world trade (10.5 percent) set this crisis apart from previous global recessions when trade growth decelerated markedly or contracted only mildly. Indeed, in the 1982 recession global trade expanded by 1.2 percent, while in the 1998 and 2001 crises it grew by 5.4 percent and 0.6 percent, respectively. These numbers reflect in part the increased interconnectedness of and responsiveness to global supply chains (Freund 2009).

Key Transmission Channels to Developing Countries

The global financial crisis was propagated to developing countries through various channels. The trade and financial channels were key transmission points for the developing economies, but changes in levels of risk aversion and the expectations of investors and consumers also played a critical role. The collapse in external demand caused export volumes to decline sharply in many countries in the region, and it also triggered a collapse in commodity prices. Demand for trade-related services also suffered, as did demand for tourism-related services.

Generally, transmission of the crisis through the trade channel was more intense for countries that were trading heavily with the United States, the epicenter of the crisis, and for countries whose exports of manufactured goods made up a large share of total exports—the crisis significantly affected the demand for manufactured goods. However, the contraction in external demand affected virtually every country, with all but a handful recording declines in exports.

Transmission through the financial channel was intensified by the increased interconnectedness of financial markets and institutions and more correlated financial risks. Liquidity pressures, equity sell-offs, and the depletion of banking capital were some of the international spillover channels (Claessens et al. 2010). Emerging markets that relied more heavily on external financing experienced capital account and bank funding pressures. Global deleveraging by banks and nonbank financial institutions, triggered by a dry-up in wholesale funding markets, markedly slowed credit growth, but credit growth did not turn sharply negative as in previous crises (despite large precrisis credit booms), in part because of the absence of currency and banking crises (Gray et al. 2010). Financial factors, and in particular the existing domestic financial vulnerabilities, determined the extent to which the global shock was amplified within countries. High leverage, gauged by the credit to deposit ratio, and rapid cumulative credit growth were associated with larger growth revisions (Berkmen et al. 2009).

Meanwhile, depressed business expectations and tighter financing conditions constrained fixed investment. Similarly, the collapse in consumer confidence in conjunction with the reduced credit demand and availability, in particular for finance-sensitive big-ticket items, explained the dramatic downward shifts in private consumption. As shown in figure 2.4, remittances in countries with a large share of migrants to the United States were also negatively affected (Sirkeci, Cohen, and Ratha 2012). Capital flows were affected as well, with foreign direct investment (FDI) recording sharp declines in selected economies.

Figure 2.4 Remittances: Latin America and the Caribbean, 2008–12
Percent, year on year

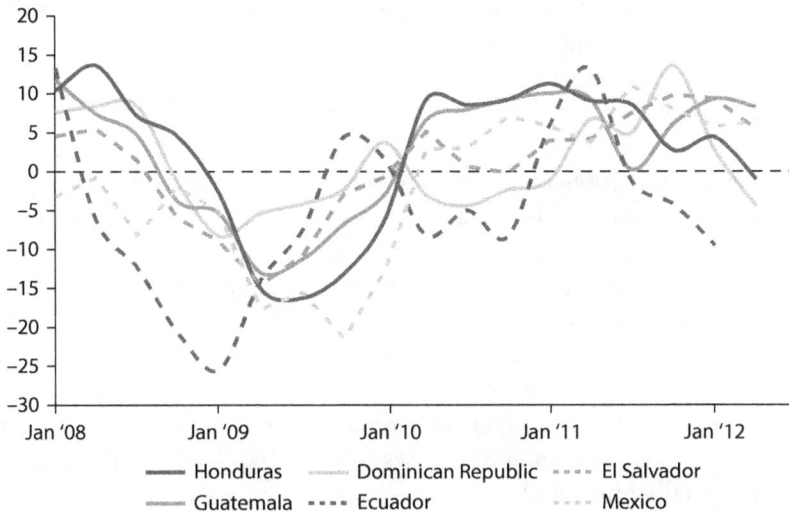

Source: World Bank.

The reversals in capital flows put pressure on exchange rates, which depreciated markedly at the height of the crisis and caused international reserves to decline.

The 2008–09 Crisis: A Break with the Past

Marked improvements in macroeconomic and financial policy frameworks in the precrisis period, in conjunction with lower external vulnerability, cushioned the external shock and allowed governments in the region to respond with countercyclical policies (Didier, Hevia, and Schmukler 2011). Notably, sounder monetary policy frameworks, including exchange rate flexibility and more independent central banks, sounder and better-regulated banking systems, significantly lower currency and rollover risks, deeper local currency debt markets, and lower net public sector borrowing requirements, played a crucial role. Improved current account balances and larger foreign exchange liquidity buffers helped the region weather the crisis as well.

Countercyclical macroeconomic policies, especially monetary policy and in a few cases countercyclical fiscal policies, contributed to a quick recovery. The monetary stimulus was significant, with emerging countries in the region reducing policy rates by 360 basis points on average from August 2008 to October 2009—the largest reduction among developing regions. The fiscal response (as measured by the change in the primary deficit) was stronger than expected given past performances during crises (De la Torre et al. 2010b). It did not include slashing spending in response to the decline in revenues. Rather, it allowed the automatic stabilizers to work and introduced new discretionary

Understanding the Poverty Impact of the Global Financial Crisis in Latin America and the Caribbean
http://dx.doi.org/10.1596/978-1-4648-0241-6

spending or revenue measures (Gray et al. 2010). The fiscal impulse varied across countries and depended crucially on the available fiscal space.

Despite a marked deterioration in economic activity, the LAC region did not experience systemic financial crises unlike in previous crises when currency mismatches and deficient regulatory frameworks underlay and amplified financial crises. During 1994–98, for example, the region experienced 11 systemic banking crises,[1] a foreign currency debt crisis, and three currency crises. In stark contrast with the past, in the 2008–09 crisis there were no systemic banking, foreign currency debt, or currency crises. Bank and corporate balance sheets were not severely impaired during the 2008–09 crisis because of the absence of currency crises, and more generally because of the lower financial and corporate sector vulnerabilities when compared with previous precrisis periods.

The global coordinated response to the crisis and the prompt provision of significant financing from international institutions limited the fall in output. Even in highly vulnerable emerging economies, the initial fall in economic activity was less pronounced than in past crises (IMF 2010). The growth collapse was larger in financially integrated economies in the region.

Furthermore, because there were no systemic banking crises output began to recover faster than in previous crises and when compared with the middle-income country average, the recovery was stronger. The resilience was also reflected in the stronger labor market performance, with unemployment increasing far less than in previous crises, controlling for the decline in GDP. Furthermore, real average wages remained constant or increased, and the trend of labor market formalization was not reversed.

The impact of the crisis on poverty was also less than in past economic downturns. The effects on poverty were heterogeneous within the region. Poverty increased mainly in Mexico and some Central American countries, whereas it actually declined in Brazil, Peru, and Uruguay.

Effects of the Crisis on the LAC Countries

During the 2008–09 crisis, the LAC region was tipped into a mild and for the most part short-lived recession. Economic activity in the region contracted 1.9 percent in 2009, compared with average annual growth of 4.5 percent over the 2003–08 period. Countries that reduced their external vulnerabilities and improved their policy fundamentals in the period prior to the crisis were less affected by it (Gray et al. 2010). Furthermore, many countries in Latin America entered the crisis from a position of cyclical strength, with their economies operating at or above potential[2] (figure 2.5). Had this not been the case, the contraction in output could have been much more significant. A recent World Bank study estimates that for every 1 percentage point decline in the income of high-income countries, Latin American and Caribbean exports might fall 1.4 percent, and output might decline 0.4 percent (World Bank 2012).

In the LAC countries, the aggregate regional growth masked a high degree of heterogeneity among countries with respect to the timing and magnitude

Figure 2.5 Output Gaps as Indicators of Strong Cyclical Positions: Latin America and the Caribbean, 2008 and 2009

Impact of the crisis mitigated by above-potential growth

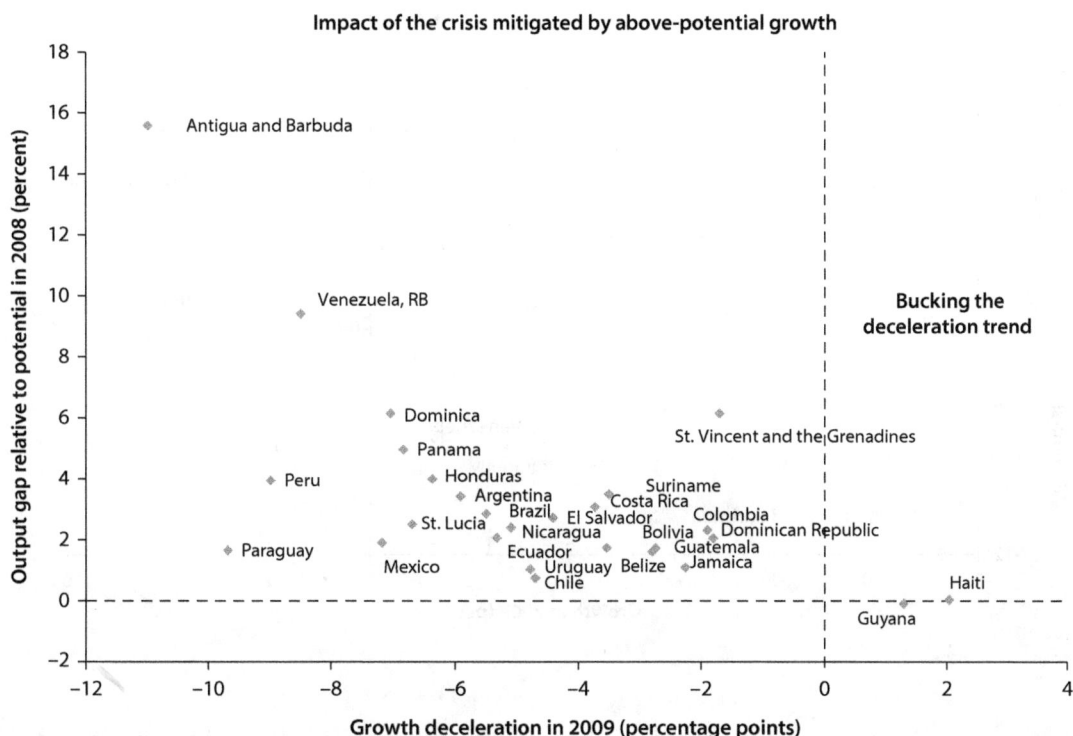

Source: World Bank.

of the recession. As noted, the duration of the recession was short-lived in most countries, and, with a few exceptions, it was mild. However, more than half of the LAC countries entered the recession in 2009 (figure 2.6) with a median output contraction rate of 2.2 percent, while the median growth rate for the remainder of the economies was a meager 2.4 percent (figure 2.1). Generally countries with more open economies, a higher degree of financial openness, stronger trade and financial links to high-income countries (and the United States in particular), and a larger share of manufacturing exports to total exports were affected most (De la Torre 2010a). Controlling for trade and financial openness, countries with stronger precrisis fundamentals and lower vulnerabilities experienced less pronounced output contractions (IMF 2010). Idiosyncratic shocks (droughts, political uncertainty, etc.) also depressed output in some of the economies in the region, with the global financial and economic crisis compounding the negative impacts of these shocks. This was, for example, the case in Paraguay and to a lesser extent in other Southern Cone countries, where a severe drought slashed agricultural output and exports. Meanwhile, in Honduras heightened political tensions also affected economic performance (figure 2.7).

The forgone output resulting from the 2008–09 crisis is, however, much larger than suggested by the annual rate of change in domestic output. Indeed, if the

Figure 2.6 Countries in Recession and Avoiding Recession: Latin America and the Caribbean, 2008–09

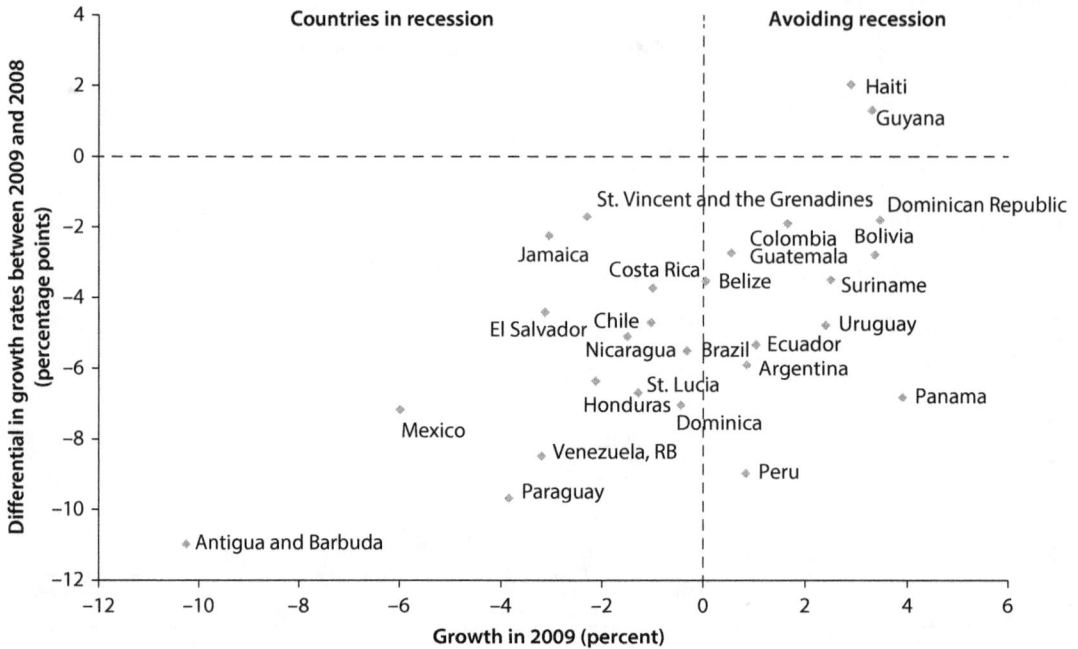

Source: World Bank.

Latin American economies had grown at a pace similar to the one recorded in the precrisis period, output would have been markedly higher in 2009. The growth differential with respect to 2008, for example, is 5.9 percentage points for the Latin America and the Caribbean region, and it is 5.1 percentage points for the 1998–2007 period.

The greatest collapse in growth occurred in Central America (6.8 percentage points), followed by South America (5.6) and the Caribbean (1.8). Part of this deceleration was part and parcel of the normal business cycle, with many economies operating above potential following several years of strong economic expansion. In most countries, however, most of the observed deceleration can be attributed to the crisis.

Collapse in External Demand in Major Export Markets

The collapse in demand in the United States and other main export markets (e.g., Canada for some of the Caribbean countries and Central America for some of the Central American countries) played a major role in the decline in the region's exports of goods and services. The decline in exports contributed 2.3 percentage points to the regional output contraction, and was the largest negative contribution to growth (figure 2.8). Because of its strong links with the U.S. economy, the Mexican economy was the first to feel the impact of the crisis, and its recession was the deepest and longest in Latin America, lasting five quarters. Output contracted 6.0 percent in 2009, on the

Figure 2.7 Real GDP Growth: Latin America and the Caribbean, 2008–09

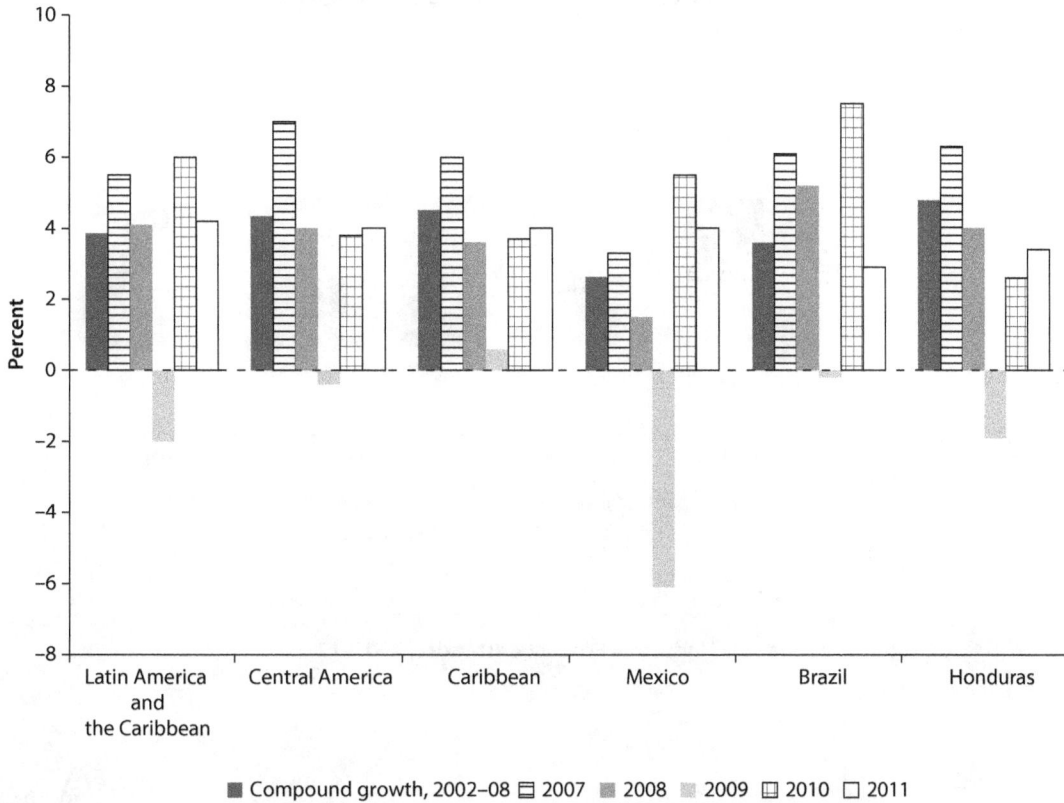

Legend: ■ Compound growth, 2002–08 ▤ 2007 ▨ 2008 ▦ 2009 ⊞ 2010 □ 2011

Source: World Bank.

heels of weak 1.2 percent growth in 2008, and accounted for more than 90 percent of the decline in the LAC region's GDP. Mexico's tight trade links with the U.S. economy (80 percent of all merchandise exports are shipped to the United States) and the composition of its exports (about two-thirds of Mexico's merchandise exports consists of exports of manufactured goods to the United States) made Mexico particularly vulnerable to the crisis. Services related to the manufacturing industries also contracted sharply in Mexico.

The economy slipped into recession in the second quarter of 2008, but the contraction was the sharpest in the first quarter of 2009, when output dropped 6.5 percent (seasonally adjusted annualized rate). The peak-to-trough contraction in output was a staggering 8.3 percent, comparable to the 10 percent contraction in output recorded during the "Tequila crisis" (1995) over the span of two quarters, and much deeper than the 2001 recession when output contracted 2.7 percent over the span of six quarters. It was not until the second quarter of 2011 that the Mexican economy returned to its precrisis output levels. In terms of composition, surprisingly private consumption began to contract in the third quarter of 2008, preceding the contraction in trade and

Understanding the Poverty Impact of the Global Financial Crisis in Latin America and the Caribbean
http://dx.doi.org/10.1596/978-1-4648-0241-6

Figure 2.8 Contribution of Private and Government Consumption, Fixed Investment, and Net Exports to Growth: Latin America and the Caribbean, 2001–10

Percentage points

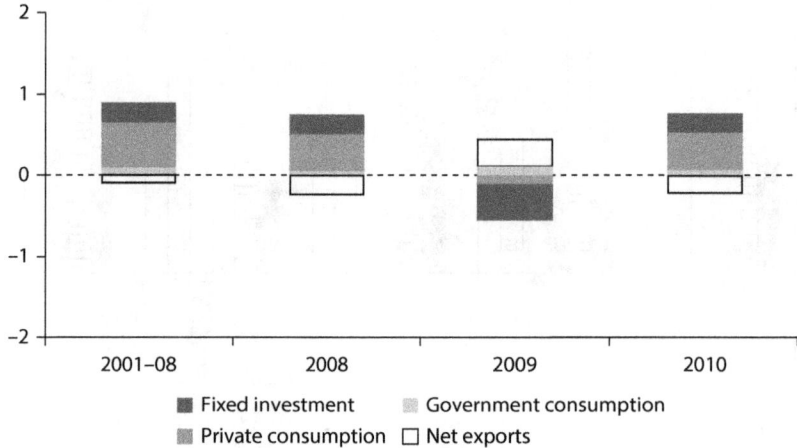

■ Fixed investment   ▨ Government consumption
▨ Private consumption □ Net exports

Source: World Bank.

Figure 2.9 Trade and Industrial Production: Mexico, 2007–12

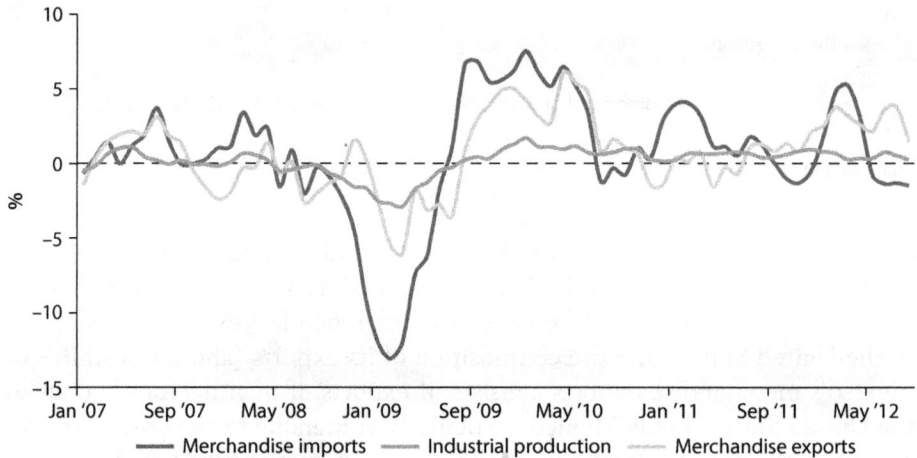

—— Merchandise imports —— Industrial production —— Merchandise exports

Source: World Bank.

investment, which began the following quarter. Over a four-quarter period, private consumption dropped a whopping 11 percent. The contraction in exports, imports, and investment lagged one quarter, but it was sharper, with peak-to-trough declines of 22.3 percent for exports, 28.5 percent for imports, and 14.2 percent for investment. The recovery in exports was swifter; they regained their precrisis levels by the second quarter of 2010 (figure 2.9). By contrast, investment and private consumption remained depressed for an extended period of time, reaching precrisis levels only in the latter part of

2011, thereby delaying the recovery in imports. Meanwhile, government spending rose almost 8 percent between the second quarter of 2008 and the second quarter of 2010.

Other economies with strong links to the United States also entered the recession in the first half of 2008. Central American countries that had a free trade agreement with the United States were severely affected (figure 2.10). Because of a sharp decline in *maquila*[3] exports, El Salvador's export volumes collapsed by 16 percent in 2009, in large part because of weaker demand from the United States, which buys almost half of El Salvador's exports, and in particular *maquila* exports. An even sharper collapse in imports (23.3 percent) attenuated the impact of the net exports on growth. Honduras's export volumes declined by more than 12 percent in 2009 as *maquila* exports declined. Guatemala, the largest Central American economy, also saw its exports decline in 2009 as demand in the United States and El Salvador, its major export markets, collapsed. Reliance on the United States as a major export market also caused exports to decline strongly in the Dominican Republic, which sends almost 60 percent of its exports to the United States, and in Jamaica, which also relies heavily on trade with the United States (half of its merchandise exports and nearly two-thirds of its services exports). Conversely, although Haiti relies heavily on exports to the United States, its exports, mainly apparel and textile products, continued to expand through the crisis.

Countries with large tourism sectors were also hard-hit, albeit with a lag. In Antigua and Barbuda, Jamaica, St. Vincent and the Grenadines, and St. Lucia stayover arrivals recorded large declines. The tourism sector in Antigua and Barbuda contracted sharply (10.3 percent) in 2009, and the recession remained deep throughout 2011 as the global financial crisis accentuated the decline in tourism receipts and FDI, and the global liquidity crunch contributed to the collapse of two large financial conglomerates, causing a marked decline in

Figure 2.10 Trade: Latin America and the Caribbean, Excluding Mexico, 2007–12

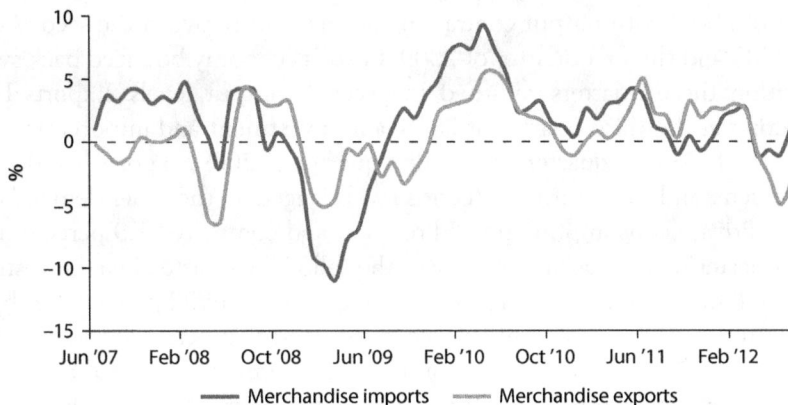

Source: World Bank.

Understanding the Poverty Impact of the Global Financial Crisis in Latin America and the Caribbean
http://dx.doi.org/10.1596/978-1-4648-0241-6

employment and activity. In the end, the country experienced the most severe fiscal and balance of payments crisis in its history. Costa Rica, where about 40 percent of tourists are from the United States, also saw a marked decline in tourism revenues. In Honduras, tourism receipts declined at a moderate pace because of a decline in tourists from the United States and Central America, the domestic political turmoil, and the rapid rise in crime rates. Tourism to the Caribbean was also affected, although less severely. Travel receipts fell slightly in the Dominican Republic in 2009, although North American tourists account for more than half of the tourists that visit that country. Jamaica, where U.S. tourists account for almost 60 percent of tourists and tourism and where tourism accounts for 13 percent of GDP, also saw a slight decline in tourism receipts because of lower prices and the decline in cruise ship arrivals. Tourist arrivals actually increased in Jamaica because of the deep discounts offered by hotel operators.

The decline in external demand also affected commodity exporters, although the decline in export volumes of commodities was relatively smaller in magnitude. Exports in Brazil, Argentina, and Chile declined 9.1 percent, 6.4 percent, and 4.5 percent, respectively, in 2009, whereas the declines in export volumes in Colombia and Peru were relatively small. The case of Colombia, however, masks a large variation; exports had fallen 9.3 percent by the third quarter of 2009 from the precrisis peak, and imports had declined by almost double peak to trough because of lower investments and weaker consumption. Export diversification by destination and exports to rapid-growth markets in Asia helped Peru and Chile to weather the crisis better. Ecuador, which normally exports 35 percent of its exports to the United States, exported 6.6 percent less in 2009. The impact was felt primarily through sharp declines in commodity prices rather than volumes because the price inelasticity of commodities in the short term means that the adjustment to lower demand is through lower prices. Non-oil commodity prices declined by 22 percent in 2009.

Brazil's economy, which by comparison was less open and had weaker links to the U.S. economy than Mexico's, slipped into a short-lived recession in the fourth quarter of 2008, with output contracting 5.5 percent between the second quarter of 2008 and the first quarter of 2009. Brazil's economy bounced back swiftly and within three quarters returned to precrisis output levels. Exports began contracting in the third quarter of 2008, and investment and imports started to decline the following quarter. By the first quarter of 2009, exports had declined 16.4 percent, and the return to precrisis levels lagged all the other demand components. Private consumption proved resilient and contracted 1.9 percent in the fourth quarter before starting to recover the following quarter. Fixed investment contracted more sharply, with a peak-to-trough decline of 22 percent, but by the first quarter of 2010 investment levels had returned to precrisis levels. As a result and because of the import intensity of investment, imports declined by a similar magnitude, and by the first quarter of 2009 they were 21 percent below their precrisis peak.

Understanding the Poverty Impact of the Global Financial Crisis in Latin America and the Caribbean
http://dx.doi.org/10.1596/978-1-4648-0241-6

Effects on Domestic Demand, in Particular Fixed Investment and Private Consumption

Increased uncertainty about the economic outlook, greater risk aversion, difficulties in obtaining capital, more expensive external financing, and sharply lower FDI inflows led to a 9.1 percent plunge in fixed investment in Latin America and the Caribbean in 2009, compared with the double-digit rates in the previous years. Fixed investment, the most cyclical component of domestic demand, contributed negative 2 percentage points to the overall decline in GDP, the second largest contribution after exports (figure 2.11). This contribution was, however, only about half that recorded in 1983, when investment plunged close to 20 percent. Fixed investment declined in almost every country in the region, whether or not a country was financially integrated in the world economy, a commodity exporter, or an open economy. More than half of countries recorded double-digit declines. Honduras and Jamaica saw some of the most dramatic contractions in investment. Indeed, two of the three largest economies in the region recorded double-digit declines in investment. FDI, usually a more stable source of financing, also collapsed during the crisis. For the region as a whole, FDI amounted to $73.6 billion in 2009, down 42 percent from $127.9 billion the previous year. However, this level is comparable with the average net FDI inflows received over the 2000–2006 period. FDI dropped almost across the board. In Argentina, FDI plunged 63 percent in 2009 from the previous year.

After growing at a very robust rate during the commodity boom years in the region, private consumption, one of the most important contributors to growth, collapsed in 2009 because of greater uncertainty about the economic

Figure 2.11 Components of Growth: Latin America and the Caribbean, 2009

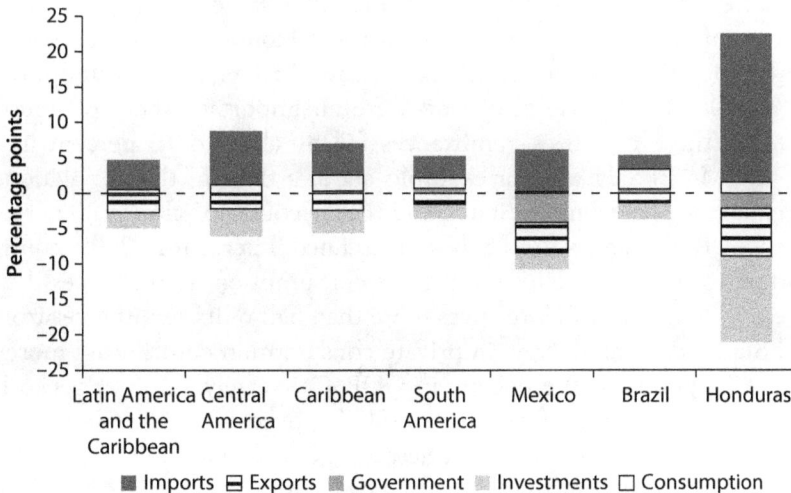

Source: World Bank.

outlook, rising unemployment rates, reduced credit availability, lower remittances, and several country-specific shocks. Private consumption, which is generally the most stable domestic demand component, declined 0.6 percent in 2009, making it the largest negative contribution to growth since at least 1960, and exceeding that of 1983 (because its share of GDP has increased since the 1980s).

The decline in private consumption contributed 2 percentage points or more to the contraction of GDP in Honduras, Paraguay, and República Bolivariana de Venezuela. The decline was severe in Mexico, where it reached a remarkable 7.3 percent, contributing 5.1 percentage points to the decline in GDP. Meanwhile, because of the sharp increase in unemployment in the construction sector in the United States, Mexican workers' remittances dropped 15 percent. Even though remittances account for a mere 2.1 percent of GDP in Mexico, the decline negatively affected the consumption of poorer households. In selected economies, country-specific shocks were significant determinants of the contraction in private demand. Indeed, private consumption in Paraguay (and other countries in the Southern Cone) was undermined by the severe drought that affected its agriculture sector, while in Honduras the uncertain political situation negatively affected consumer spending.

The contraction in domestic demand translated into a 15 percent contraction in import volumes. Not surprisingly, imports of goods and services contracted the most in countries that saw the largest contraction in private consumption (Honduras, Jamaica, El Salvador, Paraguay, and St. Lucia). In countries such as Honduras, the collapse of imports of goods and services was much bigger in magnitude than the collapse in exports, resulting in a staggering 14.1 percent positive contribution to growth of net exports. At the regional level, as a result of the compression in domestic demand and in imports, the contribution of net exports to growth was negative in only three countries: St. Vincent and the Grenadines, Haiti, and Bolivia.

Countries in which remittances represent a large share of GDP (over 15 percent of GDP in El Salvador, Jamaica, and Honduras) and that have large migrant populations in the United States saw their private consumption collapse in 2008–09 because remittances are an important share of household incomes. In these countries, remittances fell by close to 10 percent in 2009 (figure 2.4). In El Salvador, for example, about a third of the population lives abroad, mainly in the United States, and they account for almost 90 percent of remittances. Remittances to El Salvador declined 9 percent in 2009, contributing to the 10 percent collapse in private consumption. Remittances declined 9 percent in Jamaica, which receives more than half of its remittances from the United States, and the decline in private consumption contributed more than 2 percentage points to the decline in GDP. Conversely, remittances to Haiti, which account for about 20 percent of GDP, proved somewhat more resilient, remaining relatively stable in 2009, despite the fact that almost 75 percent of remittances originate in the United States. Similarly, private consumption proved much more resilient in Haiti; it expanded 1.9 percent in 2009.

Figure 2.12 Unemployment Rate: Latin America and the Caribbean, 2007–12

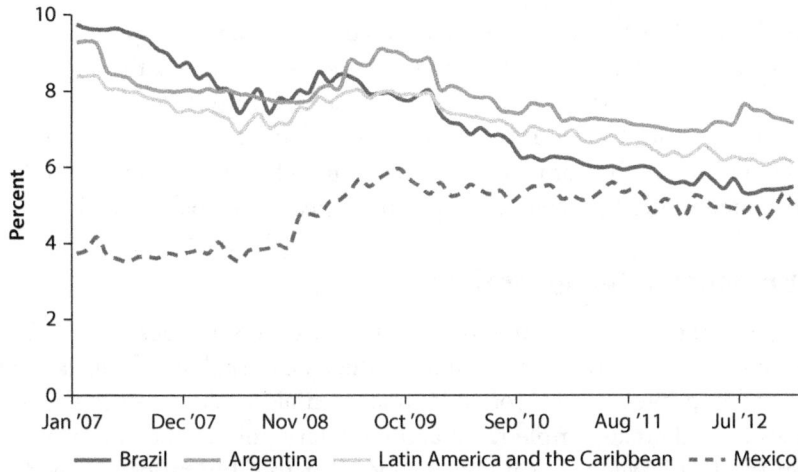

Sources: International Labour Organization and World Bank staff calculations.

Private consumption was also affected by job losses. Jobs were destroyed during the global financial and economic crisis, thereby pushing up unemployment rates in many Latin American and Caribbean countries (figure 2.12). If one controls for the size of the decline in economic activity the region experienced significantly milder adjustments than in previous crises (De la Torre et al. 2010a). The median unemployment rate (based on unemployment rates for Argentina, Brazil, Chile, Colombia, Mexico, Peru, Uruguay, and República Bolivariana de Venezuela, which account for more than 80 percent of the region's population) bottomed out in the second quarter of 2008 at 7.1 percent, down more than 3 percentage points from its long-term average. During the most acute phase of the crisis, the median unemployment rate rose by 1.3 percentage points relative to the precrisis low. The peak-to-trough increase in the unemployment rate in the eight countries with available data ranged from 3.6 percentage points in Chile to 0.7 percentage points in Uruguay. Mexico saw its unemployment rate increase 2.1 percentage points between the second quarter of 2008 and the third quarter of 2009, and even more than three years after the crisis the unemployment rate had yet to fall to below crisis levels. Colombia saw an increase of 1.4 percentage points between the second quarter of 2008 and the fourth quarter of 2009. By contrast, in Brazil unemployment inched up only 0.6 percentage points. Meanwhile, employment declined from peak to trough by between 0.8 percent (seasonally adjusted) in Brazil and 1.7 percent (seasonally adjusted) in Mexico. Employment began to decline in the third quarter of 2008 in Mexico, in the first quarter of 2009 in Brazil and Peru, and in the second quarter of 2009 in Argentina, and lasted for about two quarters in each case. In addition, in some countries the numbers of hours worked by employed workers were reduced to avoid massive layoffs,

Understanding the Poverty Impact of the Global Financial Crisis in Latin America and the Caribbean
http://dx.doi.org/10.1596/978-1-4648-0241-6

especially those of skilled workers in highly specialized sectors, in order to retain them because the crisis was perceived as temporary.

The decline in economic activity also led to declines in capacity utilization ratios, which played a role in delaying investments. In Mexico, the capacity utilization ratio declined almost 6 percent (seasonally adjusted) from peak to trough, to 74.5 percent in March 2009. In Peru, the decline was almost double that observed in Mexico. By comparison, in the United States the capacity utilization ratio declined to 68.2 percent, a decline from peak to trough of 20.7 percent.

Policy Responses during the Crisis

Some governments were better prepared than others to tackle the crisis and responded in a countercyclical fashion. Reduced external and financial vulnerabilities and improved macroeconomic fundamentals in place before the onset of the crisis helped create ample fiscal and monetary policy space in many economies in the LAC region. Fiscal deficits and debt to GDP ratios declined in the years leading up to the crisis in many countries (figures 2.13 and 2.14), reducing public sector borrowing requirements and creating fiscal space. Improved policy frameworks and stronger fundamentals also improved access to international capital markets for several countries. As a result, the region weathered the 2008–09 global financial crisis remarkably well (when compared with the global recessions of 1982, 1998, and 2001), especially in view of the magnitude of the shock and the increased openness to trade and financial and economic integration of the region.

Figure 2.13 General Government Balances as a Share of GDP: LAC, Major High-Income, and Developing Countries, 2002–11
Percentage of GDP

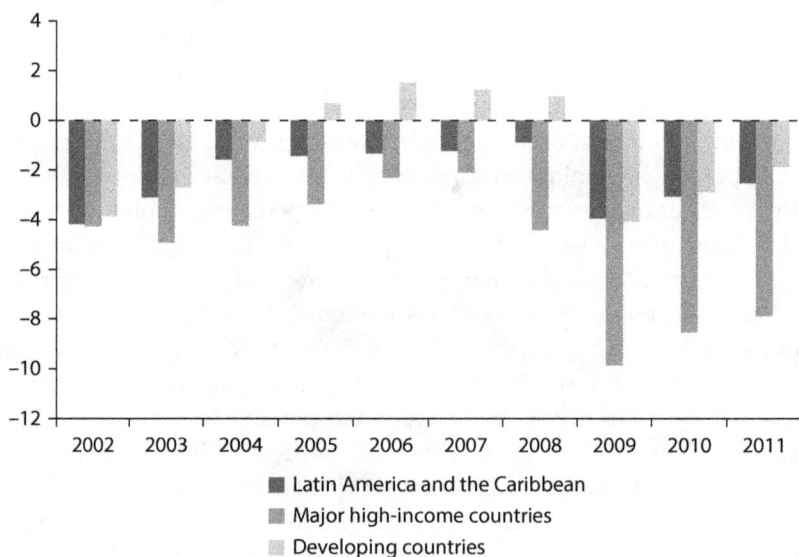

Source: World Bank.

Figure 2.14 General Government Debt as a Share of GDP: LAC, Major High-Income, and Developing Countries, 2002–11

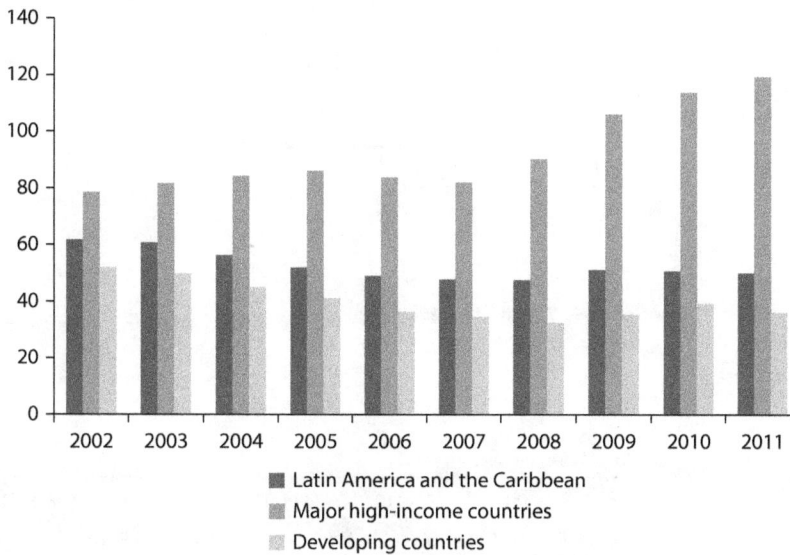

Source: World Bank.

Some countries, in particular those with stronger policy frameworks, were able to ease monetary policy to stimulate domestic demand to help smooth the impact of the global financial crisis (figure 2.15). Countries in Latin America and the Caribbean were among the most aggressive in using monetary stimulus, cutting policy rates by about 360 basis points on average by October 2009 (compared with 320 basis points in high-income countries), and most of the easing was implemented in the first half of 2009. Unconventional monetary policy measures such as credit and quantitative easing were also used, but more sparingly than in high-income countries. Countries that had more space to cut policy rates also allowed larger currency depreciations.

Ample fiscal accommodation followed this crisis in sharp contrast with past crises. Fiscal accommodation as measured by the one-year change in the primary general government balance amounted to 2.2 percent of GDP on average in Latin America and the Caribbean, or about half that of high-income countries. In the past, governments in the region had tended to adopt procyclical fiscal policies when a crisis hit because of their very limited or inexistent fiscal buffers, high public debt levels, and restricted access to financial markets during the crisis (Gavin 1997; Reinhart 2003).

In particular, commodity-exporting, financially integrated countries in the region benefitted from several years of high commodity prices. However, the primary expenditure grew at a slower pace than overall revenues and was more in line with the contribution of noncommodity revenues to total revenue growth. Other commodity-exporting countries tended to act in a procyclical fashion during the boom years, increasing the primary expenditure at a rapid pace, and much

Understanding the Poverty Impact of the Global Financial Crisis in Latin America and the Caribbean
http://dx.doi.org/10.1596/978-1-4648-0241-6

Figure 2.15 Monetary Policy Easing: Selected Latin American Countries, 2008–12

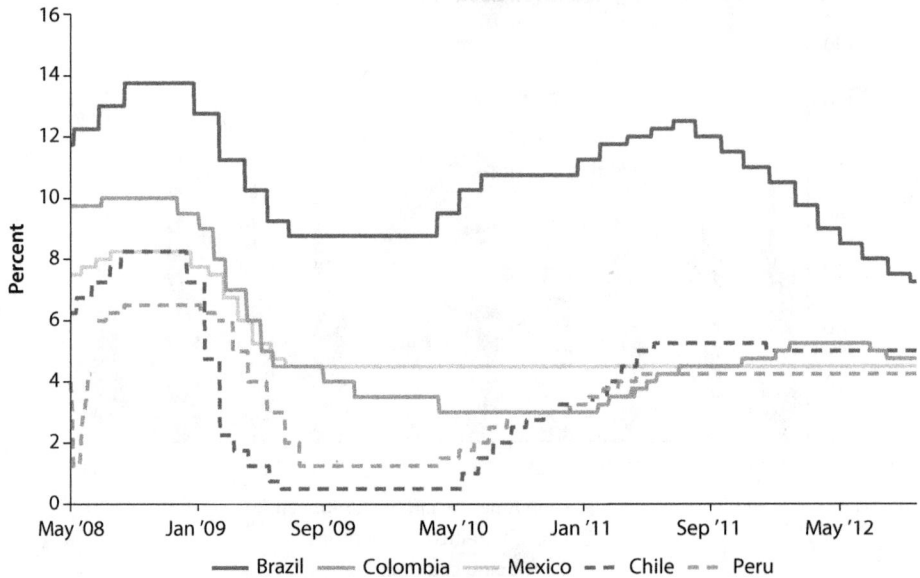

Sources: Central Banks and Datastream.

faster than the growth in noncommodity revenues. By contrast, in commodity-importing countries primary spending tended to grow at a slower pace than revenues, except in countries with large tourism sectors.

When the 2008–09 crisis hit, many countries announced fiscal stimulus packages composed of both on-budget and off-budget measures. Most fiscal packages were concentrated on increasing expenditures or transfers. Some countries announced temporary tax reductions or administrative measures deferring tax obligation payments. In addition, some countries introduced tax measures and improved tax administration to help deal with falling revenues. In general, the measures requiring only administrative decisions were implemented relatively quickly. Limited implementation capacity and delays in approving budgets or budget reforms and in approving external debt contracting delayed the increases in spending.

In many of the commodity-exporting countries, most of the decline in government revenues during the crisis was linked to lower commodity-related revenues as commodity prices plunged. Because tax revenues made up just a small share of GDP, only a relatively small part of the decline in total revenues stemmed from the decline in economic activity. By contrast, in commodity-importing countries the decline in revenues seems to be explained by lower levels of economic output, and in particular the sharp drop in imports. This drop has in many cases affected custom collections, in particular in Central American and Caribbean economies.

Understanding the Poverty Impact of the Global Financial Crisis in Latin America and the Caribbean
http://dx.doi.org/10.1596/978-1-4648-0241-6

Because most countries in the LAC region have relatively small automatic stabilizers, most changes in expenditures are likely to represent discretionary policy actions. In countries such as Argentina, Chile, Costa Rica, and Peru, the primary expenditure continued to grow in 2009 at a pace similar to that in the previous year. By contrast, some of the countries hardest hit by the reversal of terms of trade, in particular energy-exporting countries, had slashed real spending in a procyclical fashion (especially Ecuador and República Bolivariana de Venezuela).

Countries that were more capital-constrained faced a more challenging policy environment because of the difficulties in obtaining external capital at a time when government revenues were falling. In Central America, the fiscal space was for the most part more limited and quickly depleted, whereas the Caribbean countries, which have high public debt levels, had almost no room for countercyclical fiscal policy and were generally forced to adopt procyclical policies.

Notes

1. Systemic banking crises occurred during 1994–98 in Bolivia, Brazil, Costa Rica, Haiti, Mexico, and República Bolivariana de Venezuela in 1994; Argentina and Paraguay in 1995; Jamaica in 1996; and Colombia and Ecuador in 1998. Antigua and Barbuda suffered a foreign currency debt crisis in 1996, and Mexico, Suriname, and República Bolivariana de Venezuela experienced currency crises in 1994.

2. Potential GDP is the trend in actual GDP, smoothing out business cycle fluctuations.

3. According to Jansen et al. (2007), "maquila is a system of production, generally undertaken through subcontracting, through which semicompleted, intermediate supplies are transformed through processes that in many cases have added value, and whose final products are generally sold abroad."

References

Almunia, M. A., A. S. Bénétrix, B. Eichengreen, K. H. O'Rourke, and G. Rua. 2009. "From Great Depression to Great Credit Crisis: Similarities, Differences and Lessons." Working Paper 15524, National Bureau of Economic Research, Cambridge, MA.

Berkmen, P., G. Gelos, R. Rennhack, and J. P. Walsh. 2009. "The Global Financial Crisis: Explaining Cross-Country Differences in the Output Impact." Working Paper 280, International Monetary Fund, Washington, DC.

Claessens, S., G. Dell'Ariccia, D. Igan, and L. Laeven. 2010. "Lessons and Policy Implications from the Global Financial Crisis." Working Paper 10/44, International Monetary Fund, Washington, DC.

De la Torre, A., C. Calderon, T. Didier, J. Messina, and S. Schmukler. 2010a. *From Global Collapse to Recovery: Economic Adjustment and Growth Prospects in Latin America and the Caribbean.* LAC Semi-annual Report, World Bank, Washington, DC.

De la Torre, A., C. Calderon, T. Didier, E. L. Yeyati, and S. Schmukler. 2010b. *Globalized, Resilient, Dynamic: The New Face of Latin America and the Caribbean.* LAC Semi-annual Report, World Bank, Washington, DC.

Didier, T., C. Hevia, and S. L. Schmukler. 2011. "How Resilient Were Emerging Economies to the Global Crisis?" Policy Research Working Paper 5637, World Bank, Washington, DC.

Freund, C. 2009. "Trade Response to Global Downturns: Historical Evidence." Policy Research Working Paper 5015, World Bank, Washington, DC.

Gavin, M., and R. Perotti. 1997. "Fiscal Policy in Latin America." In *NBER Macroeconomics Annual 1997*, edited by B. Bernanke and J. Rotemberg. Cambridge, MA: MIT Press.

Gray, G., B. Joshi, P. Kehayova, R. Llaudes, G. Presciuttini, and M. Saenz. 2010. *How Did Emerging Markets Cope in the Crisis?* International Monetary Fund, Washington, DC.

Jansen, H. G. P., S. Morley, G. Kessler, V. Piñeiro, M. Sánchez, and M. Torero. 2007. "The Impact of the Central America Free Trade Agreement on the Central American Textile Maquila Industry." Discussion Paper 00720, International Food Policy Research Institute, Washington, DC.

Reinhart, C. M., K. S. Rogoff, and M. A. Savastano. 2003. "Debt Intolerance." Brookings Papers on Economic Activity, Brookings Institution, Washington, DC.

Sirkeci, I., J. H. Cohen, and D. Ratha. 2012. *Migration and Remittances during the Global Financial Crisis and Beyond.* Washington, DC: World Bank.

World Bank. 2012. *Global Economic Prospects, 2012.* Washington, DC: World Bank.

CHAPTER 3

Changes in Poverty and Inequality in Latin America during the Great Recession

Samuel Freije

Poverty is one of the most important indicators of social welfare. The World Bank's *World Development Report*s of 2000 and 2010 highlighted the prominence of poverty reduction as the main objective of developing economies. In the Millennium Development Goals established by the United Nations in 2000, poverty reduction is designated a specific global target to achieve within a precise time frame. Setting goals and targets has resulted in a global agenda of poverty reduction, and important advances have been achieved in that area. However, economic crises, even though usually short-lived, may delay the achievement of poverty reduction targets and have ripple effects on other areas of welfare beyond monetary poverty.[1]

This chapter gauges the impact of the 2008–09 global financial crisis on monetary poverty in Latin America. It compiles microdata for 12 Latin American countries and makes comparable estimates of poverty and inequality measures before and after 2009. The purpose of this study is to describe what happened to poverty and establish stylized facts about the sources of changes in poverty during the period of study.

The chapter has five main sections. The section "Tools of the Trade for Measuring Poverty" describes indices for measuring poverty and inequality in the region. It also describes the selection process for the countries and data sets featured in this study, as well as the methods adopted for measuring and analyzing poverty trends. The section "How Much Poverty Was There and Among Whom?" presents a general overview of before-and-after estimates of poverty changes

The author acknowledges with thanks the research assistance of the Team for Statistical Development of the Poverty and Gender Unit for the Latin American Region and the World Bank, led by João Pedro Azevedo and Louise Cord. Above all, appreciation is extended to Gabriel Facchini Palma, who produced most of the estimates that accompany this chapter and without whom the compilation and production of these data would not have been possible. Special thanks also go to Rebecca Fair and Andrés Castañeda Aguilar, who helped with the early drafts of this chapter.

for 2009. It also provides measures of moderate and extreme poverty at the national level and profiles of different population groups of interest, such as urban, rural, and female-headed households. The section "Sources of Changes in Poverty" that follows describes in detail the sources of poverty changes during the recession. This section relies on a series of decomposition techniques that allow identification of the different forces driving poverty trends for the period under study. The influences of economic growth, demographic changes, labor market dynamics, and social policy are explored as the main explanatory causes of the changes observed in poverty. The section "The Poverty Reduction That Could Have Been" provides a measure of the impact of the crisis by estimating changes in poverty in the region had the crisis not occurred. These estimates are based on a counterfactual exercise using growth and inequality elasticities of poverty. The final section summarizes and concludes.

Tools of the Trade for Measuring Poverty

The countries included in this section of the study are Argentina, Brazil, Chile, Colombia, Costa Rica, the Dominican Republic, Ecuador, El Salvador, Mexico, Paraguay, Peru, and Uruguay. For most countries, data are taken from the annual household surveys conducted in 2008 and 2009. However, the surveys for Mexico and Chile span a longer period of time. For Chile, we utilize survey data from 2006 to 2009 and for Mexico from 2008 to 2010. Other countries in the region are not included because either they do not have annual surveys (e.g., Nicaragua and Guatemala), or they do not make microdata publicly accessible on a regular basis, and recent data sets were still not available when this study commenced (e.g., Bolivia, República Bolivariana de Venezuela, and Panama).

The data are accessed through the Socio-Economic Database for Latin America and the Caribbean (SEDLAC),[2] a joint data collection and harmonization project between the Universidad Nacional de la Plata's Center for Distributive, Labor, and Social Studies (CEDLAS) and the World Bank's Poverty and Gender Unit for Latin America and the Caribbean (LCSPP). The SEDLAC database includes poverty statistics for Latin American and the Caribbean countries based on microdata from over 200 household surveys (see table 3.1 for the surveys used in this report). CEDLAS receives household surveys from national statistics institutes, and the data are harmonized so they are comparable across time and countries. The exception to this rule is Mexico, where we have used the new Encuesta Nacional de Igresos y Gastos de los Hogares (ENIGH, National Household Income and Expenditure Survey). Since 2008, it has included an expanded sample labeled Modulo de Condiciones Socioeconómicas (Module on Socioeconomic Conditions). This newly expanded survey has not yet been fully harmonized by CEDLAS, and for that reason we do not use a harmonized data set for Mexico.[3]

Analysis of poverty and inequality requires defining three main components: (1) the welfare aggregate, (2) the unit of observation, and (3) the statistical index. The first component refers to the deprivation or inequality of the welfare variable (e.g., health, education, life expectancy, or consumption) that is

Table 3.1 Sources of Household Survey Data

Country	Survey	Acronym	Fieldwork	Circa 2008	Circa 2009
Argentina	Encuesta Permanente de Hogares-Continua (Continuous National Household Survey)	EPH-C	2nd semester	2008	2009
Brazil	Pesquisa Nacional por Amostra de Domicílios (National Household Survey)	PNAD	October	2008	2009
Chile	Encuesta de Caracterización Socioeconómica Nacional (National Socioeconomic Characteristics Survey)	CASEN	November	2006	2009
Colombia	Gran Encuesta Integrada de Hogares (Integrated Household Survey)	GEIH	2nd semester	2008	2009
Costa Rica	Encuesta de Hogares de Propósitos Múltiples (Multipurpose Household Survey)	EHPM	July	2008	2009
Dominican Republic	Encuesta Nacional de Fuerza de Trabajo (National Labor Force Survey)	ENFT	October	2008	2009
El Salvador	Encuesta de Hogares de Propósitos Múltiples (Multipurpose Household Survey)	EHPM	Continuous	2008	2009
Ecuador	Encuesta de Empleo, Desempleo y Subempleo (Employment, Unemployment, and Underemployment Survey)	ENEMDU	December	2008	2009
Mexico	Encuesta Nacional de Ingresos y Gastos de los Hogares (National Income and Household Survey)	ENIGH	August/November	2008	2010
Paraguay	Encuesta Permanente de Hogares (Permanent Household Survey)	EPH	October/December	2008	2009
Peru	Encuesta Nacional de Hogares (National Household Survey)	ENAHO	Continuous	2008	2009
Uruguay	Encuesta Continua de Hogares (Continuous Household Survey)	ECH	Continuous	2008	2009

Source: SEDLAC data, 2012 (CEDLAS and World Bank).

the subject concern. The second component is the person or group of persons who are subject to deprivation or inequality—that is, individuals, families, or localities. The third component is the formula to be applied to the population of the unit of analysis for gauging deprivation or inequality in the welfare variable of concern. This section explains the specific choices made in the study about these three components.

In the Latin America region, income, not consumption, is the aggregate used to measure welfare because many household surveys in Latin America do not include questions about consumption and expenditures, only income. Expenditure surveys are conducted in some countries in the region. In some cases, they are conducted with enough regularity, but in others only every 10 years—a time frame that does not lend itself well to precise estimates for evaluating short-term changes in poverty.

The welfare aggregate is computed by adding all income sources for each individual, excluding noncurrent income, sales, and income from gifts, gambling, inheritance, and life insurance. For a nonresponse or negative income reporting, earnings are imputed by a matching process or by applying the coefficient of a Mincer equation. When zero income is reported, it is taken into account for computing poverty statistics. Other adjustments are made to address underreporting and lack information on the very rich. Real income is always used, and rural incomes are boosted by 15 percent to account for price differences in rural and urban areas. Official consumer price indexes (CPIs) are used to adjust for inflation.[4]

The unit of analysis is the individual person. However, poverty is computed at the family level. The total income of the family is the summation of all income sources earned or not earned by all family members. This aggregate is then divided by the number of household members, thereby defining the income aggregate at the individual level. We do not adjust for household composition or structure.

The indicators used for poverty are the poverty headcount and the poverty gap, and for inequality the Gini index, 90th, 50th, and 10th decile ratios. The *poverty headcount index* is the percentage of a population living below the poverty line. The formula is $H = q/n$ where H is the headcount index, q is the number of people living below the poverty line, and n is the total population. The *poverty gap index* is the mean shortfall from the poverty line (the nonpoor are counted as having zero shortfall), expressed as a percentage of the poverty line. This index measures not only poverty incidence but also depth. The formula is $PG = I * H$ where PG is the poverty gap index, H is the poverty headcount index, and I represents the income gap $[(z - yq)/z]$ where z is the poverty line and yq is the average income for the poor.

This study evaluates those people classified as living in extreme poverty and moderate poverty. The poverty lines we use are US$2.50 a day (extreme) and US$4.00 a day (moderate) in purchasing power parity (PPP) dollars. Extreme poverty is interpreted as the income needed to cover basic food requirements, and moderate poverty as the income needed to cover food and other basic necessities such as clothing and shelter. These international poverty lines differ from official poverty lines. Moreover, income aggregates from SEDLAC's harmonized databases may differ from income aggregates used in different countries. We adopt international poverty lines and a cross-country harmonized database in order to compare across countries and over time. However, this approach does not by any means imply a criticism of official statistics. It simply means that SEDLAC uses different methodologies, such as accounting only for last month's income, and standardizes the moderate and extreme poverty line across countries, among other things. The purpose is to avoid methodological differences that would render cross-country comparisons untenable (see box 3.1).

The *Gini index* measures the extent to which the distribution of income among individuals within an economy deviates from a perfectly equal distribution. A Gini index of 0 represents perfect equality; an index of 1 implies perfect inequality. Despite its generalized use in inequality studies, the Gini coefficient is neither a unique nor the most self-explanatory measure of the distribution of income. *Income ratios* are a plainer description. They represent the ratio of the mean income of a certain percentile of a population to another. For example, if a population were sorted by income level and divided into 100 groups, a 90:50 ratio would compare the mean income of the people in the 90th percentile with those in the 50th percentile. We also include the FGT(2), a index of the Foster-Greer-Throbecke family of poverty indexes that measures income inequality among the poor.[5]

Box 3.1 On the Limits of Harmonization and Comparable Poverty Numbers

Adoption of a harmonized database and a common poverty line helps to ensure that poverty numbers are comparable across countries and over time. If different income aggregates and different poverty lines are used, individuals with similar standards of living may be considered poor in one country but not poor in another. Thus neither cross-country comparisons nor regional aggregates would make any sense.

However, despite considerable efforts, harmonization does not necessarily solve all the problems, largely because of the different quality and extension of surveys. The fact that different surveys gather different data implies that some income sources are collected in some surveys but not in others. This implies in turn that income aggregates do not measure the same sources of income in every country. Even if a common income aggregate is devised using only the subset of income sources available from every survey, some variables may not be collected in some years, making the aggregates not comparable over time. For example, in our study Costa Rica's survey for 2009 failed to include the usual question about income from transfers, making the aggregate for that year not strictly comparable with those in the surveys for other years.

Even for identical surveys, comparable poverty estimates are difficult to obtain. The first hurdle is the reference period. Some surveys capture incomes from the previous month, or the previous quarter, or even the previous year. This raises the problem of survey comparability, but it also raises the issue of whether the data capture the economic forces under study. If the survey collects incomes from last month but the crisis ended 6 or 12 months ago, the survey will fail to register the impact of the crisis.

The second hurdle is the definition of the unit of observation and the use or nonuse of adult equivalence scales. The decision to adopt no adult equivalence scale may have little impact on poverty estimates for countries with low fertility rates, but it may have a significant impact for countries with a large youth population. Furthermore, the same adult equivalence scale needs to be applied to every country, even though the consumption patterns of families with children relative to adult-only families may differ from one country to another. The same problem occurs with the use of an international poverty line. Even though standards of living are then comparable across countries, the poverty threshold may be too high or too low for a certain country given its general standard of living. In these cases, making the estimates comparable across countries may produce estimates that are unrepresentative at the national level.

We illustrate these dilemmas using Mexico's National Household Income and Expenditure Survey (ENIGH). Figure B3.1.1 shows the cumulative distribution of income and moderate and extreme poverty rates under different methods for 2010. On the basis of an international poverty line of US$4.00 per day (which at purchasing power parity equals Mex$1,074.12 per person and per month), moderate poverty applies to 22.4 percent of the urban population if no adult equivalence scale is adopted and the average income of the last six months is used as an income aggregate. The adoption of adult equivalence scales, which in Mexico means that individuals under the age of 18 represent about

---

box continues next page

Understanding the Poverty Impact of the Global Financial Crisis in Latin America and the Caribbean
http://dx.doi.org/10.1596/978-1-4648-0241-6

Box 3.1 On the Limits of Harmonization and Comparable Poverty Numbers *(continued)*

Figure B3.1.1 **Measuring Moderate and Extreme Poverty in Urban Mexico, by Different Methods, 2010**

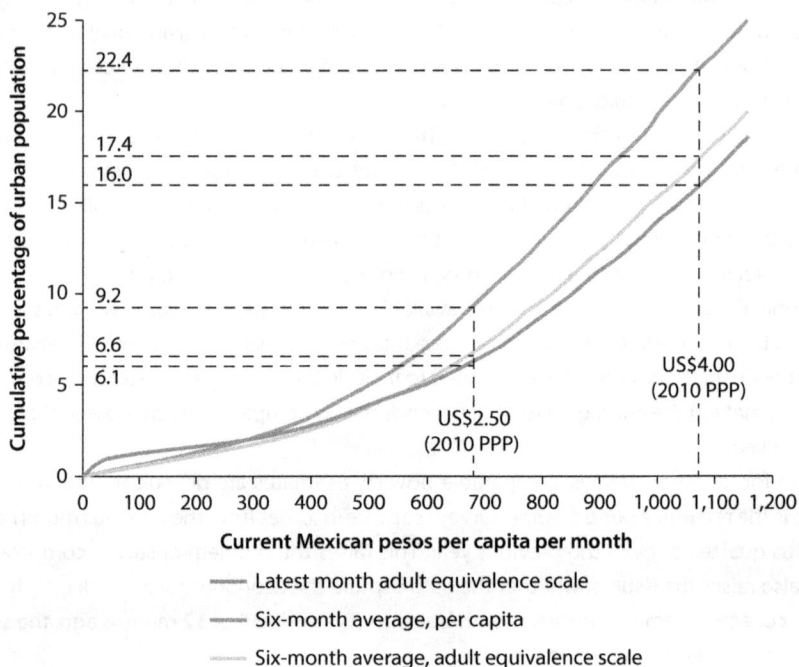

Source: ENIGH, 2010.

70 percent of individuals aged 19 and over, causes the urban poverty rate to fall, using the same poverty line and the same income aggregate, to 17.4 percent. In addition, if income from the only last month is considered (i.e., income from around August 2010 rather than the average from around the period March–August 2010), then moderate poverty in urban areas falls to 16.0 percent. In other words, using the same poverty line, assumptions about equivalence scales and income aggregates make a difference of more than 6 percentage points in poverty estimates. The differences are less pronounced in the case of extreme poverty (US$2.50 per day, which equals Mex$671.33 per month) because fewer people live with so little.

To estimate poverty rates in Mexico comparable to our estimates of poverty rates in other countries in the region, we adopt international poverty lines of US$2.50 and US$4.00 instead of the official poverty lines and income per capita estimates instead of the official adult equivalence scales. However, we adopt the official six-month income average in Mexico instead of the last-month estimate used for the other countries in order to capture some of the effects of the 2008–09 crisis. Figure B3.1.2 illustrates the implications of these assumptions as compared with the official poverty rates by the El Consejo Nacional de Evaluación de la Política de Desarrollo Social (CONEVAL,

box continues next page

Box 3.1 On the Limits of Harmonization and Comparable Poverty Numbers *(continued)*

Figure B3.1.2 Measuring Extreme Poverty in Urban Mexico, by Different Methods, 2008 and 2010

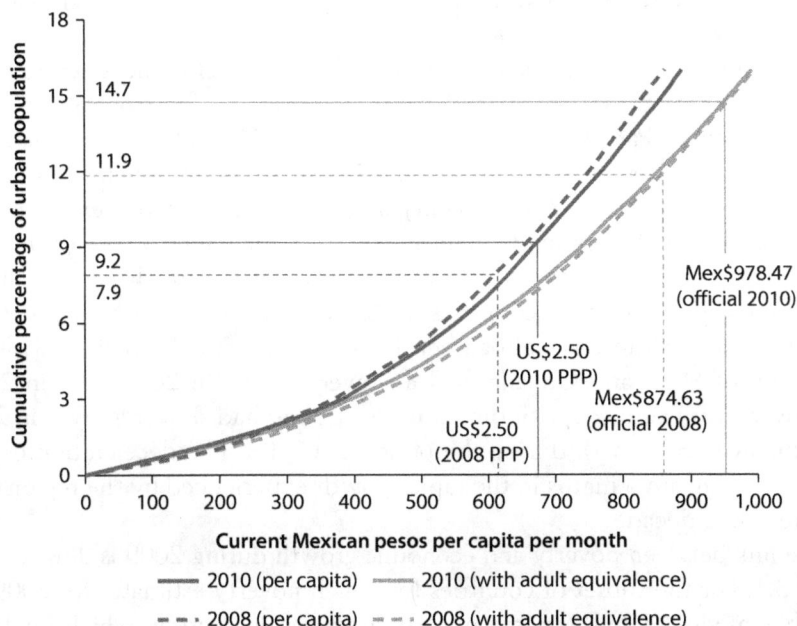

Source: ENIGH, 2008 and 2010.

National Council for the Evaluation of Social Development Policy). Official poverty estimates for urban Mexico show an increase in monetary extreme poverty (labeled Bienestar básico by CONEVAL) from 11.9 percent to 14.7 percent between 2008 and 2010. Our estimates show an increase in extreme poverty from 7.9 percent to 9.2 percent. The difference stems from the use of different poverty lines and different adult equivalence scales.

These results reveal that methodological options may produce important differences in poverty levels and trends. For every country in this study, we chose international poverty lines, opted for no adult equivalence scales, and selected income aggregates as close to the crisis period as possible. These choices are intended to make poverty rates comparable across countries and over time, and are not intended to imply any criticism of official or other estimates.

How Much Did Poverty Change during the Crisis?

The global financial crisis of 2008–09 affected Latin American countries in an important manner. According to World Bank estimates, the global gross domestic product (GDP) declined 2.2 percent in 2009 (World Bank 2012).[6] The impact of the crisis ranged from declines in GDP of 6.5 percent for countries in Eastern Europe and Central Asia and of 3.91 percent for members of the Organisation for Economic Co-operation and Development (OECD), the two regions most affected, to an expansion of 7.4 percent in South Asia and 7.5 percent in East Asia and the Pacific, the two regions least affected. Latin America had an average GDP decline of 1.9 percent, which was very close to the global average.

The Latin American average hides very important differences across countries. Some countries experienced severe recessions—for example, Mexico (−6.0 percent), Paraguay (−4.9 percent), and República Bolivariana de Venezuela (−3.2 percent). Others sustained positive growth, such as Colombia (+1.7 percent), Bolivia (+3.45 percent), and Panama (+3.85 percent). The dispersion is even wider among Caribbean countries, ranging from −11.9 percent in Antigua and Barbuda to +5.9 percent in Dominica. This dispersion should not be interpreted as some countries in the region, because of having positive growth, avoiding the crisis altogether. Every country in the region, with the exception of Haiti and Guyana, had a slower growth in 2009 than in 2008. Moreover, every country, with the same exceptions, had slower growth in 2009 than the average growth during the period 2003–08. The deceleration caused by the crisis meant a hiatus in the rapid growth experienced by the region over the preceding decade.

The link between poverty and economic growth during 2009 is illustrated in figure 3.1. For the subset of countries for which poverty estimates for 2009 are available, moderate and extreme poverty increased in those in which GDP per capita declined (Costa Rica, El Salvador, and Mexico). All countries with positive GDP per capita growth saw poverty decline. No country experienced positive growth and an increase in poverty.

A very clear negative relationship exists between economic growth and changes in poverty. There are some perplexing cases, however. Some countries with negative growth also saw a decline in moderate poverty. How did Brazil and Peru manage to reduce moderate and extreme poverty despite a decline in GDP per capita? As explained later in this chapter, the reduction in poverty was the consequence of a disconnect between GDP and survey data—that is, in these countries GDP per capita declined but average earnings as reported in household surveys did not. Other countries showed a differential impact between the bottom and the middle of the distribution. Why did moderate poverty decline while extreme poverty increased in Paraguay? Why did the opposite happen in Ecuador? The relative incidence of changes in income along the income distribution explains these patterns.

The average (nonweighted) moderate poverty headcount observed for the 12 selected countries in the Latin America region moved from 29.9 to 28.8 between 2008 and 2009, with an overall decrease of 1.1 percentage points.[7] However, the regional averages hide important differences in trends and incidence across countries. In 2009, Argentina, Chile, and Uruguay had the lowest incidence of moderate poverty (below 20 percent), but Colombia and El Salvador top out at rates

Figure 3.1 Changes in Moderate and Extreme Poverty and GDP Per Capita: Latin America, 2009

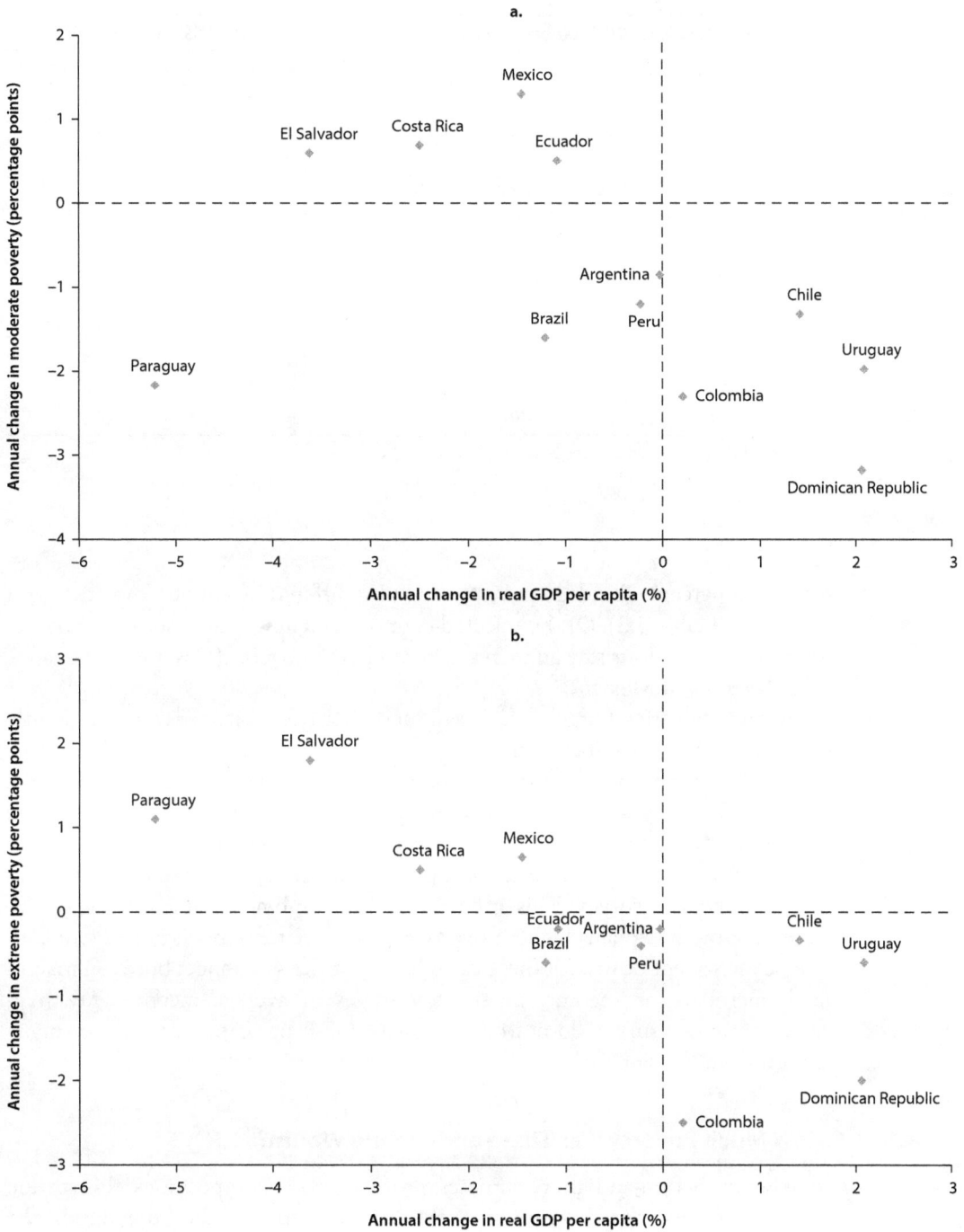

Sources: SEDLAC and World Bank's World Development Indicators (database).
Note: Data for Mexico refer to the annual average of a two-year change (2008–10) in poverty and in GDP per capita growth. Data for Chile refer to a three-year (2006–09) annual average change.

Understanding the Poverty Impact of the Global Financial Crisis in Latin America and the Caribbean
http://dx.doi.org/10.1596/978-1-4648-0241-6

Table 3.2 Changes in Poverty: Latin America and the Caribbean, 2008–09
Percentage points

	Moderate poverty (US$4.00/person/day)		Extreme poverty (US$2.50/person/day)	
	Change in headcount	*Change in poverty gap*	*Change in headcount*	*Change in poverty gap*
Argentina	−0.9	−0.2	−0.2	−0.1
Brazil	−1.6	−0.4	−0.6	0.0
Chile[a]	−4.0	−1.0	−1.0	−0.1
Colombia	−2.2	−2.0	−2.5	−1.7
Costa Rica	**0.7**	**0.4**	**0.5**	**0.5**
Dominican Rep	−3.2	−1.4	−2.0	−0.7
Ecuador	**0.5**	**0.1**	−0.2	0.0
El Salvador	**0.6**	**2.2**	**1.8**	**2.6**
Mexico[b]	**2.6**	**1.1**	**1.3**	**0.7**
Paraguay	−2.2	**0.6**	**1.1**	**1.1**
Peru	−1.2	−0.5	−0.4	−0.4
Uruguay	−2.0	−0.6	−0.6	−0.1

Sources: SEDLAC harmonized data sets and ENIGH, 2008 and 2010.
Note: Poverty increased in the countries highlighted.
a. Data refer to the period 2006–09.
b. Data refer to the period 2008–10.

above 40 percent. Trends in poverty rates also differed by country over the crisis period (see table 3.2). Of the selected countries, eight had less moderate poverty overall, whereas four saw an increase in moderate poverty (Costa Rica, Ecuador, El Salvador, and Mexico).

A few countries (Argentina, Brazil, and Peru) experienced zero or slightly negative GDP per capita growth, and yet poverty rates went down. In these three countries, national account figures show stagnant or negative growth, but the household survey shows continued income growth and declining poverty. In Paraguay, a severe recession of more than 5 percent decline in GDP per capita contrasts with the mild decline of 0.2 percent in per capita household income as reported by the survey. This mild reduction combined with very regressive income growth explains higher poverty gaps and extreme poverty while moderate poverty went down. All these cases highlight the disconnect between macro- and microdata on income. In effect, changes in average income growth as reported in the survey do not coincide with GDP per capita growth for many countries in the sample.[8]

How Much Poverty Was There and among Whom?

Relying on before-and-after estimates, profiles, and decompositions, this section provides a fine-print description of the characteristics of the poor during the 2008–09 global financial crisis.

The figures given in the previous section refer to national aggregates and nonweighted regional averages of national aggregates. These national aggregates, however, may hide important differences in the incidence of poverty among population groups. Tables 3.3 and 3.4 present the poverty rates and changes, respectively, for six categories of individuals:

1. Type of area in which individuals live, urban or rural.
2. Sex of the head of household.
3. Education of the head of household (unskilled heads have less than a complete primary education).
4. Employment status of the head of household, classifying family members according to whether the household head is employed in the formal sector, employed in the informal sector, or not employed at all.
5. Sources of household income, depending on whether the family receives income other than labor earnings.
6. Sources of household income, depending on whether the family receives some public sector transfers or subsidies.

In terms of the urban-rural divide, the stylized fact is that during the crisis moderate poverty remains much higher in rural areas than in urban areas (with the exception of Uruguay, where the areas are almost equal) and rural poverty declines faster than urban poverty in some countries but not in others. The trend of faster moderate poverty reduction in rural areas holds except for El Salvador, Paraguay, and Uruguay, where rural poverty increases while urban poverty declines, and in Mexico where rural poverty rises faster than urban poverty.

Disaggregating poverty by sex of the head of household reveals that female-headed households tend to have higher moderate poverty rates than male-headed households, with the exception of those in El Salvador, Mexico, and Paraguay. In several countries, women's moderate poverty rates decline faster, or increase more slowly, than men's. In all other countries, the opposite is true. This finding indicates that no systematic pattern of poverty dynamics by household head gender characterizes this crisis.

As for the education of household heads, members of families whose household heads completed at least primary school (skilled) consistently have lower moderate poverty rates than those who did not finish primary school (unskilled). In most cases, poverty declines faster among the unskilled than the skilled. In some countries with an increase in national poverty, households with skilled household heads see a higher increase in poverty than others. This is true of Costa Rica and Ecuador, but not of Mexico and El Salvador. Again, no systematic pattern can be discerned across countries regarding changes in poverty rates by education of the household heads.

In the case of employment status, moderate poverty is always the lowest among those living in households whose head is employed in the formal sector. This difference is stark: in most countries moderate poverty rates for this group are half or even less than half the moderate poverty rates of those for household heads working in the informal sector or heads who are jobless (i.e., unemployed/inactive). There is no regular pattern in moderate poverty dynamics by the head of household's employment status, however. This indicates that although formal

Table 3.3 Profile of Moderate Poverty Rates: Latin America, 2009

Percent

		Argentina	Brazil	Chile	Colombia	Costa Rica	Dominican Republic	Ecuador	El Salvador	Mexico[a]	Paraguay	Peru	Uruguay
National		16.4	27.6	11.8	42.6	19.6	34.7	37.6	42.7	30.1	34.9	35.7	12.0
By area	Urban	16.4	24.1	11.2	34.9	15.2	31.3	29.6	29.9	22.4	21.0	17.8	12.0
	Rural	—	46.1	16.1	66.6	25.7	41.8	53.2	64.4	55.6	54.6	67.4	11.7
By sex of household head	Male	15.0	26.7	9.8	42.1	18.5	33.1	37.7	43.9	31.3	37.1	34.7	11.1
	Female	19.8	29.7	16.6	44.0	22.6	38.4	37.2	40.1	25.3	29.7	35.3	13.9
By education of household head	Unskilled	30.1	37.1	18.2	62.9	33.9	44.5	51.5	53.0	46.7	54.9	53.8	17.4
	Skilled	14.6	17.1	9.9	33.1	15.6	24.3	32.3	24.3	23.6	28.7	25.1	11.0
By employment of household head	Formal employed	5.5	16.4	6.7	14.0	9.5	25.3	15.0	15.4	7.7	10.9	4.9	8.2
	Informal employed	30.1	47.6	19.3	55.2	28.3	37.9	42.6	54.0	38.3	38.0	32.1	28.0
	Inactive/unemployed	20.2	31.8	20.6	45.7	31.0	41.2	39.0	48.1	31.5	20.8	38.8	10.9
By sources of household income	Some other income	21.0	22.6	14.6	46.1	—	37.1	46.2	45.3	31.2	35.9	35.5	14.9
	Only labor income	12.4	30.5	5.8	40.4	—	31.5	27.8	40.8	27.1	34.3	35.9	2.6
By sources of household income	No public transfers	11.6	27.3	7.2	38.3	—	30.6	27.1	42.5	21.4	32.5	36.2	2.0
	Some public transfers	33.8	41.1	15.7	53.4	—	38.0	49.8	42.9	48.9	39.9	35.1	19.3

Sources: SEDLAC harmonized data sets and ENIGH, 2008 and 2010.

Note: — = not available.

a. Data for Mexico refer to 2010, not 2009.

Table 3.4 Changes in Moderate Poverty Rates: Latin America, 2008–09
Percentage points

		Argentina	Brazil	Chile[a]	Colombia	Costa Rica	Dominican Republic	Ecuador	El Salvador	Mexico[b]	Paraguay	Peru	Uruguay
National		-0.9	-1.6	-4.0	-2.2	0.7	-3.2	0.5	0.6	2.6	-2.2	-1.2	-2.0
By area	Urban	-0.9	-1.3	-3.7	-2.2	1.7	-2.0	2.4	-2.2	2.5	-5.1	-1.1	-2.2
	Rural	—	-2.7	-6.4	-2.1	-0.3	-5.7	-3.4	4.0	2.8	2.1	-2.5	1.0
By sex of household head	Male	-0.4	-1.8	-4.7	-2.3	0.8	-3.5	0.5	1.6	3.2	-1.3	-2.3	-1.4
	Female	-2.3	-1.1	-2.9	-2.2	-0.1	-2.7	0.5	-1.4	-0.2	-1.0	-1.8	-3.3
By education of household head	Unskilled	-0.4	-2.1	-6.2	-2.4	-0.6	-4.3	-2.6	0.8	4.5	-3.1	-0.7	-4.2
	Skilled	-0.9	-0.5	-3.2	-2.2	1.4	-2.2	1.4	0.3	3.0	-0.5	-1.7	-1.5
By employment of household head	Formal employed	-0.5	-1.9	-5.8	-2.6	-0.1	-1.8	0.7	-2.9	1.4	0.0	-4.5	-1.4
	Informal employed	-0.1	-1.6	-12.0	-4.5	2.1	-4.3	-3.7	1.3	3.8	0.1	-2.4	-3.4
	Inactive/unemployed	-2.3	-1.0	-2.6	-2.6	1.6	-5.0	-0.6	1.3	1.2	-1.5	-2.3	-2.3
By sources of household income	Some other income	-1.5	-0.7	-4.4	-0.1	—	-4.5	-0.3	3.8	3.2	-1.5	-0.1	-2.1
	Only labor income	-0.7	-2.0	-5.1	-3.7	—	-2.3	0.1	-1.6	1.1	-2.5	-2.0	-0.5
By sources of household income	No public transfers	-0.8	-1.6	-3.6	-3.9	—	-2.6	-0.2	1.0	1.8	-2.8	-2.0	-0.4
	Some public transfers	-1.8	-1.9	-6.7	0.1	—	-4.5	0.2	-0.2	4.8	0.3	0.0	-2.3

Sources: SEDLAC harmonized data sets and ENIGH, 2008 and 2010.

Note: — = not available.

a. Data refer to the period 2006–09.
b. Data refer to the period 2008–10.

employment is associated with lower poverty rates, it is not necessarily associated with faster (or slower) changes in poverty.

Moderate poverty profiles that characterize households by sources of income show that households with only labor income generally have lower moderate poverty rates than households with other sources of income. Sources of income other than labor range from pensions to rents, dividends, remittances, or public sector transfers from social programs. Different surveys have different ways of capturing these nonlabor sources of income, and therefore this decomposition may be indicating differences in survey design rather than actual sources of income. Concentrating on public sector transfers, which all surveys capture in some way, the profile shows that for 2009 moderate poverty is higher among households receiving public transfers.[9] The exception is Peru, where rates are very similar between the two groups. Over time, changes in poverty observed across all these groups show no regular pattern. These profiles indicate that public transfers are more common among households living in poverty, but those households do not necessarily have faster or slower poverty changes than other households.

In summary,[10] moderate poverty profiles show that poverty is regularly higher in rural areas and among households whose head is female or unskilled or not employed in the formal sector. Households with access to public transfers also have higher poverty rates. No regular pattern in poverty changes, however, is observed among these categories.

Box 3.2 Poverty Numbers in Other Countries

The description of poverty trends and profiles in this section makes use of available microdata from a subset of countries in the region that produce regular surveys for measuring poverty. Other countries were not included in this subset for several reasons. Some countries such as Bolivia, Panama, and República Bolivariana de Venezuela produce annual household surveys, but microdata were not available when we were preparing this report. In other countries, too wide a period elapses between surveys to be useful for analyzing the impact of the global financial crisis in 2009. For example, Guatemala's Encuesta de Condiciones de Vida (Survey on Living Conditions) was conducted in 2006 and 2011, and Nicaragua's Encuesta Nacional de Hogares sobre Medición de Nivel de Vida (National Survey of Living Standards of Households) was undertaken in 2005 and 2009. Jamaica produces an annual survey of living conditions, but it uses a consumption aggregate rather than an income aggregate to measure poverty. Panama's household survey was conducted in 2009 and 2010 but not in 2008.

More serious, many Caribbean countries have no recent surveys. For example, in the Bahamas the most recent survey of living conditions took place in 2001. No reporting or analyses of poverty trends can be undertaken in these circumstances, despite the fact that these countries are among those that endured wider swings in economic growth as a result of the 2008–09 global financial crisis.

---

box continues next page

Box 3.2 Poverty Numbers in Other Countries *(continued)*

Table B3.2.1 Official Poverty Headcount: Selected Countries, Latin America, Various Years

Country	Year	Official poverty headcount (percentage of total population)		GDP per capita growth (%)
		Extreme poverty	Moderate poverty	
Bolivia	2008	30.1	57.3	
	2009	26.1	51.3	1.7
Jamaica	2008	—	16.5	
	2009	—	17.6	—
Guatemala	2006	15.2	51.0	
	2011	13.3	53.7	4.2
Honduras	2008	44.1	65.7	
	2009	42.4	64.5	−4.1
Nicaragua	2005	17.2	48.3	
	2009	14.6	42.5	5.4
Panama	2008	15.3	33.8	
	2009	15.3	33.4	2.2
Venezuela, RB	2008	9.2	31.8	
	2009	8.8	32.5	4.7

Sources: SEDLAC (http://sedlac.econo.unlp.edu.ar/eng/index.php) and Diéguez and Alvarado 2012.
Note: GDP per capita growth refers to the accumulated growth for corresponding the period; — = not available.

In some of these cases, we can report official poverty numbers, based on official methodologies, for the most recent years for which data are available. Interestingly, all these countries show a decline in extreme poverty. Only Guatemala, Jamaica, and República Bolivariana de Venezuela report an increase in moderate poverty. Table B3.2.1 summarizes these official estimates.

Do Extreme Poverty Rates and Moderate Poverty Rates Exhibit Different Patterns?

Over the period 2008–09, the average (nonweighted) extreme poverty rate in the region moved from 15.1 to 14.9, an overall decline of 0.2 percentage points.[11] In other words, extreme poverty shows a much slower decline than moderate poverty for the period under study. Again, Argentina, Chile, Costa Rica, and Uruguay exhibit the lowest extreme poverty rates (all below 10 percent), whereas Colombia, El Salvador, and Paraguay have extreme poverty rates above the 20 percent mark (see table 3.5). As for poverty changes, some interesting variations can be observed. Most countries show a decline in extreme poverty that mirrors their declines in moderate poverty (table 3.6). In Costa Rica, El Salvador, and Mexico, the increases in extreme poverty follow the increases in moderate poverty. However, Ecuador shows a decline in extreme poverty in contrast to its increase in moderate poverty, whereas Paraguay shows an increase in extreme poverty in contrast to its decline in moderate poverty.

Understanding the Poverty Impact of the Global Financial Crisis in Latin America and the Caribbean
http://dx.doi.org/10.1596/978-1-4648-0241-6

Table 3.5 Profile of Extreme Poverty Rates: Latin America, 2009
Percent

		Argentina	Brazil	Chile	Colombia	Costa Rica	Dominican Republic	Ecuador	El Salvador	Mexico[a]	Paraguay	Peru	Uruguay
National		8.1	15.1	4.3	24.8	8.1	16.4	19.4	23.1	15.1	20.6	20.0	3.4
By area	Urban	8.1	12.6	4.0	18.8	5.3	14.0	13.7	12.3	9.2	10.5	6.6	3.5
	Rural	–	28.1	6.1	43.3	11.9	21.4	30.4	41.6	34.6	34.8	43.9	2.6
By sex of household head	Male	7.1	14.0	3.1	23.7	6.9	15.6	19.5	25.2	15.9	21.0	20.6	2.8
	Female	10.5	17.3	7.0	27.4	11.0	18.3	18.8	18.9	11.9	15.8	20.5	4.9
By education of household head	Unskilled	15.8	21.1	6.8	40.3	15.8	22.1	27.4	29.8	22.0	33.9	34.2	5.0
	Skilled	7.1	8.3	3.5	17.5	5.9	10.3	16.3	11.3	7.9	15.0	13.5	3.2
By employment of household head	Formal employed	1.6	4.6	0.9	2.8	1.8	8.6	3.5	3.7	0.9	2.5	0.3	1.5
	Informal employed	15.4	26.8	5.0	28.0	11.0	16.7	18.0	26.0	15.6	16.8	11.8	9.0
	Inactive/unemployed	11.4	21.4	10.5	31.1	17.0	22.0	22.2	28.7	13.4	10.5	23.9	3.9
By sources of household income	Some other income	11.1	14.9	5.5	29.5	–	16.9	25.1	27.0	16.1	22.7	21.4	4.3
	Only labor income	5.5	15.1	1.6	21.8	–	15.6	12.8	20.4	12.4	19.2	19.0	0.8
By sources of household income	No public transfers	5.4	14.9	3.2	21.5	–	15.1	13.4	24.1	9.2	18.7	19.3	0.6
	Some public transfers	17.8	24.4	5.2	32.8	–	17.5	26.3	21.1	27.7	24.5	21.0	5.6

Sources: SEDLAC harmonized data sets and ENIGH, 2008 and 2010.

Note: – = not available.

a. Data for Mexico refer to 2010, not 2009.

Table 3.6 Changes in Extreme Poverty Rates: Latin America, 2008–09
Percentage points

		Argentina	Brazil	Chile[a]	Colombia	Costa Rica	Dominican Republic	Ecuador	El Salvador	Mexico[b]	Paraguay	Peru	Uruguay
National		-0.2	-0.6	-1.0	-2.5	0.5	-2.0	-0.2	1.8	1.3	1.1	-0.4	-0.6
By area	Urban	-0.2	-0.2	-0.9	-1.7	0.0	-0.9	1.1	-0.8	1.2	-0.1	0.1	-0.7
	Rural	–	-2.7	-1.6	-4.7	1.3	-4.3	-2.8	5.2	1.6	2.9	-2.0	0.4
By sex of household head	Male	0.0	-0.8	-1.2	-2.4	0.4	-1.6	0.3	3.0	1.7	-0.6	0.5	-0.5
	Female	-0.8	-0.3	-0.8	-2.7	0.2	-3.3	-2.2	-0.5	-0.3	0.6	2.8	-0.8
By education of household head	Unskilled	1.1	-1.0	-2.2	-3.9	0.5	-3.3	-4.0	1.9	-1.6	-1.6	2.8	-2.0
	Skilled	-0.3	0.1	-0.5	-1.9	0.7	-0.9	1.1	1.5	-1.3	0.1	1.0	-0.3
By employment of household head	Formal employed	0.2	-1.0	-1.5	-1.7	-0.4	-1.6	-0.8	-0.6	-0.4	0.2	-0.9	-0.2
	Informal employed	1.4	-0.8	-7.6	-5.2	2.7	-2.9	-3.0	0.2	-2.2	1.8	-2.4	-0.9
	Inactive/unemployed	-1.2	0.3	0.3	-2.6	0.9	-4.5	-0.7	2.9	-2.4	-0.3	4.2	-0.3
By sources of household income	Some other income	-0.4	0.2	-1.2	-1.8	–	-4.1	-0.5	6.2	1.9	4.4	0.6	-0.7
	Only labor income	-0.2	-1.1	-1.5	-3.2	–	0.2	-0.7	-1.3	-0.1	-1.2	-1.0	0.1
By sources of household income	No public transfers	-0.1	-0.6	-0.5	-3.3	–	-0.2	-0.8	2.7	0.8	-1.2	-1.0	0.0
	Some public transfers	-0.9	-2.1	-2.2	-2.0	–	-4.1	-0.1	0.0	2.7	5.4	0.6	-0.8

Sources: SEDLAC harmonized data sets and ENIGH, 2008 and 2010.

Note: – = not available.

a. Data refer to the period 2006–09.
b. Data refer to the period 2008–10.

These different dynamics—namely, changes different in magnitude and even in direction—imply the importance of distributive forces and changes in inequality in explaining changes in poverty. In other words, those at the bottom of the distribution (the extreme poor) may have endured income shocks of a different magnitude than those in the middle of the distribution.

Most of the regularities found in the profiles of moderate poverty by group (table 3.3) are confirmed when looking at extreme poverty by group (table 3.5). Extreme poverty is higher in rural areas (except in Uruguay), in female-headed households (except in Paraguay), in households that receive some public transfers, in households headed by unskilled workers, and in households with heads not working in the formal sector. Like moderate poverty profiles, changes in extreme poverty by area, by head of household's sex, by employment, and by household income sources show no regular patterns across countries. Also like moderate poverty, households whose heads are skilled have larger poverty increases, or lower decreases, than other households (see tables 3.5 and 3.6).

And What about the Poverty Gap?

Headcount poverty rates measure only the share of the poor within the total population. Changes in headcounts are very sensitive to movements across the poverty line of families who are very close to the line, even if these movements do not entail a significant change in income and well-being. They do not indicate what happens to the actual income levels of the poor—that is, whether the poor remain as poor as before. The poverty gap, by measuring the average distance to the poverty line, reveals whether the poor are closer or farther away from the poverty line and thus whether their average standard of living has changed.

From 2008 to 2009, the nonweighted average moderate poverty gap in Latin America declined from 13.2 percent to 13.0 percent, whereas the extreme poverty gap remained at 6.8. Again, Argentina, Chile, and Uruguay had the lowest poverty gaps (table 3.7). Costa Rica joins this group, which is characterized by moderate poverty gaps below 8 percent and extreme poverty gaps below 4 percent. In other words, poverty gaps indicate roughly the same rankings among countries as poverty headcounts.

The evolution of poverty gaps is closely consistent with the evolution of poverty headcounts. Over the period studied, Costa Rica, El Salvador, and Mexico showed an increase in moderate and extreme poverty rates as well as an increase in both moderate and extreme poverty gaps. In Paraguay, both poverty gaps increased, which is consistent with the increase in extreme poverty. In Ecuador, the rise in the moderate poverty gap is consistent with the increase in moderate poverty. For all the remaining countries, the decline in poverty gaps is consistent with the declines in moderate and extreme poverty (see table 3.7).

The evidence from poverty gaps indicates that from 2008 to 2009 reductions in poverty were accompanied by a narrowing of the distance between the average income of the poor and the poverty line. In countries where poverty increased, the poverty gaps did so as well, leaving more people in poverty.

Table 3.7 Poverty Gaps: Latin America, 2008 and 2009

Percent

	Argentina	Brazil	Chile[a]	Colombia	Costa Rica	Dominican Republic	Ecuador	El Salvador	Mexico[b]	Peru	Paraguay	Uruguay
In 2008												
Poverty gap (US$4.00-a-day poverty line)	6.8	12.8	4.8	21.6	6.8	14.0	15.4	16.6	11.1	15.5	15.0	3.8
Poverty gap (US$2.50-a-day poverty line)	3.3	7.0	1.7	12.6	3.1	5.5	7.6	7.4	5.4	7.5	7.2	0.9
In 2009												
Poverty gap (US$4.00-a-day poverty line)	6.6	12.4	3.9	19.6	7.2	12.6	15.5	18.8	12.2	15.0	15.6	3.3
Poverty gap (US$2.50-a-day poverty line)	3.2	6.9	1.6	10.9	3.6	4.8	7.6	10.1	6.0	7.1	8.3	0.7
Changes (2009–2008)												
Poverty gap (US$4.00-a-day poverty line)	–0.2	–0.4	–1.0	–2.0	0.4	–1.4	0.1	2.2	1.1	–0.5	0.6	–0.6
Poverty gap (US$2.50-a-day poverty line)	–0.1	0.0	–0.1	–1.7	0.5	–0.7	0.0	2.6	0.7	–0.4	1.1	–0.1

Sources: SEDLAC harmonized data sets and ENIGH, 2008 and 2010.

a. Data refer to the period 2006–09.

b. Data refer to the period 2008–10.

The average income deficit also increased among the poor, and the extreme poverty gap leveled off.

This review of poverty headcounts and gaps has revealed a clear pattern. All countries in which moderate poverty fell also saw a decline in the extreme poverty headcount and in both the moderate and extreme poverty gaps. The only exception to this was Paraguay, where all the rates increased but moderate poverty declined. On the other hand, all countries in which moderate poverty increased also showed an increase in extreme poverty and in the moderate and extreme poverty gaps. The exception was Ecuador, where all the rates increased except the extreme poverty headcount which declined.

Because of the similarity in patterns and trends of moderate and extreme poverty rates and poverty gaps in most countries, we concentrate further analyses on moderate poverty rates. At times, however, we will introduce data about extreme poverty or poverty gaps, when these bring additional insights to the analysis.

But Who Bore the Brunt of the Crisis?

The profiles of poverty rates in previous sections only describe the poverty incidence of different population groups. It is also interesting to determine whether poverty changes are due to the increasing incidence of poverty in a group or to changes in the size of a group. Decomposition by demographic group allows identification of the personal characteristics of those affected by the crisis. The Huppi-Ravallion decomposition separates the total change in poverty incidence into the change in poverty incidence of each population group, the change in the relative size of each population group, and an interaction term (see box 3.3). This decomposition allows one to identify whether aggregate poverty changes are due to the change in poverty incidence of a group, the relative size of a group, or a combination of both. Table 3.8 presents a decomposition by the same demographic groups in the poverty profiles in table 3.6.

These decompositions contain two main messages. First, changes in household demographics such as the gender or education level of the household head and urbanization do not explain much between 2008 and 2009. This is to be expected because big changes in these dimensions occur over longer periods of time. On the other hand, the results show that changes in the household head's employment status and household's source of income (by income and transfer) do have a larger effect. This finding indicates that poverty changes are not associated with demographic trends but with something that happened between 2008 and 2009 in terms of social policies or labor market dynamics.

When one looks at demographic characteristics such as geographic area (urban/rural), gender of the head of household (male/female), and skills of the household head (high skill/low skill), all countries show mostly negligible interaction and population shift effects.[12] For gender and for area, usually the largest share of a change in poverty is attributed to the largest demographic group (urban households) and not necessarily the poorest demographic group (rural households).

Box 3.3 The Huppi-Ravallion Decomposition of Poverty Changes, by Population Group

Huppi and Ravallion (1990) propose a methodology to decompose changes in poverty rates by changes in the poverty incidence and relative size of population groups. Given poverty rates for final and initial year (P_f and P_i, respectively), the decomposition is

$$P_f - P_i = \sum_k (P_{k,f} - P_{k,i})N_{k,i} + \sum_k (N_{k,f} - N_{k,i})P_{k,i} + \sum_k (N_{k,f} - N_{k,i})(P_{k,f} - P_{k,i})$$

where $P_{k,f}(P_{k,i})$ stands for the poverty incidence and $N_{k,f}(N_{k,i})$ represents the population share in group k for the final (initial) period. The first right-hand term represents the *intrasectoral effect,* which is the change in poverty that can be attributed to changes in the incidence of poverty in each k group of the population, assuming that the relative size of each population group remains as it was in the initial year of the comparison. The second term stands for the *population shift effects*—that is, the change in poverty due to population changing from one group to another, assuming poverty incidence in each group stays at the level of the initial period. The third term is an *interaction effect* that indicates whether there is a correlation between poverty incidence and population movements: a negative sign would indicate that people tend to switch to groups where poverty is falling.

For example, members of male-headed households have a larger share of the population (not the highest poverty incidence), and they represent the greater share of changes in total incidence in most countries, such as accounting for the decline of moderate poverty by 3.2 percentage points in Chile (versus 0.8 for women). However, there are two main exceptions to this general rule: first, female-headed households account for declines in moderate poverty at a higher or equal rate than male-headed households in Argentina (urban) and Uruguay, and, second, in the Dominican Republic poverty reductions are mostly attributable to poverty declines in rural and unskilled head households (not the largest groups).

Decomposition by group according to employment status of the household head or by income sources does not show a regular pattern. In other words, the largest share of the poverty change cannot be regularly ascribed to either the largest group or the group with the highest poverty incidence. We interpret this heterogeneity as proof that different labor dynamics or different transfer policies by country motivate varied poverty dynamics. In contrast to slow demographic trends, which are pretty similar across countries, labor market performance and public transfer policies may differ from one country to another.

Furthermore, for household head employment or sources of income, the population shift plus interaction effect is negligible less often.[13] Some particular cases are of special significance. In Chile and Paraguay, non-negligible population shift effects increase moderate poverty; they are associated with an increase

Table 3.8 Decomposition of Changes in Moderate Poverty, by Population Group: Latin America, 2008–09

Percentage points

		Argentina	Brazil	Chile[a]	Colombia	Costa Rica	Dominican Republic	Ecuador	El Salvador	Mexico[b]	Paraguay	Peru	Uruguay
Change 2009–08		-0.9	-1.6	-4.0	-2.2	0.7	-3.2	0.5	0.6	2.6	-2.2	-1.2	-2.0
By area	Rural	–	-0.4	-0.8	-0.5	-0.1	-1.9	-1.1	1.4	0.7	0.9	-0.9	0.1
	Urban	–	-1.1	-3.2	-1.6	1.0	-1.3	1.6	-1.4	1.9	-3.0	-0.7	-2.0
	Population shift effect	–	-0.1	0.0	-0.1	-0.2	0.0	0.1	0.5	0.0	-0.1	0.4	-0.1
	Interaction effect	–	0.0	0.0	0.0	0.0	0.0	0.0	0.1	0.0	0.0	0.0	0.1
By sex of household head	Female	-0.7	-0.4	-0.8	-0.6	0.0	-0.8	0.1	-0.4	0.0	-0.5	-0.2	-1.0
	Male	-0.3	-1.3	-3.5	-1.7	0.6	-2.5	0.4	1.1	2.5	-1.7	-1.0	-1.0
	Population shift effect	0.1	0.0	0.2	0.0	0.1	0.1	0.0	0.0	0.0	0.0	0.0	0.0
	Interaction effect	0.0	0.0	0.1	0.0	0.0	0.0	0.0	0.0	0.0	0.0	0.0	0.0
By education of household head	Unskilled	-0.1	-1.1	-1.5	-0.8	-0.1	-2.2	-0.7	0.5	1.4	-0.3	-0.8	-0.7
	Skilled	-0.8	-0.2	-2.4	-1.5	1.0	-1.1	1.0	0.1	2.0	-1.1	-0.4	-1.2
	Population shift effect	0.0	-0.2	-0.1	0.1	-0.2	0.1	0.2	0.0	-0.8	-0.8	0.0	-0.1
	Interaction effect	0.0	0.0	0.0	0.0	0.0	0.0	0.0	0.0	-0.1	0.0	0.0	0.0
By employment of household head	Inactive/unemployed	-0.6	-0.7	-0.9	-1.2	0.2	-2.7	1.4	0.8	0.2	-1.8	-0.9	-1.0
	Informal employed	0.0	-0.2	-0.9	-0.7	0.3	-0.3	-1.1	0.3	2.2	-0.5	0.0	-0.3
	Formal employed	-0.2	-0.6	-2.6	-0.5	0.0	-0.5	0.1	-0.6	0.3	-0.7	0.0	-0.6
	Population shift effect	-0.1	0.0	0.3	0.1	0.2	0.3	-0.2	0.1	-0.1	0.8	-0.3	-0.2
	Interaction effect	0.0	0.0	0.1	0.0	0.0	0.0	0.2	0.0	0.0	0.0	0.0	0.0
By sources of household income	Some other income	-0.7	-0.3	-2.7	0.0	–	-2.4	-0.1	1.5	2.4	-0.7	0.0	-1.6
	Only labor income	-0.4	-1.3	-2.0	-2.4	–	-1.1	0.0	-1.0	0.3	-1.4	-1.2	-0.1
	Population shift effect	0.2	-0.1	0.6	0.1	–	0.4	0.6	0.0	0.0	0.0	0.0	-0.3
	Interaction effect	0.0	0.0	0.1	0.1	–	-0.1	0.0	0.1	0.0	-0.1	0.0	0.0
By sources of household income	No public transfers	-0.6	-1.5	-2.0	-2.9	n.a.	-1.3	-0.1	0.7	1.2	-1.7	-1.2	-0.1
	Some public transfers	-0.4	0.0	-3.0	0.0	n.a.	-2.3	0.1	-0.1	1.5	0.1	0.0	-1.4
	Population shift effect	0.2	0.0	1.3	0.5	n.a.	0.5	0.5	0.0	-0.1	-0.4	0.0	-0.5
	Interaction effect	0.0	0.0	-0.3	0.2	n.a.	-0.1	0.0	0.0	0.0	-0.3	0.0	0.1

Sources: SEDLAC harmonized data sets and ENIGH, 2008 and 2010.

Note: – = not available; n.a. = not applicable.

a. Data refer to the period 2006–09.

b. Data refer to the period 2008–10.

in the share of households with unemployed or inactive heads.[14] Similarly, Chile, Colombia, the Dominican Republic, and Ecuador show non-negligible population shift effects increasing moderate poverty; they are associated with a large increase in the population share that lives in households with access to public transfers.[15]

Chile shows the largest effects overall because the data span a three-year period, and it is an interesting example to explore further. Moderate poverty declined by 4 percentage points between 2006 and 2009. In this case, the largest component is poverty reduction among households whose heads have formal employment (2.6 percentage points), followed by declines in poverty in the other two groups (informal and jobless household heads) of equal size (0.9 percentage points). The population shift effect raises poverty by 0.3 percentage points because of an increase in the share of people living in households with a jobless head (this group increased by 4 percentage points for the period of reference).

Alternatively, Chile's total change in moderate poverty of 4.0 percentage points can be decomposed by sources of income of the household. This decline is a combination of a reduction of 2.0 percentage points for households receiving no public transfers and a cutback of 3.0 percentage points for households receiving some public transfers. However, there is a positive shift effect of 1.3 percentage points. It is the result of an increase in the population share of households receiving public transfers (almost 11 percentage points for the three-year period). Because this group has a higher incidence of poverty (which seems natural because they receive public transfers), we observe an increase in the relative size of the group with higher, but falling, poverty incidence. For that reason, the population shift effect is positive (1.3 percentage points), and the interaction effect is negative (−0.3 percentage points).

We see something similar in the expansion of the population with access to public transfers in Colombia, Ecuador, the Dominican Republic, Honduras, and Mexico, but of smaller magnitude. In Paraguay and Uruguay, by contrast, the population shift effect is negative, which means that there is a reduction in the population group with higher poverty incidence. This is true of the population with access to public transfers; its share fell during the study period in these countries. Similarly, Ecuador, the Dominican Republic, and Paraguay show shifts in the head's employment status group as large as those of Chile.

In general, population plus interaction effects are larger when decomposing poverty changes by income source than by the head of household's employment status. In fact, changes in the share of households with some public transfers are always higher than changes in the share of households with a jobless head. Therefore, the dynamics of public transfers is larger than changes in employment.[16] This finding indicates the relative importance, as compared with all the other decompositions, that changes in the number of households with sources of income other than labor earnings, and particularly public transfers, had on poverty changes during the global financial crisis.[17]

Understanding the Poverty Impact of the Global Financial Crisis in Latin America and the Caribbean
http://dx.doi.org/10.1596/978-1-4648-0241-6

Sources of Changes in Poverty

As we have now seen, from 2008 to 2009 poverty declined in Latin America in most countries and for most population groups. This finding seems to indicate that among countries where poverty declined, this reduction was pervasive, and few distinctive trends, by country or population group, are apparent. However, in countries where poverty increased (Costa Rica, Ecuador, El Salvador, Mexico, and Paraguay) some divergent trends can be identified. For example, in Costa Rica and Ecuador the increase in moderate poverty is associated with an increase in poverty in urban areas, whereas in El Salvador it is due to an increase in poverty in rural areas, and in Mexico both urban and rural areas show an increase. In the case of extreme poverty, however, every country experiencing an increase in poverty did so because of an increase in rural poverty. Are there then specific forces accounting for poverty changes in different counties? Is it possible to identify the driving force behind changes in poverty?

This section further analyzes the observed poverty changes by applying decomposition techniques that separate and gauge the influence of demographic groups, income sources, and changes in economic growth and inequality. The main idea is to estimate how much of the poverty change observed at the national level can be ascribed to different forces. Several methods can be used to determine to what degree a change in poverty can be allocated to different groups or factors.

This section of the study uses three types of decomposition to identify the components of poverty changes observed. These decomposition methods do not prove causality, but do account for the size of different components and their contributions to changes in poverty. The application of all these methods is akin to comparing a political map with an orographic map or a road or a rainfall map. All of them refer to the same territory but highlight different aspects of it. What is shown in one of them is not seen in the others, but to have full knowledge of the territory one must read them all.

Is It All Due to Economic Growth?

The close link between economic growth and poverty reduction has been widely documented worldwide.[18] The evidence for the countries selected for this study confirms the close link between economic growth and poverty changes. Several studies have documented the successful poverty reduction associated with the sustained growth observed in the Latin America region over the last decade. These studies also highlight the importance of redistributive policies in explaining this decline in poverty—see World Bank (2011a); Lustig, Lopez-Calva, and Ortiz (2013); and López-Calva and Lustig (2010). It is thus natural to begin our analysis by trying to ascertain how much of the poverty changes observed during the 2008–09 global financial crisis can be ascribed to changes in growth or changes in inequality.

The growth-redistribution decomposition described in box 3.4 shows that in the majority of countries growth is the dominant factor explaining changes

Box 3.4 Datt-Ravallion Decomposition of Poverty Changes, by Growth and Distribution

The Datt and Ravallion (1992) decomposition is

$$P_f - P_i = G(f, i; r) + D(f, i; r) + R(f, i; r)$$

where $G(.)$, $D(.)$, and $R(.)$ stand for the growth, distribution, and residual components as measured in the final (f) and initial (i) periods and a reference level (r) for comparisons. The first two components are defined as

$$G(f, i; r) = P(z, \mu_f, L_r) - P(z, \mu_{fi}, L_r)$$

$$D(f, i; r) = P(z, \mu_r, L_f) - P(z, \mu_r, L_{ri}).$$

The *growth component* of a change in the poverty measure is defined as the change in poverty due to a change in the mean income (from μ_i to μ_f) while holding the Lorenz curve—a summary depiction of the income distribution—constant at some reference level (L_r). The *redistribution component* is the change in poverty due to a change in the Lorenz curve (from L_i to L_f) while keeping the mean income constant at a reference level (μ_r). The poverty line is kept at a constant level z. Finally, the residual can be interpreted as the difference between the growth (redistribution) components evaluated and the poverty change. If the mean income or the Lorenz curve remains unchanged over this period, the residual would be zero.

To deal with changes in the poverty line, an extension of this method has been proposed by Kolenikov and Shorrocks (2005). By allowing several different reference levels for more than two parameters in each component, different decompositions are possible, depending on the sequence (or path) taken, and none are preferable a priori. To deal with this problem, Shorrocks (1999) applies what is known as the Shapley approach, deriving a single decomposition that is always exact and treats all possible routes symmetrically—see Kolenikov and Shorrocks (2005) for an empirical implementation of this method. Changes in inflation rates and thus in real poverty lines were not significant in 2009 unlike in other periods (for example, during the 2007 food price crisis). Therefore, we do not present this type of decomposition in this study.

in both moderate and extreme poverty. This decomposition shows how much poverty would have changed had inequality remained the same (the so-called growth effect) and how much if growth had remained constant (the redistribution effect). In every country in which poverty declined (Argentina, Brazil, Chile, Colombia, the Dominican Republic, Peru, and Uruguay), growth was the predominant factor driving the decline. Similarly, in every country where poverty rose (Ecuador, El Salvador, and Mexico), lack of growth was the predominant factor explaining such a rise. The exceptions were Costa Rica and Paraguay, where poverty increases were mostly driven by redistribution forces (see table 3.9).

This decomposition also presents evidence of a disconnect between GDP per capita growth and average income growth as reported in household surveys. It provides a first explanation of some of the odd links between GDP per capita

Understanding the Poverty Impact of the Global Financial Crisis in Latin America and the Caribbean
http://dx.doi.org/10.1596/978-1-4648-0241-6

Table 3.9 Growth Redistribution Decomposition of Poverty Changes: Latin America, 2008–09

Percentage points

		Argentina	Brazil	Chile[a]	Colombia	Costa Rica	Dominican Republic	Ecuador	El Salvador	Mexico[b]	Paraguay	Peru	Uruguay
Moderate poverty	Growth	−0.7	−1.0	−3.2	−1.9	−2.2	−2.9	2.2	1.6	2.1	0.1	−1.2	−2.0
	Redistribution	−0.2	−0.6	−0.8	−0.3	2.9	−0.2	−1.7	−1.0	0.5	−2.3	0.0	0.1
	Total change 2008–09	−0.9	−1.6	−4.0	−2.2	0.7	−3.2	0.5	0.6	2.6	−2.2	−1.2	−2.0
Extreme poverty	Growth	−0.3	−0.5	−1.0	−1.5	−1.0	−1.9	1.5	1.1	1.2	0.2	−0.9	−0.8
	Redistribution	0.1	−0.2	0.0	−1.0	1.5	−0.2	−1.7	0.7	0.1	0.9	0.5	0.2
	Total change 2008–09	−0.2	−0.6	−1.0	−2.5	0.5	−2.0	−0.2	1.8	1.3	1.1	−0.4	−0.6

Sources: SEDLAC harmonized data sets and ENIGH, 2008 and 2010.

a. Data refer to the period 2006–09.

b. Data refer to the period 2008–10.

growth and poverty changes illustrated in figure 3.1. Argentina, Brazil, and Peru had negative or null GDP per capita growth in 2009, but the Datt-Ravallion decomposition shows that income growth induced most of the poverty decline. This decomposition, which is based on survey data, refers to income growth as reported in the surveys and thus suggests that income growth as reported in the surveys was positive.

In effect, changes in average income growth as reported in surveys do not coincide with growth in GDP per capita. In most cases, both go in the same direction, although magnitudes may differ. In Argentina, Brazil, Peru, and Paraguay, the difference is big enough to make the trends diverge in sign. In these countries, income growth was positive but GDP per capita growth was negative in 2009. This finding explains why, despite a recession in 2009, moderate poverty declined in these four countries. Table 3.10 summarizes the changes in average income growth as reported in the surveys and compares them with the changes in GDP per capita growth.

Often, the redistribution effect and the growth effect go in different directions. In half the countries considered in this study, the redistribution effect partly compensates for the growth effect, and in the other half it intensifies the growth effect. In Costa Rica, the growing inequality more than compensates for positive income growth and increases both moderate and extreme poverty. In Ecuador, the redistribution effect compensates for the decline in growth—it moderates the increase in moderate poverty and reduces extreme poverty. In Uruguay, the redistribution effect is regressive and has the opposite sign of the effect of growth—it moderates the decline in poverty. In Argentina, Brazil, Chile, and Colombia, the redistribution effect goes in the same direction as the growth effect, enhancing the reduction of moderate poverty.

What Is the Role of Changes in Inequality?

The previous section revealed that changes in poverty are mostly driven by changes in economic growth, but changes in the distribution of income can enhance or hinder the effects of growth. What, then, happened to inequality during the crisis? The inequality indexes in this section show whether changes in inequality occurred at the top or the bottom of the distribution. It is mostly those at the bottom of the distribution who may have an effect on poverty dynamics.

A further look at the growth redistribution decomposition shows that changes in the income distribution effect did increase extreme poverty in Costa Rica, El Salvador, Mexico, and Paraguay. Actually, almost all the inequality measures included in this study rose in these four countries from 2008 to 2009, which is fully consistent with the enhancing effect of the redistribution effect on poverty (see table 3.11). In Costa Rica, income differentials increased at the bottom as well as at the top of the distribution. In Mexico, however, worsening inequality was concentrated at the bottom of the distribution: FGT(2) measures increased for both the moderate and extreme poverty lines, but the decile ratios stayed unaltered. El Salvador and Paraguay experienced a serious worsening in inequality at the bottom of the distribution, which intensified extreme poverty,

Table 3.10 Comparison of GDP Per Capita versus Average Income Growth: Latin America, 2008–09

	Argentina	Brazil	Chile[a]	Colombia	Costa Rica	Dominican Republic	Ecuador	El Salvador	Mexico[b]	Paraguay	Peru	Uruguay
GDP per capita growth	0.0%	−1.2%	4.3%	0.2%	−2.5%	2.1%	−1.1%	−3.5%	−7.1%	−5.2%	−0.2%	2.1%
Income per capita growth (as reported in surveys)	2.8%	2.9%	11.0%	5.5%	8.0%	6.2%	−4.8%	−3.4%	−5.1%	−0.3%	3.0%	6.9%
Difference (percentage points)	2.8	4.1	6.7	5.3	10.5	4.1	(3.7)	0.1	2.0	4.9	3.2	4.8

Sources: SEDLAC harmonized data sets; ENIGH, 2008 and 2010; and World Bank's World Development Indicators (database).
a. Data refer to the period 2006–09.
b. Data refer to the period 2008–10.

Table 3.11 Inequality Measures: Latin America, 2008 and 2009
Percent

		Argentina	Brazil	Chile[a]	Colombia	Costa Rica	Dominican Republic	Ecuador	El Salvador	Mexico[b]	Peru	Paraguay	Uruguay
In 2008	Percentile 90/percentile 10	10.0	13.1	8.7	15.2	8.7	8.3	10.1	8.8	11.0	10.5	9.9	8.4
	Percentile 90/percentile 50	2.9	3.5	3.3	3.6	3.1	3.0	3.2	3.0	3.2	3.1	3.1	3.0
	Percentile 50/percentile 10	3.5	3.8	2.6	4.2	2.8	2.7	3.2	2.9	3.4	3.4	3.2	2.8
	FGT(2) (moderate)	3.9	7.9	2.3	13.8	3.8	7.0	8.9	9.0	6.0	8.7	8.4	1.5
	FGT(2) (extreme)	2.0	4.6	0.9	8.1	2.0	2.4	4.6	3.8	3.0	3.8	3.8	0.3
	Gini coefficient	46.3	55.1	51.8	57.2	48.9	49.0	50.6	46.8	51.8	49.0	52.0	46.3
In 2009	Percentile 90/percentile 10	10.3	13.1	8.3	13.8	9.9	8.5	9.7	10.0	11.1	10.6	11.0	8.3
	Percentile 90/percentile 50	2.8	3.4	3.2	3.6	3.4	3.1	3.1	2.9	3.3	3.1	2.9	3.0
	Percentile 50/percentile 10	3.6	3.9	2.6	3.8	2.9	2.8	3.2	3.5	3.4	3.4	3.7	2.8
	FGT(2) (moderate)	3.8	7.8	2.0	12.1	4.2	6.2	9.0	11.4	7.0	8.3	9.4	1.3
	FGT(2) (extreme)	2.0	4.7	1.0	6.8	2.4	2.1	4.5	6.3	3.5	3.5	4.9	0.3
	Gini coefficient	45.2	54.7	52.1	56.7	50.7	48.9	49.4	48.3	52.1	49.1	51.0	46.3
Change 2009–08	Percentile 90/percentile 10	0.3	0.0	-0.4	-1.4	1.2	0.1	-0.4	1.3	0.1	0.0	1.1	-0.1
	Percentile 90/percentile 50	-0.1	-0.1	-0.1	0.0	0.2	0.0	-0.1	-0.2	0.1	0.0	-0.1	0.0
	Percentile 50/percentile 10	0.2	0.1	-0.1	-0.4	0.2	0.0	0.0	0.6	0.0	0.0	0.5	0.0
	FGT(2) (moderate)	-0.1	-0.1	-0.3	-1.6	0.4	-0.8	0.0	2.4	1.0	-0.4	1.0	-0.2
	FGT(2) (extreme)	0.0	0.1	0.1	-1.3	0.4	-0.3	0.0	2.5	0.5	-0.3	1.1	0.0
	Gini coefficient	-1.0	-0.4	0.2	-0.6	1.9	-0.1	-1.2	1.6	0.3	0.1	-1.0	0.0

Sources: SEDLAC harmonized data sets and ENIGH, 2008 and 2010.

a. Data refer to the period 2006–09.

b. Data refer to the period 2008–10.

but a reduction in inequality was evident at the top of the distribution (as measured by the 90:50 decile ratio). This reduction was enough to revert the effect of negative income growth and induce a reduction in moderate poverty. This finding explains the odd pattern in Paraguay.

Colombia and Ecuador are the only two countries in which all inequality measures declined, confirming the poverty reduction impact of redistribution in these countries. In Colombia, inequality declined because of a reduction of income differences at the bottom of the distribution, as seen in the decline of the FGT(2) for both the moderate and extreme poverty lines, as well as in the reduction of the 50-to-10 deciles income gap. In the latter, the reduction of inequality is more pronounced at the top of the distribution. In these two countries, reductions in inequality continue the decline in poverty brought about by income growth. In Ecuador, the reduction in inequality more than compensates for the decline in growth so that extreme poverty declines. This explains why extreme poverty declines in this country despite a drop in both GDP per capita and survey income growth.

In other countries, the results are not so consistent: some inequality indexes go up, others go down, and most changes are very small. In these cases, inequality indexes, because they focus on a specific part of the income distribution, may fail to capture the redistribution component that affects poverty dynamics. Growth incidence curves shed more light on the redistribution effect on poverty changes. The inequality measures shown earlier gauge inequality at specific levels of the income distribution, whereas the growth incidence curve shows relative changes over the entire income distribution, and particularly among those people living close to the poverty lines. We identified four types of growth incidence curve for the countries in the study.

First, for the country with the lowest extreme poverty headcount rate, Uruguay, all deciles increased their average income by a large amount. That is an almost flat growth incidence curve. Thus the trend was neither pro-poor nor pro-rich in Uruguay because the poorest deciles gained about as much as the middle and upper deciles. Peru also showed this general trend in which the income growth of all deciles increased close to the average income growth (see figure 3.2).[19]

Costa Rica, the Dominican Republic, El Salvador, and Mexico have growth incidence curves with a positive slope—that is, in these countries those at the bottom of the distribution had lower income gains (or larger income losses) than those in the middle and at the top of the distribution (figure 3.3). In these countries, the redistribution effect increased extreme poverty during the crisis.

Argentina, Brazil, and Paraguay have growth incidence curves with a stylized inverted-U shape—that is, those at the bottom of the distribution had lower income gains (or larger income losses) than those in the middle, and the latter had larger income gains than those at the top (figure 3.4). Interestingly, this finding is consistent with all these countries having a redistribution effect that reduced moderate poverty. In Argentina and Paraguay, however, the redistribution effect increased extreme poverty because, as shown in the figures, those at the bottom of the distribution did worse than those in the middle.

Figure 3.2 Neutral Growth Incidence Curves: Peru and Uruguay, 2008–09

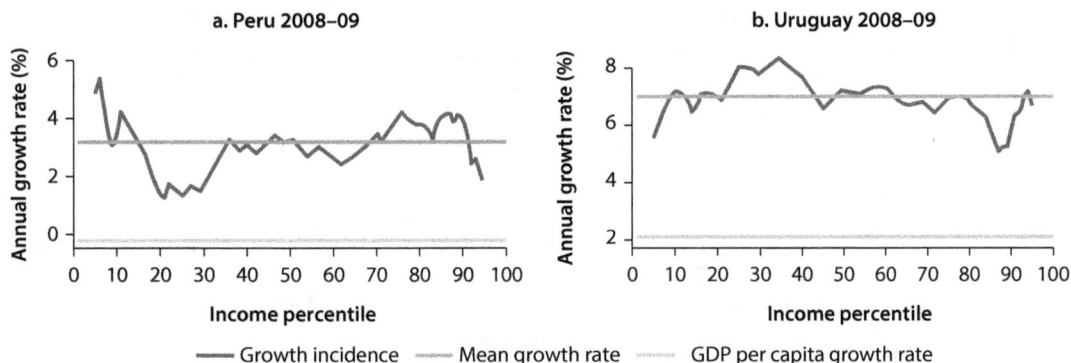

a. Peru 2008–09

b. Uruguay 2008–09

Growth incidence ——— Mean growth rate ——— GDP per capita growth rate

Source: SEDLAC data (World Bank and CEDLAS).

Figure 3.3 Regressive Growth Incidence Curves: Costa Rica, Dominican Republic, and El Salvador, 2008–09, and Mexico, 2008–10

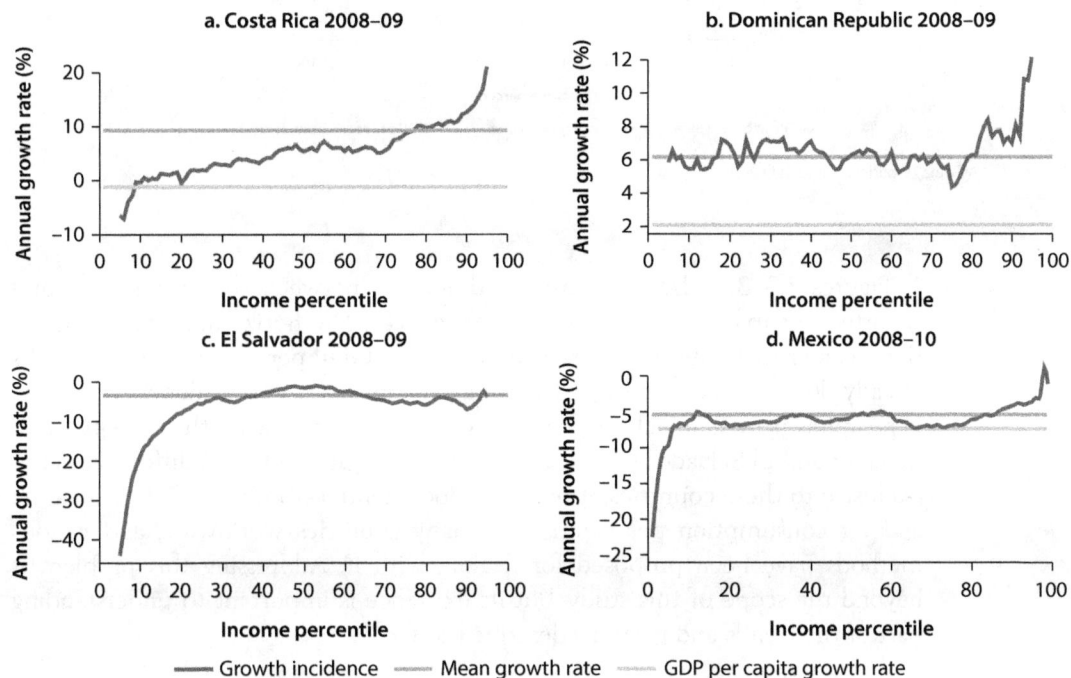

a. Costa Rica 2008–09

b. Dominican Republic 2008–09

c. El Salvador 2008–09

d. Mexico 2008–10

Growth incidence ——— Mean growth rate ——— GDP per capita growth rate

Source: SEDLAC data (World Bank and CEDLAS).

Finally, Chile, Colombia, and Ecuador have incidence curves with a negative slope—that is, those at the bottom of the distribution had larger income growth than those in the middle or at the top of the distribution (figure 3.5). These are all countries in which the redistribution effect reduced moderate and extreme poverty during the crisis.

Understanding the Poverty Impact of the Global Financial Crisis in Latin America and the Caribbean
http://dx.doi.org/10.1596/978-1-4648-0241-6

Figure 3.4 Inverted-U Growth Incidence Curves: Argentina, Brazil, and Paraguay, 2008–09

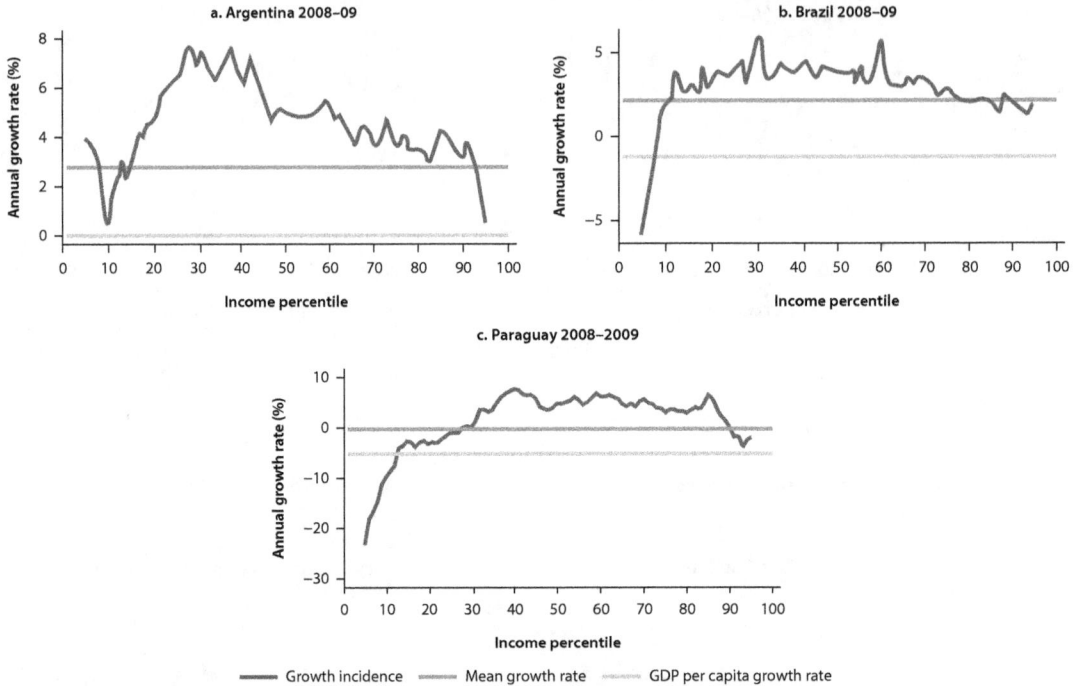

a. Argentina 2008–09

b. Brazil 2008–09

c. Paraguay 2008–2009

——— Growth incidence   ——— Mean growth rate   ⋯⋯ GDP per capita growth rate

Source: SEDLAC data (World Bank and CEDLAS).

Figures 3.3–3.5 also illustrate the difference between the average earnings reported in surveys and GDP per capita growth. The horizontal lines represent the mean growth rate from survey data and the GDP per capita growth rate. As already documented in table 3.10, average earnings growth is higher than GDP per capita growth in all the countries of the sample with the exception of Ecuador and El Salvador where they are almost equivalent. This difference is not exclusive to these countries; it has been documented—both for GDP per capita and for consumption per capita—for many countries worldwide, and various methods have been proposed for dealing with it. Addressing this problem is beyond the scope of this study, but its existence is important to understanding part of the trends and patterns described so far.[20]

Was It Earnings or Transfers?

The evidence described in the previous section suggests that changes in inequality may play an important role in poverty changes, and particularly on those to extreme poverty. An obvious question is whether public or private transfers, as opposed to earnings, play any role in this effect. Evidence from the decomposition by population group hints at the importance of households receiving transfers and the employment status of household heads in explaining changes in poverty (see table 3.8). However, in order to investigate which

Figure 3.5 Progressive Growth Incidence Curves: Chile, 2006–09, and Colombia and Ecuador, 2008–09

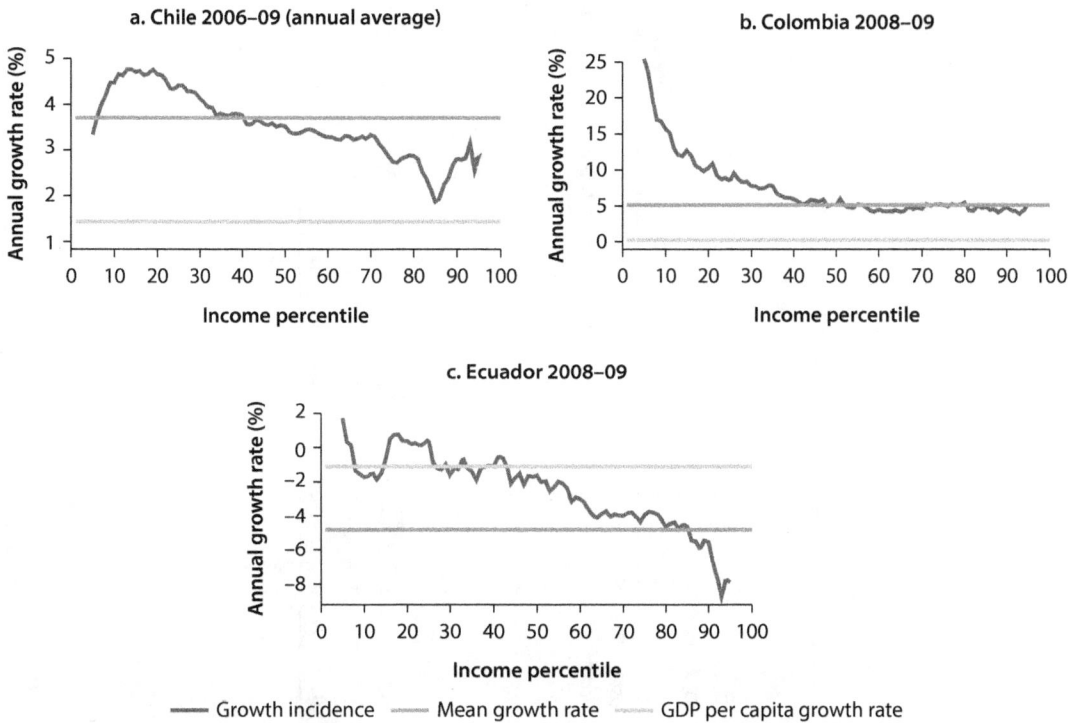

a. Chile 2006–09 (annual average)

b. Colombia 2008–09

c. Ecuador 2008–09

— Growth incidence ---- Mean growth rate ---- GDP per capita growth rate

Source: SEDLAC data (World Bank and CEDLAS).

source of income had the largest influence on poverty changes independent of the type of population group, a different type of analysis is needed. A basic decomposition by income source explains how much of the change in poverty can be ascribed to changes in labor income or to changes in nonlabor income (see table 3.12 and box 3.5).

This decomposition for moderate poverty reveals that average labor income has a larger effect on poverty than nonlabor income and rank correlation effects (see table 3.12). Changes due to labor income range from a large portion of the reduction in poverty in Chile to a large part of the increase in poverty in Mexico and Costa Rica. In 10 out of the 12 countries, the changes in labor income go in the same direction and account for the largest share of changes in moderate poverty. The only exceptions to this are Argentina, where nonlabor income has a larger effect than labor income, and El Salvador, where the rank correlation component is predominant, but in the opposite direction to labor income. More important, in all cases, where moderate poverty increased (Costa Rica, Ecuador, El Salvador, and Mexico), the rise can be mostly ascribed to a reduction in labor income, with nonlabor income playing a partially compensating role in Costa Rica and Ecuador but having a worsening effect in El Salvador and Mexico. A similar pattern is observed in countries that

Table 3.12 Decomposition of Poverty Changes, by Source of Income: Latin America, 2008–09

Percentage points

		Argentina	Brazil	Chile[a]	Colombia	Costa Rica	Dominican Republic	Ecuador	El Salvador	Mexico[b]	Paraguay	Peru	Uruguay
Moderate poverty	Labor income	-0.1	-0.7	-2.2	-1.2	2.3	-1.8	0.7	3.5	1.6	-1.5	-1.3	-2.1
	Nonlabor income	-0.4	-0.5	-1.4	-0.7	-0.4	-1.3	-0.3	1.0	1.0	-0.5	0.4	0.3
	Rank correlation	-0.3	-0.4	-0.4	-0.3	-1.2	0.0	0.1	-3.9	0.0	-0.1	-0.3	-0.1
	Total change 2008–09	-0.9	-1.6	-4.0	-2.2	0.7	-3.2	0.5	0.6	2.6	-2.2	-1.2	-2.0
Extreme poverty	Labor income	0.4	-0.1	0.4	-1.4	1.9	-1.2	0.6	5.0	0.8	1.0	-1.2	-0.9
	Nonlabor income	-0.2	-0.2	-0.8	-0.8	-0.2	-1.1	-0.4	1.3	0.5	0.1	0.4	0.3
	Rank correlation	-0.3	-0.3	-0.6	-0.3	-1.1	0.3	-0.4	-4.6	0.0	0.0	0.4	0.1
	Total change 2008–09	-0.2	-0.6	-1.0	-2.5	0.5	-2.0	-0.2	1.8	1.3	1.1	-0.4	-0.6

Sources: SEDLAC harmonized data sets and ENIGH, 2008 and 2010.

a. Data refer to the period 2006–09.

b. Data refer to the period 2008–10.

Box 3.5 Fournier Decomposition of Poverty Changes, by Income Source

A decomposition of poverty and inequality measures by income source is particularly intricate. Shorrocks (1982) and later Lerman (1999) show that decomposing a given income distribution or its change by income source depends not only on how each income source is distributed, but also on how one income source interacts with another. Several methods have been proposed for decomposing specific inequality measures by income source (see Lerman and Yitzhaki 1995; Shorrocks 1982; and Fei, Ranis, and Kuo 1978).

In this study, we use a method proposed by Fournier (2001), who develops a decomposition by factor components for an entire distribution of income, and thus it is applicable to any poverty or inequality index. This decomposition uses *rank correlation* instead of statistical correlation to address the problem of how to include the interaction between different sources of income. It allows for examination of the effects of changes in the sources of marginal distribution of each income source, as well as the change in correlation between those sources. Fournier argues that if total income consists of two different sources, the change in the distribution of total income is due to (1) a change in the marginal distribution of the first income source; (2) a change in the marginal distribution of the second income source; and (3) changes in the correlation of the two income sources. The implementation of this method follows a nonparametric technique that creates hypothetical income distributions and the differences between them. For each individual or household observed at time *t*, the population is sorted by income source, and each individual or household is ranked. A counterfactual income is created for each possible combination by keeping either marginal distributions or rank correlation between sources unchanged.

---

experienced an increase in extreme poverty rates. Again, growth incidence curves can help to elucidate the different patterns of the contribution of labor and nonlabor incomes to poverty changes. In this case, we produce growth incidence curves that represent changes in average income by decile, separating the labor and nonlabor components of each group.[21]

The first group consists of Argentina, Brazil, and Chile, where nonlabor income compensates for part of the decline suffered in labor income among those at the bottom of the distribution (see figure 3.6). This nonlabor income (which includes public transfers, but may also include other sources of income such as pensions, gifts, and remittances) makes the growth incidence curve less regressive than it would have been without it. In these countries, people at the bottom of the distribution (in the first and even second or third deciles) experienced an absolute decline in labor income, which was partly compensated for by nonlabor income, thereby reducing poverty increases.[22]

In the second group—Costa Rica, El Salvador, Paraguay, and Mexico—labor income also exhibits a very regressive pattern, but nonlabor income fails to compensate for the income decline at the bottom of the distribution (see figure 3.7). Nonlabor income in these countries barely or did not help at

Figure 3.6 Growth Incidence Curve, by Income Source: Argentina and Brazil, 2008–09, and Chile, 2006–09

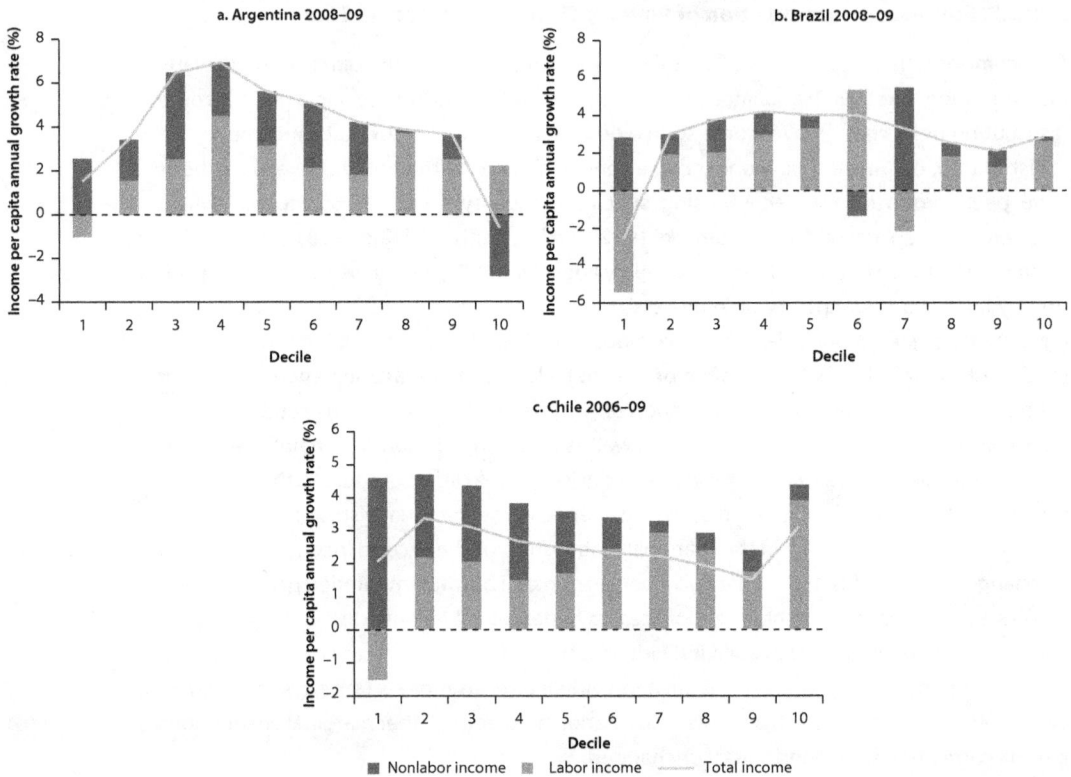

Sources: SEDLAC harmonized data sets and ENIGH, 2008 and 2010.

all the poor to ameliorate their income losses. In El Salvador, Mexico, and Paraguay, nonlabor income failed to compensate for the severe decline in labor income among those at the bottom of the distribution. In Costa Rica, what appears to be regressive nonlabor income is simply the result of the 2009 survey not including a question on transfers as part of nonlabor income, and so Costa Rica's figure is not comparable with those of the other countries.

The third group consists of countries such as Colombia and Ecuador, where labor income growth was progressive—that is, those at the bottom of the distribution had larger labor income gains (or smaller labor income losses, as in Ecuador) than those in the middle and at the top of the distribution (see figure 3.8). Nonlabor incomes were also progressive, and thus both sources played a role in reducing moderate and extreme poverty in Colombia (but only extreme poverty in Ecuador).

Finally, the Dominican Republic, Peru, and Uruguay constitute a residual group.[23] On the one hand, Uruguay shows quite even income growth across deciles for both labor and nonlabor income. Both components reduce moderate and extreme poverty. Peru also shows uniform growth in labor income, but

Figure 3.7 Growth Incidence Curve, by Income Source: Costa Rica, El Salvador, and Paraguay, 2008–09, and Mexico, 2008–10

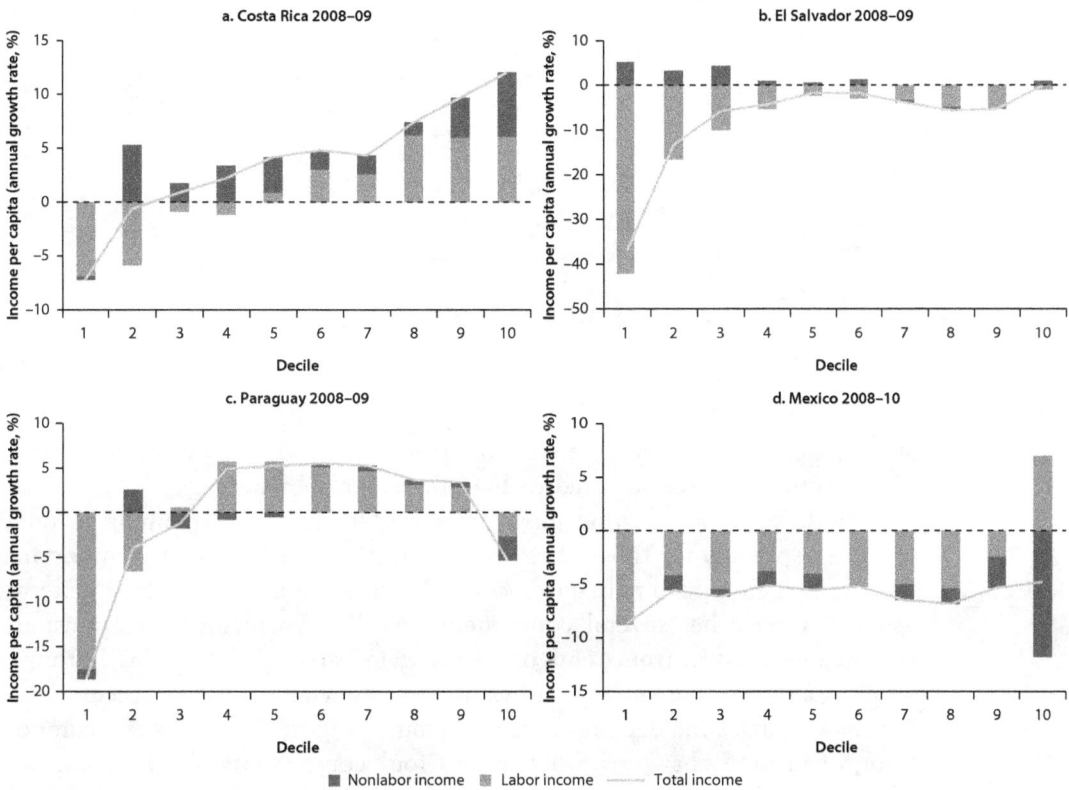

Sources: SEDLAC harmonized data sets and ENIGH, 2008 and 2010.

nonlabor income has a null or negative effect on deciles at the bottom of the distribution, thereby contributing to a dampening of the poverty reduction. The Dominican Republic shows a U-shaped pattern of labor income growth by decile—that is, those at the bottom and top ends of the distribution see larger increases than those in the middle, whereas the growth of nonlabor income shows the opposite pattern. The combination of these two patterns results in uniform across-decile income growth in this country. Again, both components contribute to moderate and extreme poverty as shown in the Fournier decomposition.

In summary, this evidence indicates that changes in labor income account for the biggest share of total changes in income for most decile groups in every country. Changes in labor incomes were regressive in most countries (i.e., larger in the middle or at the top of the distribution than at the bottom), with the exception of Colombia and Ecuador, where it was progressive, and Peru and Uruguay, where it was neutral. In many countries, however, nonlabor income represents a large component of income growth for those at the bottom of the distribution, and in these cases nonlabor income explains a less regressive growth

Figure 3.8 Growth Incidence Curve, by Income Source: Colombia and Ecuador, 2008–09

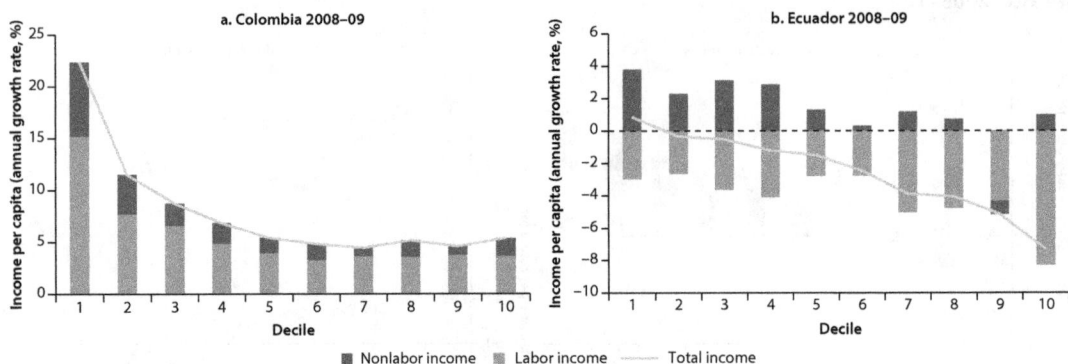

Nonlabor income   Labor income   ——— Total income

Sources: SEDLAC harmonized data sets and ENIGH, 2008 and 2010.

incidence curve and therefore reductions in extreme and even moderate poverty, which would not have occurred without these nonlabor earnings.

Because nonlabor income plays an important role in explaining income changes, especially for those at the bottom of the distribution, it is important to reveal which type of nonlabor income drives the observed results. The term *nonlabor income* has several components: public transfers, private transfers, and income derived from rents or capital gains, among other things. From a public policy point of view, it is of value to know what role government transfers play in offsetting declines in labor incomes. Figure 3.9 shows a decomposition of income changes by decile into four components for the countries where these disaggregated data are available. Public transfers observed in the data include a range of social protection programs. Private transfers include remittances, domestic intra-household transfers, and transfers from charities and private institutions. Other sources of income are grouped into "other income changes."[24]

In Mexico, Ecuador, and Uruguay, public transfers represent the largest component of nonlabor income and thus define the compensatory role of nonlabor income at the bottom of the distribution. Increases in public transfers during the period of study were concentrated in the lower deciles and were large enough to offset declines in other nonlabor income for the poorest decile. Public transfers prevented income losses for the poorest decile in Ecuador, but were insufficient to do so in Mexico. In Mexico, public transfers could barely compensate for the decline in remittances and other income received by those at the bottom of the distribution. Data in El Salvador do not indicate that public transfers played any redistributive role.[25]

It's Labor Income, But What Part of It?

When decomposing by income source, labor income appears to be the most important component of poverty changes. These changes in labor income may result from either job losses (i.e., the head of household or any member

Figure 3.9 Growth Incidence Curve, by Four Income Sources: Ecuador, El Salvador, Mexico, and Uruguay, 2008–09

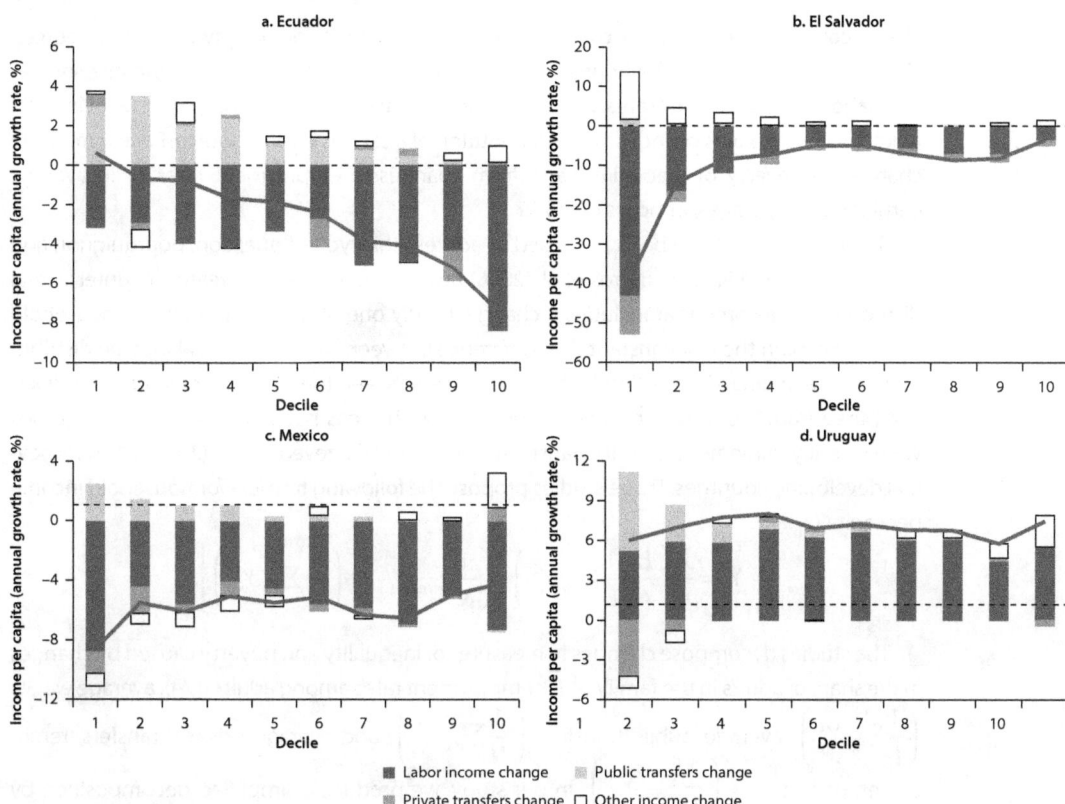

a. Ecuador

b. El Salvador

c. Mexico

d. Uruguay

■ Labor income change   ■ Public transfers change
■ Private transfers change □ Other income change

Sources: SEDLAC harmonized data sets and ENIGH, 2008 and 2010.
Note: Data for Mexico are for 2008–10.

becoming jobless) or earnings losses (i.e., working members of the household earning less). A refinement of the decomposition sources can expose the role of each of these factors (see box 3.6).

In this case, we decompose the change in moderate and extreme poverty into three main components (see figure 3.10). The first component is the number of jobs per household member. This indicator gauges the impact of joblessness on poverty changes. In particular, it refers to what economists call the extensive margin—that is, the loss of jobs rather than changes in the hours of work (also known as the intensive margin). The second component is the labor income per job in the household. This indicator measures changes in productivity and earnings associated with the global financial crisis. It may be the result of an actual wage drop, an increase in the number of hours with same earnings, or lower earnings due to fewer hours of work. We do not separate these effects. And the third component is nonlabor income per adult. This indicator aggregates all nonlabor income such as pensions and transfers. As explained earlier, this component may include different sources of income, but, because of the limitations of the

---

Box 3.6 Further Refinements of Decomposition, by Income Source

The decomposition proposed by Fournier (2001) accounts for only two income sources. However, total income at the household level may consist of more than two income sources (e.g., labor earnings, capital rents, public transfers, remittances). Moreover, it may be of interest to know what explains changes in the distribution of a certain income source. For example, do changes in poverty or inequality stem from changes in employment rates or in average earnings, hourly wages, or hours of work?

Several methods have been proposed to address this type of question. Bourguignon and Ferreira (2005) and Paes de Barros et al. (2006) propose methods that create a counterfactual distribution of income that includes a change in only one of the components of household income, keeping the rest constant. The difference between the hypothetical income distribution and the original distribution (or the difference between the poverty or inequality indexes computed from them) is attributed to the variable that has been changed. These methods were recently implemented by Inchauste et al. (2012) and Azevedo et al. (2012, 2013) for several developing countries. These studies propose the following formula for household income per capita (Y_h):

$$Y_h = \frac{A}{N}\left[\frac{L}{A}\left(\frac{1}{L}\Sigma_{i\in L}\,Y_i^L\right) + \left(\frac{1}{N}\Sigma_{i\in L}\,Y_i^T\right) + \left(\frac{1}{N}\Sigma_{i\in L}\,Y_i^R\right)\right].$$

The studies decompose changes in measures of inequality and poverty caused by changes in the share of adults in the family (A/N), employment rates among adults (L/A), average wages $\left(\frac{1}{L}\Sigma_{i\in L}\,Y_i^L\right)$, average public transfers $\left(\frac{1}{N}\Sigma_{i\in L}\,Y_i^T\right)$, and average private transfers, remittances, or pensions $\left(\frac{1}{N}\Sigma_{i\in L}\,Y_i^R\right)$. In our study, we produce a simplified decomposition by income source in which only three components are considered: average wage per worker, employment rate per household member, and nonlabor income per household member.

This type of exercise has two main limitations. First, the order in which the impact of each component is simulated affects the results of the decomposition exercise. When more than two components are considered, there is a large number of possible ways in which the decomposition can be computed. To address this problem, a technique proposed by Shorrocks (1999, 2012) known as the Shapley decomposition is adopted. Second, these are accounting simulations, which assume that when one income source changes all the others remain constant. However, it is well known that changes in economic conditions lead individuals and households to react and generate other sources of income. Thus this type of decomposition fails to include economic behavior.

---

region's household surveys in collecting capital incomes, it is mostly a measure of transfers and pensions.

This decomposition reveals two main facts. First, nonlabor income is an important share of poverty reduction, both moderate and extreme, in many countries in the region. In Argentina, Brazil, Chile, Colombia, and the Dominican

Figure 3.10 Decomposition of Changes in Extreme and Moderate Poverty, by Income Source, 2008–09

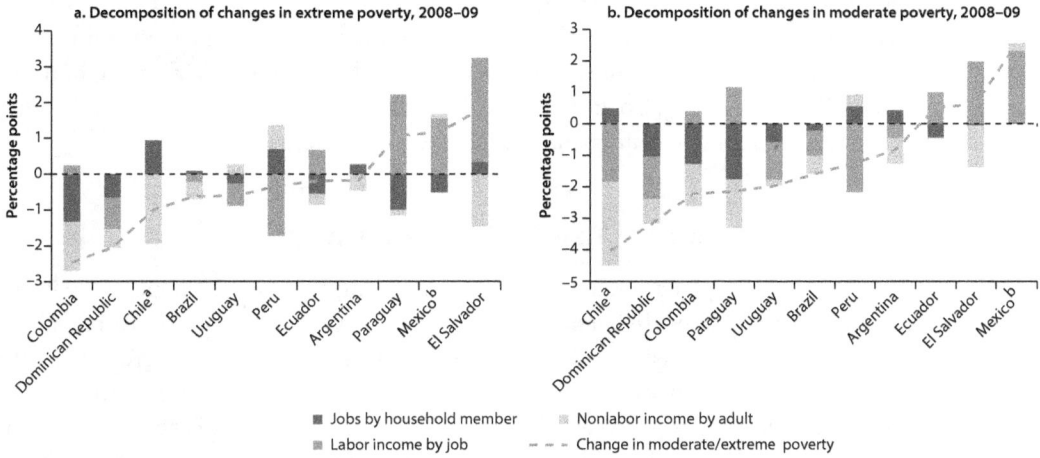

Sources: SEDLAC harmonized data sets and ENIGH, 2008 and 2010.
a. Data refer to the period 2006-09.
b. Data refer to the period 2008-10.

Republic, nonlabor sources of income have reduced both moderate and extreme poverty, while in El Salvador these income sources have curbed its increase. Nonlabor income was not very relevant to, or even contrary to, poverty reduction in Peru and Uruguay. In Ecuador, nonlabor income helped to reduce extreme poverty, but it had no impact on moderate poverty, whereas in Paraguay the opposite was true. These results are fairly consistent with those shown in table 3.12.

Second, changes in jobs by household member (a measure of the impact of joblessness) are smaller than changes in labor income by job in most countries. The exception is Colombia, where poverty changes are associated with a large increase in jobs in the household. Argentina and Chile are also exceptions of interest. In both countries, job losses increase poverty, but increases in labor income per job reduce moderate poverty (no impact on extreme poverty). In Paraguay, the opposite occurs—that is, new jobs reduce poverty, but declines in earnings per job increase extreme poverty and dampen the decline in moderate poverty. In all the remaining countries, changes in earnings per job are larger than changes in jobs per household member. Thus apart from the exceptions described, changes in poverty are mainly driven by changes in earnings derived from work rather than by changes in the access to jobs.

Moreover, countries with an increase in poverty are those who endured large changes in average earnings per job. Figure 3.10 shows that for both extreme and moderate poverty, countries with a poverty increase also show changes in average earnings as the main component of such an increase in poverty. On the other hand, poverty reductions are mostly explained by changes in employment or in nonlabor income (for extreme poverty) or by a combination of all three factors (for moderate poverty).

Understanding the Poverty Impact of the Global Financial Crisis in Latin America and the Caribbean
http://dx.doi.org/10.1596/978-1-4648-0241-6

The preceding evidence highlights the importance of understanding how labor markets adjusted to the global financial crisis, why most countries had a large earnings impact rather than an employment impact, and why some countries were able to compensate for a decline in labor earnings with more employment. The evidence also underlines the important role that nonlabor income, particularly public transfers, played in preventing increases in poverty.[26]

The Poverty Reduction That Could Have Been

Looking only at actual changes in poverty during the global financial crisis and all the population profiles and decompositions by source may fail to reveal the full impact of the crisis on poverty. Had the crisis not occurred, growth would have been higher in every country, and, assuming that poverty declines with economic growth, poverty would have been lower than it is. Particularly among those countries that experienced a decline in poverty because of some growth in 2009, faster growth would have resulted in an even larger decline in poverty. The difference between the poverty change that actually occurred and the poverty change that would have taken place is a measure of the actual impact of the crisis.

A tool often used to estimate the link between economic growth and poverty change is the growth elasticity of poverty, which measures the change in poverty associated with a change in GDP growth. This measure has been a recurring subject of research among those interested in identifying the impact of economic growth on poverty reduction. A canonical model for this relationship is

$$\Delta P = \alpha + \beta \Delta Y$$

where ΔP is the change in poverty (usually the headcount, either moderate or extreme, but other measures such as poverty gaps could be also considered) and ΔY is changes in economic growth, normally measured by GDP per capita growth. The coefficient β is an estimate of the growth elasticity of poverty. This very simple model is then extended to include controls for inequality, level of development, and recession versus expansion years. These controls are used to assess three hypotheses: (1) higher levels of inequality prevent economic growth from eliciting more poverty reduction; (2) at higher levels of development, and lower poverty rates, growth brings slower reductions in poverty; and (3) the impact of economic growth on poverty differs between recessions and expansions.[27]

Using a data set of annual changes in poverty headcount, GDP per capita, and inequality for every country in the region with data available for the period 1989–2008, we estimate the following general model:[28]

$$\Delta P = \alpha + \beta \Delta Y + \gamma \Delta G + \delta R + \varepsilon R * \Delta Y + \theta R * \Delta G + C\mu$$

where ΔG is the change in inequality (as measured by the Gini coefficient), R is a categorical variable designating years with negative economic growth, and C is a vector of categorical variables for each country in the sample. Table 3.13 summarizes the results of several experiments using different versions of this specification and several data sets. Columns (1)–(5) show the results of ordinary least squares estimates using yearly GDP per capita growth, and columns (6)–(10) show the same specifications and estimation method but using the yearly growth of mean income as reported in the survey.[29]

Table 3.13 confirms the usual findings in the literature—that is, holding other factors constant, positive economic growth is associated with a decline in poverty, while an increase in inequality is associated with an increase in poverty. This result is statistically significant in all the specifications. Interestingly, no country categorical variable was statistically significant at less than 5 percent, which indicates that there are no country-specific poverty-growth or poverty-inequality relationships in this sample.[30]

Interestingly, when using GDP per capita as an indicator of economic growth, there seems to be no change in the association between economic growth and poverty during recessions and during periods of expansion. The results in columns (1)–(5) of table 3.13 indicate that an annual increase of 1 percent increase in GDP per capita is associated with a decline of around 0.6 percentage points in the moderate poverty headcount. However, when mean average income as computed from the surveys is used [columns (7) and (9)], a 1 percent increase of mean income growth brings about a reduction of 0.30 percentage points in moderate poverty, whereas a 1 percent decline would induce an increase of about 0.45 percentage points. Meanwhile, regressions using mean income from surveys explain a much higher percentage of the variance in poverty changes than regressions using GDP per capita.[31]

Poverty estimates are usually produced using survey data. Thus mean income per household member is a closer measure of economic growth as experienced by households, particularly among those at the lower end of the income distribution, and therefore provides a better look at poverty-growth elasticities. GDP per capita, however, has the advantage of being useful for forecasts and ex ante policy making.[32]

If we adopt the models of columns (3) and (9) in table 3.13 as appropriate for forecasting, we can use the models to interpret the impact of the global financial crisis in 2009. A first interpretation of the results of these simulations is that the poverty changes actually observed for most countries in the sample are within what would have been forecasted with 95 percent statistical confidence. This means that poverty changes in 2009 were not unusual in view of the trends observed in the region in recent years (see figure 3.11).

Figure 3.11 is a replication of figure 3.1 but with the regression lines and confidence intervals of the models shown in table 3.13 in columns (3) (see left panel) and (9) (see right panel). The dots represent the poverty and economic growth changes actually observed in the countries in 2009. The solid line represents the expected poverty change that would have been predicted by the models, and the dotted lines represent the 95 percent confidence intervals of

Understanding the Poverty Impact of the Global Financial Crisis in Latin America and the Caribbean
http://dx.doi.org/10.1596/978-1-4648-0241-6

Table 3.13 Linear Regressions of Moderate Poverty Changes on Changes in Growth and Inequality
Percentage points

Explained variable	Changes in moderate poverty									
Real GDP per capita growth	-0.683***	-0.627***	-0.624***	-0.548***	-0.733***					
	(0.057)	(0.098)	(0.059)	(0.099)	(0.125)					
Surveys' mean income						-0.385***	-0.310***	-0.368***	-0.300***	-0.390***
						(0.024)	(0.050)	(0.021)	(0.042)	(0.050)
Real GDP per capita growth *recession years (%)		-0.146		-0.159						
		(0.192)		(0.191)						
Surveys' mean income per capita growth *recession years (%)							-0.183***		-0.142**	
							(0.077)		(0.066)	
Change in Gini (Gini points)			0.495***	0.517***				0.811***	0.615***	
			(0.153)	(0.168)				(0.111)	(0.173)	
Change in Gini *recession years				-0.153					0.306	
				(0.420)					(0.224)	
Recession years		0.037		0.321			-0.214		0.078	
		(0.851)		(0.886)			(0.601)		(0.513)	
Constant	0.961***	0.724	0.876***	0.545	1.940**	0.111	-0.342	0.132	-0.333	1.003*
	(0.261)	(0.455)	(0.265)	(0.457)	(0.802)	(0.187)	(0.384)	(0.161)	(0.327)	(0.561)
Country dummies	No	No	No	No	Yes	No	No	No	No	Yes
Number of observations	184	184	173	173	184	143	137	137	137	143
R-squared (adjusted)	0.437	0.432	0.462	0.456	0.450	0.641	0.736	0.736	0.744	0.642

Sources: SEDLAC's poverty, inequality, and mean income estimates and World Development Indicators (database).

Note: Interannual poverty or inequality changes correspond to the average change in poverty between two consecutive data points within the period 1989–2008 for these variables, as long as the data points are not more than five years apart. Real GDP and mean income from survey observations correspond to the geometric rate of growth between the two years that correspond in turn to the available poverty/inequality data points. Standard errors in parentheses.

Significance level: * = 10 percent, ** = 5 percent, *** = 1 percent.

Figure 3.11 Moderate Poverty and GDP Per Capita Changes: Latin America, 2009

a. Moderate poverty and GDP/head changes in 2009 (without a structural break for recessions)

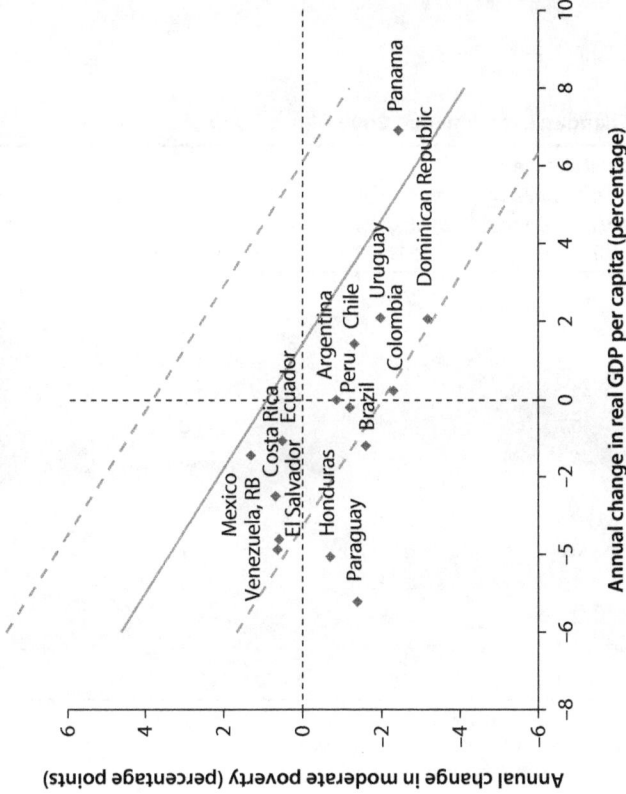

Using a linear regression of moderate poverty changes on annual GDP per capita growth

b. Moderate poverty and GDP/head changes in 2009 (with a structural break for recessions)

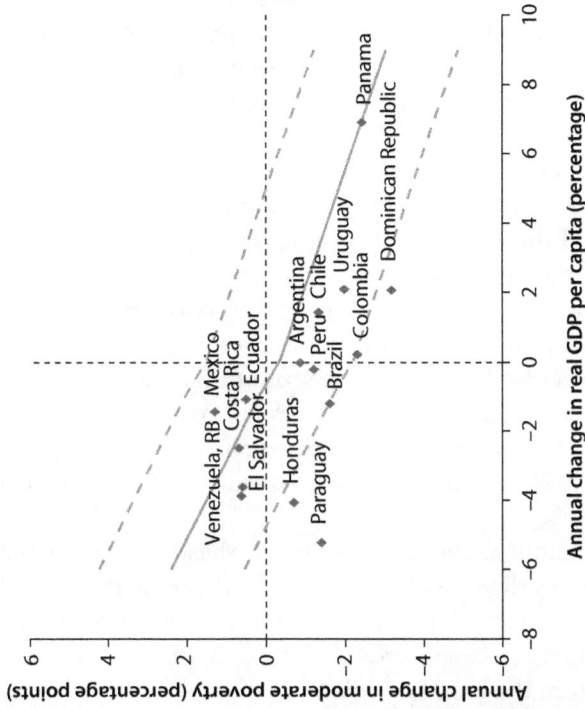

Using a linear regression, with a structural break for recessions, of moderate poverty changes on growth of mean income per household member

Source: SEDLAC's harmonized survey data and forecasts based on column (3) (left panel) and (9) (right panel) of table 3.13.

these predicted values. Interestingly, for both models Paraguay is the only country way off the lower bound of fitted poverty changes, but, as explained in previous sections, this country shows an unusual decline in moderate poverty, despite a decline in GDP and income growth, because of a decline of inequality at the top of the distribution.[33]

A second interpretation consists of forecasting poverty changes in 2009 had the crisis not occurred and the usual economic growth had taken place instead. A comparison of these forecasts with the actual poverty rates of 2009 provides an estimate of the impact of the crisis on poverty in 2009. This is a counter-factual estimate of the poverty impact of the crisis rather than the actual naïve, before-and-after poverty rate differences presented as measures of the impact of the crisis earlier in this chapter. The counterfactual in this case is the moderate poverty change predicted by the model in column (9) of table 3.13, assuming growth in 2009 would have been equal to the average GDP per capita growth between 2003 and 2008 and inequality remained constant at the 2008 level.

Table 3.14 summarizes the results of these counterfactual simulations. Column (1) shows the rate of growth in GDP per capita for 2009; column (2) the actual change in moderate poverty rates from 2008 to 2009; column (3) the average GDP per capita growth for 2003–08; and column (4) the fitted poverty rates from the model in column (9) of table 3.13.[34] Finally, column (5)

Table 3.14 Forecasted Poverty Changes: Latin America, 2009

Country	Actual GDP per capita growth, 2009	Actual change in moderate poverty, 2009 (percentage points)	Average GDP per capita growth, 2003–08	Hypothetical change in moderate poverty, 2009 (percentage points)	Estimated impact of crisis on moderate poverty (percentage points)
Argentina	0.0%	−0.9	7.5%	−2.6	1.7
Brazil	−1.2%	−1.6	3.7%	−1.4	−0.2
Chile[a]	−2.0%	−1.3	3.8%	−1.5	0.1
Colombia	0.2%	−2.2	3.9%	−1.5	−0.7
Costa Rica	−2.5%	0.7	4.2%	−1.6	2.3
Dominican Republic	2.1%	−3.2	5.5%	−2.0	−1.2
Ecuador	−1.1%	0.5	4.1%	−1.5	2.1
El Salvador	−3.6%	0.6	2.5%	−1.1	1.7
Mexico[b]	−7.1%	1.3	2.1%	−1.0	2.3
Paraguay	−5.2%	−2.2	3.6%	−1.4	−0.8
Peru	−0.2%	−1.2	6.5%	−2.3	1.1
Uruguay	2.1%	−2.0	5.9%	−2.1	0.1

Source: SEDLAC's harmonized survey data and forecasts based on column (9) of table 3.13.
a. Moderate poverty figures for Chile correspond to annualized rates for the period 2006–09.
b. Moderate poverty figures for Mexico correspond to annualized rates for the period 2008–10.

(equal to column (2) minus column (4)) shows the estimate of the impact of the crisis (i.e., the difference between the observed change in the moderate poverty rates in 2008 minus the forecast change in the moderate poverty rates in 2009).

This exercise suggests that the impact of the 2009 crisis was very heterogeneous. Some countries such as Mexico, Costa Rica, and Ecuador had poverty rates that were at least 2.0 percentage points above what would have been expected in the absence of the crisis. In other countries (Argentina, El Salvador, and Peru), this measure of the impact of the crisis was between 1.0 and 2.0 percentage points. Still others (Chile and Uruguay) had a very small impact, below 0.5 percentage points. Some countries (Brazil, Colombia, the Dominican Republic, and Paraguay) had an even faster poverty reduction during 2009 than what would be predicted by the model.[35] For the region, the observed decline in moderate poverty of −1.0 percentage point (an unweighted average on annual changes for the countries in the sample) contrasts with the forecasted decline of 1.7 percentage points had the crisis not occurred. Therefore, at the regional level the impact of the crisis is 0.7 percentage points of additional poverty.

Percentage rates and unweighted averages do not convey information about the absolute size of the impact of the crisis. In population terms, 2.4 million people left moderate poverty between 2008 and 2009. Our simulation exercise, however, would have predicted a decline in the number of the moderate poor of 5.6 million. This means that about 3.2 million people continued to live in moderate poverty (see table 3.15), which is an estimate of the impact of the crisis.

The numbers of total poor in the region are driven by the poverty dynamics of the countries with the largest populations, Brazil and Mexico. Brazil had fewer people in moderate poverty than would have been predicted by our model (300,000). Mexico, by contrast, had a 2.5 million "excess" in poverty—that is, the sum of the actual increase in moderate poverty (1.9 million) and the forecasted reductions that would have occurred had average economic growth taken place instead (690,000). In the Latin America region, most of the new poor or still poor because of the crisis in 2009 are Mexican.

This attempt at estimating the impact of the crisis has several limitations. First, it is based on a linear model assuming fast economic growth as in previous years, no changes in inequality, and the validity of past elasticities to forecast future events. Moreover, linear models based on aggregate data fail to give details of the specific groups that were more or less affected by the crisis and the channels through which the crisis affected these different groups. Chapter 5 of this study includes a more thorough counterfactual analysis of the crisis for Brazil and Mexico in 2009, indicating that the structural characteristics of these economies, such as their trade openness, export content, and trading partners, go far in explaining the different experiences of these countries in 2009 during the global financial crisis.

Understanding the Poverty Impact of the Global Financial Crisis in Latin America and the Caribbean
http://dx.doi.org/10.1596/978-1-4648-0241-6

Table 3.15 Moderate Poverty: Actual and Forecasted Population in Poverty: Latin America, 2009

	Poverty rate, 2008 (%)	Poverty rate, 2009 (%)	Hypothetical poverty, 2009 (%)	Number of poor, 2008 (millions)	Number of poor, 2009 (millions)	Actual change (millions)	Hypothetical number of poor, 2009 (millions)	Hypothetical change (millions)	Hypothetical "excess" poor (millions)
Argentina	17.3	16.4	14.7	6.85	6.57	-0.28	5.88	-0.97	0.69
Brazil	29.2	27.6	27.8	55.93	53.34	-2.59	53.63	-2.29	-0.30
Chile[a]	13.1	11.8	11.7	2.21	2.00	-0.21	1.98	-0.23	0.02
Colombia	44.8	42.6	43.3	20.17	19.45	-0.72	19.78	-0.39	-0.34
Costa Rica	18.9	19.6	17.3	0.86	0.90	0.04	0.80	-0.06	0.10
Dominican Republic	37.9	34.7	35.9	3.66	3.40	-0.26	3.52	-0.14	-0.12
Ecuador	37.1	37.6	35.5	5.21	5.36	0.15	5.07	-0.15	0.29
El Salvador	42.1	42.7	41.0	2.58	2.63	0.05	2.53	-0.05	0.10
Mexico[b]	27.5	28.8	26.5	30.42	32.27	1.84	29.74	-0.69	2.53
Paraguay	37.1	34.9	35.7	2.31	2.21	-0.10	2.26	-0.05	-0.05
Peru	36.9	35.7	34.6	10.50	10.27	-0.23	9.96	-0.54	0.31
Uruguay	14.0	12.0	11.9	0.47	0.40	-0.06	0.40	-0.07	0.00
Total				141.2	138.8	-2.4	135.5	-5.6	3.2

Sources: SEDLAC harmonized data sets and ENIGH, 2008 and 2010.

a. The poverty rate in Chile between 2008 and 2009 is derived from the average annual change from 2006 to 2009 surveys.

b. The poverty rate in Mexico between 2008 and 2009 is derived from the average annual change from 2008 to 2010 surveys.

Conclusion

This analysis of poverty measures for a selection of Latin American countries concludes with a series of stylized facts about the impact of the global financial crisis on poverty in the region in 2009. These facts refer to four general areas: (1) measures of the factual and counterfactual impacts of the crisis; (2) demographic trends; (3) the role of growth and redistribution; and (4) labor market performance and social policy.

First, estimates of the poverty elasticity of GDP growth confirm the negative association between economic growth and poverty reduction. For the countries in the region, 1.0 percentage point of annual economic growth leads to a reduction of between 0.3 and 0.6 percentage points in moderate poverty, depending on the indicator of economic growth and the econometric specification adopted. Assuming the economy grew at the usual rates (the average GDP per capita growth between 2003 and 2008) and inequality remained constant, poverty should have declined by 1.7 percentage points in 2009. The actual decline in moderate poverty of 1.0 percentage point (an unweighted average for the countries in the sample) therefore hides an impact of 0.7 percentage point of "excess" poverty due to the crisis. In population terms, moderate poverty for selected countries declined by 2.4 million people. Our simulation exercise, however, would have predicted a decline in numbers of the moderate poor of 5.7 million. This means some 3.2 million people continued to live in moderate poverty because of the crisis.

Second, poverty profiles (i.e., poverty rates and trends by population group) confirm for this crisis some well-known regularities. For almost every country in the sample, moderate and extreme poverty rates were higher among rural households, female-headed households, and households where the head was unskilled, jobless, or had an informal job. On the other hand, there were no uniform patterns for convergence of poverty changes. In other words, in a few countries groups with higher poverty rates had larger downward (or smaller upward) poverty changes, such as the rural households in Colombia or female-headed households in Mexico, but this was seldom the case. The main driver of poverty changes was the larger population groups, not the poorer groups. In most cases, the largest share of national poverty changes can be ascribed to poverty changes in large population groups such as urban households or male-headed households.

Third, average income growth is the main driver of poverty changes, but the distribution of these income changes can enhance or hinder the effects of growth. Some countries (Chile, Colombia, and Ecuador) showed a progressive growth incidence curve, which implies that in 2009 during the crisis those at the bottom of the distribution performed better than those in the middle or at the top of the distribution, thereby accelerating poverty reduction (such as in Colombia) or ameliorating the rise in poverty (such as in Ecuador). On the other hand, there were countries (Costa Rica, El Salvador, Mexico, and Paraguay)

Understanding the Poverty Impact of the Global Financial Crisis in Latin America and the Caribbean
http://dx.doi.org/10.1596/978-1-4648-0241-6

with a regressive growth incidence curve. In these cases, those at the bottom of the distribution performed worse than those in the middle or at the top of the distribution, which enhances the impact of the crisis in terms of poverty increases.

Fourth, the redistribution component described earlier can be tracked down to labor market performance or social policies. In most countries of the sample, labor earnings during the crisis showed a very regressive pattern—that is, those at the bottom of the distribution endured larger labor earnings losses (or smaller gains) than those in the middle and at the top of the distribution. In some countries such as Costa Rica, El Salvador, Mexico, and Paraguay, nonlabor income (which we interpret as a combination of mostly public or private transfers and pensions) had a very small compensatory role. In other countries such as Argentina, Brazil, and Chile, labor income also took on a regressive pattern, but nonlabor income showed a progressive pattern that helps compensate for the impact of the shock among the poorest sections of the population. And yet in other countries such as Colombia and Ecuador, labor market performance was progressive and nonlabor income was as well, thereby inducing accelerated poverty reduction. In summary, labor market performance determined how intensely the impact of the crisis was felt among those at the bottom of the distribution, but nonlabor income obtained through social policy can play a crucial compensatory role for the poor.

Further scrutiny of the characteristics of the labor income component of the crisis indicates that in the selected Latin American countries most of the change in labor income is associated with changes in earnings rather than in employment. Job gains may have some influence in explaining poverty reduction for some countries, but moderate and extreme poverty increases are mostly explained by a decline in average earnings per job. On the other hand, for the countries with available data, there is also evidence of the instrumental role played by public transfers, particularly cash transfers, in cushioning the impact of regressive changes in labor earnings during the crisis.

Notes

1. See Ferreira, Prennushi, and Ravallion (1999); Fallon and Lucas (2002); Ferreira and Schady (2008); Griffith-Jones and Ocampo (2009); Blanchard, Faruqee, and Das (2010); and World Bank (2010b). Studies documenting the impact of the 2008–09 global financial crisis on nonmonetary measures of well-being are only beginning to appear. Chang et al. (2013) find evidence of increased suicide rates among men in European and American countries with high jobless rates. Friedman and Schady (2009) have forecasted the impact of the crisis on infant mortality in African countries. Azevedo (forthcoming) shows that in Mexico the crisis had an impact on birth weight among children born during the crisis year.

2. The SEDLAC database can be found at http://sedlac.econo.unlp.edu.ar/eng/statistics .php. SEDLAC data are used in the World Bank's LAC Poverty and Labor briefs and for the online tool PovcalNet (for countries with income as their poverty measure).

We also have benefitted from the inputs of the Group for Statistical Development of the Poverty and Gender Unit for Latin America and the Caribbean at the World Bank and its recent publications on poverty during the crisis: "Did Latin America Learn to Shield Its Poor from Economic Shocks?" (World Bank 2010a) and "On the Edge of Uncertainty: Poverty Reduction in Latin America and the Caribbean during the Great Recession and Beyond" (2011b).

3. The data for Honduras were harmonized by CEDLAS, but we do not include these data in our study because of pending revisions in the harmonization process regarding over-time comparability.

4. For further details on the harmonization of surveys and other methodological aspects, see http://sedlac.econo.unlp.edu.ar/eng/methodology.php. For Mexico, we use the income aggregates defined by CONEVAL for producing its estimates of monetary poverty. For details, see http://web.coneval.gob.mx/Medicion/Paginas/Medici%C3%B3n/Programas-de-Calculo.aspx.

5. For the formula of the Gini and the FGT(2) indexes, see Sen and Foster (1997) or Cowell (2011).

6. Rates of growth of GDP are in constant 2,000 U.S. dollars (World Development Indicators code: NY.GDP.MKTP.KD.ZG). For more details on the characteristics of the global financial crisis, see chapter 2 of this study.

7. This average includes Chile and Mexico, whose data span more than a year. If a linear interpolation of poverty changes is applied to Chile and Mexico, the nonweighted average of moderate poverty rates for the region goes from 29.7 to 28.7, a 1.0 percentage point decline. A simple average of the remaining 10 countries, excluding Chile and Mexico, would render moderate poverty rates of 31.5 and 30.4, respectively, for a decrease of 1.1 percentage points between 2008 and 2009. In summary, all methods show a decline in moderate poverty of around 1 percentage point.

8. More details about this discrepancy between aggregate and survey data appear later this chapter (see table 3.10).

9. The 2009 Costa Rican survey does not provide information about public transfers so no profile by this characteristic is discussed here.

10. Several countries in the region have official poverty estimates for which no profile has been produced in this study because of lack of available microdata (see box 3.2).

11. This average includes Chile and Mexico, whose data span more than one year. If a linear interpolation of poverty changes is applied to Chile and Mexico, the nonweighted average of extreme poverty rates for the region goes from 15.0 to 14.8, for the same 0.2 percentage point decline. A simple average of the remaining 10 countries, excluding Chile and Mexico, would render extreme poverty rates of 16.2 and 15.9, respectively, for a decrease of 0.3 percentage points between 2008 and 2009.

12. In 32 of the 36 cases considered, the population shift effects are within the range [−0.2, 0.2], which indicates that changes in the demographic structure are of minimal size in explaining poverty changes. An exception is, for example, El Salvador, where these effects are high (0.6 percentage point) because of an increase in the rural population of 5 percentage points between 2008 and 2009. This finding contrasts with changes in urbanization never larger than 1 percentage point in all the other countries of the study.

13. Only 20 out of 34 decompositions had population shift plus interaction effects in the [−0.2, 0.2] range.

Understanding the Poverty Impact of the Global Financial Crisis in Latin America and the Caribbean
http://dx.doi.org/10.1596/978-1-4648-0241-6

14. In these two countries, the share of population in households with unemployed/inactive heads rose by 4 percentage points, whereas in the rest of the countries this change was never higher than 1 percentage point.

15. In these countries, the population share living in households with some public transfers rose by at least 4 percentage points, while the rest of the countries in the sample have either a smaller increase or even a reduction in the population share with access to public transfers.

16. This is consistent with very low adjustment to crises by unemployment in Latin American countries. In some of these countries, crises entail increases in informality and lower productivity rather than increases in open unemployment (see chapter 4 of this study). It is also consistent with the growing role of social policy as an anti-cyclical tool in the region (see chapter 6).

17. These decompositions show similar outcomes for extreme poverty. Results are available from the authors upon request.

18. For a thorough discussion of the links between economic growth and poverty, see Ravallion (2001, 2004, 2011).

19. In Peru, the spike of income growth at the bottom of the distribution is associated with the decline of extreme poverty.

20. Studies of this discrepancy include Ravallion (2003, 2011); Robilliard and Robinson (2003); and Bhalla (2002).

21. For each decile, each bar corresponds to the annual growth in total income. Formally, (total income$_{(final)}$ − total income$_{(final)}$)/total income$_{(initial)}$). The labor component of each bar is computed as (labor income$_{(final)}$ − labor income$_{(initial)}$/total income$_{(initial)}$). And the nonlabor income component is computed as (nonlabor income$_{(final)}$ − nonlabor income$_{(initial)}$/total income$_{(initial)}$).

22. This is precisely what the Fournier decomposition of extreme poverty shows for these countries (see table 3.12).

23. Data and figures are available upon request.

24. We use data sets for Ecuador, El Salvador, and Uruguay in which SEDLAC harmonization provides information about these categories of income. For Mexico, we use ENIGH data for 2008 and 2010, and group the original CONEVAL income aggregate into these categories using the codes provided by ENIGH technical manuals.

25. This is consistent with the negligible size of cash transfer policies in this Central American country, as compared with the relatively large programs in Mexico and Ecuador or the social pensions in Uruguay. For a discussion, see chapter 6 of this study, particularly figure 6.2.

26. Chapter 4 of this report describes a study of the reaction of Latin American labor markets to the 2008–09 global financial crisis. Chapter 6 elaborates on the advances of social policy in general and public transfers in particular during the crisis.

27. See Bourguignon (2003) and Adams (2004) for a forecasting exercise using elasticities. Also see Ravallion (2013). We actually follow a semielasticities approach suggested by Klasen and Misselhorny (2008).

28. We use SEDLAC's estimates of moderate poverty headcounts, Gini coefficients, and mean income per household member (see http://sedlac.econo.unlp.edu.ar /eng/). The data set is an unbalanced panel of 17 countries over a 30-year period. The 17 countries are Argentina, Bolivia, Brazil, Chile, Colombia, Costa Rica, the Dominican Republic, Ecuador, El Salvador, Honduras, Mexico, Nicaragua, Panama,

Paraguay, Peru, República Bolivariana de Venezuela, and Uruguay. The number of observations ranges from 25 in Brazil, 20 in Costa Rica, and 17 in Argentina, to 6 in Ecuador, 4 in Colombia, and 2 in Nicaragua. Every poverty or inequality data point refers to the annual average change between two consecutive data points within the period 1989–2008 for these variables, as long as they are not more than five years apart. Changes in real GDP per capita and mean income from survey observations correspond to the annual geometric rate of growth between the two years that corresponds in turn to the available poverty/inequality data points.

29. Results using extreme poverty as a dependent variable are qualitatively similar. These are available from the authors upon request.

30. Interactions between country categorical variables and growth (inequality) measures were also included. No interaction had a statistical significance of below 10 percent.

31. These results resemble those by Ram (2006), who found that growth-poverty elasticities derived from aggregate data are twice as big as those derived from microdata. Also see Ram (2011, 2013).

32. Table 3.10 shows that GDP per capita growth and the survey's average income growth often differ for our sample of countries in 2009. Differences in trends and levels between GDP per capita and other macroeconomic indicators of welfare as compared with the mean incomes reported by individuals in household surveys are a common finding in the literature. See Bourguignon (2003), Adams (2004), and Ravallion (2013).

33. For the regression using extreme poverty as the dependent variable, Paraguay is within the confidence intervals.

34. We chose this model because it explains a larger share of the variance in the data and produces narrower confidence intervals for the forecasts. By applying a GDP per capita average as a measure of income growth, we assume that this average is a good ex ante approximation of the change in mean household incomes from the surveys.

35. As shown in figure 3.11, these countries lie either at the lower border of the confidence intervals or way off. For these countries, the model was less able to predict poverty changes.

References

Adams, Richard. 2004. "Economic Growth, Inequality and Poverty: Estimating the Growth Elasticity of Poverty." *World Development* 32 (December): 1989–2014.

Azevedo, João Pedro. Forthcoming. "Business Cycles and Intergenerational Mobility: Evidence from the First Great Recession of the XXI Century." Policy Research Working Paper, World Bank, Washington, DC.

Azevedo, João Pedro, María Eugenia Dávalos, Carolina Diaz-Bonilla, Bernardo Atuesta, and Raul Andres Castañeda. 2013. "Fifteen Years of Inequality in Latin America: How Have Labor Markets Helped?" Policy Research Working Paper 6384, World Bank, Washington, DC.

Azevedo, João Pedro, Gabriela Inchauste, Sergio Olivieri, Jaime Saavedra Chanduvi, and Hernan Winkler. 2012. "Is Labor Income Responsible for Poverty Reduction? A Decomposition Approach." Policy Research Working Paper 6414, World Bank, Washington, DC.

Bhalla, Surjit S. 2002. *Imagine There's No Country: Poverty, Inequality and Growth in the Era of Globalization*. Washington, DC: Institute for International Economics.

Blanchard, Olivier, Hamid Faruqee, and Mitali Das. 2010. "The Initial Impact of the Crisis on Emerging Market Countries." Brookings Papers on Economic Activity, Brookings Institution, Washington, DC.

Bourguignon, François. 2003. "The Growth Elasticity of Poverty Reduction: Explaining Heterogeneity across Countries and Time Periods." In *Inequality and Growth: Theory and Policy Implications*, edited by T. S. Eicher and S. J. Turnovsky. CESIfo Seminar Series. Cambridge, MA: MIT Press.

Bourguignon, François, and Francisco H. G. Ferreira. 2005. "Decomposing Changes in the Household Distribution of Incomes: Methodological Aspects." In *The Microeconomics of Income Distribution Dynamics in East Asia and Latin America*, edited by Nora Lustig, François Bourguignon, and Francisco H. G. Ferreira.

Chang, Shu-Sen Chang, David Stuckler, Paul Yip, and David Gunnell. 2013. "Impact of 2008 Global Economic Crisis on Suicide: Time Trend Study in 54 Countries." *British Medical Journal* 347 (September): f5239.

Cowell, Frank. A. 2011. *Measuring Inequality.* 3rd ed. Oxford, U.K.: Oxford University Press.

Datt, Gaurav, and Martin Ravallion. 1992. "Growth and Redistribution Components of Changes in Poverty Measures: A Decomposition with Applications to Brazil and India in the 1980s." *Journal of Development Economics* 38 (2): 27595.

Diéguez, Julio, and Rogelio Alvarado. 2012. *Pobreza e Indigencia en 2011.* Ministry of Economics and Finance of Panama.

Fallon, Peter R., and Robert E. B. Lucas. 2002. "The Impact of Financial Crises on Labor Markets, Household Incomes, and Poverty: A Review of Evidence." *World Bank Research Observer* 17 (1): 21–45.

Fei, Johan C. H., Gustav Ranis, and Shirley W. Y. Kuo. 1978. "Growth and the Family Distribution of Income by Factor Components." *Quarterly Journal of Economics* 92 (1): 17–53.

Ferreira, Francisco H. G., Giovanna Prennushi, and Martin Ravallion. 1999. "Protecting the Poor from Macroeconomic Shocks." Policy Research Working Paper 2160, World Bank, Washington, DC.

Ferreira, Francisco H. G., and Norbert Schady. 2008. "Aggregate Economic Shocks, Child Schooling and Child Health." Policy Research Working Paper 4701, World Bank, Washington, DC.

Fournier, Martin. 2001. "Inequality Decomposition by Factor Component: A 'Rank-Correlation' Approach Illustrated on the Taiwanese Case." *Recherches economiques de Louvain* 67: 381–403.

Friedman, Jed Arnold, and Norbert Schady. 2009. "How Many More Infants Are Likely to Die in Africa as a Result of the Global Financial Crisis?" Policy Research Working Paper 5023, World Bank, Washington, DC.

Griffith-Jones, Stephany, and Jose Antonio Ocampo. 2009. "The Financial Crisis and Its Impact on Developing Countries." Working Paper 53, International Policy Center for Inclusive Growth, Brasilia.

Huppi, Monika, and Martin Ravallion. 1990. "The Sectoral Structure of Poverty during an Adjustment Period: Evidence for Indonesia in the Mid-1980s." Policy Research Working Paper Series 529, World Bank, Washington, DC.

Inchauste, Gabriela, Sergio Olivieri, Jaime Saavedra, and Hernan Winkler. 2012. "What Is Behind the Decline in Poverty since 2000? Evidence from Bangladesh, Peru and Thailand." Policy Research Working Paper 6199, World Bank, Washington, DC.

Klasen, Stephan, and Mark Misselhorny. 2008. "Determinants of the Growth Semi-Elasticity of Poverty Reduction." Discussion Paper 176, Ibero-America Institute for Economic Research, Georg-August-Universität Göttingen.

Kolenikov, S., & Shorrocks, A. (2005). "A Decomposition Analysis of Regional Poverty in Russia." Review of Development Economics 9(1): 25–46, 02.

Lerman, Robert I. 1999. "How Do Income Sources Affect Income Inequality?" In Handbook of Income Inequality Measurement, edited by Jacques Silber. London: Kluwer Academic Publishers.

Lerman, Robert I., and Shlomo Yitzhaki. 1995. "Changing Ranks and the Inequality Impacts of Taxes and Transfers." National Tax Journal 48 (1): 45–60.

López-Calva, Luis F., and Nora Lustig. 2010. "Explaining the Decline in Inequality in Latin America: Technological Change, Educational Upgrading and Democracy." In Declining Inequality in Latin America: A Decade of Progress? edited by Luis F. López-Calva and Nora Lustig. Washington, DC: Brookings Institution Press and United Nations Development Programme.

Lustig, Nora, Luis F. Lopez-Calva, and Eduardo Ortiz. 2013. "Declining Inequality in Latin America in the 2000s: The Cases of Argentina, Brazil, and Mexico." World Development 44 (April): 129–41.

Paes de Barros, Ricardo, Mirela de Carvalho, Samuel Franco, and Rosane Mendonça. 2006. "Uma análise das principais causas da queda recente na desigualdade de renda brasileira." Econômica 8 (1).

Ram, Rati. 2006. "Growth Elasticity of Poverty: Alternative Estimates and a Note of Caution." Kyklos 59 (4): 601–10.

———. 2011. "Growth Elasticity of Poverty: Direct Estimates from Recent Data." Applied Economics 43 (19).

———. 2013. "Income Elasticity of Poverty in Developing Countries: Updated Estimates from New Data." Applied Economic Letters 20 (6).

Ravallion, Martin. 2001. "Growth, Inequality and Poverty: Looking Beyond Averages." World Development 29 (11): 1803–15.

———. 2003. "Measuring Aggregate Welfare in Developing Countries: How Well Do National Accounts and Surveys Agree?" Review of Economics and Statistics 85 (3): 645–52.

———. 2004. "Pro-Poor Growth: A Primer." Policy Research Working Paper 3242, World Bank, Washington, DC.

———. 2011. "A Comparative Perspective on Poverty Reduction in Brazil, China and India." World Bank Research Observer 26 (1): 71–104.

———. 2013. "How Long Will It Take to Lift One Billion People Out of Poverty?" Policy Research Working Paper 6325, World Bank, Washington, DC.

Robilliard, Anne-Sophie, and Sherman Robinson. 2003. "Reconciling Household Surveys and National Accounts Data Using a Cross Entropy Estimation Method." Review of Income and Wealth 49 (3).

Sen, Amartya, and James E. Foster. 1997. On Economic Inequality. 2nd ed. Oxford, U.K.: Oxford University Press.

Shorrocks, A. F. 1982. "Inequality Decomposition by Factor Components." Econometrica 50: 193–211.

————. 1999. "Decomposition Procedures for Distributional Analysis: A Unified Framework Based on the Shapley Value." University of Essex.

————. 2012. "Decomposition Procedures for Distributional Analysis: A Unified Framework Based on the Shapley Value." *Journal of Economic Inequality* 11 (1): 99–126.

World Bank. 2010a. *Did Latin America Learn to Shield Its Poor from Economic Shocks?* Washington, DC. http://go.worldbank.org/HGK34AJW00.

————. 2010b. *From Global Collapse to Recovery: Economic Adjustment and Growth Prospects in Latin America and the Caribbean.* Office of the Chief Economist, Latin America and the Caribbean, World Bank.

————. 2011a. *A Break with History: Fifteen Years of Inequality Reduction.* Latin America and the Caribbean Labor and Poverty Brief. http://go.worldbank.org/HGK34AJW00.

————. 2011b. *On the Edge of Uncertainty: Poverty Reduction in Latin America and the Caribbean during the Great Recession and Beyond.* Washington, DC: World Bank

————. 2012. *World Development Indicators, 2012.* Washington, DC: World Bank.

CHAPTER 4

Labor Market Adjustment in Latin America during the Great Recession

Samuel Freije

The Great Recession of 2008–09 had a particularly strong impact on labor markets worldwide. Initial estimates indicated that nearly 20 million jobs were lost during the first year of the crisis (ILO 2009).[1] More recent estimates indicate that by the end of 2011 most countries had employment rates that were below precrisis levels. This impact, however, was stronger in advanced economies than in emerging and developing countries. According to International Labour Organization (ILO) estimates, advanced economies would not regain precrisis employment levels and employment rates until 2016, whereas emerging and developing economies would do so by 2013. This differential impact is also seen in poverty rates, which have persistently declined in developing countries, even during the crisis years, whereas most developed economies have experienced either flat or rising poverty levels (ILO 2012, 12–13, 18–19).[2]

Some developing countries fared much better than others in economic growth and employment during the 2008–09 global financial crisis. Countries with a stronger macroeconomic and fiscal stance at the beginning of the crisis, particularly regarding foreign debt, were less affected or were able to restart growth sooner (Blanchard, Faruqee, and Das 2010; IMF 2010a). Furthermore, labor market adjustment to the crisis in developing countries reportedly occurred mostly through changes in productivity or in hours of work rather than through changes in number of jobs. However, the relative size of these components among developing countries differs significantly, depending on the severity of the crisis, the structure of a country's economy, and the nature of its labor market institutions (Khanna, Newhouse, and Paci 2011; Banerji et al. 2014). In the Latin America region, unemployment increased in 2009 but at a similar pace than in

The author is grateful for the research assistance of the Team for Statistical Development of the Poverty and Gender Unit for the Latin America and the Caribbean Region at the World Bank led by João Pedro Azevedo and Louise Cord. Appreciation is extended in particular to Gabriel Facchini Palma, who produced most of the estimates that accompany this chapter and without whom the compilation and production of these data would have not been possible. Special thanks also go to Maria Dávalos who helped with early drafts of this chapter.

former recessions. Furthermore, real wages did not decline, and informal employment did not rise. The regional average, however, hides country differences, so that those countries with higher trade exposure and specialized in manufacturing experienced larger declines in growth and consequently more severe changes in unemployment and real wages.[3]

This chapter gauges the impact of the 2008–09 global financial crisis on labor markets in Latin America. It compiles microdata for eight Latin American countries and makes comparable estimates of unemployment and participation rates, as well as changes in labor productivity and wages, before and after the crisis. The purpose of this chapter is to describe what happened to labor markets and establish stylized facts about how these economies adjusted to the global crisis.

The chapter has three main sections. The section "Stylized Facts about Labor Markets in Latin America during the Crisis" presents unemployment and participation rates for a sample of countries in Latin America in comparison with other regions of the world. The section "Adjustment through Employment or through Labor Productivity?" describes how the global financial crisis affected employment in the region in 2009, highlighting its differential impact on unemployment and participation rates by gender and age group. This section revisits an estimation of Okun's Law coefficients for the selected countries and confirms that adjustment to crises does not occur mainly through an increase in unemployment. In many countries of the region, an increase in female participation rates partly compensated for youth and male unemployment, rendering rather stable gross employment rates. Because of the limited impact on total employment, the section "What Happened to Earnings?" of this chapter explores the impact of the crisis on labor productivity and wages. This section underlines that the crisis brought about severe wage declines for only a few countries in the sample, but also underscores pending data limitations that require further research. The final section summarizes and concludes.

The countries in the sample examined in this chapter of the study are those with high-frequency labor surveys: Argentina, Brazil, Chile, Colombia, Ecuador, Mexico, Peru, and Uruguay. We rely on data from the Labor Database for Latin America and the Caribbean (LABLAC).[4] The database includes information from over 400 household surveys carried out in several Latin American countries covering more than 82 percent of the population of Latin America. LABLAC surveys produce harmonized monthly or quarterly labor statistics (see table 4.1 for the surveys used in this study).[5]

Stylized Facts about Labor Markets in Latin America during the Crisis

The Basic Structure: Participation, Unemployment, and Informality

In this study, labor force participation, unemployment, and informality rates are used as the main markers for describing the evolution of labor markets during the global financial crisis. Table 4.2 shows these rates for 2007–10.[6]

These three rates merit definition. *Labor force participation rate* is the share of the working-age population (defined as individuals aged 15 and over) that is

Table 4.1 Surveys with Monthly or Quarterly Labor Data, Latin America

Country	Survey	Date rate	Abbreviation	Coverage
Argentina	Encuesta Permanente de Hogares (Permanent Household Survey)	Quarterly	EPH-C	Urban areas
Brazil	Pesquisa Mensual de Emprego (Monthly Employment Survey)	Monthly	PME	Urban areas for metropolitan regions (Recife, Salvador, Belo Horizonte, Rio de Janeiro, São Paulo, Porto Alegre)
Chile	Encuesta Nacional de Empleo y Nueva Encuesta Nacional de Empleo (National Labor Survey and New National Labor Survey)	Moving quarters	ENE/NENE	National (urban and rural)
Colombia	Gran Encuesta Integrada de Hogares (Integrated Household Survey)	Monthly	GEIH	National (urban and rural)
Ecuador	Encuesta de Empleo, Desempleo y Subempleo (Employment, Unemployment, and Underemployment Survey)	Quarterly	ENEMDU	National (urban and rural)
Mexico	Encuesta Nacional de Ocupacion y Empleo (National Employment and Occupation Survey)	Quarterly	ENOE	National (urban and rural)
Peru	Encuesta Permanente de Empleo (Permanent Employment Survey)	Moving quarters	EPE	Urban (only metropolitan Lima)
Uruguay	Encuesta Continua de Hogares (Continuous Household Survey)	Monthly	ECH	National (urban and rural)

Table 4.2 Participation, Unemployment, and Informality Rates: Latin America, 2007–10

	Levels (%)				Changes (percentage points)		
	2007	2008	2009	2010	2008	2009	2010
Argentina							
Labor force	60.5	61.0	60.9	60.0	0.5	(0.2)	(0.8)
Employed	92.5	92.7	91.6	92.7			
Formal	59.0	61.2	59.3	62.3			
Informal	41.0	38.8	40.7	37.7	(2.2)	1.9	(2.9)
Unemployed	7.5	7.3	8.4	7.3	(0.2)	1.1	(1.1)
Out of labor force	39.5	39.0	39.1	40.0			
Brazil							
Labor force	63.2	62.6	62.5	62.8	(0.6)	(0.1)	0.3
Employed	90.5	92.4	91.9	93.3			
Formal	67.1	68.4	68.7	69.9			
Informal	32.9	31.6	31.3	30.1	(1.3)	(0.3)	(1.2)
Unemployed	9.5	7.6	8.1	6.7	(1.9)	0.5	(1.3)
Out of labor force	36.8	37.4	37.5	37.2			
Chile							
Labor force	53.9	54.8	54.6	59.6	0.8	(0.2)	5.0
Employed	93.3	93.7	91.6	91.5			
Formal	64.8	65.2	64.3	68.1			
Informal	35.2	34.8	35.7	31.9	(0.4)	0.9	(3.8)

table continues next page

Table 4.2 Participation, Unemployment, and Informality Rates: Latin America, 2007–10 *(continued)*

	Levels (%)				Changes (percentage points)		
	2007	*2008*	*2009*	*2010*	*2008*	*2009*	*2010*
Unemployed	6.7	6.3	8.4	8.5	(0.4)	2.1	0.1
Out of labor force	46.1	45.2	45.4	40.4			
Colombia							
Labor force	62.8	63.4	65.5	67.4	0.6	2.1	1.9
Employed	89.9	89.2	88.9	89.4			
Formal	40.7	38.8	38.6	37.9			
Informal	59.3	61.2	61.4	62.1	1.9	0.2	0.7
Unemployed	10.1	10.8	11.1	10.6	0.7	0.3	(0.5)
Out of labor force	37.2	36.6	34.5	32.6			
Ecuador							
Labor force	70.3	68.4	66.0	64.8	(1.9)	(2.5)	(1.2)
Employed	92.8	92.7	90.6	92.5			
Formal	45.0	46.1	48.2	47.5			
Informal	55.0	53.9	51.8	52.5	(1.1)	(2.1)	0.7
Unemployed	7.2	7.3	9.4	7.5	0.0	2.2	(1.9)
Out of labor force	29.7	31.6	34.0	35.2			
Mexico							
Labor force	60.0	60.1	60.7	60.3	0.2	0.5	(0.4)
Employed	96.1	95.8	93.8	94.4			
Formal	49.6	49.4	47.9	48.5			
Informal	50.4	50.6	52.1	51.5	0.2	1.5	(0.6)
Unemployed	3.9	4.2	6.2	5.6	0.3	2.1	(0.6)
Out of labor force	40.0	39.9	39.3	39.7			
Peru							
Labor force	70.0	69.1	68.8	71.3	(0.9)	(0.3)	2.6
Employed	92.1	92.1	92.3	92.2			
Formal	53.5	54.9	55.0	53.8			
Informal	46.5	45.1	45.0	46.2	(1.4)	(0.1)	1.2
Unemployed	7.9	7.9	7.7	7.8	–	(0.2)	0.1
Out of labor force	30.0	30.9	31.2	28.7			
Uruguay							
Labor force	63.8	63.2	65.1	65.0	(0.5)	1.9	(0.1)
Employed	91.5	92.5	92.7	93.8			
Formal	57.9	59.3	59.9	60.1			
Informal	42.1	40.7	40.1	39.9	(1.4)	(0.6)	(0.2)
Unemployed	8.5	7.5	7.3	6.2	(1.0)	(0.3)	(1.1)
Out of labor force	36.2	36.8	34.9	35.0			

Sources: Database for Latin America and the Caribbean, LABLAC (CEDLAS and World Bank).
Note: Labor force and out of labor force are expressed as a percentage of the working-age population. Employed and unemployed are expressed as a percentage of the labor force. Formal and informal employed are expressed as a percentage of employed. *Informality* is defined as salaried workers in small firms, nonprofessional self-employed, and zero-income workers.

actually employed or actively looking for employment. *Unemployment rate* adheres to the ILO definition—that is, persons not employed, as a percentage of the labor force, who would have accepted a job or started an enterprise during the reference period (usually the previous week or month), and who had actively looked for ways to obtain a job or start an enterprise.[7] Finally, the *informality rate* is the share of informal workers within total employment. An individual is considered an informal worker if she or he falls into any of the following categories: (1) a nonprofessional self-employed; (2) a salaried worker in a small private firm; or (3) a zero-income worker. Implementing this definition requires the following assumptions: (1) individuals are defined as nonprofessional if they do not have a tertiary or superior education degree; (2) small firms are those with five or fewer employees; and (3) because an individual could have more than one job, the classification is applied only to the main occupation.[8]

The selected Latin American countries have quite similar labor market structures. By the 2010, they had participation rates of about 60 percent, with the exception of Peru and Colombia, which had rates closer to 70 percent. These rates were very similar to the participation rates of developed economies and Eastern European economies (around or slightly below 60 percent), but lower than the average rates in East Asia (higher than 70 percent) and higher than those in North African and Middle Eastern countries (below 50 percent).[9]

For the period 2007–10, unemployment rates ranged from about 5 percent in Mexico to about 11 percent in Colombia. The other six countries had unemployment rates within the narrower range of 6–8 percent. These numbers were again similar to the rates in most developed economies for the same period. At the same time, these rates were higher than those in East and South Asia, where average unemployment rates hovered around 4 percent, but lower than those in North Africa and the Middle East, whose rates were around or above 10 percent.

In terms of informality, the countries can be organized into three categories: (1) low, or around 30 percent (Brazil, Chile, and Uruguay); (2) intermediate, or around 40 percent (Argentina and Peru); and (3) high, or more than 50 percent (Colombia, Ecuador, and Mexico). These numbers must be viewed with caution, however, because of the different scope of the surveys used. Colombia and Mexico have national surveys, whereas Argentina, Brazil, and Peru have urban surveys, which may explain why the informality rates are much higher in Colombia and Mexico than in Argentina, Brazil, and Peru. However, countries such as Chile and Uruguay had the lowest informality rates, even for national surveys.

It is difficult to compare these numbers with global figures because definitions of informality vary across countries and from one source to another. The selected Latin American countries appear to fall in a middle range, with figures not as high as in India or Mali (reported at 80 percent) but higher than the lower-end figures in Serbia, Poland, and Moldova (all with informality rates below 10 percent).[10]

In summary, the selected Latin American countries show labor market characteristics of middle-income and even high-income economies. Participation and unemployment rates are similar to the ones seen in high-income economies. Informality rates are higher than those in middle- and high-income countries, but not as high as those in low-income countries.

Some regularities can be observed in changes in these rates for the countries selected. Participation rates declined slightly in 2009 for Argentina, Brazil, Chile, and Peru. Colombia stands apart because the year 2009 did not interrupt a continuous increase in female participation rates since the middle of the decade among both young and prime-age women. Ecuador, by contrast, saw participation rates decline from 2007 to 2010. This was a sort of convergence from high (70 percent) participation rates to the regional average participation rates. This process was led by a rapid decline in participation rates among youth, both males and females, that had been under way since the early 2000s.

All countries in the sample, with the exception of Peru and Uruguay, saw unemployment rates increase in 2009. The changes in unemployment, however, were very different. These increases ranged from 0.3 percentage point in Colombia, which represents a mere 3 percent rise, to 2.2 percentage points in Mexico, an almost 50 percent increase for this country. Peru had a slight increase of 0.4 percentage point in 2008 but an actual decline in unemployment in 2009. Uruguay only had a deceleration in the regular decline in unemployment rates that the country had been experiencing since 2006.

This heterogeneity of results is only partly linked to the differences in the growth of the gross domestic product (GDP) in 2009. That year, Uruguay and Peru experienced positive GDP growth and their unemployment rates declined. Mexico, by contrast, had a severe recession and the largest unemployment increase in the region. Brazil and Chile had approximately the same decline in GDP in 2009, but Brazil had a very small increase in unemployment, whereas Ecuador and Chile saw an increase in unemployment almost as large as Mexico's, despite having much higher growth rates. Also puzzling are Argentina and Colombia, where unemployment rates increased despite positive, yet small, GDP growth (see figure 4.1).

Another way to summarize the evolution and the content of the crisis is through the gross employment rate. This rate is the percentage of employment among the working-age population (people aged 15 and over). It combines the effect of unemployment rates and participation rates. Formally:

$$\frac{E}{W} = \frac{E}{L} * \frac{L}{W} = \left(1 - \frac{U}{L}\right) * \frac{L}{W}$$

where E is total employment, W is the population aged 15 and over (also known as the working-age population), L is the labor force (i.e., those with employment or looking for one), and U is total unemployment. Lower participation rates and higher unemployment rates imply a lower gross employment rate. Interestingly, these two rates need not go in the same direction and may compensate for one another, keeping gross employment rates unaltered.

Figure 4.1 Unemployment and Growth: Latin America, 2009

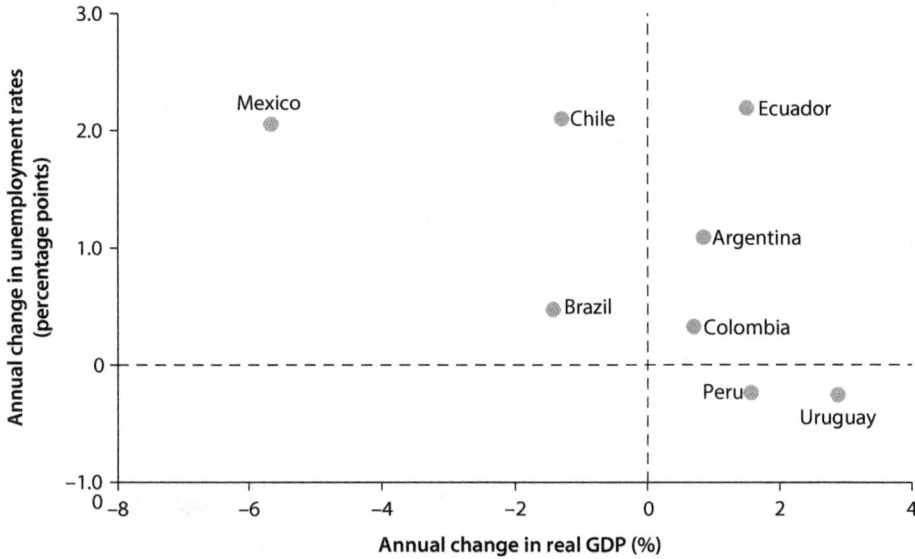

Sources: LABLAC (CEDLAS and World Bank) and International Monetary Fund, International Financial Statistics (database), various years; real GDP for Argentina: El Instituto Nacional de Estadística y Censos (INDEC, National Institute of Statistics and Census), http://www.indec.gov.ar.
Note: Changes in the unemployment rates correspond to year-to-year differences in the unemployment rate by the third quarter of 2009 (except for Argentina where it corresponds to the fourth quarter of 2009). Changes in GDP growth correspond to the year-to-year percentage change in annual real GDP by the third quarter of 2009 (fourth quarter for Argentina).

Like unemployment rates, gross employment rates are partly linked to the differences in GDP growth in 2009. Countries with positive economic growth in 2009 (Colombia, Peru, and Uruguay) experienced increases in gross employment rates, whereas countries with negative economic growth (Brazil, Chile, and Mexico) saw a decline in gross employment rates. The odd cases are Argentina and Ecuador. In Argentina, economic growth was accompanied by a decline, though slight, in its gross employment rate. Ecuador is a clear outlier, with a large decline in employment despite positive economic growth (see figure 4.2). As explained later in this chapter, Ecuador is somehow exceptional among these countries. It is the only country with a large decline in its participation rates (due to a secular decline toward regional convergence) and a large increase in its unemployment rate, both of which led to a noticeable reduction in employment despite some positive economic growth.

The previous figures suggest a tenuous linear connection between employment and economic growth. Higher economic growth is associated with additional employment growth and less unemployment, but how much additional or less employment per unit of GDP growth varies a great deal from one country to another. Actually, some countries experienced almost no change in employment together with some economic growth (e.g., Peru), which must have entailed an increase in average productivity, while others experienced the opposite and should therefore have seen declining productivity (e.g., Brazil).

Understanding the Poverty Impact of the Global Financial Crisis in Latin America and the Caribbean
http://dx.doi.org/10.1596/978-1-4648-0241-6

Figure 4.2 Gross Employment Rate and Growth: Latin America, 2009

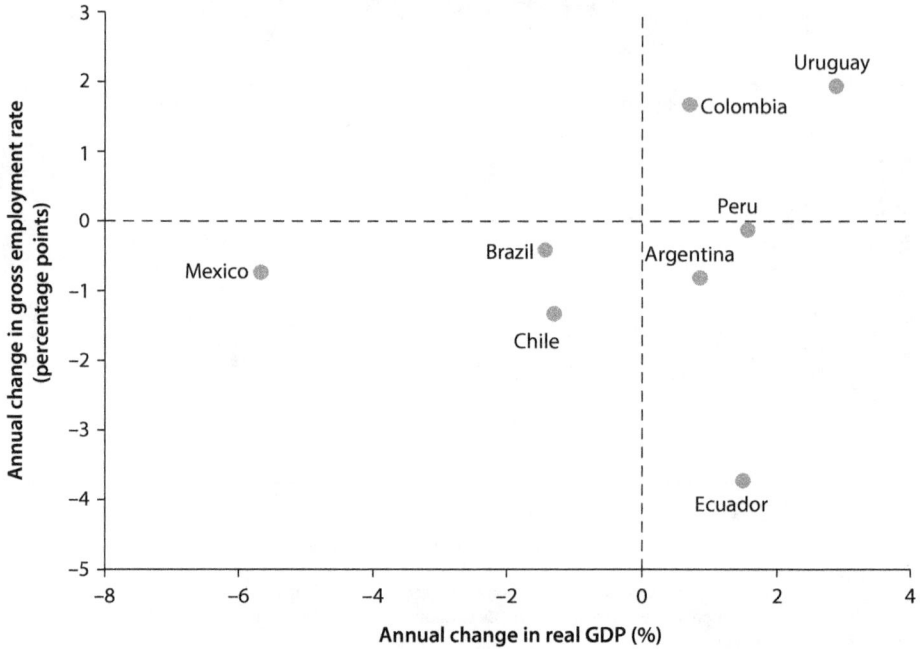

Sources: LABLAC (CEDLAS and World Bank) and International Monetary Fund, International Financial Statistics (database), various years; real GDP for Argentina: INDEC.
Note: Changes in the gross employment rates correspond to year-to-year differences in the gross employment rate for the third quarter of 2009 (except for Argentina where it corresponds to the fourth quarter of 2009). Changes in GDP growth correspond to the year-to-year percentage change in annual real GDP by the third quarter of 2009 (fourth quarter for Argentina).

Adjustment through Employment or through Labor Productivity?

A simple decomposition can link macroeconomic performance, as measured by GDP per capita, to the main indicators of labor market performance. The decomposition is

$$\Delta(Y/P) = \Delta(Y/E) + \Delta(E/W) + \Delta(W/P) \qquad (4.1)$$

where Y is real GDP, P is the total population, W is the working-age population, E is employment, and Δ is the percentage change.[11] This decomposition allows us to identify how changes in GDP per capita are a combination of three main components. The first component indicates how a crisis turned into a change in labor productivity.[12] The second component, the gross employment rate, which is developed in the following section of this chapter as a combination of both participation and unemployment rates, indicates how the crisis affected employment. The third component is the ratio of the working-age population to total population (W/P). In the short term, the W/P term tends to move slowly because it is driven by the age structure of the country. In this regard, the W/P rate is more a result of long-term demographic forces than short-term labor market adjustments.[13] Given this decomposition, the first question is whether the observed changes in GDP per capita in our sample were associated mostly with changes in labor productivity or mostly with changes in gross employment rates or with a combination of both.

During the first year of the crisis, in Argentina, Brazil, Mexico, and Peru changes in productivity were larger (in absolute value) than changes in gross employment rates (see table 4.3). In these countries, labor markets adjusted to the crisis through a reduction in labor productivity rather than a reduction in employment. On the other hand, Chile experienced changes in its gross employment rate that were larger than those in labor productivity. This country saw its labor market adjust to the crisis through employment, avoiding a decline in labor productivity. Interestingly, in Colombia, Ecuador, and Uruguay, changes in productivity and gross employment rates went in opposite directions. In Colombia and Uruguay, increases in gross employment were able to partially or fully compensate for the decline in product per worker. In Ecuador, the opposite was true.

In summary, the crisis had a heterogeneous productivity impact versus employment impact on the countries in the sample. On the one hand, in Argentina, Brazil, Peru, and Mexico most of the adjustment occurred through changes in labor productivity. On the other hand, Colombia, Chile, Ecuador, and Uruguay experienced wider oscillations in employment rates than in average productivity.

The estimates in table 4.3 are based on end of year data. Quarter after quarter data give a more detailed description of the performance of the labor market during this crisis—in particular, how rapidly the crisis evolved, its duration, and its impact on the labor market through changes in productivity or changes in employment. Figure 4.3 shows the evolution of the employment component of equation (4.1) using quarterly GDP data and quarterly labor surveys for the eight countries selected—the evolution of the productivity component appears later in this chapter. To facilitate analysis of this component, all series are indexed to a value of 100 in the fourth quarter of 2008.[14]

The gross employment rate (E/W) is represented by a green line in figure 4.3. As explained in the previous section, this gross employment rate is the

Table 4.3 Decomposition of Changes of GDP Per Capita: Latin America, 2009
Percent

Country	GDP per capita	GDP per worker	Worker/working-age population	Working-age population/ total population
			Four quarters after	
Argentina	−1.3	−1.1	−0.7	0.5
Brazil	−2.3	−2.0	−0.7	0.5
Chile	−3.0	−0.4	−2.6	0.0
Colombia	−0.1	−3.7	3.0	0.7
Ecuador	−2.1	3.2	−5.9	0.6
Mexico	−3.4	−3.2	−1.3	1.1
Peru	−1.4	−2.3	−0.2	1.0
Uruguay	1.6	−1.3	3.3	−0.5

Sources: LABLAC (CEDLAS and World Bank) and International Monetary Fund, International Financial Statistics (database), various years; real GDP for Argentina: INDEC.
Note: Data refer to percentage changes from the third quarter of 2008 to the third quarter of 2009.

Understanding the Poverty Impact of the Global Financial Crisis in Latin America and the Caribbean
http://dx.doi.org/10.1596/978-1-4648-0241-6

Figure 4.3 Quarterly Trends in Participation and Employment Rates: Latin America

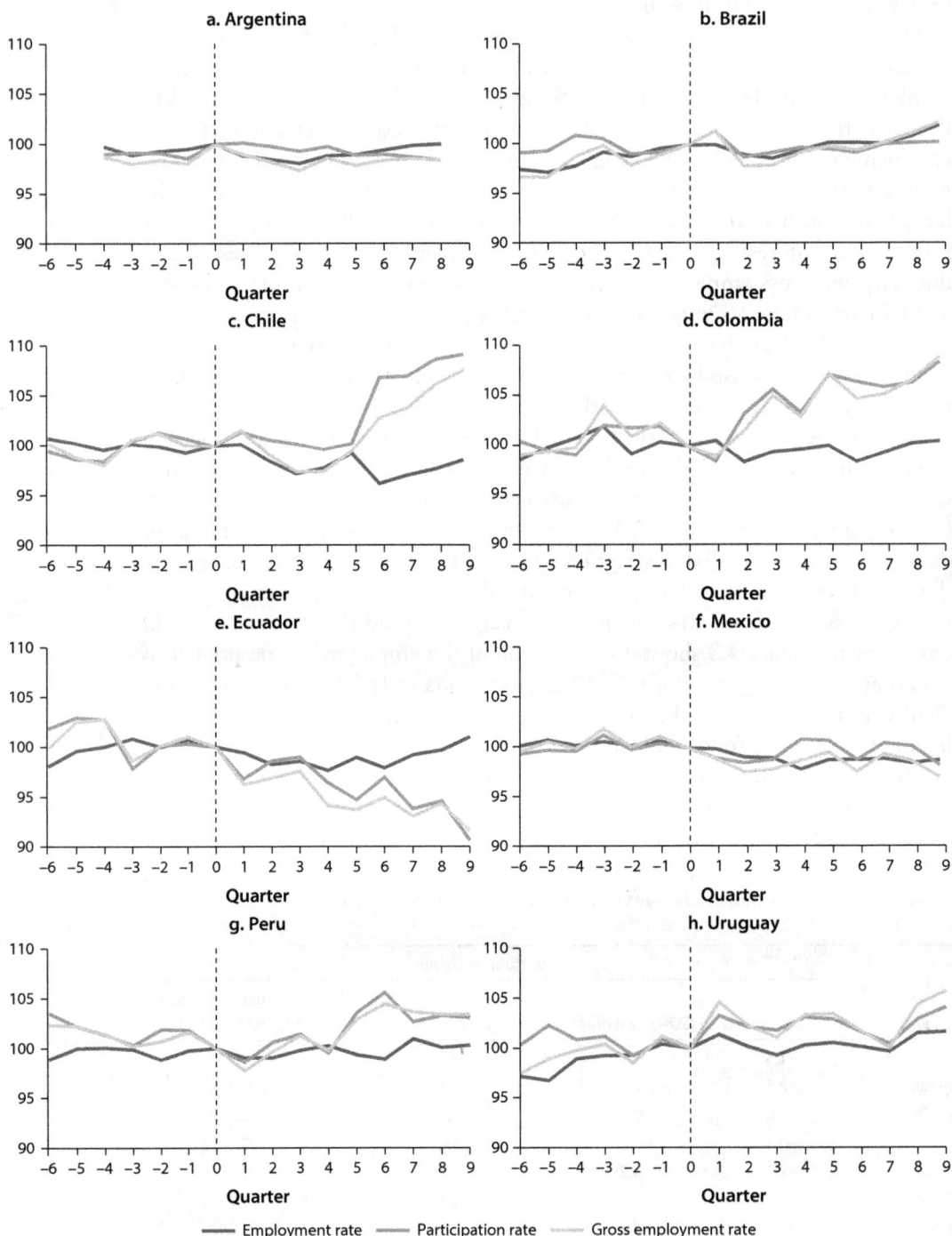

Employment rate   Participation rate   Gross employment rate

Source: LABLAC (CEDLAS and World Bank).
Note: The x-axis refers to quarters after or before the quarter of reference (second quarter of 2008). On the y-axis, the index equals 100 at the third quarter of 2008 (except for Argentina where it corresponds to the fourth quarter of 2008).

combination of two rates. The figure also shows the evolution of employment rates (*E/L*, blue lines), which move in the opposite direction of the unemployment rate, as well as the participation rate (*L/W*, orange line), for all countries under study. In other words, trends in gross employment rates can be explained by trends in unemployment rates or in participation rates.

The gross employment rate is mostly driven by the participation rate in every country of the sample. The increase in gross employment rates in Colombia, Peru, and Uruguay eight and even four quarters after the crisis began was the consequence of a persistent rise of participation rates, which more than compensated for rather stable employment rates. In Chile, the gross employment rate declined during the first four quarters because of growing unemployment and a flat participation rate. From the fifth quarter onward, the rapidly growing participation rate compensated for unemployment, and the gross employment rate regained its precrisis levels.[15] In Ecuador, the persistent decline in the participation rate that had been observed for several years even before the crisis began was the main force behind the drop in the gross employment rate. By contrast, Argentina, Brazil, and Mexico saw a decline in gross employment rates that was the combination of an increase of unemployment and a slight increase in participation rates.

In Brazil, Colombia, Peru, and Uruguay, the unemployment impact of the crisis was short-lived, and by the fourth or fifth quarter after the onset of the crisis unemployment rates were back to their precrisis levels. On the other hand, Argentina, Chile, Ecuador, and Mexico experienced deeper and longer increases in their unemployment rates. In Chile and Mexico, two years after the onset of the crisis unemployment rates had still not regained their precrisis levels.

In summary, both participation and unemployment rates are important factors in the reaction of Latin American labor markets to the 2008–09 global financial crisis. The following sections explore further the dynamics of participation and unemployment rates in Latin America, in particular how female participation rates compensated for youth unemployment rates.

Evolution of Employment in the Crisis: Youth to the Bench, Women to the Rescue

For the period 2007–10, labor force participation rates by gender in the selected countries are similar to the rates in most developing regions and higher than the rates in developed economies. Among prime-age males (ages 25–64), labor force participation is above 90 percent for all countries in the sample, except Brazil where it stands at around 85 percent. By contrast, in developed economies the rate hovers in the 70 percent range. Prime-age female labor force participation is between 65 percent and 70 percent for all countries in the sample, except for Mexico and Chile where it remains around 50 percent.[16] These rates are close to the participation rates of females in developed countries, Eastern Europe, and East Asia (between 50 percent and 60 percent), but higher than those in South Asia and the Middle East (between 20 percent and 35 percent).

The dynamics of participation rates during the global financial crisis exhibited important differences by age and gender, but these were very similar across countries in the sample. The year 2009 was characterized by a decline in participation rates among youth and higher participation among prime-age adults. Within the latter, female labor participation grew much faster than male participation, which in some cases (Chile, Ecuador, and Mexico) even declined (see table 4.4). Participation rates among seniors (people aged 65 and over) declined or remained the same in all countries except Peru and Uruguay, where the crisis was less intense. This indicates that the crisis induced a sort of substitution effect in which the young and the old withdrew from the labor market, whereas prime-age females entered the labor market to support the family economy.

Table 4.4 Age and Gender Profiles of Participation Rates: Latin America, 2007–10

	Rate (%)				Change (percentage points)		
	2007	2008	2009	2010	2008	2009	2010
Argentina							
National	60.4	61.0	60.9	60.0	0.6	−0.2	−0.8
By age							
15–24	43.6	42.8	41.3	40.8	−0.8	−1.6	−0.5
25–64	76.1	77.5	78.0	77.1	1.4	0.4	−0.8
65+	16.5	15.5	15.2	14.5	−1.0	−0.3	−0.7
By gender[a]							
Female	61.8	64.0	64.9	63.0	2.2	0.9	−1.9
Male	92.3	92.6	92.7	92.7	0.3	0.1	0.0
Brazil[b]							
National	63.2	62.6	62.5	62.8	−0.6	−0.1	0.3
By age							
15–24	56.9	56.2	55.1	55.3	−0.7	−1.0	0.2
25–64	73.2	72.5	73.0	73.3	−0.7	0.6	0.3
65+	12.4	13.1	12.0	12.5	0.7	−1.1	0.4
By gender[a]							
Female	62.5	61.9	62.7	62.9	−0.6	0.7	0.3
Male	85.6	84.9	85.4	85.7	−0.6	0.4	0.4
Chile							
National	53.9	54.8	54.6	59.6	0.8	−0.2	5.0
By age							
15–24	30.8	32.4	31.1	38.2	1.6	−1.3	7.0
25–64	69.8	70.7	71.0	75.3	0.9	0.3	4.3
65+	16.1	16.3	16.3	21.1	0.3	0.0	4.7
By gender[a]							
Female	49.2	51.0	51.8	60.1	1.8	0.8	8.3
Male	91.0	91.1	90.9	91.1	0.1	−0.1	0.2
Colombia							
National	62.8	63.4	65.5	67.4	0.6	2.1	1.9
By age							
15–24	46.0	46.6	50.0	52.3	0.7	3.4	2.2
25–64	75.4	75.9	77.8	79.1	0.5	1.8	1.4
65+	22.9	24.4	24.3	27.8	1.5	−0.1	3.5

table continues next page

Table 4.4 Age and Gender Profiles of Participation Rates: Latin America, 2007–10 *(continued)*

	Rate (%)				Change (percentage points)		
	2007	*2008*	*2009*	*2010*	*2008*	*2009*	*2010*
By gender[a]							
Female	59.6	59.7	62.9	65.3	0.1	3.3	2.3
Male	92.6	93.6	93.8	94.1	1.0	0.2	0.3
Ecuador							
National	70.3	68.4	66.0	64.8	−1.9	−2.5	−1.2
By age							
15–24	55.1	51.9	46.9	44.8	−3.1	−5.1	−2.1
25–64	82.0	80.9	79.5	78.9	−1.1	−1.4	−0.6
65+	39.7	37.5	32.8	32.3	−2.2	−4.7	−0.5
By gender[a]							
Female	69.2	67.4	65.5	65.1	−1.8	−1.9	−0.4
Male	96.5	96.3	95.5	94.5	−0.3	−0.8	−0.9
Mexico							
National	60.0	60.1	60.7	60.3	0.2	0.5	−0.4
By age							
15–24	48.3	48.5	47.8	48.4	0.2	−0.8	0.6
25–64	69.5	69.5	70.8	70.0	0.0	1.3	−0.8
65+	28.4	28.7	28.2	27.9	0.3	−0.6	−0.3
By gender[a]							
Female	49.5	49.5	52.1	51.0	0.1	2.6	−1.1
Male	92.8	92.5	92.2	91.6	−0.3	−0.3	−0.6
Peru							
National	70.0	69.1	68.8	71.3	−0.9	−0.3	2.6
By age							
15–24	58.9	57.8	54.6	56.8	−1.2	−3.2	2.2
25–64	81.4	80.6	81.5	83.9	−0.8	0.9	2.4
65+	23.5	22.9	23.7	30.5	−0.6	0.8	6.8
By gender[a]							
Female	69.6	68.3	69.9	73.2	−1.3	1.6	3.2
Male	93.9	93.8	94.0	95.4	−0.1	0.2	1.4
Uruguay							
National	63.8	63.2	65.1	65.0	−0.5	1.9	−0.1
By age							
15–24	55.9	51.6	52.9	52.8	−4.3	1.3	−0.1
25–64	80.5	81.8	82.9	82.8	1.3	1.0	0.0
65+	15.4	16.9	18.1	17.9	1.6	1.2	−0.2
By gender[a]							
Female	69.9	72.9	73.4	73.6	3.0	0.5	0.2
Male	92.7	92.2	93.9	93.4	−0.5	1.8	−0.6

Source: LABLAC (CEDLAS and World Bank).
Note: Table refers to labor force and out of labor force as a percentage of working-age population.
a. Population aged 25–64.

Understanding the Poverty Impact of the Global Financial Crisis in Latin America and the Caribbean
http://dx.doi.org/10.1596/978-1-4648-0241-6

Female labor force participation grew in all countries during the crisis. In Argentina, Brazil, and Mexico, the female participation rates increased momentarily, only to decline or level off again after the crisis. Chile had a recurrent increase in the female participation rate (always higher than the rate for males), and Peru saw accelerated participation rates for males and females (but faster for females) in both 2009 and 2010.

In 2009 Colombia, Ecuador, and Uruguay departed from the general pattern. In Ecuador, the participation rates of all age and gender groups declined. This trend can be associated with the trend of Ecuador's participation rates converging with the regional average. The trends have been recorded since the beginning of the decade and can be confirmed in our data for 2007 through 2010. However, youth and senior participation rates declined faster in 2009 than in previous and subsequent years, indicating a pattern of adjustment to the crisis similar to that in the other selected countries. In Colombia, in contrast to Ecuador, youth increased their participation faster than other groups. In Uruguay, youth and male prime-age males increased their participation faster than seniors and female prime-age workers. In these two cases, it seems that continued positive economic growth prevented a decline of youth participation in the labor market.

Evolution of Unemployment Rates by Groups

The first and most prominent regularity in the sample of Latin American countries is that the youth unemployment rate during the global financial crisis was at least 2.5 times higher than that for prime-age adults (see table 4.5). The unemployment rates for youth (people aged 15–24) in 2009 ranged from 11.8 percent in Mexico to 22.6 in Colombia, but this range hides the wide gaps between the youth and prime-age unemployment rates. The youth to prime-age ratios in Mexico, Colombia, and Ecuador stay within the 2.5–3.0 range. In some countries, the ratio is above 3.0 (Argentina, Brazil, Chile, and Peru) and is five times higher in Uruguay in 2010. These findings put these countries in the upper rank of the youth to adult unemployment ratios in the world.[17]

Not only is youth unemployment very high in all the countries, but it also increased the most in 2009 during the crisis. For every country that experienced an increase in unemployment during 2009, youth unemployment had the largest increase among all population groups. For example, in Mexico youth unemployment grew 3.4 percentage points, while prime-age adults experienced an increase of 1.8 percentage points and seniors (people aged 65 and over) a 1.1 percentage point increase. Similar trends were evident in Argentina, Brazil, Chile, Colombia, and Ecuador. By contrast, in Peru and Uruguay, countries that experienced declines in unemployment, youth unemployment also declined faster. This finding indicates that youth employment is the swing variable of the economic cycle. It is the young who proportionately lose more jobs during recessions, but it is also the young who proportionately are hired more often during expansions: in five out of the eight countries in the sample, the youth had the largest declines in unemployment rates in 2010.

Understanding the Poverty Impact of the Global Financial Crisis in Latin America and the Caribbean
http://dx.doi.org/10.1596/978-1-4648-0241-6

Table 4.5 Age and Gender Profiles of Employment Rates: Latin America, 2007–10

	Rate (%)				Change (percentage points)		
	2007	2008	2009	2010	2008	2009	2010
Argentina							
National	7.5	7.3	8.4	7.3	−0.2	1.1	−1.1
By age							
15–24	16.5	17.0	20.2	19.0	0.5	3.2	−1.2
25–64	5.5	5.4	6.3	5.1	−0.1	0.8	−1.2
65+	9.2	4.5	5.0	5.6	−4.7	0.5	0.6
By gender[a]							
Female	7.5	6.8	7.6	6.4	−0.6	0.7	−1.1
Male	4.1	4.4	5.3	4.2	0.3	0.9	−1.1
Brazil[b]							
National	9.5	7.6	8.1	6.7	−1.9	0.5	−1.3
By age							
15–24	21.9	16.9	18.6	16.3	−5.0	1.7	−2.3
25–64	6.6	5.5	5.9	4.8	−1.1	0.4	−1.1
65+	1.4	2.2	1.5	1.0	0.7	−0.7	−0.5
By gender[a]							
Female	8.6	7.1	7.3	6.3	−1.6	0.3	−1.0
Male	4.9	4.1	4.6	3.5	−0.8	0.4	−1.1
Chile							
National	6.7	6.3	8.4	8.5	−0.4	2.1	0.1
By age							
15–24	17.1	17.0	19.5	18.9	−0.1	2.6	−0.7
25–64	5.3	4.8	7.1	7.0	−0.5	2.2	−0.1
65+	0.8	1.0	1.2	3.3	0.2	0.2	2.1
By gender[a]							
Female	5.1	4.7	6.0	8.2	−0.4	1.3	2.2
Male	5.5	4.9	7.7	6.1	−0.5	2.7	−1.5
Colombia							
National	10.1	10.8	11.1	10.6	0.7	0.3	−0.5
By age							
15–24	20.0	22.0	22.6	21.0	2.1	0.6	−1.6
25–64	7.9	8.4	8.5	8.1	0.4	0.2	−0.4
65+	3.8	3.8	3.4	5.5	−0.1	−0.3	2.1
By gender[a]							
Female	9.8	10.8	11.5	10.8	1.0	0.7	−0.7
Male	6.6	6.7	6.3	6.1	0.0	−0.3	−0.2
Ecuador							
National	7.2	7.3	9.4	7.5	0.0	2.2	−1.9
By age							
15–24	16.4	17.0	19.9	18.2	0.6	2.9	−1.7
25–64	4.9	4.8	7.2	5.4	−0.1	2.4	−1.7
65+	2.5	3.7	4.5	2.2	1.2	0.8	−2.3

table continues next page

Understanding the Poverty Impact of the Global Financial Crisis in Latin America and the Caribbean
http://dx.doi.org/10.1596/978-1-4648-0241-6

Table 4.5 Age and Gender Profiles of Employment Rates: Latin America, 2007–10 *(continued)*

	Rate (%)				Change (percentage points)		
	2007	2008	2009	2010	2008	2009	2010
By gender[a]							
Female	6.9	7.5	9.0	6.3	0.6	1.6	−2.7
Male	3.3	2.6	5.7	4.7	−0.7	3.1	−1.0
Mexico							
National	3.9	4.2	6.2	5.6	0.3	2.1	−0.6
By age							
15–24	8.0	8.4	11.8	11.0	0.4	3.4	−0.8
25–64	2.9	3.2	5.0	4.4	0.3	1.8	−0.6
65+	1.2	0.8	2.0	1.5	−0.3	1.1	−0.5
By gender[a]							
Female	3.2	3.2	5.4	4.3	−0.1	2.2	−1.0
Male	2.7	3.2	4.7	4.4	0.5	1.5	−0.3
Peru							
National	8.1	8.5	7.8	7.6	0.4	−0.7	−0.2
By age							
15–24	14.1	16.8	15.1	16.0	2.7	−1.7	0.9
25–64	6.1	5.8	5.7	5.2	−0.3	−0.1	−0.6
65+	6.2	5.8	4.4	4.2	−0.4	−1.5	−0.2
By gender[a]							
Female	7.6	8.5	7.2	6.4	0.9	−1.4	−0.8
Male	5.0	3.7	4.5	4.1	−1.3	0.8	−0.4
Uruguay							
National	8.5	7.5	7.3	6.2	−1.0	−0.3	−1.1
By age							
15–24	23.1	20.7	19.3	19.1	−2.5	−1.4	−0.1
25–64	5.7	5.1	5.0	3.8	−0.5	−0.1	−1.2
65+	4.5	2.1	4.5	2.5	−2.4	2.4	−2.1
By gender[a]							
Female	8.7	7.0	6.5	6.0	−1.8	−0.4	−0.5
Male	3.0	3.5	3.6	1.9	0.5	0.1	−1.7

Source: SEDLAC (CEDLAS and World Bank).
Note: Table presents unemployed as a percentage of the labor force.
a. Population aged 25–64.

Another important regularity is that unemployment rates were systematically higher for females than males. The difference was usually 2–4 percentage points higher for women with two interesting exceptions. In Mexico, unemployment rates were only slightly higher for women: less than half a percentage point. In Chile, unemployment rates were slightly lower for women until 2009. But from 2010 onward, a new survey design captured a higher unemployment rate for women. The dynamics of unemployment rates by gender during the crisis showed that unemployment rates grew faster among men than women.

Again, the exception was Mexico, which in 2009 had a larger increase in female unemployment rates. By 2010, however, both rates were again equal.

The gender gap in unemployment rates did not change over the course of this cycle. Only in Mexico did the gap close: male unemployment rates rose to the same level as the higher, female rates in the second quarter of 2009, and the rates remained practically equal during 2010. In the rest of the countries under study, unemployment rates moved in parallel over the course of the crisis.

Finally, unemployment rates for seniors were the lowest in every country in the sample. In addition, changes in the unemployment rate of this group were almost always the lowest among all rates, indicating that seniors were less likely to become unemployed. As indicated in table 4.4, if the crisis affected them, they left the labor market rather than remain unemployed.

Accounting for the Total Change in Employment

The foregoing descriptions of trends in participation and unemployment rates do not explain how much of the total change in gross employment rates during the crisis can be attributed to different groups. Prime-age females increased their participation, while that of other groups declined. However, prime-age females also endured larger increases in unemployment in some countries. The young saw a decline in participation and an increase in unemployment. Did one trend compensate for the other? What about the movements by prime-age males? Because of their predominance in labor markets, do they define the evolution of those markets?

The gross employment rate can be decomposed as a weighted average of the employment rates of youth, prime-age males and females, and senior workers, where the weights correspond to the population shares of these four groups. Formally:

$$\frac{E}{W} = \frac{E_Y}{W_Y} * \frac{W_Y}{W} + \frac{E_F}{W_F} * \frac{W_F}{W} + \frac{E_M}{W_M} * \frac{W_M}{W} + \frac{E_S}{W_S} * \frac{W_S}{W}$$

where the subscripts Y, F, M, and S correspond to youth, prime-age females, prime-age males, and seniors. Changes in this formula of the gross employment rates can be decomposed into changes ascribed to each of the population groups. These changes are due to changes in employment rates or changes in the relative size of each of the group. Figure 4.4 shows this decomposition for changes in the gross employment rates for 2008, 2009, and 2010 for the eight countries in our sample.[18]

The stylized picture of labor adjustment is that Latin American countries that endured a decline in gross employment rates did so mostly through youth and prime-age male employment, which was partly compensated for by a rise in prime-age female employment. Three main messages emerge from this figure. First, in every case in which the gross employment rate declined from 2008 to 2012, this decline was mostly due to a fall in employment among the youth. The exceptions were Chile and Mexico in 2009, where there was also a decline among prime-age males. In 2008 Peru saw a decline in gross employment rates because of both youth and prime-age females.

Understanding the Poverty Impact of the Global Financial Crisis in Latin America and the Caribbean
http://dx.doi.org/10.1596/978-1-4648-0241-6

Figure 4.4 Decomposition of Changes in Gross Employment Rates: Latin America, 2008–10

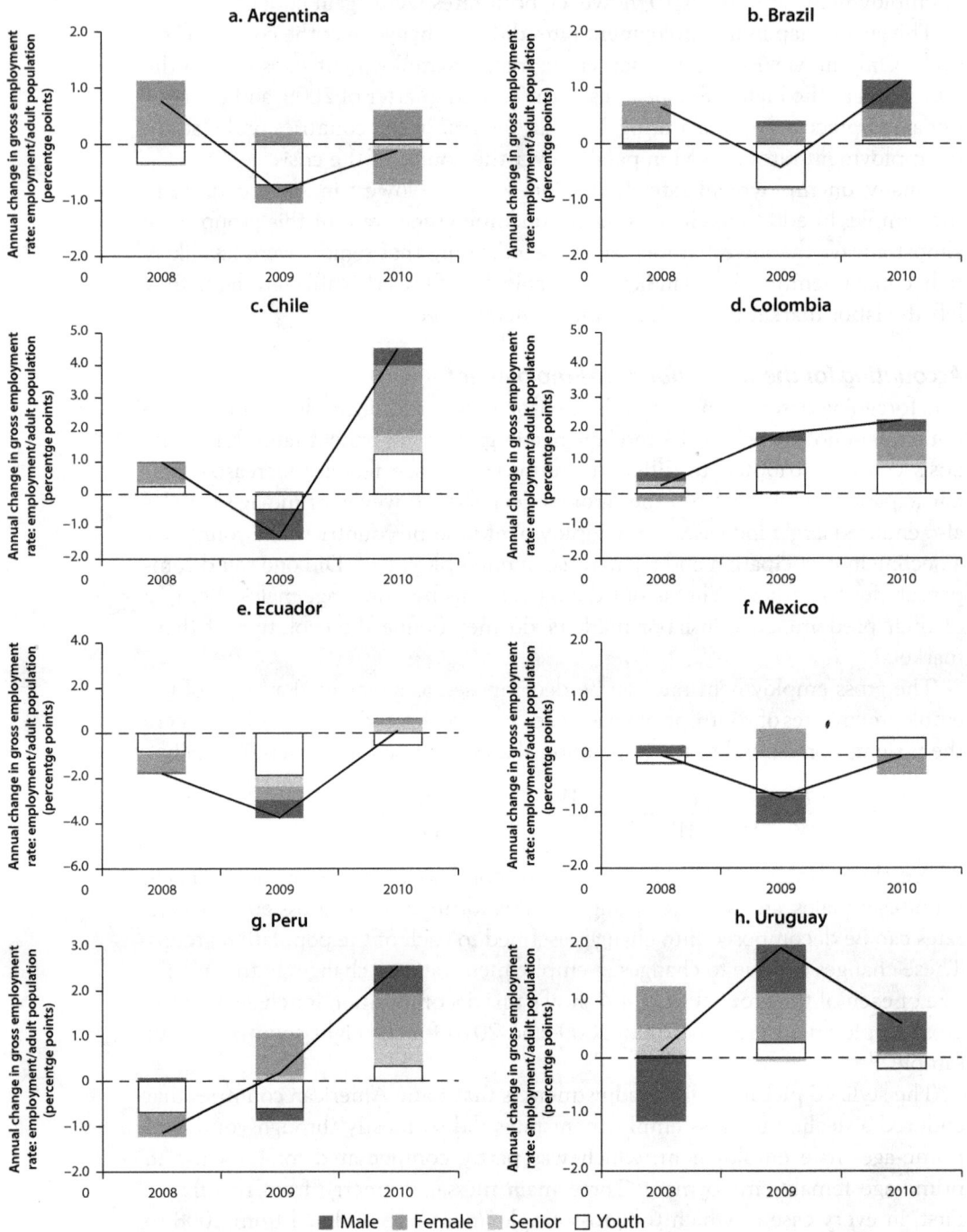

Source: LABLAC (CEDLAS and World Bank).
Note: Graphs depict decomposition of gross employment rates by population group for the third quarter of each year (except for Argentina where it corresponds to the fourth quarter).

Second, these declines in the gross employment rates were partly compensated for in Argentina, Brazil, and Mexico by an increase in employment rates among prime-age women. In Peru, prime-age females fully compensated for the declines in youth and prime-age male employment, and so 2009 was a year with no decline in growth employment rates. Chile is again an exception because prime-age women underwent no change in employment in 2009. In Ecuador, female employment reinforced the employment decline among males and youth.

Third, countries that had positive growth in 2009 (Colombia and Uruguay) had no decline in employment for any group. To the contrary, employment rates grew for youth and prime-age males and females.

These findings seem to indicate that in most countries of the region families protected themselves against the loss of employment among men and the young by the higher labor participation of women. Interestingly, the country with the most extensive and mature unemployment insurance system in the region, Chile, is the only one that saw no increase in female employment during the crisis.[19]

In any case, no country in the sample had a large decline in gross employment rates one year after the onset of the crisis (2010). Among those that endured a decline in 2009, the gross employment rate fell less than, or around 1 percentage point. Colombia and Uruguay saw their rates grow in 2009, and the deceleration in 2008—perhaps due to an early response to the crisis—was also below the 1 percentage point mark.

Not Much Change in Unemployment: The Usual Small Crisis?

Recessions produce two possible outcomes for family members. On the one hand, because of the decline of economic activity, an individual tends to lose his or her job and enter the ranks of the unemployed or even stop searching for a job and leave the labor market. On the other hand, employment losses reduce the family income, which prompts other family members to look for sources of income. These two forces move in opposite directions, and thus there is no a priori answer to which effect will predominate during a crisis. This chapter has presented evidence that in Latin America the second force partly compensated for the first. Participation rates, particularly among females, mostly explain changes in gross employment during the recent crisis in the region. This, however, is in part due to the rather limited effect of the crisis on unemployment.

The link between unemployment and short-term growth in Latin America is usually at the lower end of the range observed in developed countries—that is, Latin American countries are not usually characterized by large changes in unemployment in response to changes in GDP growth. Linear projections of unemployment rates on GDP growth, using annual data, find coefficients of unemployment change to GDP change that range from −0.16 for Ecuador to −0.37 for Colombia. Thus a decline in GDP growth of 1 percent would forecast an average rise of 0.16–0.37 percentage point in unemployment (see figure 4.5).

This connection between short-term economic growth and changes in unemployment is usually known as Okun's Law (see box 4.1).

Understanding the Poverty Impact of the Global Financial Crisis in Latin America and the Caribbean
http://dx.doi.org/10.1596/978-1-4648-0241-6

Figure 4.5 Unemployment and GDP over a 20-Year Period: Latin America

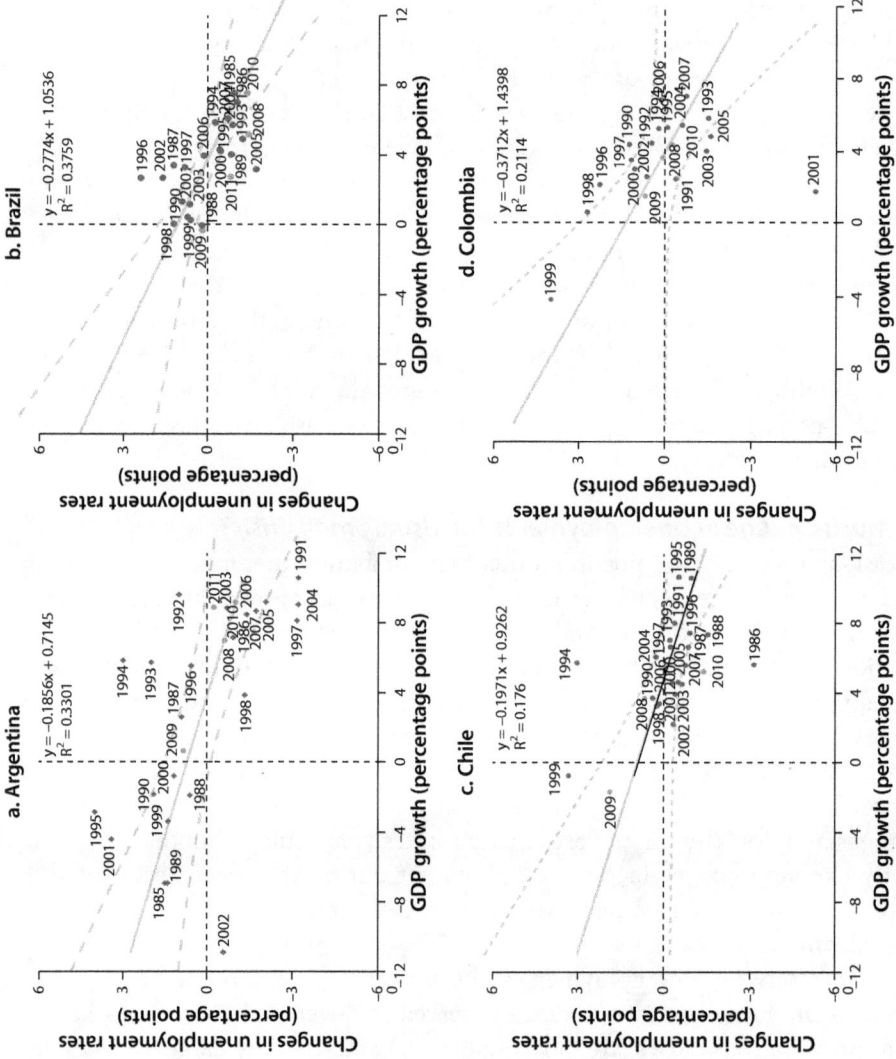

a. Argentina

$y = -0.1856x + 0.7145$
$R^2 = 0.3301$

Changes in unemployment rates (percentage points)

GDP growth (percentage points)

2001 1995
1990
1999 2000
1985 1989
2000 2009 1987
1988
1998
1994
1993
1996
1992
2011 2003
2010
2008 2006
2007
2005
1997 1991
2004
2002

b. Brazil

$y = -0.2774x + 1.0536$
$R^2 = 0.3759$

Changes in unemployment rates (percentage points)

GDP growth (percentage points)

1996
2002
1990 1987
2001 1997
1998 2000 2006
1999 2003
2002 1988
1994
1995
1989 1993 1986
2011 2004 2007
2005 2008 2010

c. Chile

$y = -0.1971x + 0.9262$
$R^2 = 0.176$

Changes in unemployment rates (percentage points)

GDP growth (percentage points)

1999
2009
1994
2008 1990 2004
1998 1997
2002 2005 2006 1993 1991 1995
2003 2000 1992 1996 1989
2001 1987 1990
2010 1988
1986

d. Colombia

$y = -0.3712x + 1.4398$
$R^2 = 0.2114$

Changes in unemployment rates (percentage points)

GDP growth (percentage points)

1999
1998 1996
1997 1990
2000 1992
2002 2006
2009 1994 1995
2008 2004 2007
1991 2010 1993
2003 2005
2001

figure continues next page

figure continues next page

134

Figure 4.5 Unemployment and GDP over a 20-Year Period: Latin America *(continued)*

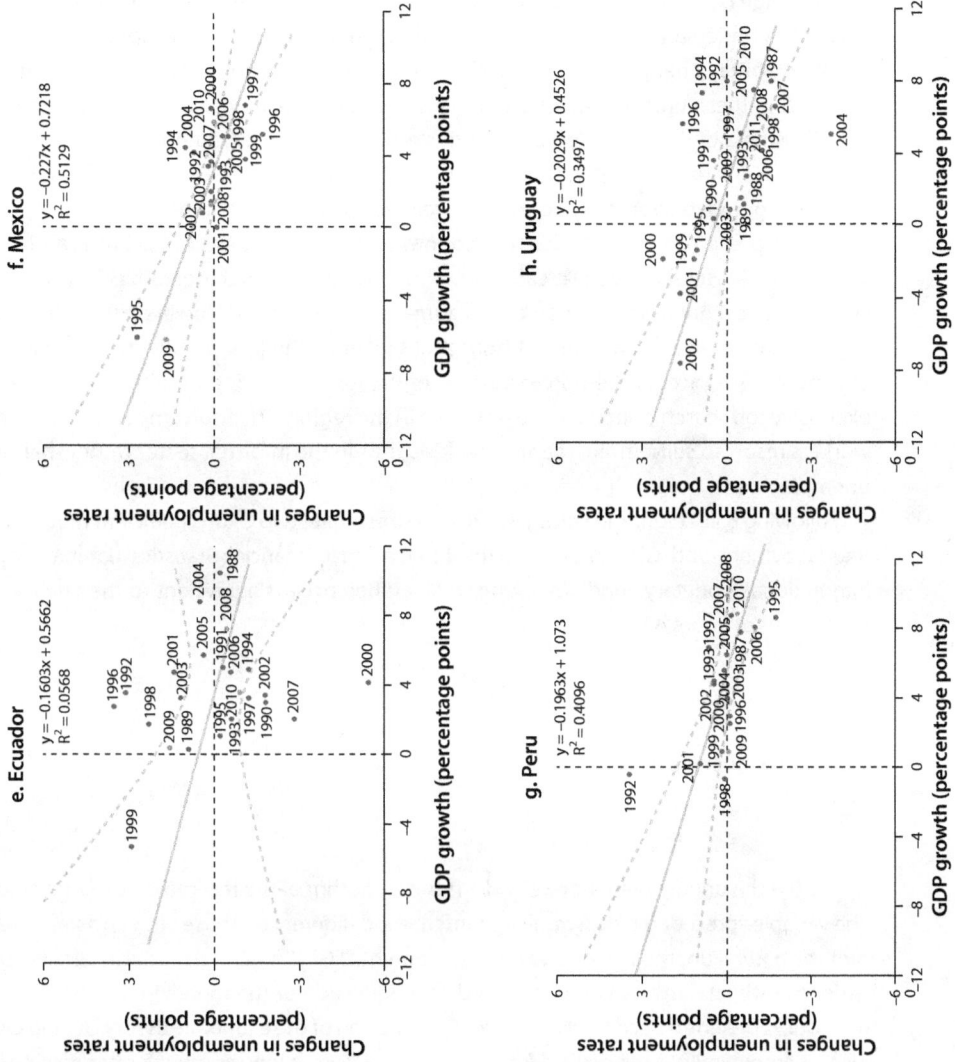

e. Ecuador

$y = -0.1603x + 0.5662$
$R^2 = 0.0568$

(scatter plot: Changes in unemployment rates (percentage points) on y-axis, from −6 to 6; GDP growth (percentage points) on x-axis, from −12 to 12)

Data points labeled: 1996, 1992, 1998, 2009, 2003, 2001, 2005, 2004, 1989, 1991, 2008, 1988, 1995, 1993, 2010, 2006, 1997, 1994, 1990, 2002, 2007, 2000, 1999

GDP growth (percentage points)

f. Mexico

$y = -0.227x + 0.7218$
$R^2 = 0.5129$

(scatter plot: Changes in unemployment rates (percentage points) on y-axis, from −3 to 6; GDP growth (percentage points) on x-axis, from −12 to 12)

Data points labeled: 1994, 2004, 2010, 2002, 2003, 1992, 2007, 2000, 2001, 2008, 1993, 2005, 1998, 2006, 1999, 1997, 1996, 1995, 2009

GDP growth (percentage points)

g. Peru

$y = -0.1963x + 1.073$
$R^2 = 0.4096$

(scatter plot: Changes in unemployment rates (percentage points) on y-axis, from −6 to 6; GDP growth (percentage points) on x-axis, from −12 to 12)

Data points labeled: 2002, 1993, 1997, 2001, 1999, 2000, 2004, 2005, 2007, 2008, 1998, 2009, 1996, 2003, 1987, 2010, 2006, 1995, 1992

GDP growth (percentage points)

h. Uruguay

$y = -0.2029x + 0.4526$
$R^2 = 0.3497$

(scatter plot: Changes in unemployment rates (percentage points) on y-axis, from −3 to 6; GDP growth (percentage points) on x-axis, from −12 to 12)

Data points labeled: 1994, 1996, 1991, 1992, 2005, 2010, 1990, 2009, 1997, 1987, 2000, 1995, 1993, 2011, 2008, 1998, 2007, 1999, 1989, 1988, 2006, 2001, 2002, 2004

GDP growth (percentage points)

Sources: International Monetary Fund, International Financial Statistics (database), various years, and ILO 2013.

Note: The y-axis measures changes in annual unemployment rates in percentage points. The x-axis measures annual GDP growth.

135

Box 4.1 Okun's Law

Okun's Law refers to an empirical relationship between changes in unemployment and output. Used in macroeconomic modeling since its introduction by Okun (1962), the term is usually interpreted as the main link between growth and employment in the short term. For the U.S. economy, Okun found that an approximate increase (decrease) in output of 3 percentage points induced a decrease (increase) in unemployment of 1 percentage point. This link is understood as an empirical regularity that captures both supply and demand effects that may change over time and differ from one country to another. In addition to scrutinizing these time and place differences, a large literature has been developed to test the robustness of this relationship to various econometric specifications.

The reasons for the dispersion in Okun coefficients across countries are the subject of an ongoing debate. Some argue that it is related to labor market institutions and regulations that prevent dismissals during economic downturns—see IMF (2010b) and Cazes, Verick, and Al Hussami (2011). Latin American countries are characterized by restrictive labor market regulations, and so this argument could apply.[20] However, it could also be argued that relatively low levels of household income, the lack of fully developed unemployment insurance, and enforcement of regulations make open unemployment a very expensive job search option for most people in the region. Therefore, most Latin American workers resort to self-employment or salaried jobs in the informal sector rather than open unemployment.

Following Ball, Leigh, and Loungani (2012), we estimate two Okun coefficient models using unemployment and GDP data from the International Financial Statistics database of the International Monetary Fund (IMF). One, in first differences, is equivalent to the one used for illustrations of figure 4.5:

$$\Delta U_t = \alpha + \beta \Delta Y_t + \in_t.$$

And the other is in levels:

$$U_t - U_t^* = \beta(Y_t - Y_t^*) + \in_t$$

where U is the unemployment rate and Y is the logarithm of the real gross domestic product. The variables preceded by a Δ represent interperiod differences; those with an asterisk represent the natural unemployment rate and the potential GDP level. The model in "differences" is easier to estimate and can be interpreted as a derivation of the model in "levels." The latter, however, is preferred because it is a better specification of the economic theory behind Okun's idea: unemployment rates deviate from their natural level as long as growth rates deviate from their potential.

The model in "levels" requires estimates of the natural unemployment rates and potential GDP growth trends, which are approximated here using the Hodrik-Pescott smoothing procedure (see table B4.1.1). Estimates of these models using quarterly data for six countries in the sample are also shown in table B4.1.2.

box continues next page

Box 4.1 Okun's Law (continued)

Table B4.1.1 Estimates of Okun's Coefficient Using Annual Data

	Equation in first differences			Equation in levels (HP filter 100)			Equation in levels (HP filter 1,000)		
		Adjusted R²	Obs.		Adjusted R²	Obs.		Adjusted R²	Obs.
Argentina	−0.1891***			−0.1254**			−0.1425***		
	(0.0578)	0.288	25	(0.0479)	0.190	25	(0.0486)	0.233	25
Brazil	−0.2944***			−0.1118**			−0.1303**		
	(0.0780)	0.376	23	(0.0516)	0.170	18	(0.0559)	0.198	18
Chile	−0.2437***			−0.0656			−0.0790*		
	(0.0845)	0.234	25	(0.0396)	0.065	25	(0.0419)	0.093	25
Colombia	−0.4050**			−0.1027			−0.1434*		
	(0.1486)	0.211	25	(0.0780)	0.028	25	(0.0822)	0.076	25
Ecuador	−0.1825			−0.0760			−0.0869		
	(0.1396)	0.031	23	(0.0903)	0.013	23	(0.0908)	0.037	23
Mexico	−0.2019***			−0.1183**			−0.1195**		
	(0.0429)	0.540	19	(0.0410)	0.278	19	(0.0431)	0.260	19
Peru	−0.1698***			−0.0443			−0.0493		
	(0.0543)	0.316	20	(0.0381)	0.018	19	(0.0385)	0.032	19
Uruguay	−0.2145***			−0.1226***			−0.1628***		
	(0.0541)	0.380	25	(0.0393)	0.258	25	(0.0422)	0.357	25

Sources: LABLAC (CEDLAS and World Bank) and International Monetary Fund, International Financial Statistics (database), various years; real GDP for Argentina: INDEC.
Note: HP = Hodrik-Pescott.
Significance level: * = 10 percent, ** = 5 percent, *** = 1 percent.

Table B4.1.2 Estimates of Okun's Coefficient Using Quarterly Data

	Equation in first differences			Equation in levels (HP filter 1,600)			Equation in levels (HP filter 1,000)		
		Adjusted R²	Obs.		Adjusted R²	Obs.		Adjusted R²	Obs.
Brazil	−0.0429*			−0.0426			−0.0423		
	(0.0220)	0.061	44	(0.0303)	0.024	40	(0.0305)	0.029	40
Chile	−0.1202***			−0.1090***			−0.1100***		
	(0.0276)	0.183	81	(0.0261)	0.169	81	(0.0262)	0.170	81
Colombia	−0.4660			−0.2997			−0.2986		
	(0.3309)	0.015	68	(0.2691)	0.003	68	(0.2702)	0.003	68
Mexico	−0.0770***			−0.0770***			−0.0765***		
	(0.0173)	0.290	47	(0.0173)	0.292	47	(0.0170)	0.291	47
Peru	−0.0884***			−0.0841***			−0.0843***		
	(0.0179)	0.422	33	(0.0172)	0.409	33	(0.0172)	0.410	33
Uruguay	−0.0741***			−0.0667***			−0.0670***		
	(0.0160)	0.463	27	(0.0156)	0.392	27	(0.0156)	0.392	27

Sources: LABLAC (CEDLAS and World Bank) and International Monetary Fund, International Financial Statistics (database), various years; real GDP for Argentina: INDEC.
Note: HP = Hodrik-Pescott.
Significance level: * = 10 percent, ** = 5 percent, *** = 1 percent.

box continues next page

Box 4.1 Okun's Law *(continued)*

Equations in differences show some cross-country differences. Using both yearly and quarterly data, Colombia has the highest coefficient (although it loses statistical signifi-cance because of insufficient quarterly data).[21] Chile is below Colombia but among the higher coefficients in both types of data. The other countries change ranks depending on the data used.

For both yearly and quarterly data, estimates from equations in levels are smaller than those in differences because the latter estimates report changes in unemployment due to actual changes in GDP, whereas the former report changes in GDP above or below a long-term trend of GDP growth.

Moreover, when using the equation in levels, the range of Okun's coefficient narrows to the point that there seems to be no substantive difference across the countries. These results enhance the main finding from models in differences, which is that Latin American countries have very low Okun coefficients: approximately a 0.15 percentage point increase in unemployment for a 1 percent decline in GDP growth with respect to the long-term trend in potential GDP growth.

Results using quarterly data and more sophisticated techniques reveal that Okun's coefficients are very similar across several countries in the region, approx-imating a 0.15 increase in unemployment for a 1 percent decline in GDP growth. In all cases, the estimates are at the lower end of the range for developed coun-tries. Recent estimates of Okun's coefficients for developed countries range from about −0.10 in countries such as Japan and Austria, to −0.45 in Canada, the United States, and the United Kingdom, to −0.80 in Spain.[22]

Interestingly, the growth-unemployment link observed in Latin America dur-ing the crisis does not seem to be very different from those of previous years. In Argentina, Colombia, and Uruguay, the observed changes in unemployment for 2008, 2009, and 2010 are almost on a simple regression line (see figure 4.5)—that is, an analyst could have almost perfectly forecasted changes in unemploy-ment given the observed changes in GDP and the experience accumulated in previous years.[23] For Chile, Ecuador, and Mexico, the 2009 increase in unem-ployment is not exactly on the regression line, but still falls within the confi-dence intervals of the projection: slightly higher than the expected value in Chile and Ecuador and slightly lower in Mexico. In other words, the 2008–09 global financial crisis was not special in the sense that observed changes in unemployment were not different from what statistical regression analysis would have forecasted for these six countries. A few outliers can be spotted, however. In Brazil, changes in unemployment were lower than expected between 2008 and 2011, and so Brazil performed better than usual during this recession. In Peru, the unchanged unemployment rate in 2009 was unexpected, and unemployment declines in 2010 were within confidence margins.

Figure 4.5 also shows that in 2009 the crisis led to a large decline in output (as measured by real GDP growth), but only in Chile and Mexico. All the other countries in the sample experienced a deceleration in output growth in 2009 that was not as bad as in other years. In Brazil, Colombia, Ecuador, and Peru, output growth was among the smallest in the 20-year period considered, but no large recession was involved. Finally, Argentina and Uruguay faced output growth of only 0.7 percent and 2.4 percent, respectively, in 2009, which was much lower than the 7 percent growth both countries observed in 2008. However, those results are not as bad as those encountered in the recessions in the mid-1990s or the early 2000s when output declined more than 4 percent in some years.

In summary, for the Latin American countries under study, the 2008–09 global financial crisis did not have an unusual impact on unemployment, first, because the crisis was not as severe as at other times in some countries (Argentina, Peru, and Uruguay) and, second, because the rise in unemployment was not larger than expected in those countries with a large shock (Chile and Mexico) or with a moderate deceleration (Colombia and Peru). The most interesting case, however, is Brazil. In 2009 it endured one of the largest growth decelerations in its recent history, but its unemployment growth was minimal.[24]

The combination of limited unemployment changes and compensatory female labor force participation led to limited changes in total gross employment rates during the 2009 recession. This limited employment change, as implied in equation (4.1), may lead to larger changes in productivity and wages during recessions. However, it has been documented that the region has also experienced, because of macro policies leading to lower inflation, less wage volatility and particularly downward rigidity of wages.[25] What happened to productivity and wages during 2009?

What Happened to Earnings?

For any given change in output, the smaller the changes in gross employment, the larger will be the changes in labor productivity and vice versa. Changes in gross employment rates indicate only the "employment" side of the impact of the crisis. The "productivity" side is the difference between changes in GDP per capita and changes in gross employment—see equation (4.1).

GDP per capita is an indicator of living standards, whereas GDP per worker is a measure of labor productivity. The difference between the two is, precisely, the gross employment rate, discussed extensively in previous sections.[26] In countries in which the gross employment rate increased during the crisis, changes in GDP per capita were larger than changes in GDP per worker. In other words, the less labor productivity was affected by the crisis, the more employment took the brunt of the adjustment, and vice versa. The distance between the red and orange lines in figure 4.6 shows that in Argentina, Brazil, and Mexico GDP per capita and GDP per worker have moved very closely together over the period under study. Thus labor productivity carried almost all the burden of the adjustment (the blue and orange lines are almost

Figure 4.6 Quarterly Trends in GDP Per Capita, GDP per Worker, and Average Earnings: Latin America

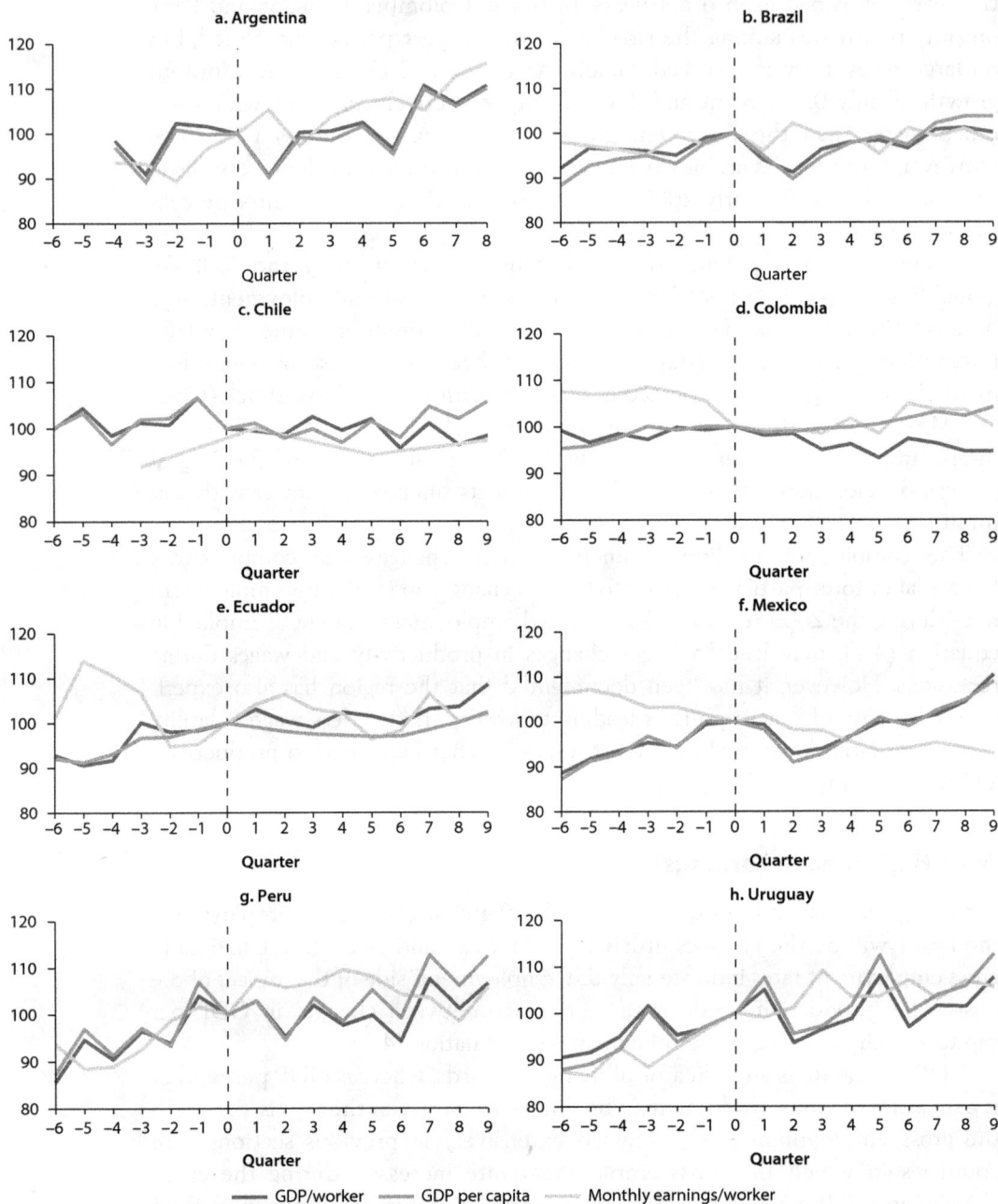

a. Argentina

b. Brazil

c. Chile

d. Colombia

e. Ecuador

f. Mexico

g. Peru

h. Uruguay

GDP/worker ——— GDP per capita ——— Monthly earnings/worker

Source: LABLAC (CEDLAS and World Bank).

Note: The x-axis refers to quarters after or before the quarter of reference (second quarter of 2008). On the y-axis, the index equals 100 at the third quarter of 2008 (except for Argentina where it corresponds to the fourth quarter of 2008). Chile's earnings data correspond to fourth quarter only of 2007, 2008, 2009, and 2010. All variables are defined in real terms using the implicit GDP deflator.

identical). In the rest of the countries, part of the adjustment was undertaken through changes in employment (the gap between the blue and orange lines widens).

In all the countries under study, GDP per capita declined from the first quarter of 2009. This decline was very abrupt in Argentina, Brazil, and Mexico and less so in other countries. The decline lasted one or two quarters in Argentina, Peru, and Uruguay and longer in Brazil, Ecuador, and Mexico, where precrisis GDP per capita levels were not reached until seven or eight quarters after the onset of the crisis. The orange line in figure 4.6 shows this evolution of GDP per capita for the selected countries.

Changes in labor productivity, as measured by GDP per worker, are of special interest because labor earnings and wages are expected to closely follow changes in labor productivity. In the long term, wages are expected to evolve with labor productivity. However, in the short term there can be discrepancies because of market imperfections but also because of problems with data collection.

Evidence of the disconnect between GDP per worker and earnings per worker, or between macro and survey data is apparent in figure 4.6. During the recent crisis, the evolution of average earnings as reported from labor surveys did not necessarily follow changes in labor productivity.[27] In Argentina, Brazil, Ecuador, Peru, and Uruguay, average real earnings as reported in surveys increased despite declines in output per capita or in labor productivity during the initial quarters of the crisis. On the other hand, real earnings in Mexico declined despite the recovery of labor productivity as of the fifth quarter after the onset of the crisis. Finally, reported earnings in Colombia followed a trend similar to that of labor productivity; they declined during the initial quarters of the crisis and increased afterward. Data for Chile are incomplete, but they seem to indicate first a decline and then a rise in real earnings that goes in the same direction as the decline in GDP per worker.[28]

The disconnect may stem from misreporting, or the fact that surveys capture only labor income, whereas macroeconomic GDP figures capture all income. Misreporting of labor income can play a role in the differences. Especially when there are high rates of informality and unemployment and people do a lot of short-term work, it can be difficult to track exact wages over a long period of time. It is difficult to identify the causes of this disconnect without further inquiry into the methods used for national accounts and labor surveys in each country.[29] In any case, we report these trends to highlight the need to recognize different trends in earnings and labor productivity during the recent crisis.

The difference in trends between GDP per worker from national accounts and average labor earnings from household labor surveys could arise from either misreporting in surveys or changing factorial distribution. These components can be represented as

$$(Y/E) = (Y/C) \ (C/R) \ (R/E) \qquad (4.2)$$

Understanding the Poverty Impact of the Global Financial Crisis in Latin America and the Caribbean
http://dx.doi.org/10.1596/978-1-4648-0241-6

where Y and E have the same meaning as in equation (4.1), C is total workers' compensation, and R is survey-reported labor earnings.[30] The first term represents the factorial distribution of income: the inverse of the share of labor within total output. The third term represents the average wage reported in surveys. The second term then represents mismatches between the *System of National Accounts* and labor surveys because of misreporting or methodological differences.[31]

The ratio of GDP to workers' compensation can be analyzed using data on factorial distribution of income available from the *System of National Accounts*,[32] particularly from what is known as the income approach to total output—that is, any production activity that generates an income that is shared between factors of production. The ratio of workers' compensation to GDP is a measure of the distribution of income into labor and other factors of production. Workers' compensation in national accounts is defined as "total remuneration, in cash or in kind, payable by an enterprise to an employee for work done by the latter during the accounting period" (United Nations et al. 2009, 131). This definition disregards the remuneration earned by the self-employed or those who work in a family firm where an employer-employee relationship is not formal. We can then add to workers' compensation the national accounts concept of "mixed income" as a measure of the earnings of these other workers. It is not pure labor income because it may contain a combination of labor earnings and capital rents, or, as stated in the definition, "it implicitly contains an element of remuneration for work done by the owner, or other members of the household, that cannot be separately identified from the return to the owner as entrepreneur" (United Nations et al. 2009, 132).

From the United Nations Statistics Division, we collected data on the components of GDP based on the income approach. These data allow us to analyze how different income components changed over the crisis and what happened to the share of labor during this period. Unfortunately, data from the income approach to GDP are produced with a lag, and so we show results for only a subset of four countries.

For every country with available data, the share of labor income within GDP increased in 2009 because workers' compensation was the least-affected income component of GDP during the 2009 recession. Assuming that workers' compensation and mixed incomes, as defined in the *System of National Accounts*, accrued to all workers, the share of workers increased by 0.6 percentage point in Chile, Colombia, and Mexico and 1.1 percentage points in Brazil. If only the share of workers' compensation within GDP is considered, the increase is even higher: 1.1 percentage points in Chile, 1.2 percentage points in Colombia and Mexico, and 1.8 percentage points in Brazil (see table 4.6).

This rise in the share of labor within total GDP in 2009 was the consequence of workers' compensation being less affected by the crisis than other income. Figure 4.7 shows the decomposition of changes in GDP by income components of output according to national accounts. In figure 4.7, the blue bar represents

Table 4.6 Evolution of Workers' Share in GDP over the Crisis: Brazil, Chile, Colombia, and Mexico, 2007–10

Percent

Country	Workers' compensation as share of GDP				Labor income as share of GDP			
	2007	*2008*	*2009*	*2010*	*2007*	*2008*	*2009*	*2010*
Brazil	41.3	41.8	43.6	—	50.4	50.6	51.7	—
Chile	35.2	39.4	40.6	—	41.2	45.2	45.8	—
Colombia	32.0	31.7	32.8	32.8	56.1	55.1	55.7	55.3
Mexico	28.1	28.1	29.2	28.2	48.1	48.7	49.3	48.7

Source: United Nations Statistics Division, National Accounts Data.

Note: Based on notation from the *System of National Accounts*, $b.1 = d.1 + b.2 + g.3 + d.2 - d.3$ where $b.1$ is GDP, $d.1$ is workers' compensation, $g.2$ is gross operating surplus, $g.3$ is gross mixed income, and $d2 - d3$ is net taxes on production. Thus workers' compensation as a share of GDP is $\dfrac{d.1}{b.1}$ and labor income as a share of GDP is $\dfrac{d.1}{b.1} + \dfrac{b.3}{b.1}$; — = not available.

Figure 4.7 Decomposition of GDP Changes, by Income Components: Brazil, Chile, Colombia, and Mexico

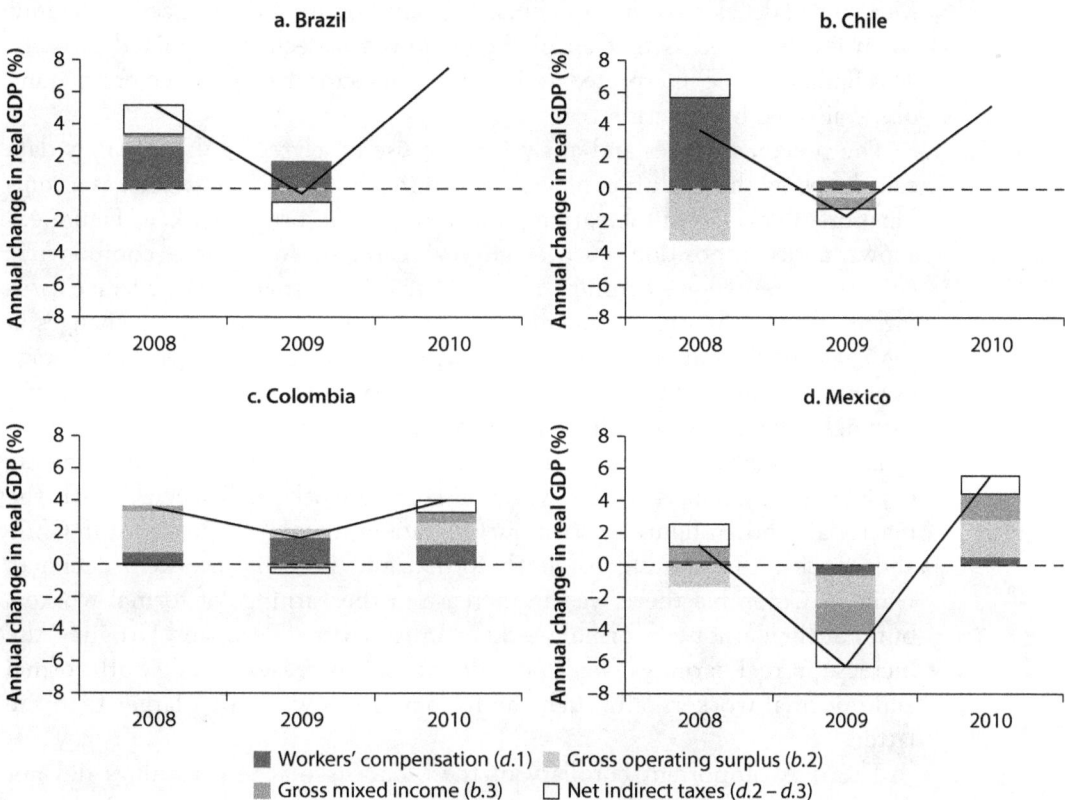

a. Brazil

b. Chile

c. Colombia

d. Mexico

■ Workers' compensation (*d.*1)   ▨ Gross operating surplus (*b.*2)
▨ Gross mixed income (*b.*3)   □ Net indirect taxes (*d.*2 – *d.*3)

Source: United Nations Statistical Division.

Note: Bars are missing for Brazil and Chile because data for total GDP change are available but not its components for these two countries. In this decomposition, if $b.1 = d.1 + b.2 + g.3 + d.2 - d.3$ where $b.1$ is GDP, $d.1$ is workers' compensation, $b.2$ is gross operating surplus, $b.3$ is gross mixed income, and $d.2 - d.3$ is net taxes on production, then the percentage change in GDP can be decomposed as

$$\frac{\Delta b.1}{b.1} = \frac{\Delta d.1}{b.1} + \frac{\Delta b.2}{b.1} + \frac{\Delta b.3}{b.1} + \frac{\Delta(d.2 - d.3)}{b.1}.$$

Understanding the Poverty Impact of the Global Financial Crisis in Latin America and the Caribbean
http://dx.doi.org/10.1596/978-1-4648-0241-6

output changes accruing to changes in workers' compensation, the orange bar represents changes in income from informal firms, the green bar represents changes in capital gains, and the white bar represents net indirect taxes.[33]

The decline in the share of capital in GDP implies that the recession, as measured by negative growth in GDP per worker, did not fully translate into a decline in average earnings. Given the decomposition shown in equation 4.2, the larger is a decline in the share of capital, the lower is the decline in average earnings for a given drop in GDP per worker.[34] In any case, the changes in the functional distribution of income reported in table 4.6 are relatively small, so that if the ratio of macro to survey data does not change, changes in GDP per worker must translate into changes in survey-reported earnings.

From 2007 to 2010 (figure 4.7), workers' compensation declined in absolute terms only in Mexico; it decelerated in Brazil and Chile and even increased in Colombia. On the other hand, gross operating surplus (i.e., the contribution of capital from incorporated firms to value added) declined in Brazil, Chile, and Mexico and decelerated in Colombia. The only common pattern across the four countries described is that all of them showed a decline in "mixed income." This finding can be interpreted as the "informal sector" being the sector unequivocally affected by the crisis.

The previous figures and analysis make use of aggregate data. Survey data can also show the evolution of average earnings and can be described as a combination of changes in the earnings of formal and informal workers. Figure 4.8 shows a decomposition of average real earnings into three components: changes in the average earnings of formal workers, changes in the average earnings of informal workers, and the interaction terms accounting for changes in the share of formal employment.[35] This decomposition reveals that average earnings increase with an increase in formal earnings, an increase in informal earnings, or an increase in the size of the formal sector.[36]

In all countries in the sample, changes in real earnings are mostly explained by changes in the wages of formal workers. In accord with the macrodata shown figure 4.7, the survey data in figure 4.8 show that in Chile and Mexico the earnings of both formal and informal workers declined, while in Colombia there was an increase in the earnings of formal workers but a decline among informal workers. In Argentina, Peru, and Uruguay, the increase in real earnings was a combination of increases among both formal and informal workers, although the former group was much larger than the latter.

The most important corollary of these data is that real earnings did not decline in 2009 largely because of an increase in informality or a decline in informal earnings. Falling or stagnant informal earnings exacerbated the declines in average earnings in Brazil, Colombia, Chile, and Mexico, but that does not explain the totality of the declines in earnings in these countries where formal workers also experienced declines in real earnings or no growth at all, such as in Brazil.

Figure 4.8 Decomposition of Average Earnings, by Formal and Informal Earnings: Latin America, 2008–10

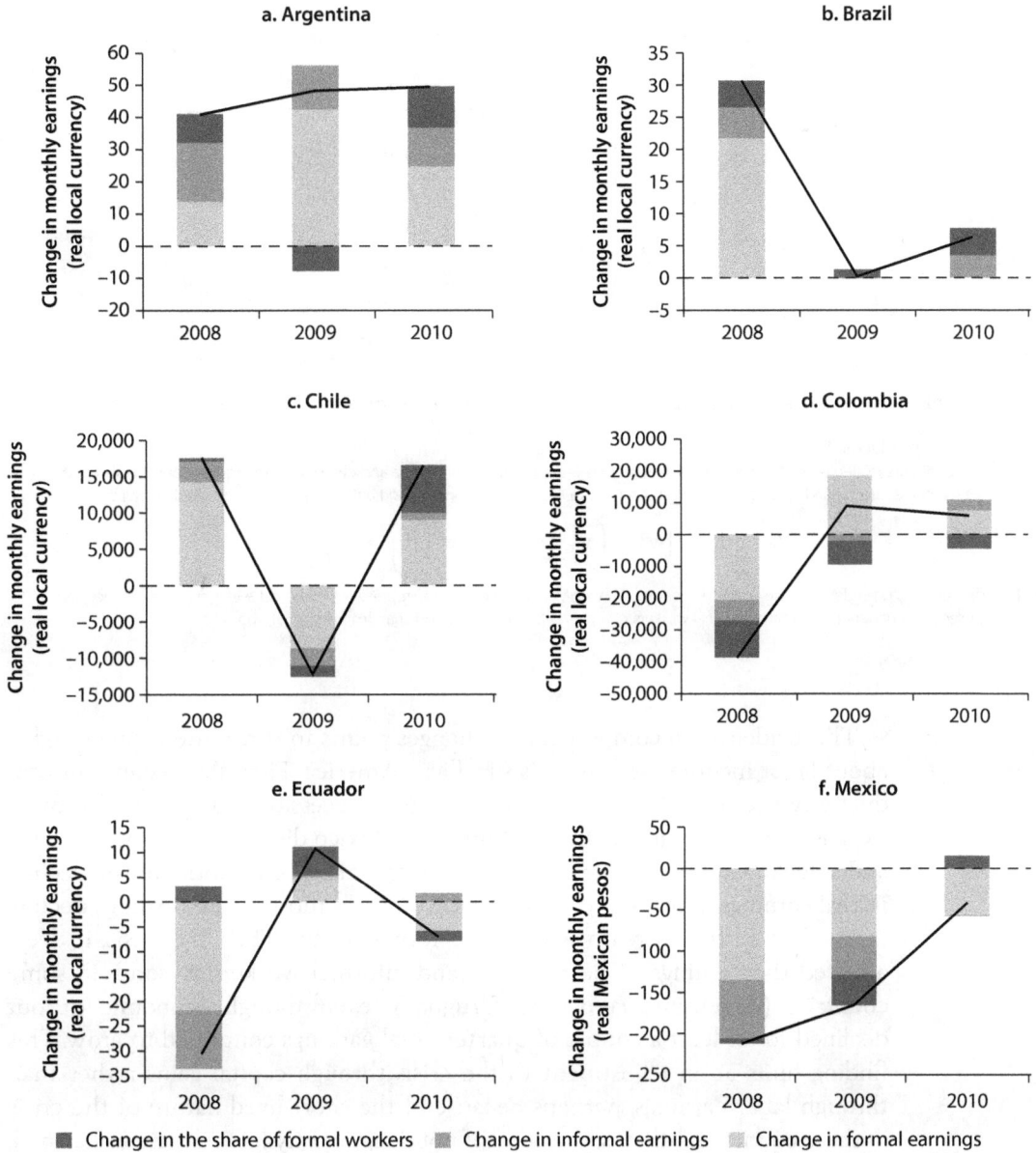

a. Argentina

b. Brazil

c. Chile

d. Colombia

e. Ecuador

f. Mexico

■ Change in the share of formal workers ▨ Change in informal earnings ▨ Change in formal earnings

figure continues next page

Understanding the Poverty Impact of the Global Financial Crisis in Latin America and the Caribbean
http://dx.doi.org/10.1596/978-1-4648-0241-6

Figure 4.8 Decomposition of Average Earnings by Formal and Informal Earnings: Latin America, 2008–10
(continued)

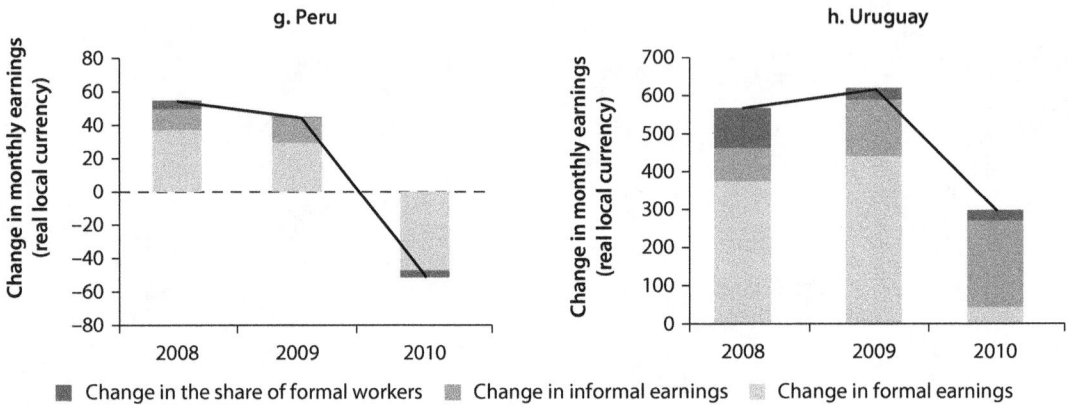

g. Peru

h. Uruguay

■ Change in the share of formal workers   ■ Change in informal earnings   ▦ Change in formal earnings

Source: LABLAC (CEDLAS and World Bank).
Note: All changes are related to the third quarter of the previous years (except for Argentina and Chile where they correspond to the fourth quarter). All variables are defined in real terms using the implicit GDP deflator. The interperiod difference in wages can be defined as

$$[W]_{t=1} - [W]_{t=0} = \left(\Delta\frac{E_f}{E}\right)\left(\overline{W}_f - \overline{W}_i\right) + \Delta W_f\left(\frac{\overline{E}_f}{E}\right) + \Delta W_i\left(\frac{\overline{E}_i}{E}\right)$$

where the variables preceded by Δ are time changes and the variables with a bar on top represent two-period averages. The difference can be decomposed into changes in the share of formal workers, changes in formal wages, and changes in informal wages.

This evidence on components of changes points to three interesting insights about labor incomes and the crisis in Latin America. First, the declines in productivity and in real earnings during the 2009 recession did not arise from an expansion of informality. Only in Chile and Mexico did a larger informal sector and a decline in the average earnings of these workers contribute to the decline in real earnings. However, even in these countries most of the earnings decline accrued to a drop in real wages in the formal sector. Thus, the crisis, if deep, affected the earnings of both formal and informal workers. Second, in some countries (Argentina, Peru, and Uruguay), even though economic output declined for at least a couple of quarters, real earnings continued to grow. This finding hints at an adjustment to the crisis through capital gains rather than through labor earnings, perhaps because of the short-lived nature of the crisis in these countries—that is, the crisis, if not deep, mostly left workers unharmed. Third, because of the higher average wages in the formal sector and its large share of total employment (at least in the countries in our sample), changes in real earnings are mostly explained by changes in formal wages and the formal employment share. Informal wages are seldom the largest component of income growth. Large income gains are related to large formal wage gains, which explains the search for formalization in many countries in the region (see box 4.2).

Box 4.2 The Search for Formalization

One of the interesting features of the 2009 recession is that in the Latin America region the informal sector did not increase countercyclically as it often did during previous recessions. No regular cross-country pattern was observed in changes in informality rates during the 2009 recession. Some countries experienced an increase in informality (Argentina, Chile, Colombia, and Mexico), while others saw a decline (Brazil, Ecuador, Peru, and Uruguay).

As usual for the eight countries in the sample, informality rates were higher during the recession among the youth, senior workers, women, and the low-skilled.[37] Moreover, in all the countries where the informal sector increased, it was the youth who saw a much faster increase in this type of jobs. Women increased their informality rates in Mexico and Argentina, but in Chile the men did so. In 2009 the share of informal employment declined slightly in Brazil, but this decline was slower than the drop in 2008 and its continuation in 2010. Therefore, Brazil also experienced an increase in the share of informal jobs (compared with what had been the usual decline). Again the youth, but also the elderly, endured the slower decline of informality rates in Brazil. Interestingly, between 2007 and 2010 informality rates declined in Uruguay and Peru, the countries least affected by the crisis, but those rates increased in 2009 in both countries among the youth.

The evidence in this chapter points to the importance of formal employment in explaining most of the changes in average wages. It is important to highlight that these results rely on a job position rather than a social protection definition of *informality*.[38] The data presented in this study do not make use of the definition of *informality* as workers not covered by social or legal protection. The World Bank's *World Development Report 2013: Jobs* discusses the trade-off between these two approaches (World Bank 2012a): informality as a job-position/low-productivity characteristic versus informality as a lack-of-social-protection problem. Middle-income countries such as those in our sample want to expand social protection for their workers, but also need to increase labor productivity so that social protection does not become a burden for job creation. A debate on the deregulation and flexibilization of markets has lingered for several decades, but no definite answer has emerged.[39] Some countries aim for universal social protection financed through general taxation, thereby formalizing all labor market "de jure." Others aim to enhance enforcement of regulations and promote the growth of small business as a mechanism for enhancing productivity, while others recommend a flexibilization of labor market regulations. The *World Development Report* recommends a three-pronged strategy for formalization that combines social assistance for those workers with very limited human capital accumulation, flexibilization of some regulations for small and medium-size firms with potential for becoming larger and more productive firms, and enforcement of regulations among already large firms (see World Bank 2012a, 210–13).

Understanding the Poverty Impact of the Global Financial Crisis in Latin America and the Caribbean
http://dx.doi.org/10.1596/978-1-4648-0241-6

Conclusion

This analysis of employment and earnings indicators for a selection of Latin American countries concludes with a series of stylized facts about the impact of the 2008–09 global financial crisis on labor markets in the region.

In 2009 most countries saw a small decline in their gross employment rate (i.e., employment as a share of the working-age population), and this decline is mostly explained by a reduction in employment among the youth, followed by a reduction in employment among prime-age males. This reduction in employment was partly but not totally compensated for by an increase in the employment of prime-age females. Increases in employment rates (Chile and Colombia) or a large decline (Ecuador) were also driven by changes in female participation rates.

The evolution of employment rates during the period under study is mostly explained by trends in participation rates rather than in unemployment rates. Not only did the participation rates of women rise, but also the region had a very low unemployment to growth relationship (i.e., Okun's Law coefficient). In this sense, the crisis did not have an unusual impact on unemployment in 2009, first, because for most countries the crisis was not as severe as earlier ones, and, second, because the increase in unemployment was not larger than expected. Two countries can be singled out, however. Mexico and Chile saw a very unusual decline in output and therefore experienced a significant increase in unemployment.

In many countries, changes in employment were relatively smaller than changes in output per worker. However, changes in labor productivity, as measured by GDP per worker, and average labor earnings do not necessarily parallel declines in GDP per capita in the short term. This explains the fact that in several countries real average earnings did not decline in 2009, even if the country had negative GDP per capita growth.

Countries with the larger declines in GDP—Mexico and Chile—were the ones with the larger declines in productivity and earnings. In these two countries, the crisis also brought on a decline in employment. Average earnings declined as well. Indeed, the recession was strong enough to drive a combination of a decline in formal wages and a decline in informal wages. In countries where GDP declines were smaller or short-lived, the adjustment to the crisis seems to have been based on a reduction in capital gains rather than through labor earnings, perhaps because of the short-lived nature of the crisis in these countries.

The short-term disconnect between GDP per capita, labor productivity, and average earnings can be explained in part by methodological differences between macroeconomic aggregates and survey data, but it also may be the consequence of the larger impact of the crisis on capital returns than on labor incomes. For a subset of four countries with available data, there is some evidence that this is the case. All countries showed a rise in the share of labor within total GDP in 2009 because workers' compensation was less affected by the crisis than other incomes. On the other hand, the gross operating surplus (i.e., the contribution of capital from incorporated firms to value added) declined or decelerated in all countries in the subsample. The only common pattern across the four countries described is that all of them saw a decline in "mixed income." This can be interpreted as confirming that the informal sector was the sector unequivocally affected by the crisis.

Survey data indicate that earnings among informal workers certainly declined among countries with large drops in income. Informal wages, however, were not the largest component of income growth or decline. On the contrary, because of the higher average wages among formal workers and their large share of total employment—at least in the countries in our sample—changes in real earnings are mostly explained by changes in formal wages.

Notes

1. These estimates correspond to a sample including all member countries of the Organisation for Economic Co-operation and Development (OECD) and 20 large developing countries.

2. These estimates include a sample of 22 high-income countries, 26 middle-income countries, and 16 lower-middle-income countries.

3. For an early study on the reaction of labor markets to the crisis in Latin America, see World Bank (2010).

4. This database is the result of collaboration between the Universidad Nacional de la Plata's Center for Distributive, Labor, and Social Studies (CEDLAS) and the World Bank's Poverty and Gender Unit for Latin America and the Caribbean (LCSPP). The LABLAC database can be found online at http://lablac.econo.unlp.edu.ar/eng/index.php. It includes quarterly information for Argentina (from 2003), Ecuador (from 2006), and Mexico (from 2005); monthly information for Brazil (from 2007), Colombia (from 2006), and Uruguay (from 2006); and moving quarter information for Chile (from 2007) and Peru (from 2007). The surveys for Argentina, Brazil, and Peru cover only urban areas.

5. This study utilizes data from every country in the LABLAC database except Paraguay because data for that country have only been available since 2010.

6. We use the third quarter (or the month of August) as the reference period because by the third quarter of 2008 the countries selected had still not experienced a decline in GDP growth, but by the same quarter of 2009 all countries had had at least one quarter of negative GDP growth. For Argentina, however, we use the fourth quarter because no survey was conducted during the third quarter of 2007.

7. The set of questions to define this job search in each country may vary, however, from one questionnaire to another.

8. For this and other definitions for LABLAC data sets, visit http://lablac.econo.unlp.edu.ar/eng/methodology.php.

9. Global and regional rates in this and following paragraphs are taken from the ILO's *Key Indicators of the Labour Market* (ILO 2013).

10. For international figures on informality, see Chen, Hussmanns, and Vanek (2012) and (ILO 2013, table 8).

11. This decomposition is based on the identity $Y/P = (Y/E)(E/W)(W/P)$. The first derivative of a logarithmic transformation of this identity is an approximation of an additive decomposition of percentage changes.

12. When hourly data are available, a further decomposition can separate productivity as value added per hour worked (Y/H) and average hours per worker (H/E). We do not have access to hourly data for all the countries in the sample. Therefore, our estimates of changes in productivity per worker hide a combination of changes in productivity and changes in hours per worker. For a discussion on the comparative performance of the Brazilian and Mexican economies during the 2009 recession, using hourly data, see chapter 5 of this study.

13. However, this rate may differ from one country to another, depending on the stage of a country's demographic transition.

14. Again, with the exception of Argentina, which we index as 100 by the fourth quarter of 2008.

15. Data for Chile have a structural break in the first quarter of 2010 when the Encuesta Nacional de Empleo (National Employment Surey) underwent an important overhaul. The reference period for questions about employment changed, and, as a consequence, the participation rates for youth (aged 15–24) and adult women (aged 25–64) increased dramatically, between 5 and 8 percentage points. The rise observed, then, should be viewed with caution because it is in part an artifact of data collection methods.

16. See the previous footnote regarding Chile's data.

17. For a study on youth unemployment, see ILO (2011).

18. It can be shown that, for a ratio defined as the weighted average of the ratios of two population groups (say, A and B),

$$\frac{E}{W} = \frac{E_A}{W_A}\frac{W_A}{W} + \frac{E_B}{W_B}\frac{W_B}{W}.$$

The time difference in the ratio can be defined as

$$\left[\frac{E}{W}\right]_{t=1} - \left[\frac{E}{W}\right]_{t=0} = \left[\Delta\frac{E_A}{W_A}\left(\overline{\frac{W_A}{W}}\right) + \Delta\frac{W_A}{W}\left(\overline{\frac{E_A}{W_A}}\right)\right] + \left[\Delta\frac{E_B}{W_B}\left(\overline{\frac{W_B}{W}}\right) + \Delta\frac{W_B}{W}\left(\overline{\frac{E_B}{W_B}}\right)\right]$$

where the ratios preceded by Δ are time changes and the ratios with a bar on top are time averages. The difference can be decomposed into changes in the participation share or in the population share of groups A (first part of right-hand side) and B (second part of right-hand side). We can extend this decomposition to our four-group definition of the gross employment rate.

19. Ecuador, as noted earlier, is an outlier with prime-age women, as well as other groups, experiencing a decline in employment, despite economic growth.

20. For the impact of regulations on labor market variables in the region, see Heckman and Pagés (2004) and Perry et al. (2007).

21. This high Okun coefficient for Colombia may be due to very high unemployment responses to GDP changes in the early 1990s. A recent study by the World Bank (2012b) reports changes in Okun coefficients over time in Colombia and finds that this coefficient has declined and is currently not much higher than those for other Latin American countries.

22. This range of estimates appears in a variety of studies using different methodologies such as IMF (2010b), Perman and Tavera (2005, 2007), and Moosa (1997).

23. The linear projections in this figure are produced using data to 2007 only.

24. For a discussion of the comparative performance of Brazil's and Mexico's economies during the 2009 recession, see chapter 5 of this study.

25. For a description of the macro stance of the region during the crisis, see chapter 2 of this study. For studies on the real and nominal rigidity of wages in Latin America, see World Bank (2012b) and Messina and Sanz (2011).

26. Plus the demographics effect of the potential labor force (i.e., the share of the working -age population to total population).

27. A similar argument is made in chapter 3 of this study where it is shown that poverty rates are explained by changes in survey incomes (which include earnings and others forms of income reported by survey respondents) and not by GDP per capita changes, which show different trends.

28. Labor surveys for Chile include data on monthly earnings only for the fourth quarter of 2007, 2008, 2009, and 2010.

29. Gollin (2002) argues that the output and income of small firms are always underestimated in national accounts, and proposes a method to account for it. For a cross-country study on the long-term evolution of the functional distribution of income and methods to address methodological problems, see Rodriguez and Jayadev (2010).

30. Aggregate measures of workers' compensations are measured in the *System of National Accounts* as account D1: "Compensation of Employees." See United Nations et al. (2009).

31. If this term equals 1, there are no mismatches. If it is greater than 1, as it usually is, the survey data are underreporting total workers' compensation from the national accounts.

32. For a detailed description of the *System National Accounts,* see United Nations et al. (2009). Lequiller and Blades (2006) is a useful primer on national accounts.

33. Each component of GDP has a code in the *System of National Accounts* (see United Nations et al. 2009). GDP is $b.1$, workers' compensation is $d.1$, gross operating surplus is $b.2$, gross mixed income is $b.3$, and net taxes on production is $d.2 - d.3$ so that

$$b.1 = d.1 + b.2 + g.3 + d.2 - d.3.$$

Figure 4.7 shows the results of the following decomposition:

$$\frac{\Delta b.1}{b.1} = \frac{\Delta d.1}{b.1} + \frac{\Delta b.2}{b.1} + \frac{\Delta b.3}{b.1} + \frac{\Delta(d.2 - d.3)}{b.1}$$

where Δ stands for first difference.

34. Assuming a fixed ratio of macro aggregate data to survey data.

35. Again, it can be shown that for average earnings defined as the weighted average of the average earnings of two population groups (say, formal and informal)

$$W = \frac{E_f}{E} W_f + \frac{E_i}{E} W_i$$

where W is the average earnings for all workers, formal workers (W_f), and informal workers (W_i), and E is total employment, with the same subscripts. Then, if $\frac{E_f}{E} = 1 - \frac{E_i}{E}$, the time difference in the ratio can be defined as

$$[W]_{t=1} - [W]_{t=0} = \left(\Delta \frac{E_f}{E} \right) \left(\overline{W_f} - \overline{W_i} \right) + \Delta W_f \left(\frac{\overline{E}_f}{E} \right) + \Delta W_i \left(\frac{\overline{E}_i}{E} \right)$$

where the variables preceded by Δ are time changes and the variables with a bar on top represent two-period averages. The difference can be decomposed into changes in the share of formal workers, changes in formal wages, and changes in informal wages.

36. This is assuming, as usual, that the wage gap between the formal sector and informal sector is positive.

37. Data on informality rates by workers' gender, age, and skill are not included, but are available from the authors upon request. Also visit LABLAC, http://lablac.econo.unlp .edu.ar/eng/index.php.

38. Alternatively, a job contract definition of informality would focus on the legality and social security coverage of a given job. LABLAC also provides data that are based on this definition (see http://lablac.econo.unlp.edu.ar/eng/index.php).

39. A landmark study on the impact of regulation upon labor markets in general, and informality in particular, for Latin America is Heckman and Pages (2004). A more recent study which revisits the evidence about regulations and labor market institutions is by Betcherman (2012).

References

Ball, Laurence, Daniel Leigh, and Prakash Loungani. 2012. "The Okun's Law: Fit at 50?" Paper presented at the 13th Jacques Polak Annual Research Conference hosted by the International Monetary Fund, Washington, DC, November 8–9.

Banerji, Arup, David Newhouse, Pierella Paci, and David Robalino. 2014. *Working through the Crisis: Jobs and Policies in Developing Countries during the Great Recession.* Directions in Development Series. Washington, DC: World Bank.

Betcherman, Gordon. 2012. "Labor Market Institutions: A Review of the Literature." Background paper for *World Development Report 2013: Jobs.* World Bank, Washington, DC.

Blanchard, O., M. Das, and H. Faruqee. 2010. "The Initial Impact of the Crisis on Emerging Market Countries." *Brookings Papers on Economic Activity,* 41 (1): 263–323.

Cazes, Sandrine, Sher Verick, and Fares Al Hussami. 2011. "Diverging Trends in Unemployment in the United States and Europe: Evidence from Okun's Law and the Global Financial Crisis." Employment Sector, Employment Working Paper 106, International Labour Organization, Geneva.

Chen, Martha, Ralf Hussmanns, and Joann Vanek. 2012. "Measuring the Informal Economy: Concepts and Definitions." Working Paper (Statistics) 2, Women in Informal Employment: Globalizing and Organizing, Cambridge, MA.

Gollin, Douglas. 2002. "Getting Income Shares Right." *Journal of Political Economy* 110 (April): 458–74.

Heckman, James J., and Carmen Pages, eds. 2004. *Law and Employment: Lessons from Latin America and the Caribbean.* Chicago, IL: University of Chicago Press.

ILO (International Labour Organization). 2009. *World of Work Report 2009: The Global Jobs Crisis and Beyond.* Geneva: International Institute for Labour Studies.

———. 2011. *Global Employment Trends for Youth.* ILO, Geneva.

———. 2012. *World of Work Report 2012: Better Jobs for a Better Economy.* Geneva: International Institute for Labour Studies.

———. 2013. *Key Indicators of the Labour Market.* 7th ed. Geneva: ILO.

IMF (International Monetary Fund). 2010a. "How Did Emerging Markets Cope in the Crisis?" IMF Policy Paper. http://www.imf.org/external/pp/longres.aspx?gsa=true&id =4459.

———. 2010b. "Unemployment Dynamics during Recessions and Recoveries: Okun's Law and Beyond." In *World Economic Output: Rebalancing Growth.* Washington, DC: IMF, April.

Khanna, Gaurav, David Newhouse, and Pierella Paci. 2011. "Fewer Jobs or Smaller Paychecks? Aggregate Crisis Impacts in Selected Middle-Income Countries." Policy Research Working Paper 5791, World Bank, Washington, DC.

Lequiller, François, and Derek Blades. 2006. *Understanding National Accounts.* Paris: OECD.

Messina, Julián, and Anna Sanz-de-Galdeano. 2011. "Wage Rigidity and Disinflation in Emerging Countries." Policy Research Working Paper 5863, World Bank, Washington, DC.

Moosa, Imad A. 1997. "A Cross-Country Comparison of Okun's Coefficient." *Journal of Comparative Economics* 24 (3): 335–56.

Okun, Arthur. M. 1962. "Potential GNP: Its Measurement and Significance." *Proceedings of the Business and Economics Statistics* 98–104.

Perman, Roger, and Christophe Tavera. 2005. "A Cross-Country Analysis of the Okun's Law Coefficient Convergence in Europe." *Applied Economics* 37 (21): 2501–13.

———. 2007. "Testing for Convergence of the Okun's Law Coefficient in Europe." *Empirica* 34 (1): 45–61.

Perry, Guillermo E., William F. Maloney, Omar S. Arias, Pablo Fajnzylber, Andrew D. Mason, and Jaime Saavedra-Chanduvi. 2007. *Informality: Exit and Exclusion.* Washington, DC: World Bank.

Rodriguez, Francisco, and Arjun Jayadev. 2010. "The Declining Labor Share of Income." Human Development Research Paper 2010/36, United Nations Development Programme, New York.

United Nations, European Communities, International Monetary Fund, Organisation for Economic Co-operation and Development, and World Bank. 2009. *System of National Accounts 2008.* New York: United Nations.

World Bank. 2010. *From Global Collapse to Recovery: Economic Adjustment and Growth Prospects in Latin America and the Caribbean.* Office of the Chief Economist, Latin America and the Caribbean, World Bank.

———. 2012a. *World Development Report 2013: Jobs.* Washington, DC: World Bank.

———. 2012b. *The Labor Market Story behind Latin America's Transformation.* Office of the Chief Economist, Latin America and the Caribbean, World Bank.

CHAPTER 5

Brazil and Mexico Facing the 2008–09 Financial Crisis: Still Fragile or Becoming Stronger?

Maurizio Bussolo, Rafael de Hoyos, Peter Dixon, Maureen Rimmer, and George Verikios

This chapter studies the incidence impact of the 2008–09 global financial crisis on Brazil and Mexico. During the last decade, Mexico has been on a slow growth path, whereas Brazil has enjoyed a sustained and accelerating expansion of its economy, accompanied by a reduction in income inequality. Because of its close commercial ties with the United States, Mexico was much more severely affected by the global crisis than Brazil, which not only trades with a more diversified set of countries, but also exports commodities and agricultural goods whose demand and prices were less affected by the crisis. During 2009, the gross domestic product (GDP) of Mexico contracted by about 6 percent but only 0.3 percent in Brazil. Compared with a counterfactual—no-crisis—scenario, Mexico lost about 9 percentage points of its GDP (instead of growing by 2.8 percent in 2009, it contracted by 6.2 percent), whereas Brazil lost 4 percentage points. The size of the crisis has thus been very different across these two countries.

The features of the macro shock were also different across the two counties. When the crisis and no-crisis scenarios are compared, changes in public consumption were not very significant in either country. Imports and exports dropped in both countries, but consumption was more resilient in Brazil than in Mexico. The relative reduction in investment demand (i.e., with respect to a 1 percent reduction in GDP) was much larger in Brazil. A large number of studies have described the reasons for these differences in aggregate demand adjustments, and this study, while not offering further explanations for this macro shock, contributes to the understanding of its incidence impacts. In fact, what matters more for distribution, and for designing adequate protective policies, is not the overall size of the shock but its incidence. A crucial (incidence-relevant) difference between Mexico and Brazil is the impact of the shock on labor markets. But this difference is not visible at once. For each percentage point reduction in GDP (when comparing the no-crisis to the crisis scenario), employment contracted by 0.2 percent in both Mexico and Brazil. However, when employment is measured in number of hours worked and not in number of people employed, the picture that emerges is quite different. Mexico experienced a sharp reduction in hours worked, whereas these were almost unaffected in Brazil. In Mexico, for the same 1 percent slowdown of GDP (the same "dose" of crisis), employment, when using the new definition of number of hours worked, contracts sixfold more, 1.2 percent instead of 0.2 percent.

These aggregate quantity adjustments mask more complex dynamics. In Mexico, more skilled jobs were hoarded while unskilled ones were shed, and this produced some widening of inequality. In Brazil, unskilled workers in the nontradable sectors (a group that is close to the bottom of the income distribution) actually experienced some employment gains, reducing income dispersion.

Wages also adjusted differently: they were less flexible in Brazil than in Mexico. Earnings changes were progressive in Mexico, as skilled workers and those in the nontradable sectors—groups with higher labor incomes—experienced a fall in their wage premia. Brazil's skill premium increased slightly and generated some unequalizing pressures.

Notwithstanding the larger magnitude of the shock in Mexico and its negative impact across all parts of the distribution, the opposing forces of change in terms of employment and earnings combined to produce a similar overall incidence of the crisis across the two countries. This incidence refers to a comparison of two scenarios, one with the crisis and another without the crisis. As explained shortly, this is quite a different comparison than one contrasting the situations before (2007) and after (2009 or 2010) the crisis (as was conducted in chapter 3 on poverty). This incidence refers to a comparison of two scenarios, one with the crisis and another without the crisis. As explained shortly, this is quite a different comparison than one contrasting the situations before (2007) and after (2009 or 2010) the crisis (as was conducted in chapter 3 on poverty). Our analysis also discovered that the transmission channels were different, which provides useful insights for designing policy measures.

Setting the Problem

From 2000 to 2012, Brazil's per capita GDP grew cumulatively by about 30 percent, achieving an average annual growth rate of 2.2 percent. By contrast, growth in Mexico was rather weak, with an average annual growth rate of GDP per capita of less than 1 percent over the same period (see figure 5.1). Between 2008 and 2009 during the global financial crisis, Mexico's GDP per capita contracted by 7.4 percent, whereas Brazil experienced a reduction of only 1.2 percent.

A large number of papers—Gray et al. (2010); Lane and Milesi-Ferretti (2010); Rojas-Suarez (2010); Devereux, Kollmann, and Roeger (2011); Chudik and Fratzscher (2011); Rose and Spiegel (2011); Hollweg, Lederman, and Reyes (2012); Lederman and Reyes (2012); Fernandez, Lederman, and Gutierrez-Rocha (2013)—have analyzed the aggregate impacts (GDP growth and aggregate demand adjustments) of the crisis. However, less is known about how these macro impacts affected poverty and the distribution of income (see Kaplan,

Figure 5.1   Growth Performances: Mexico and Brazil, 2000–12

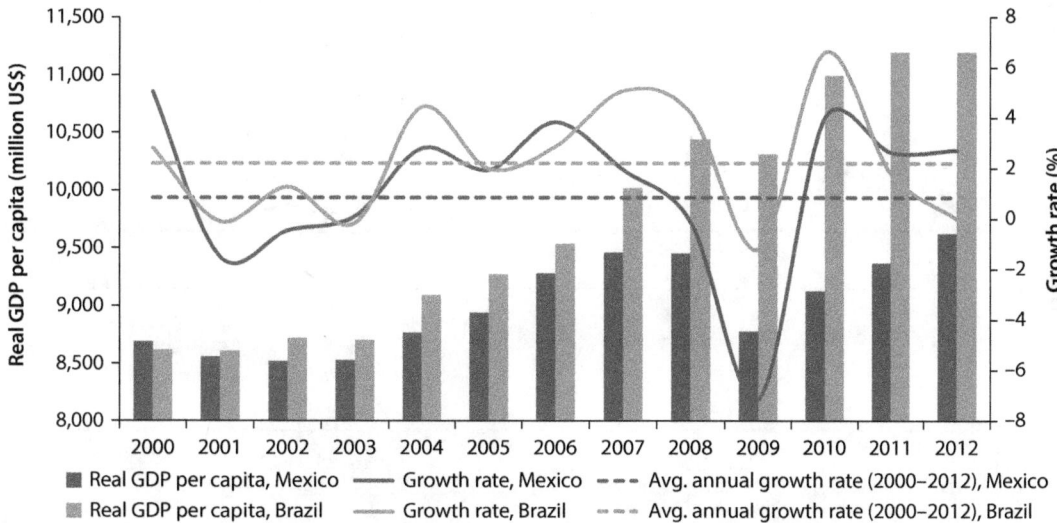

Real GDP per capita, Mexico · Growth rate, Mexico · Avg. annual growth rate (2000–2012), Mexico
Real GDP per capita, Brazil · Growth rate, Brazil · Avg. annual growth rate (2000–2012), Brazil

Source: Development Prospects Group (DECPG), World Bank.

Lederman, and Robertson 2012). The key contribution of this chapter is to shed light on the links between this macro shock and its micro consequences.

Comparing income distributions before and after the crisis shows that the incidence of the crisis was drastically different across Brazil and Mexico (as shown by the growth incidence curves (GICs) in figure 5.2). In Mexico, all households suffered a reduction in income between 2008 and 2010 (years when household surveys are available), but income reductions were more acute among households at the lower part of the distribution, and particularly so among the poorest 10 percent of the population. By contrast, household surveys in Brazil for 2008 and 2009 report positive income changes for all households, with those in the middle of the distribution enjoying the largest increases.[1] The changes in income in the different parts of the distribution are summarized by changes in the Gini index of inequality, which in Mexico increased 0.3 percentage points and in Brazil fell 0.5 percentage points.[2]

A moderately negative growth effect, not captured by household surveys, combined with a progressive change in income distribution in Brazil, explains a reduction of 1.4 and 0.5 percentage points in its poverty headcount and gap, respectively. This is in stark contrast to Mexico, which experienced a sharp reduction in economic activity and an increase in income inequality, both of which explain the increase in the poverty headcount and gap of 2.6 and 1.1 percentage points, respectively.[3]

The global financial crisis most directly affected poverty and distribution through the labor market. Monthly wages in Mexico declined by almost 10 percent during the crisis period,[4] whereas in Brazil wages rose by 3 percent. The unemployment rate in Brazil rose from 7.1 percent to 8.3 percent, a moderate increase consistent with the minor contraction in GDP. However, as shown in figure 5.3,

Figure 5.2 Growth Incidence Curve: Brazil, 2008–09, and Mexico, 2008–10

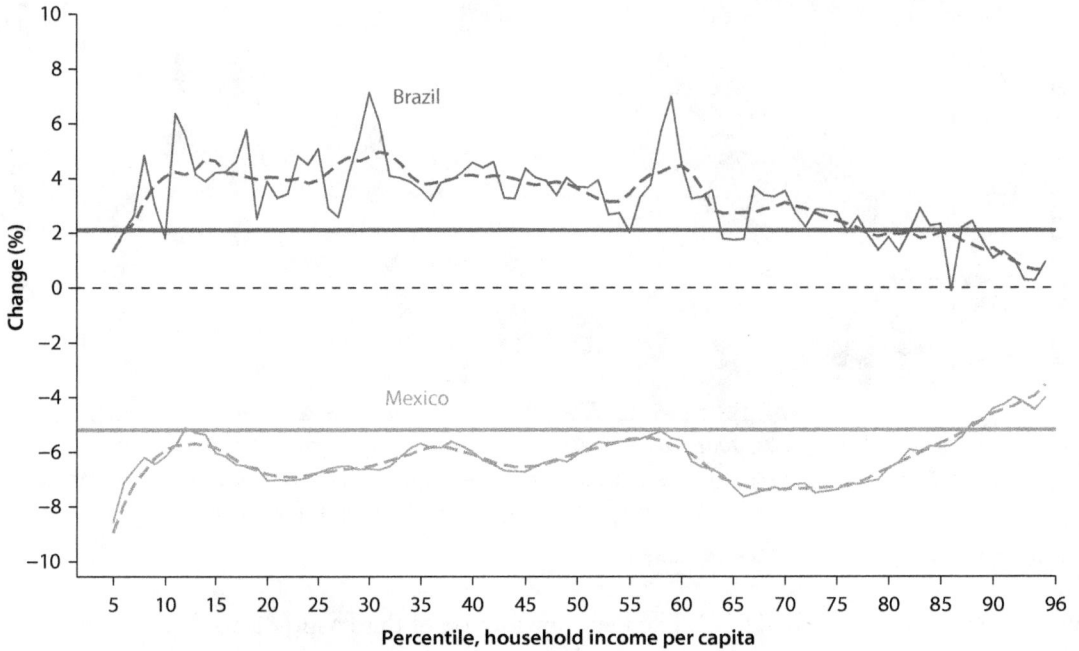

Sources: Brazil: Pesquisa Nacional por Amostra de Domicílios (PNAD, National Household Survey Sample), 2008 and 2009; Mexico: La Encuesta Nacional de Ingresos y Gastos de los Hogares (ENIGH, National Household Income and Expenditure Survey), 2008 and 2010.
Note: Straight lines represent the average change in per capita household income, jagged lines the change in per capita household income, and dashed lines the change in per capita household income, smoothed using locally weighted regressions.

Figure 5.3 Unemployment Trends: Mexico and Brazil, 2000–11

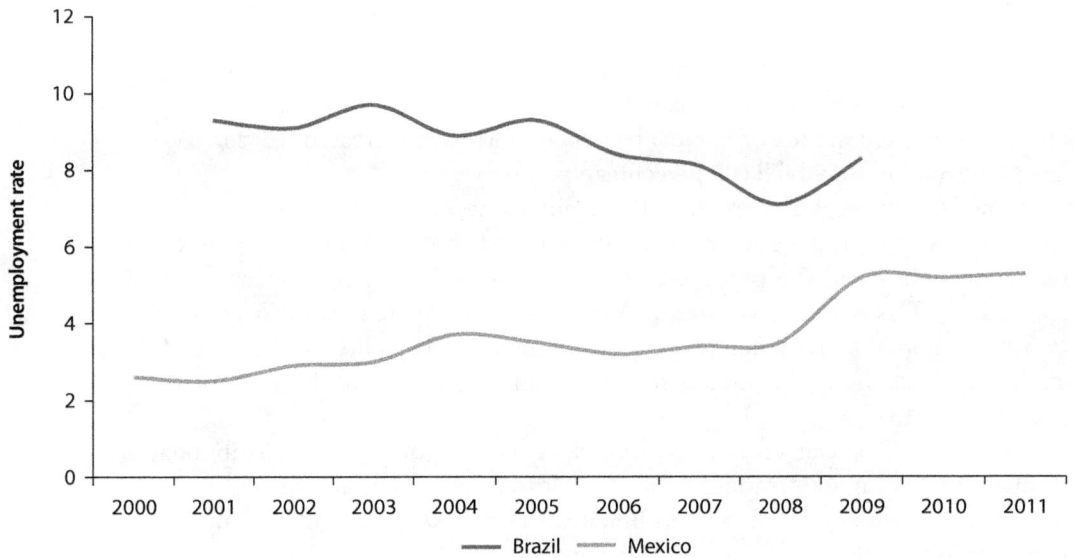

Source: World Development Indicators (database), World Bank (average yearly rates).

Understanding the Poverty Impact of the Global Financial Crisis in Latin America and the Caribbean
http://dx.doi.org/10.1596/978-1-4648-0241-6

the crisis interrupted a trend of declining Brazilian unemployment. The increase in the unemployment rate in Mexico from 3.5 percent in 2008 to 5.2 percent in 2009 was similar in magnitude to that in Brazil, despite the much larger drop in GDP. However, the genuine full employment effect in Mexico should include, as mentioned at the outset of this chapter, the loss of worked hours. When these are considered, the total loss of "full-time equivalent" employment is 5.3 percentage points (compared with a 1.1 percentage point reduction in the number of people employed).

These figures illustrate changes in GDP and employment as percent differences between their respective levels before and after the crisis. An alternative is to compare the crisis levels of GDP and employment with the levels they would have reached in the absence of the crisis. The difference between a before-and-after and a counterfactual approach is not trivial, especially when one would have expected growth to continue at the pace observed before the crisis. Similarly, the incidence, or micro, effects of the crisis can be assessed by comparing income data from household surveys undertaken before and after the crisis, or by estimating the income distribution that would have emerged in the absence of the crisis. Building macro- and microcounterfactuals or scenarios is the main methodological challenge faced in this study.

Conceptual Framework and the Macro-Micro Model

An analysis of links between a macroeconomic shock and its poverty effects cannot rely just on changes at the aggregate levels (GDP or prices). It requires an investigation of distributional changes, essentially in terms of factor market adjustments and relative price changes and their incidence at the level of the individual household. A general conceptual framework linking a macro shock to its micro impacts is summarized graphically in figure 5.4.

Economies are exposed to systemic risks that arise from different types of large shocks, or crises. The types of shocks range from natural disasters, conflicts, or civil unrest to economic crises. In the first group of shocks, one normally observes the destruction of physical and human capital with dire consequences for the affected countries. This study does not focus on this type of crisis; rather, it focuses on economic crises. These crises can be a consequence of either supply or demand side shocks. At the macro level (top panel of figure 5.4), demand and supply shocks can have the same effect—a reduction in aggregate output—but their impact on relative prices determines the reallocation of resources, the effects on input prices, and ultimately the incidence of the shock. Other things being equal, the magnitude of the initial shock and the slopes of aggregate demand and supply (which embed deep structural parameters of the affected economy) will determine how much GDP will contract and changes in relative prices.

Moving from the macro to the "meso" level (middle panel of figure 5.4), the fall in aggregate output can be mapped in the shrinkage of individual sectors and related contractions of factor incomes. For the sake of simplicity, assume that the

Figure 5.4 Conceptual Framework: Linking a Macroeconomic Shock to Its Microeconomic Impacts

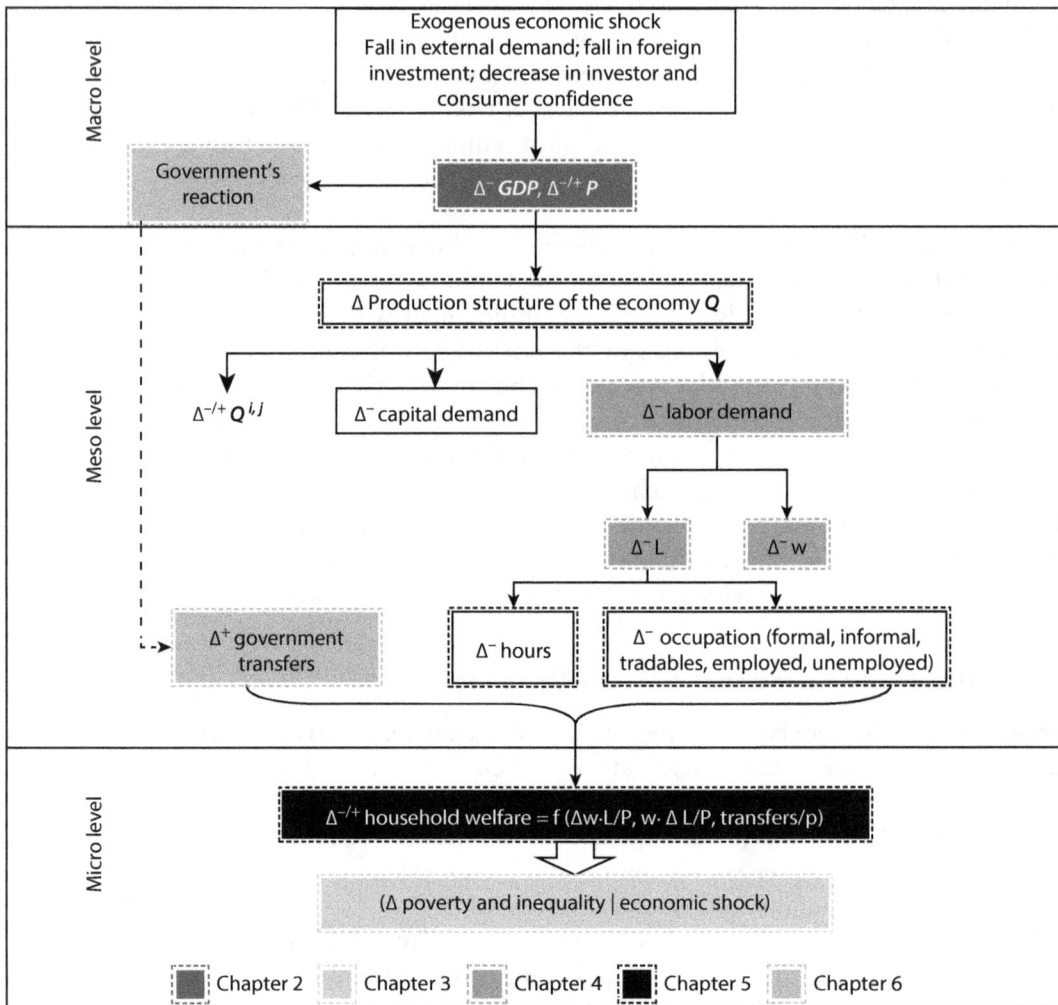

economy has just two factors of production: capital and labor. A reduction in factor income can thus be the result of a fall in profits or a fall in the wage bill. These reductions may stem, for example, from a drop in export demand for a sector that uses more intensively one factor or the other factor. Once again, the structure of the economy, in particular the degree of competition and the functioning of the labor markets, will determine the size of the final income contraction. In turn, a lower demand for labor can be accommodated through a reduction in employment, a reduction in wages, or a combined reduction in both, or by shifting workers from formal (full-time, well-paid) jobs to informal (part-time, lower-paid) ones.

Given their relevance to the lower tail of the income distribution, this study focuses on labor market adjustments rather than on adjustments affecting capital incomes. Lack of good household-level data on capital endowments and income presents additional obstacles in moving beyond labor in modeling household income dynamics.

Changes in factor income and public and private transfers are mapped onto changes of household per capita real income or consumption, poverty, and income distribution at the micro level (bottom panel of figure 5.4). *Real* is used here to take into account the changes in prices of the bundle of goods consumed by households.

The strength of the transmission channels—from a shock to its poverty impacts—between the macro, meso, and micro levels and within them depends on structural characteristics of the economy such as the level of competition and contestability of relevant markets, the dynamism of labor markets, the ex ante risk management tools, and the ex post coping strategies of individual agents. The macro features of an economy—that is, its macroeconomic policies, institutions, and initial macro fundamentals—can be interpreted as risk management tools. On the eve of the 2008–09 global financial crisis, the degree of macro preparedness of most Latin American economies was fairly good. And similarly, at the micro level improvements in social protection programs provided an additional line of defense against risks. The responses to the shock also affected the strength of the transmission channels. Most governments responded at the macro level by adopting countercyclical fiscal stances and accommodative monetary policies and at the micro level by expanding different types of programs and transfers.

To operationalize the conceptual framework, this chapter develops a structural macro-micro model that can be best described as a sequential two-step process. In the first step, a computable general equilibrium (CGE or macro) model is used to create two scenarios, one in which the crisis does not take place and a second in which the observed outcome of the crisis is reproduced. In a second step, three sets of general equilibrium effects, also called linking aggregate variables (LAVs)—growth, wages, and employment by sector and skill—are mapped to households in a microsimulation model. This procedure generates macro- and microcounterfactuals.

The approach taken in this chapter is based on macro-micro simulation methodologies developed in the recent literature—Bourguignon, Bussolo, and Pereira da Silva (2008) describe its advantages and drawbacks. Variants of this methodology have been used in various contributions to this literature. These range from ex post studies, such as Robilliard, Bourguignon, and Robinson (2008), to ex ante simulation studies, such as Bourguignon, Ferreira, and Leite (2002); Chen and Ravallion (2004); Bussolo, Lay, and Van der Mensbrugghe (2006); and Bourguignon and Savard (2008). Comprehensive surveys are found in Bourguignon and Pereira da Silva (2003); Bourguignon, Bussolo, and Pereira da Silva (2008); and Davies (2009). A 2010 special edition of the *International Journal of Microsimulations* was fully dedicated to macro-micro modeling frameworks.[5]

The Macro Model

A MONASH-style[6] CGE model is used as the top macro model in this study. Production takes place under perfect competition and constant returns to scale, and it is modeled in a nested constant elasticity of substitution (CES) fashion to reflect various substitution possibilities across inputs. All labor and capital income accrues to the households.

The output of production activities is transformed into consumed commodities by means of a transition matrix, which takes into account the fact that multiple activities can produce the same commodity and that multiple commodities can be the output of a single activity. Household demand is allocated across commodities according to the linear expenditure system (LES), in which consumers maximize a Stone-Geary utility function subject to the disposable income constraint. Other final demand agents—government and investment— use the CES expenditure system.

International trade is modeled using the nested Armington specification, in which consumer products are differentiated by region of origin and combined using CES functions. World import prices are fixed, which means that any increase in import demand can be satisfied without affecting global prices (a small-country assumption). On the supply side, producers allocate output for domestic and export markets according to a constant elasticity of transformation (CET) specification. In contrast with the import side, exporters have some degree of market power and therefore face a downward sloping demand curve.

The aggregate stock of capital is allocated across various sectors with a finite elasticity of transformation, resulting in imperfect capital mobility. Skilled and unskilled workers are freely mobile throughout the economy. Although international migration is likely to be an important element in the dynamics of the Mexican labor market, it is not considered here. Finally, the model allows for changes in the degree of resource utilization or unemployment for labor (via short-term wage stickiness) and excess capacity for capital.

The volumes of government current spending are fixed as shares of real GDP, as is the deficit (in real terms). Public revenues adjust to clear the government balance by means of a flexible household direct tax rate. Investment demand, derived from the production function, has to equal investment financing; the latter is represented by an upward sloping curve with respect to rates of return. Financing comes from a pool of domestic and international savings. Indeed, the current account balance is endogenous and equals the difference between domestic investment and domestic saving.

The model is solved in a recursive dynamic mode in which subsequent end-of-period equilibria are linked with a set of equations that update the main macroeconomic variables. There are three determinants of real GDP growth in the model: labor supply growth, capital accumulation, and increases in productivity. The volumes of skilled and unskilled labor grow exogenously at the growth rate of the working-age population (aged

15–64 years) obtained from population forecasts. The capital stock in each period is the sum of depreciated capital from the period before and new investment. For all sectors, total factor productivity (TFP) is exogenous, but can be switched to endogenous, depending on the simulation closure rule.

In addition to the productivity case, switching variables from endogenous to exogenous according to the type of simulation is one of the major advantages of using a MONASH-style model. Three distinct simulation modes (and related closure rules) are used in this study: historical, forecast, and decomposition. These are described as follows:

- The *historical* mode switches naturally endogenous variables[7] such as consumption, investment, government spending, exports, imports, employment, and capital stocks at the detailed commodity/industry level to exogenous and sets them equal to their respective levels observed in a specific year. Correspondingly, historical simulations produce estimates of many naturally exogenous, but often unobservable, variables representing investor and consumer confidence, positions of export demand and import supply curves, industry technologies, household preferences, and required rates of return on capital.

- The *forecast* mode is used in simulations designed to produce a baseline picture of a future or counterfactual evolution of the economy. The underlying philosophy of this simulation mode is similar to the historical one. In both modes, we exogenize variables for which we have information with no regard for causation. Rather than exogenizing variables for which we have historical observations, in the forecast mode we exogenize variables for which we have forecasts, or counterfactual levels. This might include macro variables, exports by commodity, and demographic variables.

- The *decomposition* mode is used to assess the contribution of each individual transmission mechanism—represented, for example, by changes in confidence, export demand, technology—to the full change in the naturally endogenous variables of interest such as income, employment, and wages of different categories of workers. In this mode, confidence parameters, export demand curve positions, technology, preferences, and other such variables are set exogenous and are shifted, one at the time, with the movements estimated for them in the comparison between historical and forecast (or counterfactual) simulations.

By using these three simulation models, the CGE model assesses the relative importance of the various transmission mechanisms (such as drop in export demand, investors confidence, etc) of the crisis. In addition, with these simulations, the CGE model provides the LAVs to run the appropriate counterfactual microsimulations, thereby allowing investigators to go beyond the imprecise before and after approach.

From Macro to Micro

The CGE-generated LAVs are used to "shock" the bottom micro module so that a counterfactual income distribution can be estimated.[8] The following equations represent the core of the micro module:

$$W_h = f(Y_h, P_h) \cong \frac{Y_h}{P_h} \qquad (5.1)$$

$$Y_h = \sum_l \theta_{h,l}^\ell \theta_{h,l}^e w_l + Y_h^o \qquad (5.2)$$

$$P_h = p_f \theta_{f,h} + p_{nf}(1 - \theta_{f,h}) \qquad (5.3)$$

The welfare of household h, W_h, is defined as a function of income and a household-specific price index, P_h. The income of household h, Y_h, is defined as the sum of labor remunerations $\left(\sum_l \theta_{h,l}^\ell w_l\right)$, and an exogenous nonlabor income (Y_h^o). For the sake of simplicity, the household-specific price index is defined as the sum of economy-wide food and nonfood price indexes weighted by the household's budget allocated to these consumption items. Welfare effects are approximated by the following general expressions:

$$dW_h = \frac{\partial W_h}{\partial Y_h} dY_h + \frac{\partial W_h}{\partial P_h} dP_h \qquad (5.4a)$$

$$dW_h = \frac{\partial W_h}{\partial Y_h} \left\{ \frac{\partial Y_h}{\partial \theta_{h,l}^l} + \frac{\partial Y_h}{\partial \theta_{h,l}^e} + \frac{\partial Y_h}{\partial w_l} \right\} + \frac{\partial W_h}{\partial P_h} dP_h. \qquad (5.4b)$$

Therefore, changes in welfare are determined by changes in household income and the household-specific price index. In turn, changes in the household price index, dP_h, are solely determined by changes in the food and nonfood price indexes, keeping the budget shares, θ_f, constant. Changes in household income are solely determined by changes in labor remunerations, and these in turn are allowed to vary as a result of changes in the allocation of workers in the different labor market segments (i.e., employed versus unemployed and, if an individual is employed, the sector of occupation), tradable and nontradable sectors ($\Delta\theta_{h,l}^\ell$), hours worked ($\Delta\theta_{h,l}^e$), and the returns to skilled and unskilled labor in the different labor market segments (Δw_l). A new household welfare aggregate is computed by adding the exogenous household income to the sum of simulated labor incomes for each member of the household (given his or her skill endowments, employment status, and sector of employment) and deflating the new total household income by the new household-specific price index. Based on the simulated welfare aggregate, a counterfactual distribution of income is generated and compared with the initial distribution. Finally, growth effects are distribution-neutral changes in per capita household income.

A key issue in this modeling framework is the connection between the macro CGE part and the micro module, and therefore a major difficulty is satisfactorily mapping the sources of incomes from the CGE model to the micro model. For example, the microsimulation module defines an exogenous household income (Y_h^o) as all nonlabor income components such as transfers, imputed rents, and capital remuneration. This exogenous income is not modified during the simulations. Thus, although consistency between macro and micro is always pursued, the changes in capital remunerations predicted by the CGE are not reflected in the microdata.[9]

A structuralist feature introduced in the model is the assumption of labor market segmentation. Some degree of labor segmentation is allowed between the tradable and nontradable sectors. The labor market segmentation assumption gives rise to wage differentials across labor market segments.[10] At the micro level, workers are reallocated among employment and unemployment and tradable and nontradable sectors by means of a probit model, where the probability of losing or getting a job (or switching sectors) is estimated as a function of several personal and household characteristics. Workers are allowed to switch between labor market segments until the CGE-estimated differences in labor allocations between the crisis and no-crisis scenarios are achieved. For workers who switch, a labor income is imputed on the basis of observable characteristics and the return of them prevailing in the receiving labor market segment. For example, if a worker abandons unemployment, that worker will be imputed a wage based on his or her observable characteristics such as age, gender, and education. If a worker loses his or her job, that worker's labor income will be set to zero.

The top-down approach used here takes into account important sources of household heterogeneity such as the structure of income by labor segment and the composition of consumption in food versus nonfood items—θs in equations (5.2) and (5.3). In other words, although only a handful of variables link the macro and the micro, macro shocks will have different welfare impacts across households. In addition, allowing for full heterogeneity means that in the new, *simulated* distribution, households, as well as individuals, can be identified according to the complete set of socioeconomic characteristics recorded in the survey. It is thus easier to identify a specific characteristic—such as region of residence, employment status, gender, education, or age—that may strongly correlate with larger than average losses from the global crisis and then use this information in designing targeted compensatory measures.

Explaining the Welfare Effects of the Crisis

Macroeconomic and Aggregate Labor Market Effects

The macroeconomic and the aggregate labor market impacts of the crisis, when compared with a noncrisis counterfactual, were quite different in Mexico and Brazil. Mexico's labor market adjusted via a robust drop in hours worked and a moderate reduction in hourly wages. Employment measured in hours worked shrank by 7 percent, but only 2.1 percent of people lost their jobs.[11] Clearly, working fewer hours had a negative effect on incomes, but it generally represented a transitory and less severe loss than the one associated with becoming unemployed. In Brazil, the inflexibility of the real wage did not support employment when aggregate demand dropped. In terms of job losses, the crisis had a relative impact (i.e., for each 1 percent reduction of GDP) that was similar across the two countries. This and the next subsection focus on these cross-country differences at the macro and meso levels (see figure 5.4), and the third subsection considers the micro (poverty and distribution) impacts.

If the global financial crisis had not happened, the economies of Mexico and Brazil would have expanded by about 3 and 4 percent, respectively, during the simulation period, as shown in table 5.1. These "forecasts," or counterfactuals, impose GDP growth rates slightly higher than the trend growth rate observed in the recent past (2001–07) because they are based on the view of the world prevailing prior to the global financial crisis. In this view, Latin American countries—specifically those that have natural resources and that underwent structural reforms and have reached and maintained a stable macroeconomic framework—were considered likely to enjoy strong growth.[12]

Growth rates of supply of primary factors are also exogenously imposed. For Mexico, employment growth is projected at a little under 2 percent a year. Projected investment growth is above that of GDP. For Brazil, labor input growth is projected at about 2 percent a year, and investment growth at around that of GDP. Given this investment growth and the high initial (2008) investment to capital ratio, capital growth is projected at about 6 percent.

By fitting these paths, the model estimates endogenously the changes in a set of (normally exogenous) variables. For example, given a target in terms of growth of factor inputs and GDP, the model calculates the growth in TFP. For Mexico, TFP growth is estimated at 0.2 percent for 2009 and 0.7 percent a year for 2010. This would have been enough to support steady wage growth of about 1 percent a year in real terms. For Brazil, given the targeted GDP growth and the evolution of factors of production, the implied growth of TFP is about −0.2 percent for 2009 and −0.3 percent for 2010. The small decrements in TFP over 2009–10 support zero wage growth in real terms.

Other endogenous results from these forecast simulations include: changes in investor confidence, propensity to consume, preferences across domestic or imported goods, international prices, and related foreign demand and supply of goods and services.[13]

In the historical or crisis run, Mexico's GDP and all of its expenditure components, except public consumption, contracted in 2009. The drop in investment and trade were, because of the nature of the crisis, substantial. Exports declined by 14 percent, in contrast with a no-crisis expansion of 5 percent, and imports collapsed by almost 20 percent,[14] compared with a no-crisis increase of nearly 7 percent. Public consumption grew by 3 percent, compared with baseline

Table 5.1 Evolution of Main Macroeconomic Variables in the No-Crisis and Crisis Scenarios (Growth Rates): Mexico and Brazil

Percent

	Average, 2001–07	No-crisis or forecast simulation			Crisis or historical simulation			Difference		
		2008	2009	2010	2008	2009	2010	2008	2009	2010
Mexico										
Real private consumption	3.8	1.8	3.3	3.5	1.8	−7.2	5.0	0.0	−10.2	−8.8
Real investment	3.8	5.9	4.4	4.4	5.9	−12.1	6.2	0.0	−15.8	−14.3
Real public consumption	0.5	1.0	1.5	1.5	1.0	3.2	2.4	0.0	1.7	2.6
Real exports	5.1	0.5	5.2	5.5	0.5	−13.5	21.7	0.0	−17.8	−5.2
Real imports	5.6	2.8	6.4	5.0	2.8	−18.6	20.5	0.0	−23.4	−12.2
Inventories[a]		−0.6	0.0	0.0	−0.6	−0.6	−0.6	0.0	−0.6	−1.2
Real GDP	2.3	1.2	2.8	3.5	1.2	−6.0	5.3	0.0	−8.5	−7.0
Aggregate employment in hours[b]	1.8	4.4	1.8	1.8	4.4	−5.3	5.4	0.0	−7.0	−3.7
Aggregate capital input		3.2	3.5	3.4	3.2	0.4	5.0	0.0	−3.0	−1.5
Total factor productivity[c]		−2.2	0.1	0.7	−2.2	−2.7	−0.2	0.0	−2.8	−3.7
Average real hourly wage rate[d]		−3.7	1.3	1.2	−3.7	−1.6	−4.5	0.0	−2.9	−8.3
Aggregate employment[e]	1.7	2.1	1.4	1.5	2.1	−1.1	3.0	0.0	−2.5	−1.0
Total factor productivity[c]		−0.7	0.2	0.7	−0.7	−5.2	0.1	0.0	−5.4	−6.0
Average real wage rate[d]		−1.6	1.0	1.0	−1.6	−7.5	−3.5	0.0	−8.4	−12.5
Brazil										
Real private consumption	3.3	5.7	3.8	3.8	5.7	4.4	6.9	0.0	0.6	3.7
Real investment	3.9	13.6	3.9	3.9	13.6	−6.7	21.3	0.0	−10.2	4.9
Real public consumption	3.3	3.2	3.3	3.3	3.2	3.1	4.2	0.0	−0.1	0.8
Real exports	9.1	0.5	9.1	9.1	0.5	−9.1	11.5	0.0	−16.7	−14.9
Real imports	6.9	15.4	6.3	6.3	15.4	−7.6	35.8	0.0	−13.1	11.1
Inventories[a]		−0.6	0.0	0.0	−0.6	−0.6	−0.6	0.0	−0.6	−1.2

table continues next page

167

Table 5.1 Evolution of Main Macroeconomic Variables in the No-Crisis and Crisis Scenarios (Growth Rates): Mexico and Brazil *(continued)*

Percent

	Average, 2001–07	No-crisis or forecast simulation			Crisis or historical simulation			Difference		
		2008	2009	2010	2008	2009	2010	2008	2009	2010
Real GDP	3.4	5.2	4.0	4.0	5.2	–0.3	7.5	0.0	–4.1	–0.9
Aggregate employment[e]	3.0	5.0	1.4	1.7	5.0	0.4	3.6	0.0	–0.9	0.9
Aggregate capital input		5.0	6.0	5.6	5.0	3.5	4.7	0.0	–2.3	–3.1
Total factor productivity[c]		–0.4	–0.2	–0.3	–0.4	0.0	1.7	0.0	0.2	2.2
Average real wage rate[d]		1.3	0.0	0.0	1.3	0.6	0.0	0.0	0.6	0.6

Source: World Bank data.

a. Inventory change as a percentage contribution to GDP.

b. Employment measured as full-time equivalent number of people (derived from the hours worked).

c. GDP per unit of primary factor input.

d. Calculated as a weighted average of the percentage movements in wage rates by occupation and sector, with the weights in the year *t* calculation reflecting wage bill shares halfway between those in years *t* – 1 and *t*.

e. Measures labor input as number of people employed.

growth of 1.5 percent. A higher public expenditure was part of the Mexican government's response to the global financial crisis.

In 2009, trade and investment also collapsed in Brazil, confirming that the crisis this time around was originating outside of Latin America. However, GDP and private consumption were much less affected in Brazil than in Mexico. This is an important difference: in Mexico, a 6 percent contraction in GDP was accompanied by a 12 percent reduction in investment (a 1:2 relationship). In Brazil, a less than half a percent slowdown in GDP growth was accompanied by a drop of 7 percent in investment (a 1:20 relationship). The crisis-related adjustments in the structure of aggregate demand were very different across the two countries, with important consequences for the differential adjustment of the factor markets and especially of the labor markets (see the next subsection).

By contrasting the forecast scenario and the historical scenario—that is, the no-crisis scenario with the crisis one—the model unveils the size of the change in key unobservable variables. For both countries, the magnitudes of the loss of investor confidence, the shift of export demand curves, and changes in consumer behavior as related to the drops in I (investment), X (exports), M (imports), and C (consumption) are summarized in table 5.2. The crisis also featured changes on the supply side. Mexico and Brazil experienced a reduction in the use of capital, changes in the intensity of use of different types of labor, and wage adjustments. For example, the recession of 2009 had little effect on the capital stocks available to Mexican and Brazilian businesses, but it did affect the amount of capital in use. According to the available estimates, in 2009 recession-related excess capacity (capital not in use) was about 3.0 percent for Mexico and 2.5 percent for Brazil. The implied effects on unobservable variables, such as technological and productivity shifts, of these supply-side changes were also estimated comparing the two scenarios and are shown in table 5.2.

What Explains the Different Labor Market Impacts of the Crisis in Mexico and Brazil?

The aggregate labor market impacts of the crisis have already been described. However, to fully capture the micro consequences of the main cross-country differences in terms of adjustments of jobs versus hours worked and of wage increases versus reductions, adjustments at a more disaggregated level need to be analyzed. And the picture becomes slightly more complicated when these changes are analyzed for different categories of workers (skilled and unskilled) and for different sectors (tradables and nontradables)—see table 5.3.

In Mexico, workers in the tradable sectors suffer larger (hour) employment losses, but milder wage declines than workers in the nontradable sectors. These differential adjustments result in an increase in the tradable to nontradable sectoral wage premium. Similarly, unskilled workers are more likely to lose jobs than skilled ones, and, correspondingly, the unemployment rate rises more for unskilled workers than skilled ones. However, the skill wage premium is almost unaffected. A main adjustment channel of the Mexican labor market is captured by the change in the factorial intensity shown in the bottom panel of table 5.3.

Table 5.2 Summary of the Main Shocks from and Adjustments to the Global Financial Crisis Based on Contrasting the Forecast Scenario and the Historical Scenario: Mexico and Brazil

	Mexico	Brazil
Investor confidence	The crisis and its associated loss of confidence mean that for the same level of investment, investors require a higher rate of return. In a nonrecessionary situation, the average rate of return on capital in Mexico in 2009 is 8 percent. To overcome the intensified risk aversion, the increase in the rate of return is 6.25 percent—that is, to justify the nonrecessionary level of investment, the rate of return rises from 8.0 percent to 8.5 percent.	In the nonrecessionary situation, the average rate of return on capital in Brazil in 2009 is 13.9 percent. The upward movement in the capital supply schedule caused by the loss of confidence related to the recession is 15.1 percent. This implies that the rate of return required justifying the nonrecessionary level of investment moves from 13.9 percent to 16.0 percent.
Trade	A large reduction in foreign (mainly U.S.) demand for Mexican products; changes in preferences toward domestic goods and away from imports; deterioration in the terms of trade. Quantitatively, these shocks correspond to a 12.3 percent reduction in foreign demand—that is, at any foreign price Mexico could sell 12.3 percent less in the recession than it would have been able to sell in the nonrecession situation—and a change in preferences reducing the ratio of import quantities to domestic quantities by 37 percent at any ratio of import prices to domestic prices.	Reduction in demand for Brazilian products; changes in preferences toward domestic goods; deterioration in the terms of trade. These effects correspond to a 21.2 percent reduction in foreign demand and a change in preferences that reduces the ratio of import quantities to domestic quantities by 14.7 percent at any ratio of import prices to domestic prices.
Public expenditure	An increase in public expenditures of 1.7 percent.	An increase in public expenditures of 0.63 percent.
Propensity to consume	A smoothing of consumption—that is, an increase in the average propensity to consume (public and private) out of GNP. The increase in the average propensity to consume is 3.7 percent.	The increase in the average propensity to consume is 4.8 percent.
Excess capacity (Δ capital in use)	A reduction of capital in use (excess capacity) of 2.9 percent. This shock also includes the effects of a change in inventories.	A reduction in capital in use (excess capacity) of 2.35 percent. This shock also includes the effects of a change in inventories.
Productivity	A reduction in total factor productivity of 2.7 percent.	A reduction in total factor productivity of 2.0 percent. For Brazil, this shock also contains the effects of a technology change favoring labor over capital.
Wage rates	A reduction in the aggregate real wage rate of 2.8 percent.	An increase in real wage rates of 0.60 percent.
Technology shift	A shift in employer preferences in favor of skilled workers and against unskilled workers.	A shift in employer preferences in favor of unskilled and against skilled workers. The shift is about 15 percent in the nontraded sectors—that is, the ratio of unskilled employment to skilled employment increases by 15 percent because of the recession, above and beyond wage changes.

Source: World Bank.

Table 5.3 Labor Market Performance (Percentage Difference between the Crisis and No-Crisis Scenarios in 2009): Mexico and Brazil

	Mexico	Brazil
Real wages[a]		
Unskilled workers in tradables	−1.7	1.2
Unskilled workers in nontradables	−4.3	−0.3
Skilled workers in tradables	−0.7	−0.5
Skilled workers in nontradables	−4.2	1.1
Wage premia		
Skilled/unskilled workers	−0.2	0.3
Trade/nontrade	3.3	0.5
Employment[b]		
Unskilled workers in tradables	−12.3	−6.7
Unskilled workers in nontradables	−7.8	2.7
Skilled workers in tradables	−9.4	−3.7
Skilled workers in nontradables	−4.3	0.2
Unskilled workers	−9.6	−1.3
Skilled workers	−5.5	−0.6
Tradables	−10.9	−5.7
Nontradables	−5.4	1.2
Sectoral skill intensities		
Skilled/unskilled workers in tradables	3.3	3.2
Skilled/unskilled workers in nontradables	3.8	−2.4
Unskilled unemployed labor	49.1	19.4
Skilled unemployed labor	45.3	6.0
Overall real GDP (growth effect)	−8.5	−4.1

Source: MONASH model simulations based on historical and forecast runs.
a. Real wages are measured as monthly average wages for Brazil and hourly average wages for Mexico.
b. Employment is number of workers for Brazil and effective employment for Mexico (i.e., the number of worked hours per week divided by 48—equivalent to full-time employment).

For both the tradable and nontradable sectors of the economy, the skilled to unskilled employment ratio increases by about 3 percent. In the no-crisis scenario, Mexico would have normally employed 1.02 and 2.18 (effective) skilled workers per each unskilled worker in the tradable and nontradable sectors, respectively. But because of the crisis, these ratios become 1.06 and 2.26. This change in the skill intensity of Mexican labor markets is enough to save about 1 million skilled jobs during the crisis.[15]

In Brazil, employment in the tradable sectors goes down as well, and more severely for unskilled workers. The nontradable sectors react differently and register a slight increase in employment. However, the increase benefits only unskilled workers. This positive impact does not fully compensate for the job losses in the tradable sectors that are large enough to amount to a collective loss of employment of about 1 percent for unskilled workers. The adjustment in the Brazilian labor markets appears to have been the substitution of skilled by unskilled employment in the nontradable sectors and the reverse in the tradable sectors. This is highlighted by the changes in factor intensities in table 5.3. These quantity adjustments are accompanied by negligible changes in the skill and sectoral wage premia.

These cross-country differences in the labor market adjustment are the joint result of the type of shock that hit these countries, the institutional settings of their product and factor markets, and agents' reactions to the shock. A decomposition analysis (performed by using the CGE model in decomposition mode) sheds light on the contribution of these different mechanisms.

Starting with the type of shock, for Mexico loss of investor confidence, trade shocks, underutilization of capital, consumption smoothing (a temporary reduction in saving to compensate for losses of income), and expansion of public expenditures jointly explain about 60 percent of the total loss of employment.[16] This share is quite large but not uniform. Together, these mechanisms capture 70 percent of the reduction in the employment of skilled workers but only 40 percent of the employment of unskilled ones.

This finding clearly indicates that the institutional settings and the agents' reactions play an important role. Wage downward flexibility actually helps to conserve employment (more or less equally for the skilled and unskilled), and thus productivity and labor hoarding have to explain the residual share of the change (60 percent for unskilled labor and 30 percent for skilled labor). Employers' decisions to hold on to their more skilled workers (labor hoarding) and shed unskilled jobs increase the share of accounted reduction of unskilled employment by another 30 percent. The residual 30 percent of unexplained change in employment (for both skilled and unskilled workers) is dealt with by negative productivity shifts. These come from adjustments within the sectors (such as churning of firms) and are not explicitly determined by the model.

The case of Brazil is quite different. Crisis-related demand side changes account jointly for almost 500 percent of the full reduction in employment between the two scenarios—by about 300 and 800 percent of the drop in the employment of skilled and unskilled workers, respectively. This finding implies that there are very strong adjustments (conserving jobs) in the labor markets, and that they are of greater magnitude for the unskilled.

Before describing Brazil's labor market adjustments, we will consider separately the specific impacts on workers of the investment, private consumption, and trade shocks. In Brazil, the large drop in investment demand because of the loss in investor confidence by itself explains more than 400 percent of the reduction in employment of unskilled workers. Because of the concentration of very low-skilled workers in the construction sector, this fall in investment barely affects skilled employment. In fact, in Brazil the drop in investment alone explains about 140 percent of the total reduction in employment for all workers. By contrast, the same shock explains only 14 percent of the loss of employment in Mexico.

The change in private consumption and its consequences for employment are also quite different across the two countries. Because of the drop in their incomes and the relative prices they are facing, consumers in both countries adjust upward their propensity to consume (consumption smoothing), but they do so more significantly in Brazil. This private consumption shift supports GDP in both countries, but the effect on employment is of the opposite sign. Employment (both skilled and unskilled) in Mexico benefits from it, but not in Brazil. There the shift in the composition of aggregate demand—toward more private consumption—entails a reallocation of resources from the more labor-intensive production sectors (essentially tradables) to those less labor-intensive.

Finally, the trade shock decreases aggregate employment in both countries in roughly the same proportion, explaining between 40 percent and 50 percent of the total reduction in employment. But in Brazil it affects more significantly unskilled workers, whereas in Mexico skilled workers suffer larger losses.

In summary, it is clear that the *shape* of the shock affected Mexican and Brazilian labor markets quite dissimilarly. However, as mentioned earlier, in Brazil the labor market's adjustment mechanisms (wages, productivity, and hoarding) were also very different from those described for Mexico. In Brazil, the slight rise in real wages added to the difficulty in retaining workers. But, more important, productivity and labor hoarding shifts strongly contributed to conserving employment and specifically unskilled employment. First, during the crisis there was a general shift in production toward using more intensively labor versus capital. Second, and in contrast to Mexico, unskilled labor, especially in the nontradable sectors, was hoarded. However, for the tradable sectors the adjustment was similar to that observed in Mexico: exporting firms or firms producing traded goods for the domestic market competing with imports tended to preserve their more skilled workers.

Poverty and Income Distribution Effects of the Crisis

The overall welfare effect of the crisis can be decomposed into growth and distributional impacts. The growth component is simply the difference between the observed level of GDP per capita (which is also the level reproduced in the historical mode) and the level that would have been observed in the absence of the crisis (forecast mode). The global crisis caused an 8 percent contraction of GDP per capita in Mexico and a 4 percent reduction in Brazil. In the absence of the crisis, GDP per capita in Mexico and Brazil would have been US$970 and US$260 higher, respectively, than the level observed in 2009. However, the income loss was not the same for all socioeconomic groups. For example, Mexican workers in the tradable sectors of the economy suffered a milder reduction in wages but larger employment losses as a result of the crisis.

In more formal terms, the distributional impact depends on changes of (1) unemployment rates (or, more precisely, full job losses), (2) number of hours worked, and (3) hourly wages, all of which are differentiated by sector (tradables versus nontradables) and by skill level.

The full distributional impact is decomposed into the individual contributions of each of these changes and is illustrated by GICs capturing their ceteris paribus effect. A GIC with a positive slope indicates a regressive effect—that is, poorer households lose more (or gain less), in relative terms, than richer ones. Our baseline is the Mexican household survey, La Encuesta Nacional de Ingresos y Gastos de los Hogares (ENIGH, National Household Income and Expenditure Survey), for 2008 and the Brazilian survey PNAD for 2009. The Mexican survey, ENIGH 2008, is then shocked with the negative effects of the crisis captured by the difference between the historical (observed) crisis scenario and the forecast no-crisis scenario. For Brazil, the starting point is PNAD 2009, which already contains the effects of the crisis. Thus households are affected with a positive shock to construct the hypothetical scenario of Brazil in 2009 without the crisis (forecast mode).

Distributional Effects of Changes in Wages

In Mexico, the hourly wage reductions observed during the crisis were much milder in the tradable sectors than in the nontradable sectors (a reduction of more than 4 percent for both skilled and unskilled workers in nontradables, and contractions of 1.7 and 0.7 percent, respectively, for unskilled and skilled workers in the tradables—see the relevant data in table 5.3). Overall, the crisis reduced the wage gap between tradable and nontradable sectors and did not have a significant effect on the skill wage premia. Because workers in tradable sectors earn lower wages, the distributional effect through this channel was relatively mild and progressive.

Figure 5.5 shows the (growth-neutral) distributional effect of the change in hourly wages brought about by the crisis. Empirically, this microsimulation is performed by simply changing the hourly wages of all individuals in the household survey ENIGH 2008 according to their position in the labor market (skilled, unskilled, tradable, nontradable) and the shocks shown in the upper panel of table 5.3.[17]

Figure 5.5 Distributional Effects of Changes in Hourly Wages, Observed and No-Crisis Scenarios: Mexico

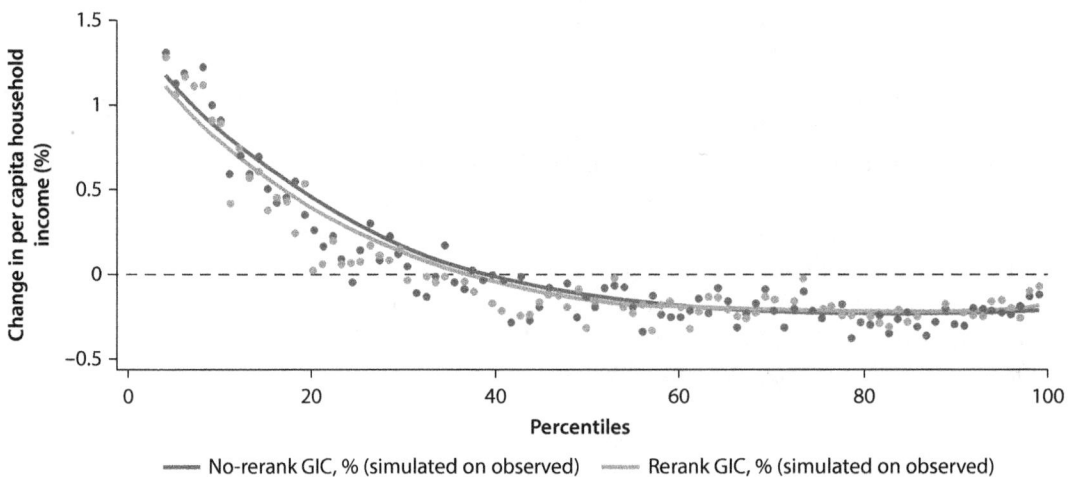

Source: Authors' own computation using the results from the microsimulation.

The negative slope of the growth incidence curve in figure 5.5 shows that had the crisis only affected hourly wages in Mexico income inequality would have declined as a consequence of the shock. The progressivity of this shock is explained by the relatively mild wage adjustment in the tradable sectors, where labor remuneration is lower than in the nontradable sectors. Much of the progressivity is determined by the differentiated income effects among the poorest households and those located in the middle of the distribution and less so between the latter and the richest households.

Figure 5.5 shows two GICs that practically overlap; one does not allow for a reranking of households along the income distribution (blue line) and the other does (orange line). Although in this particular case the two GICs are practically the same, conceptually they are quite different.[18] The blue (no-reranking) line depicts changes in average per capita household income following the same households in the observed and simulated scenarios. By contrast, the orange GIC, which allows reranking, treats households in the observed situation and simulated scenario as if they were coming from different surveys. The difference between the GICs captures changes in the position of households along the income distribution between the historical and forecast scenarios—that is, the economic mobility brought about by the crisis.

The distributional effects of changes in (monthly) wages in Brazil are significantly different from those in Mexico (figure 5.6). Because of wage inflexibility, unskilled workers in tradable sectors, the lowest earning group, and skilled workers in services, the group with the highest earnings, experienced an *increase* in real wages as a consequence of the crisis (see table 5.3). By contrast, unskilled workers in the nontradable sectors and skilled workers in tradable sectors (those located in the middle of the income distribution) experienced a decrease in real wages as a consequence of the crisis. Therefore, figure 5.6 shows a fairly flat U-shaped GIC,

Figure 5.6 Distributional Effects of Changes in Monthly Wages, Observed and No-Crisis Scenarios: Brazil

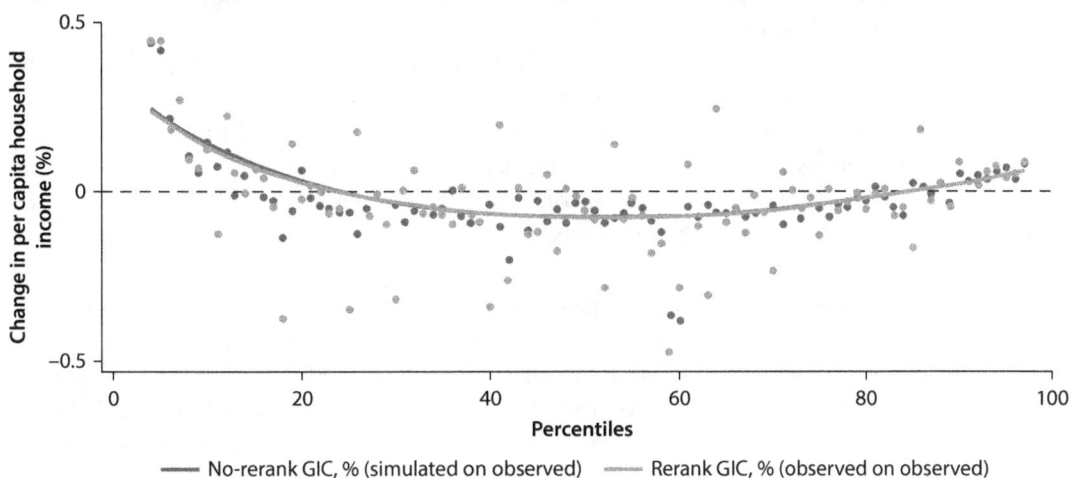

Source: Authors' own computation using the results from the microsimulation.

with those at the extremes of the per capita household income distribution benefiting from wage rigidities but not those toward the middle of the distribution.

Overall, the changes in (hourly) wages brought about in Mexico by the crisis were progressive—although all labor market segments experienced a wage loss, and in Brazil the changes in (monthly) wages were slightly regressive—that is, they increased inequality. The difference in incidence is explained by the way in which the tradable versus nontradable sectors, as well as the skilled versus unskilled wage gaps, changed in the two countries. The negative shock of the international crisis on Mexico's tradable sectors (employing workers earning on average less than workers in the nontradable sectors) was accommodated more through a reduction in quantities than in hourly wages. In fact, reducing the number of hours worked saved jobs while permitting employers to reduce costs—with no need for larger cuts in hourly wages—when facing the crisis. Adjustments in the nontradable sectors entailed both losses of hours worked (but less intensive than in the tradable sectors) and hourly wages (with larger negative magnitudes). In particular, skilled workers in the nontradable sectors, the largest group of workers in this segment and the group with the highest earners, endured a large drop in hourly wages. These adjustments entailed both an increase in the tradable to nontradable wage gap and a reduction in the skill premium. Both of these changes are equalizing and explain the progressivity of the GIC. Brazil's adjustments implied a slight increase in the skill wage gap and a very minor improvement in the intersectoral gap. The combination of an unequalizing and an equalizing pressure generated the mild U-shaped GIC shown in figure 5.6.

Distributional Effects of Changes in Total Hours Worked

In Mexico, the adjustment mechanism applied to reductions in labor demand differed between the tradable and nontradable sectors. The tradable sector adjusted mainly through quantities, with relatively mild reductions in hourly wages; the nontradable sector adjusted through wages but relatively small reductions in effective employment (see table 5.3 for details).

How do the simulated crisis-related changes in total hours worked affect the incomes of households at different parts of the distribution? Figure 5.7 answers this question using the 2008 Mexican household survey and imposing the negative shocks in effective employment as reported in table 5.3 while keeping all other variables and average income constant. Overall, the effects are regressive, but the largest negative impacts are borne by households located between the 20th and 40th percentiles. Note that there is a small difference between the GIC that allows for reranking (orange line, assuming anonymous households) and the GIC that does not allow for reranking (blue line, "following" households), showing that the crisis-mandated changes in hours worked and their implied change in income were large enough to change the ordering of some households in the lower part of the distribution. The hours worked in Brazil did not vary significantly between the crisis and no-crisis scenarios, and thus this is not included in the simulations for Brazil.

Figure 5.7 Distributional Effects of Changes in Hours Worked, Observed and No-Crisis Scenarios: Mexico

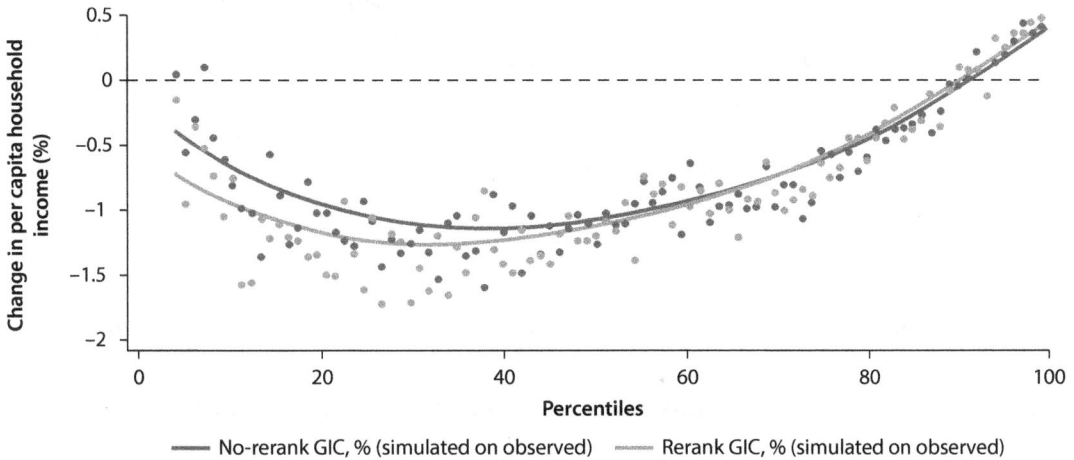

Source: Authors' own computation using the results from the microsimulation.

Distributional Effects of Increased Unemployment Rates

A reduction in total hours worked or effective employment is the outcome of a reduction in the number of people employed and, among those who kept their jobs, a reduction in hours worked (in the case of Mexico). In Mexico, the unemployment rate among unskilled workers increased from a simulated no-crisis scenario of 2.8 percent to an observed level of 4.2 percent during 2009, for an increase of 1.4 percentage points or 49.1 percent as reported in the bottom panel of table 5.3. For skilled workers, the unemployment rate increased 1.9 percentage points, from 4.1 percent in the simulated no-crisis scenario to 6.0 percent during the crisis (an increase of 45.3 percent as reported in the bottom panel of table 5.3). These changes in unemployment rates meant that 739,000 Mexican workers were pushed into unemployment, of which 232,000 were unskilled and 507,000 were skilled. The difference in the numbers of workers is explained by the larger population being classified as skilled workers (i.e., those with at least nine years of formal schooling). But who are those 739,000 workers who lost their jobs as a consequence of the crisis? Or, more specifically, were these male or female workers? Were they earning similar wages, were they of similar ages, or did they share other characteristics? Using the information at the micro (household) level, it is possible to ascertain the differential (and incidence) impact of an increase in aggregate unemployment. By means of a probit model, which estimates the probability of being unemployed as a function of sex, years of schooling, age, a rural/urban dummy, and geographic location, the microsimulation module identifies those who are most likely to lose their jobs. By construction, the workers chosen to become unemployed by the probit model are those whose characteristics are closest to those of unemployed individuals.

Understanding the Poverty Impact of the Global Financial Crisis in Latin America and the Caribbean
http://dx.doi.org/10.1596/978-1-4648-0241-6

Figure 5.8 shows the incidence of job destruction caused by the global financial crisis (compared against a no crisis case) among deciles of the income distribution, distinguishing by skill levels. Among unskilled workers, the largest effects are concentrated in deciles 5 to 8, and for skilled workers the incidence is more progressive, concentrating in deciles 5 to 9. Although the reduction in per capita income among households that experience a job loss is quite large (35 percent), the total jobs lost because of the crisis represent only 1.7 percent of the total working population of almost 43 million. For this reason, as shown in figure 5.9, the isolated distributional effect of an increase of unemployment

Figure 5.8 Distribution of Job Destruction Caused by the Global Financial Crisis, by Decile and Skills Level: Mexico

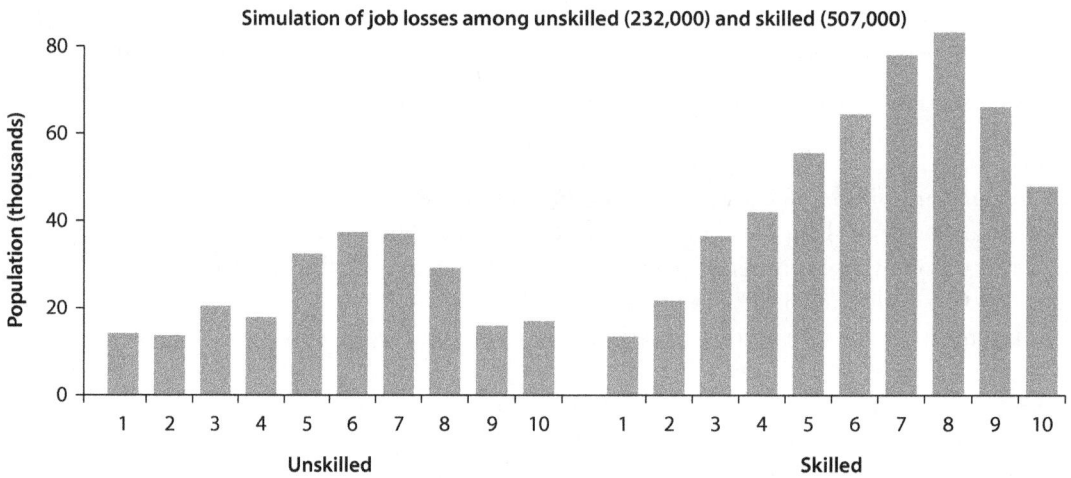

Source: ENIGH, 2008.

Figure 5.9 Distributional Effects of Job Losses, Observed and No-Crisis Scenarios: Mexico

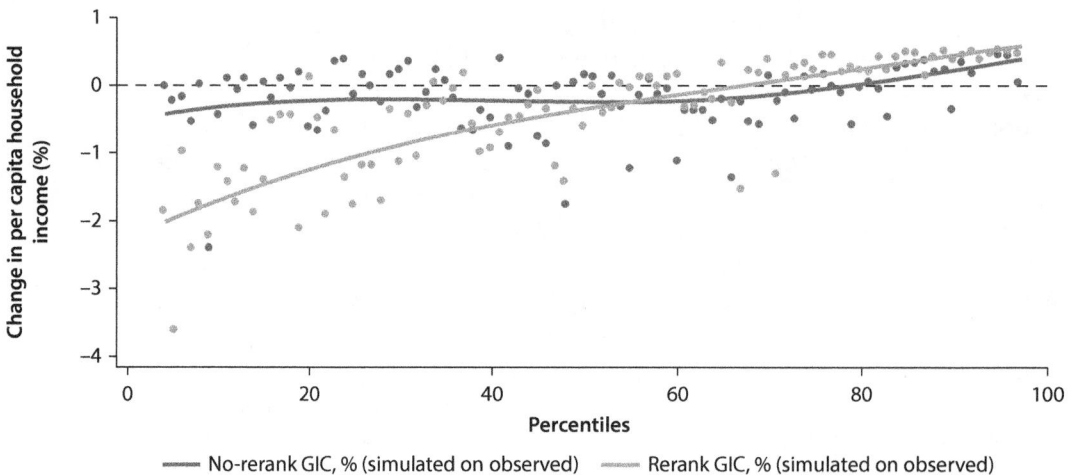

Source: Authors' own computation using the results from the microsimulation.

when following the same households in the scenarios with and without the crisis (not allowing for reranking) are quite neutral. However, when the GIC allows for reranking, the incidence of the crisis-mandated increase in unemployment rates shows a regressive effect. The difference between the two incidence curves shown in figure 5.9 reveals that unemployment has large mobility effects—in other words, every time a household experiences a job loss with its subsequent income contraction, its position in the income distribution changes.

Two other household characteristics also help explain the distributional effects of job losses: (1) heterogeneity in the source of income and (2) heterogeneity in the share of household members having a job. Labor earnings account for a lower share of total household income among households in the lowest and highest deciles of the income distribution. The poorest households in Mexico obtain a significant proportion of their income from transfers, whereas capital earnings account for a sizable proportion of the incomes of the richest households. Therefore, changes in labor income triggered by a job loss have a heterogeneous welfare effect among households located at different points in the distribution. Furthermore, the proportion of household members who have a job is significantly lower among the poorest households in Mexico. These two features explain why the largest income reductions brought about by job losses are concentrated among households located in the middle part of the income distribution.

An interesting result of the unemployment effects in Mexico is its concentration among the youth. In Mexico, being young is one of the most common characteristics of the unemployed; therefore, the probit model identifies young workers as the most likely to lose their jobs because of the crisis (figure 5.10).

Figure 5.10 Average Age of Job Keepers and Job Losers: Mexico (Results of Microsimulation)

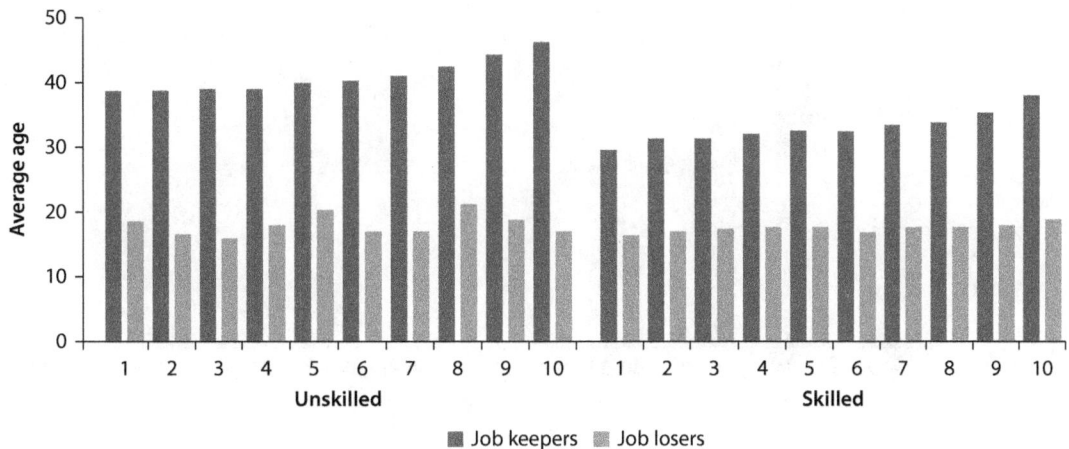

Source: ENIGH, 2008.

Understanding the Poverty Impact of the Global Financial Crisis in Latin America and the Caribbean
http://dx.doi.org/10.1596/978-1-4648-0241-6

Are these effects the outcome of the assumptions of the model (i.e., the mechanical way in which the probit model is selecting workers to become unemployed), or do they find some empirical support? Using data from the Mexican employment survey, Encuesta Nacional de Ocupación y Empleo (ENOE, National Survey of Occupation and Employment) from the first quarters of 2008, 2009, and 2010, we find that the age groups that lost more jobs during the crisis were, indeed, those between the ages of 15 and 29 (figure 5.11). Although workers of this age accounted for less than a third of total employment in Mexico, this age group filled 6 of every 10 jobs destroyed in Mexico during the first quarter of 2008 and the first quarter of 2010.[19] The incidence of job losses is not as concentrated among youth as simulated by our model, but this evidence supports the results produced by the model: youth are the group most likely to lose a job during a negative economic shock.

The distributional effects of the crisis through an increase in unemployment rates in Brazil are not very different from the effects in Mexico. If households are followed over time (growth incidence curve with reranking in figure 5.12) the effects seem to be quite mild, with households located in the middle part of the distribution suffering the largest income losses because of the increase in unemployment rates. The shape of the blue GIC in figure 5.12 (not allowing for reranking) is explained by the larger increase in the unemployment rate among unskilled workers (primarily in the nontradable sectors)

Figure 5.11   Job Destruction: Mexico, 2008–10

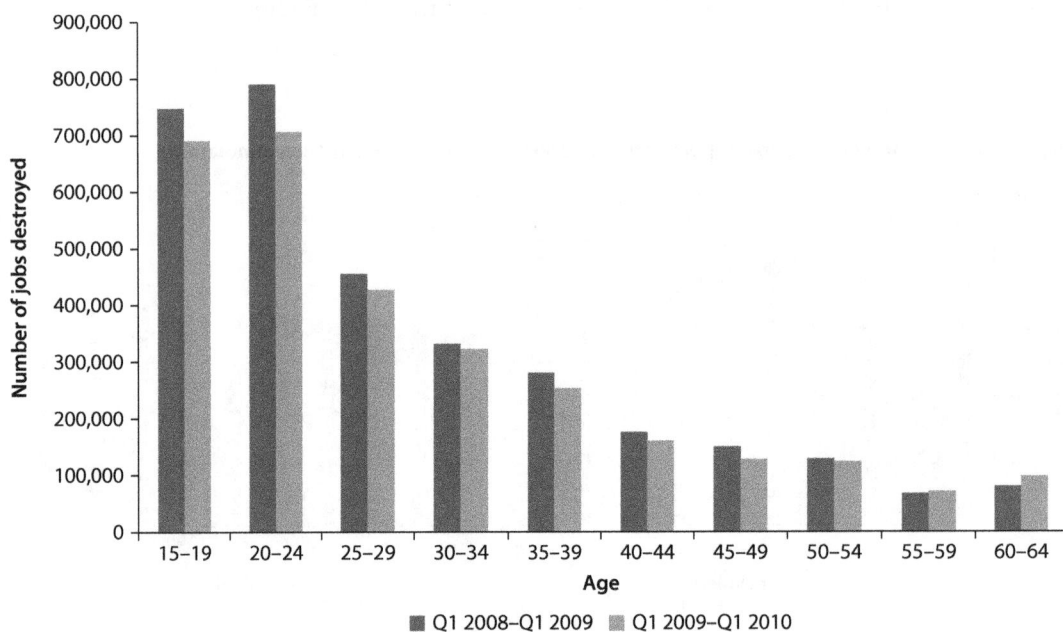

Source: Encuesta Nacional de Ocupación y Empleo (ENOE, National Survey of Occupation and Employment).

Understanding the Poverty Impact of the Global Financial Crisis in Latin America and the Caribbean
http://dx.doi.org/10.1596/978-1-4648-0241-6

Figure 5.12 Distributional Effects of Job Losses, Observed and No-Crisis Scenarios: Brazil

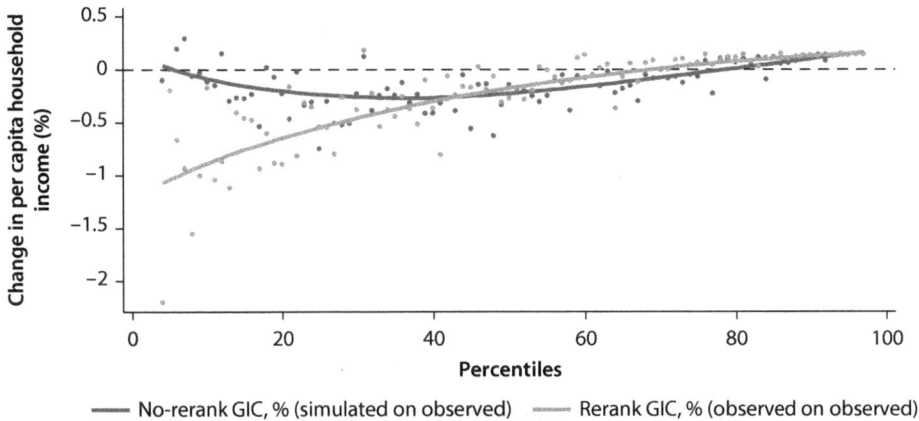

— No-rerank GIC, % (simulated on observed) ----- Rerank GIC, % (observed on observed)

Source: Authors' own computation using the results from the microsimulation.

versus the smaller increase in the unemployment rate among skilled workers (primarily those in the nontradable sectors).

As in Mexico, unemployment effects are an important determinant of changes in the position of Brazilian households along the income distribution (economic mobility). The mobility effects of the crisis-mandated changes in unemployment rates explain the difference between the two GICs depicted in figure 5.12. Another similarity between the countries in terms of the welfare effects of an increase in unemployment is related to its bias toward youth. Brazilian youth also suffered disproportionally from the increase in unemployment rates. Although the bias is not as strong as in Mexico, young workers between the ages of 15 and 29 had a larger probability of being sacked as a result of an exogenous income shock in Brazil.

Total Distributional Effects of the Crisis

When all effects, wages, hours worked (in the case of Mexico) and unemployment rates are jointly simulated, the impact of the crisis is shown to be regressive but largest among households located in the middle part of the per capita household income distribution in both Mexico and Brazil (see GICs with no-rerank in figures 5.13 and 5.14, respectively). The average household in Mexico loses 8 percent of its income as a result of the crisis (comparing the incomes in a scenario without the crisis with the observed levels) with households located in the middle part of the income distribution losing more than 9 percent of their per capita household income as a result of the crisis. For Brazil, the effect is milder, with an average loss in income of 4 percent, which is close to 5 percent among households located around the 40th percentile of the income distribution.

The crisis also causes some mobility in both Mexico and Brazil. In Mexico, reductions in hours worked are enough to push some households originally

Figure 5.13 Overall Distributional Effects of the Crisis, Observed and No-Crisis Scenarios: Mexico

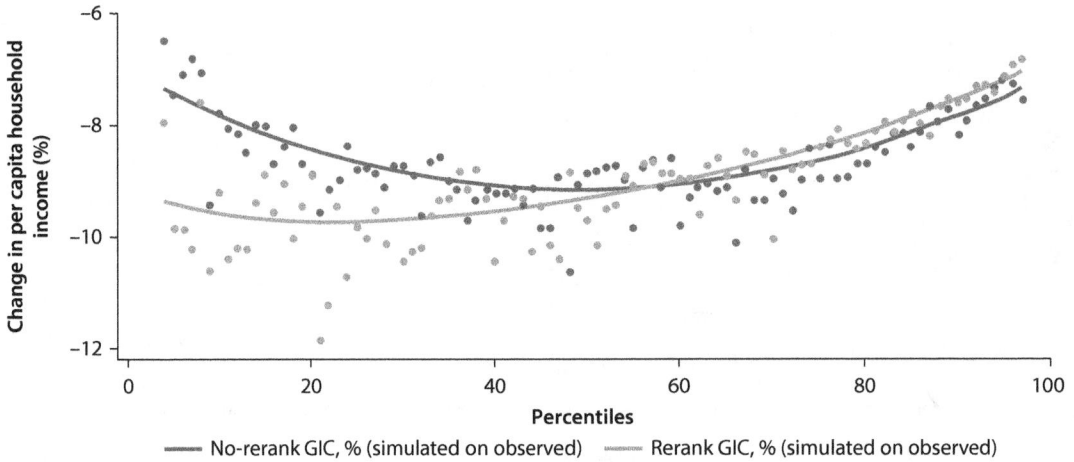

Source: Authors' own computation using the results from the microsimulation.

Figure 5.14 Overall Distributional Effects of the Crisis, Observed and No-Crisis Scenarios: Brazil

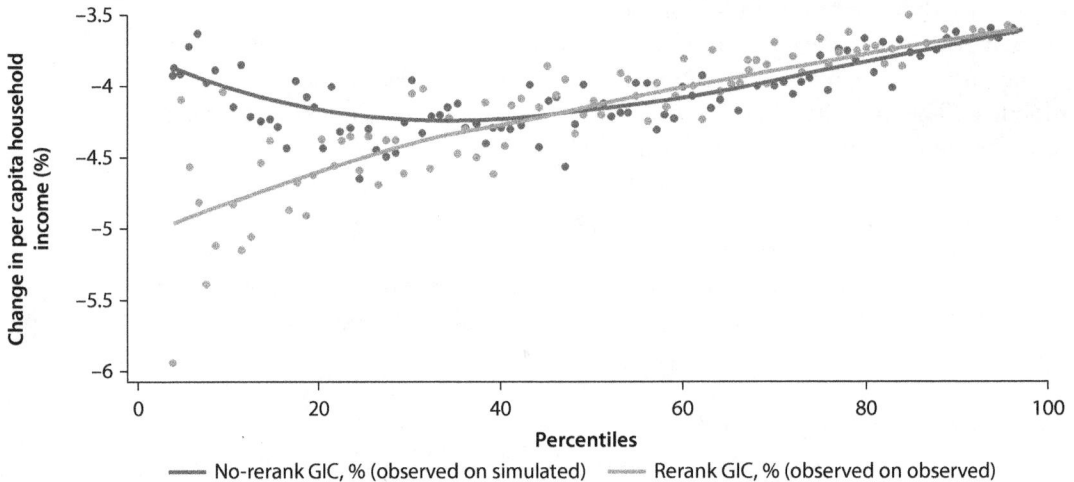

Source: Authors' own computation using the results from the microsimulation.

located in the middle part of the distribution into lower income brackets. More important, in both Mexico and Brazil increases in unemployment shift the position of households originally situated in the middle part of the income distribution toward the bottom percentiles.

Conclusion

The macroeconomic and the aggregate labor market impacts of the 2008–09 global financial crisis, when compared with a no-crisis counterfactual, were quite different in Mexico and Brazil. Mexico's labor market adjusted via a robust drop in the number of hours worked and a moderate reduction in hourly wages. Employment measured in hours worked shrank by 7 percent, but only 2.1 percent of people lost their jobs. Clearly, working fewer hours had a negative effect on incomes, but it generally represented a transitory and less severe loss than the one associated with becoming unemployed.

In Brazil, the inflexibility of the real wage did not support employment when aggregate demand dropped. In terms of job losses, the crisis had a relative impact (i.e., for each 1 percent reduction in GDP) that was similar across the two countries.

For both countries, the crisis meant a severe contraction of exports, but, notwithstanding the different sizes of the GDP contraction, investment collapsed by about 10 percent in both countries, rendering the reduction in investment relatively more severe in Brazil. Because of the diverse factor intensities (in terms of skilled and unskilled labor and capital inputs) in tradables and sectors linked to investment activities (such as construction), the decline in employment and wages affected, to varying degrees, workers and households in different parts of the income distribution.

The simulation results show that labor markets in Mexico and Brazil reacted differently to the global financial crisis, and particularly the labor market adjustments across the tradable and nontradable sectors of these two countries. The tradable sectors in Mexico adjusted mainly through a reduction in employment and average hours worked, with mild changes in wages. The nontradable sectors suffered larger losses in wages but milder ones in employment. And for both groups of sectors, unskilled workers lost relatively more than skilled workers. In Brazil, as a consequence of the crisis, the employment adjustment in the tradable sectors was similar to that of Mexico—that is, skilled workers lost relatively fewer jobs than unskilled workers (although they suffered from reduced wages). However, in the nontradable sectors unskilled workers found additional employment at almost constant wages, whereas skilled workers did record some losses.

The distributional effects of the crisis in Mexico—transmitted from a fall in external demand and through the ensuing adjustment in the labor market—are explained as follows: (1) job losses disproportionally affected unskilled workers in the tradable sectors; and (2) number of hours worked contracted more for unskilled workers, particularly among those in the tradable sectors who are typically located in the middle part of the Mexican income distribution. These two regressive effects were partly offset by a relatively milder reduction in hourly wages among unskilled workers in the tradable sectors—the groups with the lowest earnings in Mexico. The contraction in wages in Brazil was much milder and more concentrated among skilled workers in the tradable sectors and unskilled workers in the nontradable sectors, typically located in the middle or lower part of the Brazilian income distribution. The regressive effects of changes in wages were partly offset by an increase in employment among unskilled workers in the nontradable sectors, the group with the lowest earnings in the country. Finally, in Mexico, and to a lesser extent in Brazil, the simulation results show that workers between the ages of 15 and 29 were particularly vulnerable to external shocks increasing domestic unemployment.

These employment and related wage effects generated welfare effects at the level of the household. By comparing the actual crisis with a counterfactual (no-crisis) scenario, this chapter shows that in both countries households located between the 40th and 60th percentiles of the income distribution suffered the most and that income inequality widened. The overall crisis effects were therefore regressive. In Mexico, households located in the middle of the income distribution experienced a reduction in per capita household income of more than 9 percent, whereas the effect was close to 8 percent and 7 percent among the poorest and richest households, respectively. The regressive effects of the crisis are summarized by an increase in the Gini coefficient of 0.6 percentage point for Mexico and 0.3 percentage point for Brazil. The increase in income inequality (distributional effect) coupled with the significant reduction in average incomes (growth effect) resulted in an increase in the proportion of the population under the poverty line in both countries: the extreme poverty headcount ratio passed from a no-crisis level of 16.7 percent to a crisis level of 19.7, for an increase of 3 percentage points attributable to the crisis. In Brazil, the extreme poverty headcount ratio passed from 6.6 percent to 7.2 percent, an increase of 0.6 percentage point due to the crisis.

From a policy perspective, the results shown here have important implications. One of the most important findings is that, contrary to what some might have thought, the poorest households were not hit disproportionally by the external shock. The fact that households located in the middle part of the distribution, just above the moderate poverty line, bore a significant proportion of the shock poses new challenges to the governments in a region that has invested in the design of social protection programs targeting the bottom of the distribution. For example, when external shocks affect the vulnerable middle class, it limits the effectiveness of expansions in current social protection policies such as Oportunidades in Mexico and Bolsa Familia in Brazil to cushion the effects of the crisis. A second policy-relevant finding arises from the way in which the tradable sectors in Mexico adjusted to the crisis by means of job destruction and reductions in average hours worked while leaving wages almost constant. This degree of labor market flexibility in the mostly formal tradable sectors is positive as long as it is coupled with unemployment insurance or training programs for workers losing their jobs. The study's findings suggest that during times of external shocks, governments should be prepared for an increase in youth unemployment because workers between the ages of 15 and 29 are particularly vulnerable to reductions in external demand.

Annex A: Decomposition of the Global Financial Crisis Shock

Table 5A.1 Driving Factors: Decomposition of Recession-Induced Deviations in 2009, Mexico

Differences between crisis and no-crisis scenarios, percent

		Driving factor							
Variable	Total deviation (0)	Investor confidence (1)	Trade shocks (2)	Government spending (3)	Capital in use (4)	Average propensity to consume (5)	Productivity (6)	Wage shift (7)	Occupation shift (8)
L	−7.0	−1.01	−2.77	0.29	−2.48	1.89	−5.34	2.44	0.00
GDP	−8.5	−0.58	−1.93	0.11	−2.97	1.33	−5.69	1.21	0.00
I	−15.8	−4.67	−9.63	−0.09	−3.26	6.39	−7.93	3.39	0.00
C	−10.2	−2.23	−8.37	−0.28	−3.70	8.64	−6.24	2.02	0.00
X	−17.8	4.97	−5.57	0.35	1.54	−16.00	−1.06	−2.01	0.00
M	−23.4	−1.18	−21.18	0.10	−1.96	2.87	−3.13	1.03	0.00
G	1.7	0.00	0.00	1.69	0.00	0.00	0.00	0.00	0.00
W/P_c	−2.9	0.00	0.00	0.00	0.00	0.00	0.00	−2.85	0.00
Employment									
Skilled	−5.5	−0.99	−2.79	0.27	−2.25	1.93	−4.76	2.25	0.85
Unskilled	−9.6	−0.75	−1.82	0.25	−2.42	1.21	−5.58	2.31	−2.75
Employment									
Skilled, nontradables	−4.9	−1.63	−4.68	0.36	−2.36	3.57	−3.89	2.90	0.80
Unskilled, nontradables	−8.4	−1.60	−4.61	0.35	−2.32	3.51	−3.82	2.92	−2.83
Skilled, tradables	−10.0	0.85	2.76	0.07	−2.90	−3.13	−9.95	0.90	1.39
Unskilled, tradables	−12.9	0.95	3.77	0.07	−2.87	−3.45	−9.72	1.25	−2.85
Output									
Nontraded	−8.7	−0.95	−2.54	0.14	−2.65	1.90	−6.06	1.45	0.00
Traded	−6.3	0.44	0.98	0.03	−2.88	−1.59	−3.63	0.40	0.00
Employment									
Nontraded	−5.4	−1.55	−4.45	0.34	−2.24	3.39	−3.69	2.77	0.00
Traded	−10.9	0.88	3.07	0.07	−2.87	−3.21	−9.80	1.01	0.00

Note: L = employment; I = investment; C = private consumption; X = exports; M = imports; G = public consumption; and W/P_c = real wages.

Table 5A.2 Driving Factors: Decomposition of Recession-Induced Deviations in 2009, Mexico
Percent contributions

Variable	Total deviation (0)	Investor confidence (1)	Trade shocks (2)	Government spending (3)	Capital in use (4)	Average propensity to consume (5)	Productivity (6)	Wage shift (7)	Occupation shift (8)
L	100	14	40	−4	36	−27	77	−35	0
GDP	100	7	23	−1	35	−16	67	−14	0
I	100	30	61	1	21	−40	50	−21	0
C	100	22	82	3	36	−85	61	−20	0
X	100	−28	31	−2	−9	90	6	11	0
M	100	5	90	0	8	−12	13	−4	0
G	100	0	0	100	0	0	0	0	0
W/P_c	100	0	0	0	0	0	0	100	0
Employment									
Skilled	100	18	51	−5	41	−35	86	−41	−15
Unskilled	100	8	19	−3	25	−13	58	−24	29
Employment									
Skilled, nontradables	100	33	95	−7	48	−72	79	−59	−16
Unskilled, nontradables	100	19	55	−4	28	−42	46	−35	34
Skilled, tradables	100	−8	−28	−1	29	31	99	−9	−14
Unskilled, tradables	100	−7	−29	−1	22	27	76	−10	22
Output									
Nontraded	100	11	29	−2	30	−22	70	−17	0
Traded	100	−7	−16	−1	46	25	58	−6	0
Employment									
Nontraded	100	29	82	−6	41	−63	68	−51	0
Traded	100	−8	−28	−1	26	30	90	−9	0

Note: L = employment; I = investment; C = private consumption; X = exports; M = imports; G = public consumption; and W/P_c = real wages.

Table 5A.3 Driving Factors: Decomposition of Recession-Induced Deviations in 2009, Brazil

Differences between crisis and no-crisis scenarios, percent

Variable	Total deviation (0)	Investor confidence (1)	Trade shocks (2)	Government spending (3)	Capital in use (4)	Average propensity to consume (5)	Productivity (6)	Wage shift (7)	Occupation shift (8)
							Driving factor		
L	−0.9	−1.30	−0.47	−0.06	−1.77	−0.97	4.03	−0.38	0.00
GDP	−4.1	−3.75	−1.35	−0.05	−5.04	1.78	4.74	−0.46	0.00
I	−10.20	−15.13	6.91	−2.27	−0.01	2.29	−0.28	0.00	−1.72
C	0.60	−6.02	8.72	−1.71	0.02	2.32	−0.36	0.00	−2.37
X	−16.70	29.82	−36.80	−6.85	−0.02	0.81	0.42	0.00	−4.04
M	−13.70	−9.27	6.70	−10.58	−0.01	−0.02	0.20	0.00	−0.75
G	−0.14	0.00	0.00	0.00	−0.14	0.00	0.00	0.00	0.00
W/P_c	0.60	0.00	0.00	0.00	0.00	0.00	0.59	0.00	0.00
Employment									
Skilled	−0.58	0.04	−0.12	−0.05	−1.11	−0.61	2.88	−0.26	−1.36
Unskilled	−1.31	−5.50	−1.38	−0.05	−2.48	−1.22	4.16	−0.44	5.59
Employment									
Skilled, nontradables	0.24	−2.40	2.72	−0.68	−0.08	4.36	−0.42	−2.28	−0.98
Unskilled, nontradables	2.74	−12.02	7.17	−2.19	−0.04	4.82	−0.22	6.58	−1.37
Skilled, tradables	−3.75	8.20	−12.12	1.64	−0.01	−0.02	0.10	0.75	−2.29
Unskilled, tradables	−6.71	10.13	−13.85	1.18	−0.01	−0.66	−0.40	−1.06	−2.04
Output									
Nontraded	−1.80	−2.74	2.05	−0.59	−0.03	1.47	−0.19	0.00	−1.76
Traded	−1.60	5.10	−7.30	0.69	0.00	2.32	−0.06	0.00	−2.30
Employment									
Nontraded	1.24	−6.85	−1.50	−0.10	−1.52	5.43	6.29	−0.52	0.00
Traded	−5.70	10.30	1.66	−0.01	−2.51	−14.69	−0.32	−0.13	0.00

Note: L = employment; I = investment; C = private consumption; X = exports; M = imports; G = public consumption; and W/P_c = real wages.

Table 5A.4 Driving Factors: Decomposition of Recession-Induced Deviations in 2009, Brazil
Percent contributions

		Driving factor							
Variable	*Total deviation* (0)	*Investor confidence* (1)	*Trade shocks* (2)	*Government spending* (3)	*Capital in use* (4)	*Average propensity to consume* (5)	*Productivity* (6)	*Wage shift* (7)	*Occupation shift* (8)
L	100	140	51	7	190	104	−433	41	0
GDP	100	91	33	1	122	−43	−115	11	0
I	100	148	−68	22	0	−22	3	0	17
C	100	−1,003	1,453	−285	3	387	−60	0	−395
X	100	−179	220	41	0	−5	−3	0	24
M	100	68	−49	77	0	0	−1	0	5
G	100	0	0	0	100	0	0	0	0
W/P_c	100	0	0	0	0	0	98	0	0
Employment									
Skilled	100	−7	21	9	190	104	−493	44	232
Unskilled	100	421	106	3	190	93	−319	34	−428
Employment									
Skilled, nontradables	100	−1,019	1,155	−289	−34	1,851	−178	−968	−416
Unskilled, nontradables	100	−439	262	−80	−1	176	−8	240	−50
Skilled, tradables	100	−219	323	−44	0	1	−3	−20	61
Unskilled, tradables	100	−151	206	−18	0	10	6	16	30
Output									
Nontraded	100	152	−114	33	2	−82	11	0	98
Traded	100	−319	456	−43	0	−145	4	0	144
Employment									
Nontraded	100	−555	−122	−8	−123	440	509	−42	0
Traded	100	−181	−29	0	44	258	6	2	0

Note: L = employment; I = investment; C = private consumption; X = exports; M = imports; G = public consumption; and W/P_c = real wages.

Annex B: Decomposition of the Global Financial Crisis Shock Using the CGE Model

This annex describes in detail the results of the decomposition analysis shown in tables 5A.1 (Mexico) and 5A.3 (Brazil). Each column of these tables represents the individual effect of a single driving factor on the macro or labor market variables in the rows of the tables. For example, column (1) of table 5A.1 shows that the reduction in investor confidence caused a reduction in aggregate investment of 4.59 percent. This reduction is calculated as that caused by imputing the change in investor confidence from the no-crisis to the crisis scenario while leaving the average propensity to consume, trade flows, government expenditure, etc. on their no-crisis paths.

Column (0)—which equals the sum of all the other columns—represents for 2009 the full discrepancy between the values each variable takes in the crisis and no-crisis scenarios.

The decomposition of the impacts on the labor market in terms of changes in both employment and wage is embedded in this decomposition exercise. For all but one of the drivers (columns), the labor market is assumed to operate with sticky real wages. However, because a reduction in wages was actually observed in Mexico during the crisis, this is implemented in column (7) as an "outward" shift of a positively sloped supply of labor—that is, workers are willing to work the same amount of hours at a lower wage. This shift in the labor supply counterbalances the negative effect on employment generated by the other shocks (however, Brazil experienced a slight wage increase and so the reverse occurred). What follows considers the results of the decomposition in greater detail.

Investor Confidence

The effect of an "exogenous" reduction in investment demand consistent with the difference in investor confidence estimated in the historical (crisis) and forecast (no-crisis) runs of the model is shown in column (1). How is this shock transmitted through the economy? GDP is determined by the aggregate production function (i.e., by the availability of labor and capital and the level of productivity), and therefore a reduction in investment, with an initially fixed supply (fixed GDP), must be accompanied by an increase in net exports.[20] This is accomplished via a real depreciation: demand for nontradables falls—a large share of investment demand is accounted for by nontradables such as construction—and their prices, determined domestically, go down. However, prices for tradables, determined in the international market, do not fall as much, which generates the real depreciation and the incentive for producers to shift resources toward tradables (exportables and other products that compete with imports). In Mexico, exports (by volume) increase by almost 5 percent, while imports decrease by about 1 percent—see column (1) in table 5A.1.

Because Mexican exporters face a downward sloping foreign demand, they have to reduce prices to increase their volume of sales in international markets. This reduction, combined with fixed import prices,[21] generates a terms of trade loss. To remain profitable at these lower prices, firms have to reduce their costs. However, with sticky wages, the only way to do so is to reduce employment. Such a reduction, combined with a fixed stock of capital,[22] increases the marginal product of labor. With fewer but more productive workers, firms remain competitive.

Once this employment contraction is established, it is fairly straightforward to explain the reduction in GDP via the production function and the effect on consumption via a reduction in income. The reductions in employment by skill level and by sector depend on the factorial intensity of the sectors producing investment goods, and, as already stated, on the fact that a large share of investment is accounted for by the nontradable construction sector.

In Brazil, the crisis-related drop in investor confidence yields results *qualitatively* similar to those just described for Mexico. However, Brazil suffered a drop in investment activity *quantitatively* much larger than the Mexican one. This is an interesting result: had investment confidence in Brazil decreased by the same magnitude as in Mexico, the model would have been unable to account for the full observed reduction in investment activity. In fact, the loss of confidence in the case of Brazil accounts for more than the total drop in investment (148 percent, which means that other shocks supported investment by counterbalancing the loss of confidence), whereas it explains less than a third in Mexico.[23] This signals that Brazilian investment was probably already close to a ceiling perhaps because of its loose monetary policy and that the crisis caused a large retrenchment by investors.

Another interesting quantitative difference is the trade adjustment that accompanies the investment shock. Because in Brazil trade is far smaller in magnitude than in Mexico—the ratios of imports and exports to GDP are 30 and 60 percent, respectively—a reduction in investment that entails a positive impact on the trade balance generates a larger percentage change in imports and exports. Finally, when all these effects are combined they produce quantitatively larger effects on employment in Brazil.

Trade Shock

The next large crisis-related shock is a reduction in export demand.[24] This shock has the same qualitative effects in the two countries. However, these effects have larger magnitudes in Mexico. The trade shock accounts for 40 percent of the total GDP contraction in Mexico and 20 percent in Brazil.

The reduction in exports generates a terms of trade deterioration that has to be counterbalanced by a reduction in employment to moderate production costs. The reduction in employment, while increasing the marginal product of labor, lowers the marginal product of capital. Because the rental rate is not fixed, the reduction in the marginal product of capital is accompanied by falling rates of return. This outcome negatively affects investors, who are then less willing to finance investment with lower rates of return. In Mexico, as observed in column (2), *I* goes down by 9 percent. This produces a real depreciation as explained for the case of investor confidence.

The fall in employment reduces GDP and drags down private consumption and imports. Private consumption also goes down because of the real depreciation. However, these endogenous effects cannot account for the full observed drop in imports. Therefore, the model suggests that, during the crisis, there was a shift in preferences away from imports.[25] This, in turn, results in an additional contraction of imports that counteracts the real exchange rate depreciation due to a reduction in absorption (and investment in particular). The real exchange rate strengthens (or, more precisely, goes down less than it could) with negative consequences for exports. However, overall net exports improve.

The combined effect of the change in the structure of aggregate demand results in a slightly higher reduction in employment for skilled workers in relation to unskilled workers. And, because of the especially large contraction in imports, it results in a slight increase in employment in the tradable sectors (the sectors producing import-competing goods) and a loss of employment in the nontradable sectors.

Government Spending

The mild countercyclical fiscal policy accounted for in column (3) has the initial effect of shifting the structure of aggregate demand. With GDP determined from the aggregate production function, higher government consumption crowds out private consumption.

This shift in the composition of aggregate demand is relevant to the labor market because an increase in public consumption reallocates demand toward goods and services whose production is more intensive in labor inputs. Achieving the new sectoral composition of the combined private and public demand requires a larger amount of labor inputs. And because wages are fixed, this results in an increase in employment. In Mexico, the increase is similar for skilled and unskilled employment—0.3 percent—but in Brazil the demand for skilled workers increases more. For both countries, higher government expenditures result in higher employment in the nontradable sectors than in the tradable sectors.

The Capital in Use Shock

Another mechanism operating during the recession was reducing the use of capital. Firms became more risk-averse and reduced their level of production by leaving capital idle. Because of the fixed wage assumption and no effect on the terms of trade, a reduction in the capital input has to be accompanied by a proportionate reduction in labor inputs. Otherwise, the marginal product of labor would be below the fixed wage and firms would generate losses.

In Mexico, working below full capacity (a reduction of about 3 percent of capital in use) brings about a reduction in employment of about 2.5 percent and a reduction in GDP of 2.8 percent. There are negligible effects on sectoral occupation because both input types (labor and capital) go down in parallel. The capital to labor ratio does not change, and thus there is no specialization toward either tradables or nontradables.

Consumption Smoothing

The crisis-related contraction of incomes would normally entail a larger drop in private consumption than the one actually observed. This implies that, consistent with the permanent income theory, the drop in income was perceived as temporary, and households reduced their saving to smooth consumption. In terms of column (5), this is equivalent to an upsurge in the propensity to consume, which results in an increase in C of more than 8 percent for both countries.

In Mexico, an increase in consumption, other things being equal, requires a reduction in net exports and thus a real appreciation. As exports are reduced, their prices rise and the terms of trade improve. Once again, with fixed wages, the improved terms of trade make it profitable to employ more workers even if, given the fixed availability of capital, the marginal product of labor is decreasing. Additional labor inputs raise the marginal productivity of capital and thus its rate of return. This in turn stimulates investment. The joint effect of a large reduction in exports, an increase in imports, and an increase in investment in labor markets is job creation in the nontradable sectors and job losses in the tradable ones.

These transmission mechanisms operate differently in Brazil. The increased consumption results in slightly lower aggregate employment because the shift in the composition of aggregate demand—toward more private consumption, investment, and imports and fewer exports—entails a reallocation of resources from more labor-intensive to less labor-intensive production sectors.[26] However, the relative adjustment for the tradable and nontradable sectors is similar across the two countries.

Labor Market Adjustment Mechanisms: Productivity, Wage, and Skill Shifts

Changes in productivity, real wages, and occupation—the columns to the far right in the decomposition tables—are important adjustment mechanisms for both Brazil and Mexico. The starting point is the observation that in Mexico productivity changes differently across sectors with a significant fall in the nontradable segment and a rise in the tradable one.[27] Wages follow the same pattern as these productivity shifts: workers in the tradable sectors suffer lower wage losses than those in the nontradable sectors. Column (6) in table 5A.1 isolates the impact of this differential productivity shock. A reduction in productivity in the nontradable sectors generates an increase in their prices, which pushes up the real exchange rate and thus hurts the tradable sectors. Producers of exportables are negatively affected because their goods are less competitive, and producers of importables are also hurt because imports are cheaper. This real appreciation hurts employment in the tradables more than in the nontradables.

The next step in the decomposition considers the effect of the wage shift, shown in column (7). Lower real wages combined with unchanged labor productivity create an incentive to increase employment (movement along the demand for labor curve), and firms employ more workers until the decreasing productivity of the marginal worker equals the new lower wage. The increase in employment then produces an increase in output. In addition, the (aggregate demand) composition of GDP changes because an increase in employment with fixed capital stock produces an increase in the marginal productivity of capital and thus pushes up the demand for it. This push in turn propels up the rate of return, thereby allowing the economy to move up the supply of investment, which increases by 3 percent. Finally, an increase in I affects the trade balance negatively. A decrease in the average wage benefits employment in the nontradables more than in the tradables. This is explained via an appreciation in the real exchange rate.

The last run of the model, the shift in the skill intensity of employment, represents a residual. Because the changes in relative goods and factor prices and shifts in demand are observed and "exogenous," the model cannot reproduce the shift toward skilled workers, nor equivalently can it explain the bias against the unskilled. To fit the data, a change in the technology equivalent to an exogenous increase in the skill intensity of employment is assumed. The effects of this exogenous change are shown in column (8).

In the case of Brazil, the combined effect of the first five columns indicates a much larger loss of employment than the one actually observed. Moreover, the slight increase in average real wages also induced some employment loss, as shown in column (7). Thus how was Brazil's economy able to preserve employment if trade contraction, loss of investor confidence, and other crisis-related shifts in aggregate demand were causing job losses? An explanation that is consistent with the observed employment contraction is that firms chose a different input mix and used more labor and less capital. This can be represented by a technological shift that is capital-saving and labor-using. Column (8) reveals that a final twist in favoring unskilled employment, especially in the nontradable sectors, accompanied the adjustment to the crisis. For the tradable sectors, the adjustment was similar to that observed in Mexico: firms exporting or producing traded goods for the domestic market competing with imports tended to preserve their more skilled workers.

Notes

1. Note that for Brazil there is a clear inconsistency between changes in GDP per capita (measured by national accounts) and changes in household incomes per capita, as measured by the Pesquisa Nacional por Amostra de Domicílios (PNAD, National Household Survey Sample). Inconsistencies between macro- and microdata sources have been at the center of a long and still open debate. For discussions on the subject, see Robilliard and Robinson (2003) and Deaton and Kozel (2005).

2. For more details, see chapter 3.

3. For more details, see chapter 3.

4. Here the crisis period refers to 2008 and 2010 for Mexico, and 2008 and 2009 for Brazil. These are the years for which household surveys were collected for the two countries. However, in the formal model-based analysis used later in the chapter, 2009 is the crisis year for both countries.

5. For more details, see the spring 2010 special issue of *International Journal of Microsimulation*, entitled "Macro-Micro Analytics: A Guide to Combining Computable

General Equilibrium and Microsimulation Modeling Frameworks," http://www
.microsimulation.org/IJM/.

6. See, for example, Dixon and Rimmer (2002) and Dixon, Koopman, and Rimmer
(2012). For Brazil, the CGE model is a 57-sector, single-country model built around
Global Trade Analysis Project (GTAP) input-output tables for 2007 (Center for
Global Trade Analysis 2012). For Mexico, it is a 33-sector, single-country model built
around Organisation for Economic Co-operation and Development (OECD) input-
output tables for the mid-2000s.

7. By "naturally" endogenous variables we mean those that are normally explained
by CGE models. For example, for consumption quantities in a consumption
equation, consumption quantity is the naturally endogenous variable, and the
propensity to consume out of income is the parameter or naturally exogenous
variable.

8. Note that the macro-micro analytical framework used here does not contain any
explicit bottom-up feedback from the micro module to the macro model.

9. The decision to treat capital remunerations as exogenous, thereby losing some of the
macro-micro consistency, conforms with the limitations of household surveys in capturing incomes deriving from capital (see Székely and Hilgert 2007).

10. The Chow tests for equality on the Mincer equation parameters between tradable and
nontradable sectors were rejected at the 95 percent level of confidence, empirically
supporting labor market segmentation.

11. These figures are different from those reported earlier in this chapter because here
they refer to the differences between a crisis and no-crisis scenario, whereas the earlier
section was reporting the differences in levels before and after the crisis.

12. To put in perspective the growth rates of 3–4 percent assumed in the counterfactual scenario of no crisis for Mexico and Brazil, compare the forecasts
reported in the International Monetary Fund (IMF) staff reports for the Article
IV consultations in these countries. These reports were forecasting for Mexico
growth rates of 3.6–3.8 percent for the period 2008–12 (IMF 2007, 19, table
"Medium-term Staff Scenario") and for Brazil a growth rate of 4.9 percent for
2008 (IMF 2008).

13. As explained earlier, during the forecast simulation the model swaps naturally
endogenous variables with naturally exogenous ones. In the case of investment, the
model would naturally explain it as the equilibrium point where investment
demand (derived from the demand for capital in the production function) and
investment supply (financing of investment opportunities derived from savings)
meet. However, in the forecast mode this point (i.e., the level of investment) is
given, and the model calculates what happens to investor confidence, so that this
level is actually compatible with the data that underpin this investment market for
each country.

   In the case of consumption, given a target of its actual level, together with income
growth and relative prices, the model estimates the propensity to consume. For
exports, given the supply of Brazilian and Mexican products for the international
markets, the position of the foreign demand compatible with the actual observed
export flows is calculated. And so on.

14. In addition to the usual MONASH features, the model for Mexico incorporates
Mexico's manufacturing re-export activity. Re-exporting, in which large volumes of
imports are processed entirely for export, is an important aspect of the Mexican

economy. Because of the crisis, imports in Mexico contracted not only because of a fall in incomes but also because of a fall in export demand. And the second link is a direct link—that is, over and above the indirect link that a contraction of export demand has on incomes.

15. In the no-crisis scenario, employment of effective workers equals 13.6 million for unskilled workers and 23.5 million for skilled workers and an overall ratio of skilled worker per unskilled worker of 1.73. In the crisis scenario, this ratio increases to 1.81, and thus—assuming that nothing happens to the level of employment of unskilled workers—the number of employed skilled workers is estimated at 24.5 million (13.6 million × 1.81). The difference in employment for skilled workers between the two scenarios is equal to 1 million.

16. Full detail on this and other effects are provided in Annex A, tables 5A.1, 5A.2, 5A.3, and 5A.4. In this specific case, the combined effect is estimated by summing the changes in L in the first row of table 5A.1 in annex A for columns (1)–(5). This sum is equal to −4.08 percent, and it represents 58 percent of the total change, −7.0. Each column of the table represents the isolated impact of an individual driver or shock. For example, the model can identify the impact of the reduction in investor confidence (as described in table 5.2) in isolation (by imputing the change in investor confidence from the no-crisis to the crisis scenario while leaving the average propensity to consume, trade flows, government expenditure, etc. on their no-crisis paths) on GDP, employment, and wages. This impact can then be compared with the total impact to estimate the relative contribution of the reduction in investment confidence (a detailed analysis is offered in annex B).

17. In this simulation, the average per capita household income is kept constant to emphasize that changes in labor market outcomes (wages, labor allocation, and hours worked) are determining the distributional effects of the crisis, while the changes in average incomes are solely determined by the growth effect of the crisis as estimated by the macro model.

18. See Bourguignon (2011) for a detailed discussion on this topic.

19. See http://www.inegi.org.mx/est/contenidos/proyectos/encuestas/hogares/regulares /enoe/default.aspx.

20. This is evident from the equation GDP = $C + I + G + (X - M)$. With fixed GDP, a reduction in I has to be compensated for by an increase in net exports because C is a function of income (GDP) and G is fixed.

21. As described in the macro model section, the model assumes that Mexico and Brazil face downward sloping foreign demand for their exports, but that these economies have no market power on the import side.

22. The reduction in Investment affects the accumulation of capital and thus the future stock of capital but not the current one.

23. For Brazil, the share of the change in investment explained by the reduction in investor confidence is calculated from the figures in table 5A.3 as −15.1/−10.2 × 100 = 148 percent. For Mexico, the share of the change in investment is calculated (using figures from table 5A.1) as −4.7/−15.8 × 100 = 30 percent.

24. Column (2), which describes the impact of the reduction in export demand, also includes a simultaneous reduction in imports (via a shift in the preferences of Mexican demand toward domestic products). A further decomposition of this combined trade shock is available upon request. The size of the trade shocks is obtained from comparing the historical (crisis) versus the forecast (no-crisis) simulations. The change in

preferences for domestic as opposed to import varieties can be viewed as the residual change that is needed to bring about the observed reduction in imports over and above that endogenously produced by the observed relative price change. During the recession, Mexico and Brazil experienced real exchange rate depreciation, but it was not enough to account for the full reduction in imports.

25. This finding should be analyzed further. It may indeed be the result of rationing imports rather than a voluntary change in preferences. A disruption of logistics and a delay of shipments from the United States to Mexico may have caused this shift of preferences away from imports. Exporters in the United States may have been affected by the drying up of credit and may have either deferred production or decided to shift their sales to the domestic market.

26. The increase in GDP associated with a slight reduction in employment seems perplexing at first glance. However, the shift in demand toward consumption and imports implies a shift toward GDP components that have higher indirect taxation. Therefore, when measured at market prices, GDP is slightly higher in the specific shock of column (5).

27. With respect to the no-crisis scenario, the output of the tradable sectors contracts by about 6 percent and that of the nontradable sectors by almost 9 percent. These are accompanied by reductions in labor inputs of 11 and 6 percent, respectively.

References

Bourguignon, François. 2011. "Non-Anonymous Growth Incidence Curves, Income Mobility and Social Welfare Dominance." *Journal of Economic Inequality* 9 (4): 605–27.

Bourguignon, François, Maurizio Bussolo, and Luiz Pereira da Silva, eds. 2008. *The Impact of Macroeconomic Policies on Poverty and Income Distribution: Macro-Micro Evaluation Techniques and Tools*. Washington, DC: World Bank.

Bourguignon, François, H. G. Francisco Ferreira, and Phillippe G. Leite. 2002. "Beyond Oaxaca-Blinder: Accounting for Differences in Household Income Distributions across Countries." Policy Research Working Paper 2828, World Bank, Washington, DC.

Bourguignon, François, and Luiz Pereira da Silva, eds. 2003. *The Impact of Economic Policies on Poverty and Income Distribution: Evaluation Techniques and Tools*. Washington, DC: World Bank.

Bourguignon, François, and Luc Savard. 2008. "Distributional Effects of Trade Reform: An Integrated Macro-Micro Model Applied to the Philippines Labour." In *The Impact of Macroeconomic Policies on Poverty and Income Distribution: Macro-Micro Evaluation Techniques and Tools*, edited by Francois Bourguignon, Maurizio Bussolo, and Luiz Pereira da Silva, 177–212. Houndmills, U.K.: Palgrave.

Bussolo, Maurizio, Jann Lay, and Dominique Van der Mensbrugghe. 2006. "Structural Change and Poverty Reduction in Brazil: The Impact of the Doha Round Table of Contents." In *Poverty and the WTO*, edited by Thomas W. Hertel and L. Alan Winters, 249–84. Washington, DC: World Bank.

Chen, Shaohua, and Martin Ravallion. 2004. "Welfare Impacts of China's Accession to the World Trade Organization." *World Bank Economic Review* 18 (1): 29–57. http://wber .oupjournals.org/cgi/doi/10.1093/wber/lhh031.

Chudik, Alexander, and Marcel Fratzscher. 2011. "Identifying the Global Transmission of the 2007–2009 Financial Crisis in a GVAR Model." *European Economic Review* 55 (3).

Davies, James B. 2009. "Combining Microsimulation with CGE and Macro Modelling for Distributional Analysis in Developing and Transition Countries." *International Journal of Microsimulation* 2 (1): 49–56.

Deaton, Angus, and Valerie Kozel. 2005. "Data and Dogma: The Great Indian Poverty Debate." *World Bank Research Observer* 20 (2): 177–99.

Devereux, Michael B., Robert Kollmann, and Werner Roeger. 2011. "Advances in International Macroeconomics: Lessons from the Crisis." *European Economic Review* 55 (3).

Dixon, Peter, Robert B. Koopman, and Maureen T. Rimmer. 2012. "The MONASH Style of CGE Modeling: A Framework for Practical Policy Analysis." In *Handbook of Computable General Equilibrium Modeling*, edited by Peter B. Dixon and Dale Jorgenson, 23–103. Dordrecht: Springer.

Dixon, Peter, and Maureen T. Rimmer. 2002. *Dynamic General and Equilibrium Modeling for Forecasting and Policy*. Amsterdam: Elsevier.

Fernandez, Ana M., Daniel Lederman, and Mario Gutierrez-Rocha. 2013. "Export Entrepreneurship and Trade Structure in Latin America during Good and Bad Times." Policy Research Working Paper 6413, World Bank, Washington, DC.

Gray, G., B. Joshi, P. Kehayova, R. Llaudes, G. Presciuttini, M. Saenz, M. Saito, and M. Chivakul. 2010. "How Did Emerging Markets Cope in the Crisis?" Paper prepared by the Strategy, Policy, and Review Department in consultation with other departments at the International Monetary Fund, Washington, DC.

Hollweg, Claire H., Daniel Lederman, and Jose-Daniel Reyes. 2012. "Monitoring Export Vulnerability to Changes in Growth Rates of Major Global Markets." Policy Research Working Paper 6266, World Bank, Washington, DC.

IMF (International Monetary Fund). 2007. *Mexico: 2007 Article IV Consultation—Staff Report; Staff Supplement; and Public Information Notice on the Executive Board Discussion for Mexico*. IMF Country Report 07/379, Washington, DC.

———. 2008. *Article IV Consultation with Brazil*. Public Information Notice (PIN) No. 08/103, Washington, DC, August 8.

Kaplan, David S., Daniel Lederman, and Raymond Robertson. 2012. "What Drives Short-Run Labor Market Volatility in Offshoring Industries? Evidence from Northern Mexico during 2007–2009." Policy Research Working Paper 6268, World Bank, Washington, DC.

Lane, Philip R., and Gian Maria Milesi-Ferretti. 2010. "The Cross-Country Incidence of the Global Crisis." *IMF Economic Review* 59 (1): 77–110.

Robilliard, Anne-Sophie, François Bourguignon, and Sherman Robinson. 2008. "Crisis and Income Distribution: A Micro-Macro Model for Indonesia." In *The Impact of Macroeconomic Policies on Poverty and Income Distribution: Macro-Micro Evaluation Techniques and Tools*, edited by François Bourguignon, Maurizio Bussolo, and Luiz Pereira da Silva, 93–118. Washington, DC: World Bank.

Robilliard, Anne-Sophie, and Sherman Robinson. 2003. "Reconciling Household Surveys and National Accounts Data Using a Cross Entropy Estimation Method." *Review of Income and Wealth* 49 (3): 395–406.

Rojas-Suarez, Liliana. 2010. "The International Financial Crisis: Eight Lessons for and from Latin America." Working Paper 202, Center for Global Development, Washington, DC.

Rose, Andrew K., and Mark M. Spiegel. 2011. "Cross-Country Causes and Consequences of the Crisis: An Update." *European Economic Review* 55 (3): 309–24.

Székely, Miguel, and Marianne Hilgert. 2007. "What's Behind the Inequality We Measure: An Investigation Using Latin American Data." *Oxford Development Studies* 35 (2).

CHAPTER 6

The Role of Social Protection in the Crisis in Latin America and the Caribbean

Margaret Grosh, Anna Fruttero, and Maria Laura Oliveri

Social protection is a core part of the policy package for addressing poverty, vulnerability, and shocks. Under the umbrella of social protection, social assistance programs provide public transfers to supplement incomes that fall short of needs. Unemployment insurance (UI) partially replaces labor earnings for the unemployed. And active labor market policies seek to improve the employability or wages of prospective or current workers. All of these facets of social protection thus mitigate the loss of earnings and jobs as discussed in earlier chapters.

This chapter tells the story of how social protection was available or modified to assist those in the Latin America and the Caribbean (LAC) region who were affected by the 2008–09 global financial crisis. The section "Social Assistance, Unemployment Insurance, and Active Labor Market Programming in the LAC Region in the 2000s: An Overview" is a broad overview of social protection and how it changed over the 2000s. The sections "Labor Market Programs" and "Social Assistance" that follow then focus, respectively, on how the labor market and social assistance programs most pertinent to the crisis response have developed, with a bit of background on their precrisis status and more detail on the many changes in policy or programming evoked by or coincident in time with the crisis. The section "Reflections" discusses some themes particularly relevant in delivering social protection in a crisis and outlines challenges for the future.

We would like to thank Paula Cerutti, who took over from Maria Laura Oliveri as maven of the social protection expenditure database, and Claudia Rodriguez Alas, who worked on the household survey databases. Our colleagues in the Social Protection Unit of the Human Development Department in the Latin America and the Caribbean Region were very helpful in steering us to literature and putting specifics into context.

Social Assistance, Unemployment Insurance, and Active Labor Market Programming in the LAC Region in the 2000s: An Overview

The 2000s saw a significant increase in expenditures on social assistance programs in LAC (see box 6.1 for an explanation of the expenditure database on which this discussion is built).

Box 6.1 Social Protection Database of Government Expenditures and Number of Beneficiaries

The Latin America and the Caribbean Social Protection team at the World Bank has commissioned special compilations of data from budget and program sources aimed at constructing a high-quality, transparent database that will allow benchmarking of LAC social protection programs—their design, financing, and outcomes across the region and over time, including during times of crisis. The initial work was carried out by local consultants familiar with social policy in the countries and working from common terms of reference, although with diverse data sources. Information was harmonized to improve quality and comparability. Several features of how this work was conducted should be kept in mind in interpreting the numbers found here:

- In this chapter, we focus on a core set of programs for which we collected information from all countries based on a rather narrowly defined concept of social assistance. This is not a matter of conceptual principle, but a practical approach to using the data that were reasonably and readily collectible and comparable across a fairly large and diverse group of countries. This description of our approach implies that we have biased downward our measurement of the efforts governments make to protect their poor. For example, we exclude housing sector social assistance, subsidized prices of food or energy, and subsidized access to health insurance.
- We consider only federal and national government expenditures. Again, this approach is out of pragmatism rather than conviction, and it probably underestimates the assistance available to the population, especially in Argentina and Brazil.
- The ever-vexing issue of how to categorize programs plagues this and similar exercises. Fundamentally, category labels are not very important to the analysis and interpretation carried out in this study, and thus we ask readers' tolerance where we have made one choice and you might have made another. The following points should be kept in mind:
  - In this chapter, the categorization of the programs chosen for policies related to the labor market follows that used by the Organisation for Economic Co-operation and Development (OECD).
  - Income support by means of employment in labor-intensive public works programs falls under labor market programs rather than social assistance, in keeping with the OECD classification.
  - Social assistance is divided into 11 categories: conditional cash transfers (CCTs), school feeding programs, other food programs, family allowances and child benefits, social pensions, disability benefits, funeral allowances, education benefits, special benefits, emergency benefits, and other social safety network programs.

---

box continues next page

Box 6.1 Social Protection Database of Government Expenditures and Number of Beneficiaries
(continued)

  – Although categories of "conditional" and "unconditional" are commonly used and sound quite dichotomous, how programs encourage the use of social services is in reality more of a continuum. Thus a program might be categorized differently by different analysts or even the same analyst when considering how the program operates at different points in time or what the rules say as opposed to what takes place in practice.
- More vexing is the continuum between social assistance fully financed by general tax revenues and social assistance that has a very small contributory element. For example, Brazil's spending on rural pensions constitutes about 1.2 percent of GDP, which we classified as social assistance because it is mostly financed from general revenues rather than contributions. These pensions fall into a conceptual gray area, but they are large enough to materially distort the comparative view of countries' social protection efforts if they are omitted.
- GDP estimates from the International Monetary Fund's *World Economic Outlook* are used as the divisor for expenditure numbers.

The database commissioned by the Latin America and the Caribbean Social Protection team at the World Bank will eventually become publicly available alongside data from other regions at http://worldbank.org/ASPIRE. Meanwhile, the methods used to compile the database and the main findings are available in Cerutti et al. (2014).

The average spending in the 10 countries for which we have data rose from 0.4 percent of the gross domestic product (GDP) in 2000 to 1.2 percent in 2010.[1] Argentina's social assistance expenditures, for example, increased sevenfold, from 0.2 percent to 1.5 percent of GDP (figure 6.1). In 2000 all 10 countries were spending at least 0.4 percent of GDP on social assistance, and four of them (Argentina, Brazil, Chile, and Ecuador) were spending more than 1 percent, thereby entering the range of most of the Eastern European and Central Asian countries, though not of their highest spenders (World Bank ECA SPeeD Database).

Half of the countries for which we have social assistance data spend as much or more on social assistance as the value of the poverty gap (PG) for the extreme poor, but half fall well short. In 2008 spending on social assistance in Argentina, Brazil, and Chile exceeded the value of these countries' moderate PGs, whereas the levels of spending in Ecuador and Uruguay were similar to the value of the extreme PG (see table 6.1). Spending in Colombia, El Salvador, Honduras, Mexico, and Peru was much lower than even the extreme PG. Of course, in no country is social assistance meant to assist only the poorest. Many programs are intended for specific categories of individuals across the income distribution—the elderly, the disabled, or children, for example—and none can achieve perfect targeting. Thus such calculations do not imply that social assistance spending will eliminate extreme poverty in the countries that are spending more than the value of their PG. However, countries that spend less on social assistance than the value of their PG will surely not close it.

Understanding the Poverty Impact of the Global Financial Crisis in Latin America and the Caribbean
http://dx.doi.org/10.1596/978-1-4648-0241-6

Figure 6.1 Spending on Social Assistance as a Share of GDP for Selected Countries: Latin America and the Caribbean, 2000–10

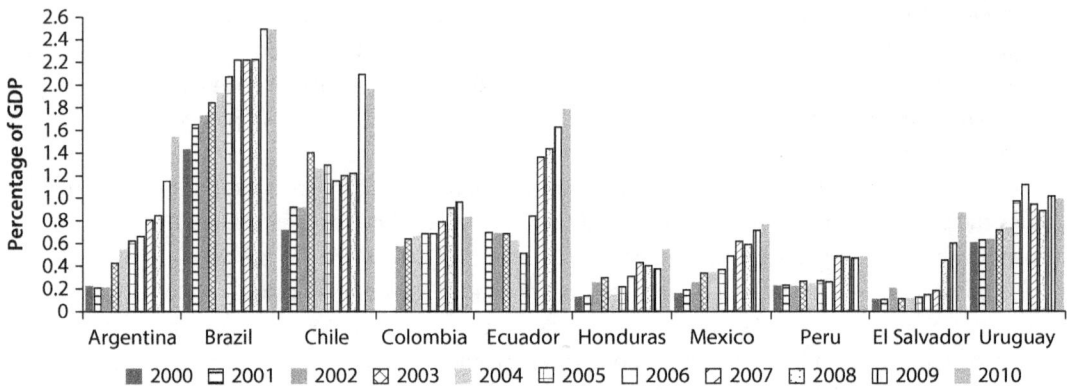

Source: Cerutti et al. 2014.
Note: The graph includes only central government–level expenditures.

Table 6.1 Poverty Gap and Social Assistance Spending: Latin America and the Caribbean, 2008

Percentage of GDP

	PG, moderate	PG, extreme	Social assistance
Argentina	0.572	0.357	0.844
Brazil	1.909	1.193	2.223
Chile	0.419	0.262	1.219
Colombia	2.935	1.834	0.912
Costa Rica	0.611	0.382	–
Dominican Republic	3.225	2.016	–
Ecuador	2.287	1.429	1.434
El Salvador	3.930	2.456	0.446
Honduras	9.504	5.940	0.399
Mexico	1.306	0.816	0.586
Paraguay	3.695	2.309	–
Peru	2.885	1.803	0.474
Uruguay	1.385	0.865	0.883

Sources: Poverty gaps: see note; social assistance: Cerutti et al. 2014.
Note: The values of the poverty gaps as a share of GDP are calculated based on the poverty gaps presented in chapter 3. They are then multiplied by the corresponding international poverty line (either US$4.00 or $2.50); converted to local currency using the purchasing power parity (PPP) index; multiplied by 365 to convert from a daily to an annual figure; multiplied by the number of poor (e.g., the headcount times the population); and divided by GDP in local currency units (LCUs); – = not available.

The overall picture of social assistance in the LAC region is that most countries have a rich and diverse set of programs, but there is a great deal of variation in the mix within each country (figure 6.2). Latin America is rightly well known for the rise of its conditional cash transfer (CCT) program. Perhaps less widely recognized but also important are the new social pensions in many countries and child allowances in a few, the ongoing school feeding programs, and the still significant presence of in-kind food programs in several countries.[2]

Understanding the Poverty Impact of the Global Financial Crisis in Latin America and the Caribbean
http://dx.doi.org/10.1596/978-1-4648-0241-6

Figure 6.2 Social Assistance Spending as a Share of GDP, by Country and Type of Program: Latin America and the Caribbean, 2000–10

a. Argentina

b. Brazil

c. Chile

d. Colombia

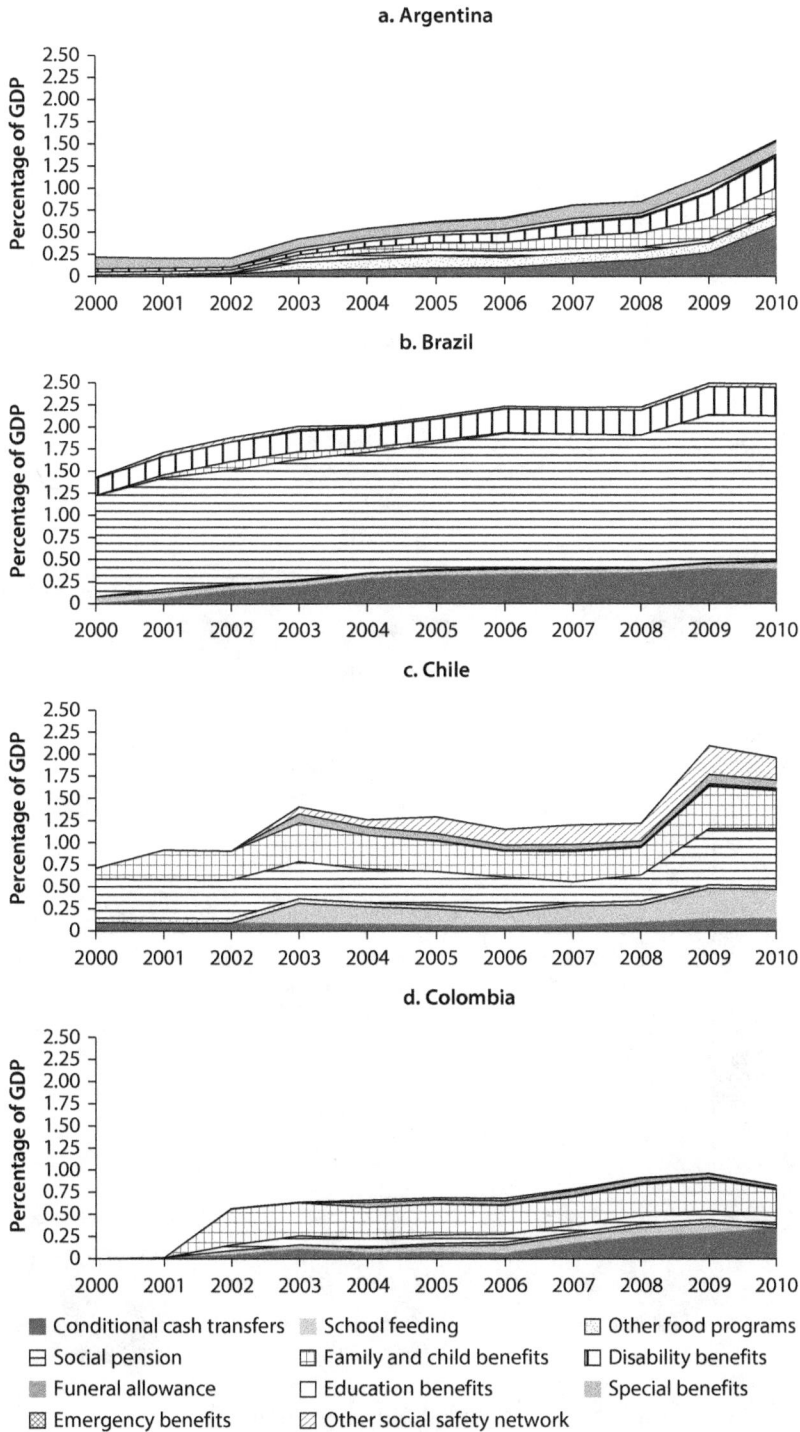

Conditional cash transfers School feeding Other food programs
Social pension Family and child benefits Disability benefits
Funeral allowance Education benefits Special benefits
Emergency benefits Other social safety network

figure continues next page

Understanding the Poverty Impact of the Global Financial Crisis in Latin America and the Caribbean
http://dx.doi.org/10.1596/978-1-4648-0241-6

Figure 6.2 Social Assistance Spending as a Share of GDP, by Country and Type of Program: Latin America and the Caribbean, 2000–10 *(continued)*

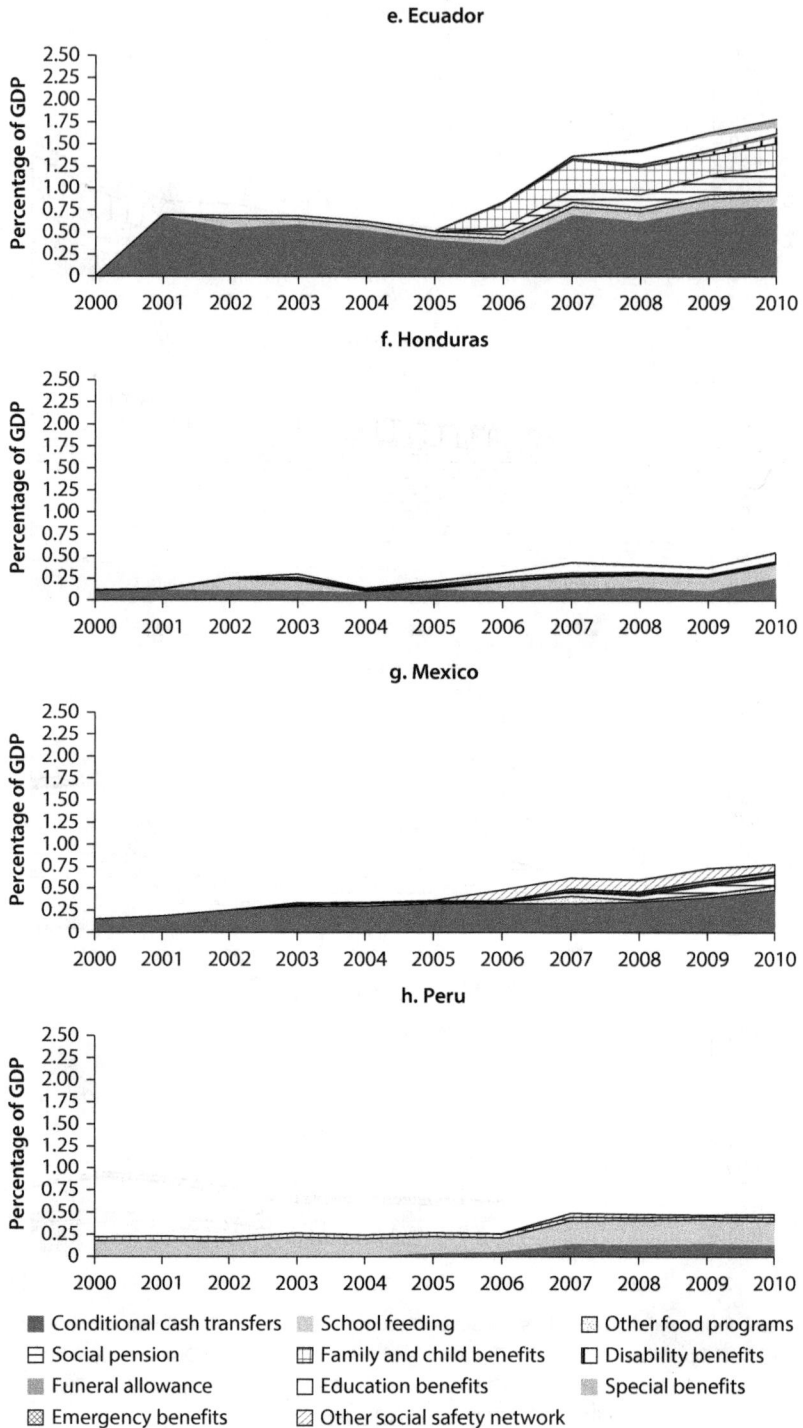

e. Ecuador

f. Honduras

g. Mexico

h. Peru

- ■ Conditional cash transfers
- ▨ School feeding
- ☐ Other food programs
- ⊟ Social pension
- ▦ Family and child benefits
- ☐ Disability benefits
- ▨ Funeral allowance
- ☐ Education benefits
- ▨ Special benefits
- ▨ Emergency benefits
- ▨ Other social safety network

figure continues next page

Figure 6.2 Social Assistance Spending as a Share of GDP, by Country and Type of Program: Latin America and the Caribbean, 2000–10 *(continued)*

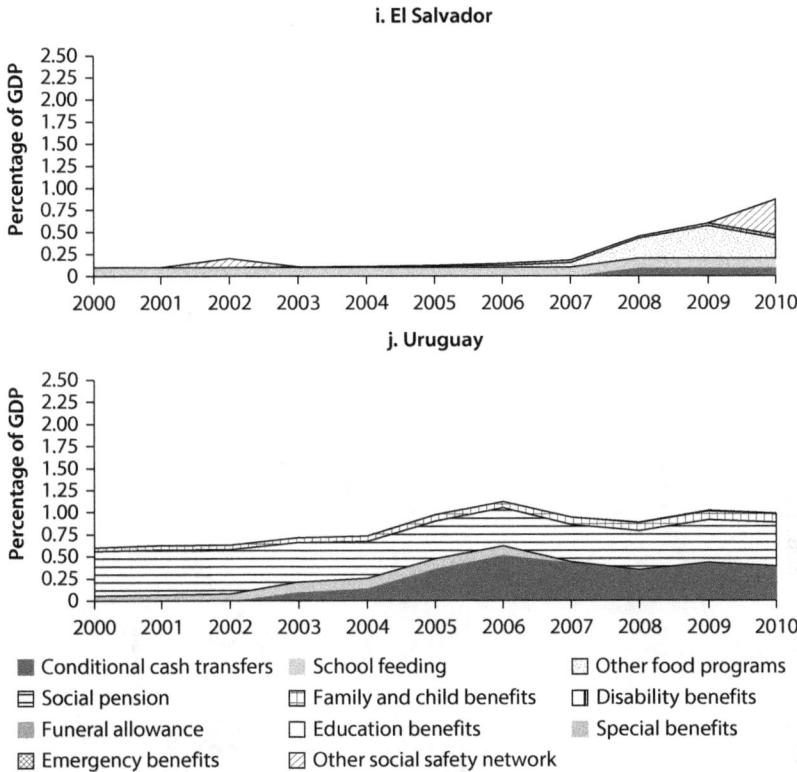

i. El Salvador

j. Uruguay

- ■ Conditional cash transfers
- ▨ School feeding
- ☐ Other food programs
- ⊟ Social pension
- ⊞ Family and child benefits
- ⊡ Disability benefits
- ▨ Funeral allowance
- ☐ Education benefits
- ▨ Special benefits
- ▨ Emergency benefits
- ▨ Other social safety network

Source: Cerutti et al. 2014.

Expenditures on labor market programs—UI, employment services, training, wage subsidies, incentives for self-employment, or direct public employment—are much lower: on the order of 1 percent of GDP in recent years in Brazil and for selected years in Argentina (see figure 6.3); on the order of 0.3–0.6 percent of GDP in Chile, Colombia, and Uruguay; and still lower in the other countries in the data set. By way of comparison, the OECD average for UI alone is in the range of 0.7–1.0 percent of GDP, depending on the year, and the active labor market policy (ALMP) ranged from 0.5 percent to 0.7 percent of GDP during the decade (OECD iLibrary[3]). ALMP spending in the 10 Eastern and Central European countries was 0.5 percent of GDP in 2008 and 1.0 percent of GDP in 2010 (Kuddo 2012). Although expenditures on labor market programs are still low in the LAC region, this has been a rather active area of social policy making over the last decade, and especially in more recent years and in the higher-income countries.

Secular expansions and changes in social protection programming dominated the 2000s, with the response to the global financial crisis playing a rather secondary role. The notable increases in social assistance spending in the 10 LAC countries at the time of the crisis seem to be explained by the secular increase

Figure 6.3 Spending on Labor Market Programs as a Share of GDP for Selected Countries: Latin America and the Caribbean, 2000–10

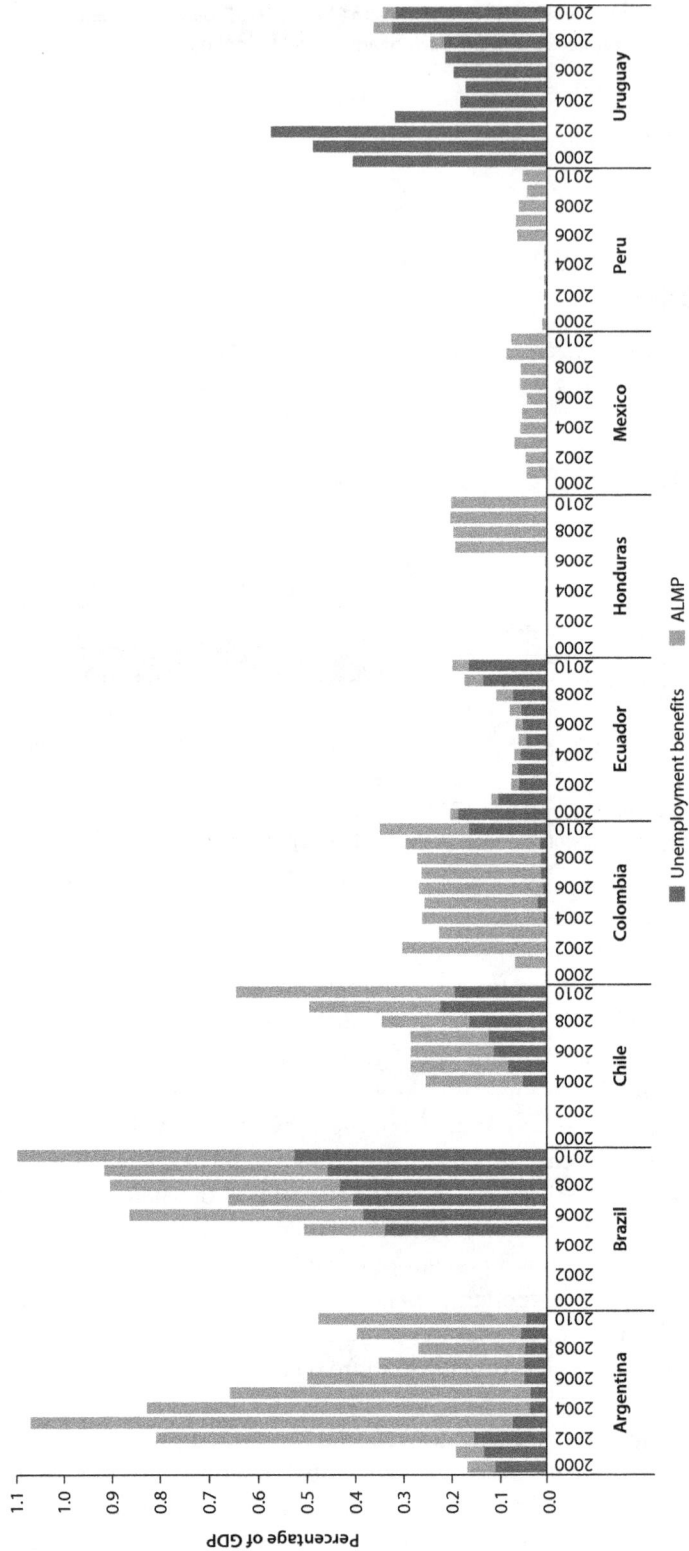

Source: Cerutti et al. 2014.

Note: ALMP = active labor market policies.

rather than by a sharp response to the crisis in 2008 or after (see figure 6.3). Even where expenditures increased from 2008 to 2010 by more than the trend for the decade, the policy story behind them was usually not one of crisis. Argentina, for example, doubled social assistance spending from 2003 to 2008, and nearly again from 2008 to 2010. However, the uptick in 2009 and 2010 was not really crisis-related. The headline change was the creation in Argentina of the Universal Child Allowance in late 2009, a reform that had been gathering momentum for some time. In Brazil, the steady increase in expenditures was largely due to the creation and expansion of Bolsa Familia (Family Grant), with more gradual increases as well in the expenditures on noncontributory pensions for the elderly and disabled. Similarly, in Ecuador the introduction of a social pension and increases in spending on Bono de Desarrollo Humano (BDH, Human Development Grant) drove the changes (see figure 6.2 for the disaggregation of the total expenditures by program).

There were, of course, some peaks in the more crisis-related expenditures, and these are clearer on the labor market side. The largest was in Argentina, where the Jefes y Jefas de Hogar Desocupados (Unemployed Heads of Household) workfare program put in place in response to the currency crisis in 2001 accounted for more than 0.9 percent of GDP in 2003 at its peak. The program and expenditures on it then declined as beneficiaries got jobs or moved on to other programs (World Bank 2010a). In response to the 2008–09 financial crisis, the largest increases in expenditures on labor programs were for unemployment benefits in Brazil, Chile, Ecuador, and Uruguay. Mexico also noticeably increased its social assistance expenditure by means of the increase in benefit levels and expansion of Oportunidades (Opportunities) and its Programa de Asistenctia Alimentaria (PAL, Program for Nutritional Assistance).

The financial crisis playing out in headlines around the world evoked an active policy response in many of the nations of LAC, and usually it was a multifaceted one. In many countries, the crisis response included expansionary monetary and fiscal policies. Within fiscal policies, stimulus packages often included a diverse range of tax measures, infrastructure spending, and increases in social protection. Within social protection, responses usually included a range of measures to increase the coverage or generosity of social assistance programs or labor market programs. Mexico's stimulus package, described in box 6.2, illustrates the multifaceted dimensions of the stimulus packages used.

Latin America relied less on social protection as part of its fiscal stimulus packages than did other countries worldwide. Zhang, Thelen, and Rao (2010) reviewed the packages in 48 countries across the income spectrum (all those for which they could find enough information for their calculation) and estimated a total fiscal stimulus of about 3.9 percent of global GDP in 2008 (ranging from 13 percent of GDP in China to 0.2 percent in Sri Lanka). Of this, about 25 percent was spent on social protection measures, with richer countries generally spending more on these programs. For the five Latin American countries in their sample (Argentina, Chile, Honduras, Mexico, and Peru), the average stimulus package was 2.6 percent of GDP, and only about 4 percent of it went to

Box 6.2   Policy Response to the 2008–09 Financial Crisis in Mexico

The 2008–09 global financial crisis dramatically affected the Mexican economy. Mexico's economic expansion from 2002 onward came to an end in the first quarter of 2008, when the economy entered a recession that became the deepest in Latin America. The contraction in GDP was considerable in the fourth quarter of 2008 and the first quarter of 2009 (at annualized rates of 7.5 percent and 24.9 percent, respectively). Consequently, there were sharp increases in unemployment, underemployment, and poverty rates.

To help strengthen the Mexican economy and mitigate the adverse effects of the rough and more volatile international environment, the government of Mexico adopted a fiscal stimulus package of almost Mex$190 billion (approximately US$14 billion) in the last quarter of 2008 and first semester of 2009 (ILO 2010). This package included programs related to growth, employment, public works, household economics, infrastructure, housing, and the influenza outbreak. Table B6.2.1 presents the breakdown of Mexico's fiscal stimulus plan. Overall, the fiscal stimulus for 2009 has been estimated at 1.5 percent of GDP by the International Monetary Fund (see SHCP 2010) and by Zhang, Thelen, and Rao (2010).

Table B6.2.1   Composition of Fiscal Stimulus Package: Mexico, 2009
Billions of pesos

	Final cost
Total	189.0
PICE	**90.3**
Program of additional expenditures	53.1
Compensation for lower revenues and major nonprogrammable expenditures	25.2
PEMEX infrastructure projects	12.0
ANEFE	**83.5**
Reduction in the price of gasoline, price of liquefied petroleum gas, and electricity fees	47.4
Investment by PEMEX and the federal states	30.0
Program for promoting the development of national suppliers and contractors for PEMEX	1.5
Employment programs (2.2 revised), expansion of medical insurance (2.6), and programs for saving energy (0.8)	5.6
Fiscal measures related to outbreak of H1N1 influenza	**15.2**
Compensation for decrease in tax revenues	10.0
Reduction of overpayment made to a Single Rate Business Tax	2.0
(IETU) against the monthly income tax (ISR)	2.2
Reduction of 20 percent in employers' contributions to Instituto Mexicano del Seguro Social (IMSS, Mexican Institute of Social Security)	0.5

Note: Subtotals appear in boldface. PICE = Programa para Impulsar el Crecimiento y el Empleo (Program to Boost Growth and Employment). ANEFE = Acuerdo Nacional en Favor de la Economía Familiar y el Empleo (National Agreement in Support of Households and Employment).

augmented social protection measures. Among the Latin American nations covered in the study, the share of the stimulus spent on social protection was highest for Honduras (37 percent of the stimulus package, or 0.38 of GDP), which is in part an artifact of how the study focused on discretionary policy or changes as opposed to automatic stabilizers.

From 2008 on, against the background of developing social protection systems, a number of policy changes were evident in the LAC region, and they were somewhat more numerous in countries that were more affected by the crisis and more heavily weighted to social assistance than to labor market programs. A good deal of policy response was also evident in some countries—in the Dominican Republic and Argentina, for example—that were not so deeply affected by this crisis, but had relatively recent scars from prior crises and would not have known at the outset of the global downturn how well their economies would fare. Table 6.2 and maps 6.1 and 6.2 briefly summarize the policy actions taken after the crisis. This tally is of policy changes, thereby discounting the support to households that flowed from ongoing programs. For example, Ecuador did not take action to change the design of its unemployment insurance savings account (UISA) after the crisis, but expenditures nearly doubled as the number of beneficiaries doubled. Of the 26 countries listed in table 6.2, 20 increased coverage (15 countries) or benefit levels (14 countries) of cash transfer programs. Fourteen countries made changes to one or more of their passive or active labor market programs.

The loose correlation of social protection responses to the economic impacts of the crisis is a pattern found beyond Latin America as well. Robalino, Newhouse, and Rother (2014), who have looked at 50 countries worldwide, document that among countries there is little systematic difference in policy responses with greater or lesser impacts on growth or on unemployment rates. The LAC region differs in its somewhat higher reliance on existing programs. Robalino et al. find that roughly two-thirds of the policy responses observed were new rather than expansions or modifications of existing programs.

Labor Market Programs

Conceptually, labor market programs are the default option to buffer reductions in growth or employment. As described in earlier chapters, unemployment rose in all countries with high-frequency data. Because labor incomes are the main driver of prosperity or poverty, labor market programs are potentially a very important social protection response.

Before the crisis, nearly every country in LAC had some sort of labor programs, and many countries modified them to better respond to the crisis. To provide the unemployed with income support, countries long ago adopted severance pay legislation, which was by far the most common tool, indeed nearly ubiquitous. Most of the upper-middle-income countries had some form of unemployment insurance (UI) programs, and a goodly handful of countries throughout the whole income range used direct employment on labor-intensive public works or community service as an alternate way of proving income support to workers who did not qualify for unemployment insurance or severance pay. A number of countries also had one or more types of active labor market programs designed to improve the employability or wages of prospective workers. Here we focus on two highly applicable

Table 6.2 Frequency of Social Protection Policy Responses to the 2008–09 Global Financial Crisis: Latin America and the Caribbean

Outcome		Cash transfer response (Conditional and unconditional)			MW	Labor market			
		Increased benefits	Increased coverage	Developed new program		Wage subsidies	UI/ UISA	Training	Temporary employment
Strong (negative growth)	Antigua and Barbuda						X		
	Mexico	X	X		X		X	X	X
	Paraguay	X	X		X			X	X
	Venezuela, RB				X				
	El Salvador	X			X				X
	Jamaica	X	X		X			X	
	St. Vincent and the Grenadines	X							
	Honduras		X	X	X				
	Nicaragua				X				
	St. Lucia								X
	Chile	X	X	X	X	X	X	X	X
	Costa Rica		X		X			X	
	Dominica	X			X				
	Brazil	X	X		X		X		
Moderate (positive growth but significant deceleration)	Peru	X	X					X	
	Panama		X	X					
	Argentina	X		X	X	X		X	X
	Ecuador		X	X	X			X	
	Uruguay	X	X		X	X	X		
	Belize			X					
Low (positive growth with moderate deceleration)	Bolivia		X	X	X				
	Guatemala	X	X	X	X				
	Colombia	X	X		X	X		X	
	Dominican Republic	X	X		X				
	Guyana				X				
	Haiti				X				

Sources: ILO/World Bank 2012 and CEPAL 2010.

Note: MW = minimum wage; UI = unemployment insurance; UISA = unemployment insurance savings account. Countries were ordered from more affected to least affected.

Map 6.1 Changes in Social Assistance Programs: Latin America and the Caribbean

COUNTRIES WITH CCT PROGRAMS
DATA NOT AVAILABLE

Honduras
- Increased transfers from 150,000 to 220,000

Mexico
- Expanded food component of Oportunidades
- Expanded coverage in 2009 of Vivir Mejor Food Support Program benefitted nearly 5.3 million households

Belize
- Introduced a CCT program

Jamaica
- Increased PATH coverage by 120,000 beneficiaries
- Increased benefits by 25%
- Expanded school feeding program

Dominican Republic
- Extended coverage to 50,000 new households
- Increased Comer Es Primero by 27%
- Created school attendance incentives for over 292,000 children

Antigua and Barbuda
- Expanded assistance for school children (uniforms, meals)

Dominica
- Increase in social welfare payments and school transfer subsidy

St. Vincent and the Grenadines
- Improved social safety net (poor students and elderly)

Barbados
- Expanded welfare grants and pensions

Guatemala
- Rapidly expanded the CCT program from launch in April 2008 to 458,000 families at end of 2009
- In April 2009, added a nutrition benefit of US$13 per family with preschool children

El Salvador
- Comunidades Solidaria program doubled the benefit per family, from US$150 to $300 for families with children in primary education

Nicaragua
- Provided food support and subsidies by strengthening or launching initiatives such as the Alimentos para el Pueblo program and the Food Distribution and Sale at Fair Prices program

Costa Rica
- Offered meals to 16,000 children in 37 of the poorest districts
- Increased beneficiaries of the Avancemos program

Panama
- Expanded Red de Oportunidades, reaching 75,000 households

Colombia
- Familias en Accion program benefitted 1,765,000 households and 4,052,000 children in more than 1,093 municipalities.
- Increased by around 1 million number of households and children registered in the program
- Expanded Proteccion Social Adulto Mayor to provide monetary subsidies to 486,211 beneficiaries

Grenada
- Began food basket distribution scheme at an approximate cost of US$8 million.
- Expanded school feeding program
- Enhanced assistance for schoolchildren
- Increased public assistance allowance

Trinidad and Tobago
- Strengthened social programs targeting the poor

Brazil
- Extended the Bolsa Familia Program (BFP) to 1.3 million additional families. Increased eligibility for benefits from a monthly income of R$120 to R$140 (US$78) and increased benefits by close to 10%, with the average benefit reaching R$95 per month (US$53)

Ecuador
- Expanded the Bono de Desarrollo Humano
- Number of recipients increased 27%

Peru
- Juntos program increased its coverage (by providing around US$35 per month for medical checkups)

Bolivia
- During 2009, the "Juana Azurduy" voucher benefitted 14,000 people

Chile
- Chile Solidario covered 332,995 families

Paraguay
- Expanded conditional transfers program from 88,000 to 120,000 families

Uruguay
- Expanded family allowances to 62,000 new beneficiaries
- Increased amount and increased differentiation by grade

Argentina
- Introduced a new transfer program for children and adolescents younger than age 18 (AUH) that extended coverage under the contributory program for family allowances to include families in the informal economy and families of unemployed persons

Falkland Islands
(Islas Malvinas)

IBRD 40807 | June 2014
This map was produced by the Map Design Unit of The World Bank. The boundaries, colors, denominations and any other information shown on this map do not imply, on the part of The World Bank Group, any judgment on the legal status of any territory, or any endorsement or acceptance of such boundaries.

Source: Authors' compilation.
Note: CCT = conditional cash transfer; AUH = Asignación Universal por Hijo (Universal Child Allowance).

responses to the crisis: "short-work" schemes intended to reduce firing and public employment services.[4]

Informal sectors are large in the LAC region, and this characteristic not only influences how labor adjustments play out in terms of unemployment, reduced wages, or increased informality, but also shapes the scope of the possible social protection measures. Figure 6.4 reports for the period 1990–2010 the share of the working population covered by social insurance, a first condition for coverage in many of the region's UI schemes. The second condition is the length or density of contributions in the months prior to a spell of unemployment. Coverage was highest in the upper-income countries and for higher deciles, but was only partial even there. Costa Rica, Uruguay, and Chile, well known for their extensive social protection systems, covered over 80 percent of their richest quintiles, but only about 40–60 percent of their poorest quintiles. The coverage of the poorest quintiles was negligible in many countries, especially in Central America. Over the 2000s, the pattern of high informality changed little in most countries, although improvement in coverage is evident in Colombia and Chile.

Understanding the Poverty Impact of the Global Financial Crisis in Latin America and the Caribbean
http://dx.doi.org/10.1596/978-1-4648-0241-6

Map 6.2 Labor Program Responses: Latin America and the Caribbean

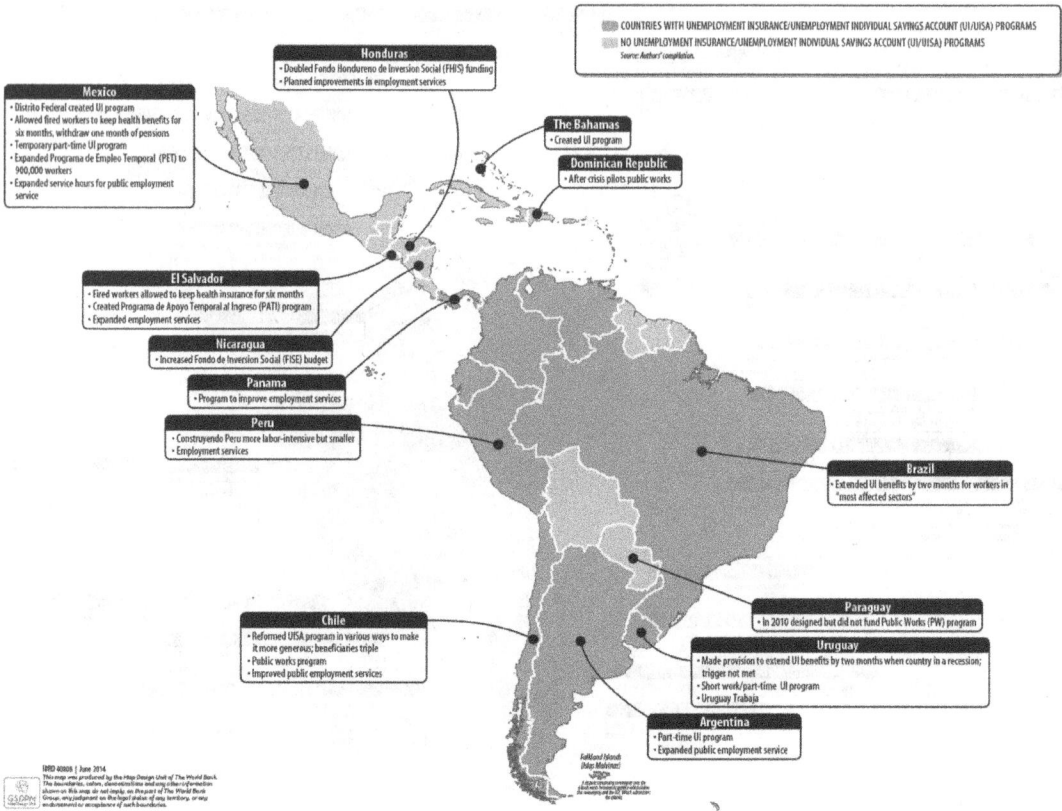

COUNTRIES WITH UNEMPLOYMENT INSURANCE/UNEMPLOYMENT INDIVIDUAL SAVINGS ACCOUNT (UI/UISA) PROGRAMS
NO UNEMPLOYMENT INSURANCE/UNEMPLOYMENT INDIVIDUAL SAVINGS ACCOUNT (UI/UISA) PROGRAMS
Source: Authors' compilation.

Honduras
- Doubled Fondo Hondureno de Inversión Social (FHIS) funding
- Planned improvements in employment services

Mexico
- Distrito Federal created UI program
- Allowed fired workers to keep health benefits for six months, withdraw one month of pensions
- Temporary part-time UI program
- Expanded Programa de Empleo Temporal (PET) to 900,000 workers
- Expanded service hours for public employment service

The Bahamas
- Created UI program

Dominican Republic
- After crisis pilots public works

El Salvador
- Fired workers allowed to keep health insurance for six months
- Created Programa de Apoyo Temporal al Ingreso (PATI) program
- Expanded employment services

Nicaragua
- Increased Fondo de Inversión Social (FISE) budget

Panama
- Program to improve employment services

Peru
- Construyendo Peru more labor-intensive but smaller
- Employment services

Brazil
- Extended UI benefits by two months for workers in "most affected sectors"

Chile
- Reformed UISA program in various ways to make it more generous; beneficiaries triple
- Public works program
- Improved public employment services

Paraguay
- In 2010 designed but did not fund Public Works (PW) program

Uruguay
- Made provision to extend UI benefits by two months when country in a recession; trigger not met
- Short work/part-time UI program
- Uruguay Trabaja

Argentina
- Part-time UI program
- Expanded public employment service

Source: Authors' compilation.
Note: DF = Distrito Federal; UI = unemployment insurance; PET = Programa de Empleo Temporal (Program for Temporary Employment); FHIS = Fondo Hondureño de Inversión Social (Honduran Social Investment Fund); FISE = Fondo de Inversion Social (Social Investment Fund); PATI = Programa de Apoyo Tempora al Ingreso (Temporary Income Support Program).

Unemployment Insurance and UISAs
Program Logic

Unemployment insurance, UISAs, and severance pay are three ways in which the income of unemployed workers can be replaced. Each program has its pros and cons and may be more suitable for some countries than others, depending on the structure of the labor market.

In formal economies, unemployment insurance is the classic program for income replacement for households, and it can be an "automatic stabilizer" for the economy. Unemployment insurance is typically formulated to replace a share of income, with payments commonly in the range of 25–75 percent of lost wages over a period three to six months. UI covers formal sector workers who contributed to UI for some minimum period before the unemployment spell (Vodopevic 2004; International Labour Organization/International Social Security Association [ILO/ISSA] social security database). Unemployment insurance is, however, unable to assist those in the informal sector, which, because of the large size of

Figure 6.4 Share of Working Population Covered by Social Insurance, by Quintile of Per Capita Income: Latin America and the Caribbean, 1990–2010

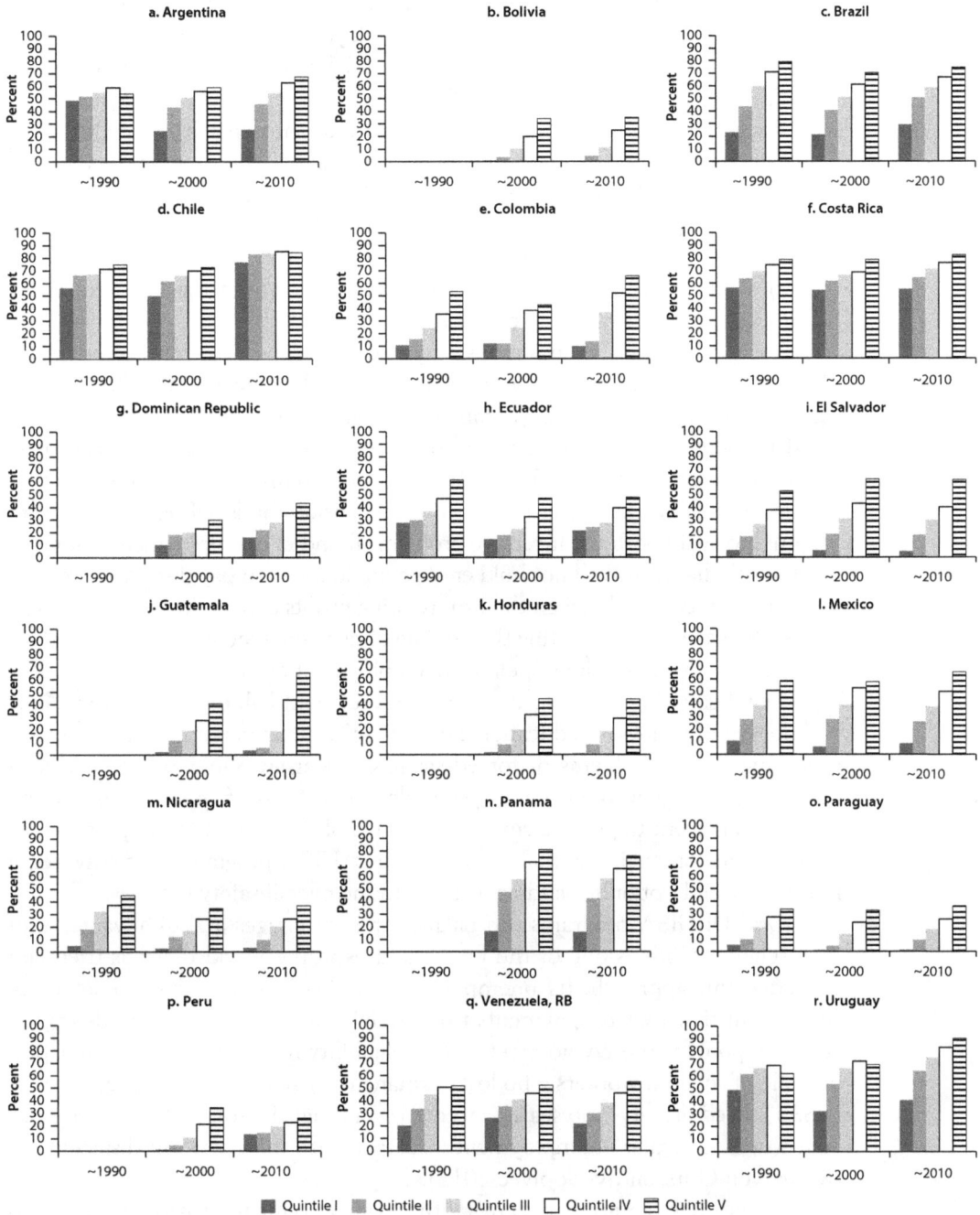

Quintile I   Quintile II   Quintile III   Quintile IV   Quintile V

Source: Rofman and Oliveri 2012, figure 8.
Note: Argentina, 1995–2006; Bolivia, 1999–2005; Brazil, 1995–2006; Chile, 1996–2006; Colombia, 1996–2006; Costa Rica, 1995–2006; Dominican Republic, 2006; Ecuador, 1995–2006; El Salvador, 1995–2005; Guatemala, 1998–2006; Honduras, 2006; Mexico, 1998–2006; Nicaragua, 2005; Panama, 2004; Paraguay, 1999–2006; Peru, 1999–2006; Venezuela, RB, 1995–2006; Uruguay, 1995–2006.

Understanding the Poverty Impact of the Global Financial Crisis in Latin America and the Caribbean
http://dx.doi.org/10.1596/978-1-4648-0241-6

the LAC region's informal sector, implies a significant limitation in coverage. The presence of substantial informal sectors also makes it difficult for Latin American unemployment insurance programs to ensure that their benefits flow only to those who are not working because unemployed formal sector workers may work in the informal sector. And even where labor markets are predominately formal, there are some disincentive effects, with workers perhaps delaying somewhat longer the search for or acceptance of alternate employment than they would in the absence of unemployment insurance. Design parameters can be selected to reduce these disincentive effects, but these adjustments also tend to limit the assistance offered by the schemes. For these reasons, UI programs are less common in poorer/more informal countries than in richer/more formal countries worldwide and are present in only a minority of the LAC countries, where they protect a minority of workers.

To escape some of the limitations of classically designed unemployment insurance, several Latin American countries have adapted a variant—the UISA. In this variant, workers accrue savings from individual or employer contributions (or both) to individual accounts, and, when unemployed, they are entitled to draw benefits over short, often fixed periods. Any balance remaining in their accounts at the end of their working lives reverts to their pension funds. UISA schemes were invented to avoid both the incentive problems found in unemployment insurance and the risk that firms will not hold enough liquid assets to pay dismissed workers severance pay, especially when the firm is losing profits and job losses are the most intense. However, in eliminating the pooling of risks, the scheme can leave workers underinsured in cases of long spells of unemployment or of low contribution density. The schemes in essence force savings, and so about half of the countries allow withdrawals of savings for education, housing, or health expenditures. This remediates some of the problems of forced savings, but again puts workers at risk of insufficient savings in the event of unemployment. Most of the schemes are too small or too recent to provide coverage to much of their countries' populations or many lessons on their optimal design features. UISA programs are, however, a much discussed option for adding a strand to the overall safety net.

Hybrid UI-UISA programs can balance the advantages and disadvantages of each scheme. Chile is one of the few countries in the world that has tried and evaluated this approach. Its unemployment savings accounts have a solidarity component that tops up payments from individual accounts with funds from a common pool for those who meet certain eligibility requirements. An evaluation in Chile of covered workers who lost permanent jobs prior to 2007 suggests that UISAs indeed preserve job search incentives and that the solidarity fund component works as regular unemployment insurance with the attendant disincentives (Reyes, von Ours, and Vodopivec 2012).

Severance pay requirements are another way of trying to provide income support for the unemployed. Such legislation demands that employers make payments, usually as lump sums, to workers when they leave employment under one or more circumstances—dismissal, redundancy, bankruptcy, disability, retirement, and end of service. Because the payments are made from one private party to another, the administrative requirements for government are lower than for UI or UISA. Workers have full incentives to work because the amount they are paid does not vary by length of unemployment. Because the protection provided is not linked to the spell of unemployment, it can be too high for those with long tenure or those who can quickly find new employment and too low for those with short tenure or a long spell of unemployment. Severance pay does raise the costs of firing and may dampen labor reallocation or absorption, although the magnitude of such effects is somewhat contested—see, for example, reviews in Holzmann and Vodopivec (2012) and Pages, Pierre, and Scarpetta (2009) of the impacts of such schemes. Moreover, there is the risk that firms, especially those with a large number of redundancies or in bankruptcy, will be unable to meet severance pay obligations, and, of course, firms always have an incentive to avoid payments, resulting in substantial litigation in the labor courts (de Ferranti et al. 2000). The limitations on coverage are quantified for Chile, where the regulations cover workers with indefinite-duration contracts and 12 months of tenure who are dismissed for the "needs of the enterprise"—a group roughly estimated to represent a little more than 6 percent of all formal and informal employees who become unemployed. Even in this small group, a significant proportion probably will receive no severance pay or less than they are entitled to because employers often persuade workers to accept a reduced amount or simply refuse to pay (OECD 2009).

UI and UISA Programs in the LAC Region

Unemployment insurance or UISA systems are in place in several of the higher-income and larger countries in LAC (see tables 6.3 and 6.4 and figure 6.5), but the LAC countries spend less on UI and UISA than OECD countries. Whereas in 2007 OECD countries spent on average about 0.6 percent of GDP on unemployment insurance programs (OECD iLibrary), in the LAC countries for which we have data only Brazil spent as much, Uruguay spent about 0.3 percent of GDP, and no other country came close.

Household surveys reveal how small the programs are in absolute size and that, surprisingly, the distribution of benefits from UI programs is relatively neutral across the income distribution (see figure 6.5). The small share of the population benefitting is expected because many workers are not in formal jobs, and many of those who are may not have met the minimum requirements for benefits or may have been unemployed longer than the duration of benefits. Jaramillo and Saavedra (2005) report that only 5–15 percent of the unemployed population receives benefits. Somewhat more surprising is the neutral distribution of benefits because those covered had stable formal jobs—a type of worker usually concentrated in the upper half of the income distribution. Two factors are at work here. As described in chapter 5, once a job is lost, many households will indeed have low incomes, which underscores the importance of the programs for those who do benefit from them. There may also be a mechanical issue in that income as shown in figure 6.5 is measured in the last month, but receipt of unemployment benefits is measured in the prior year so that a family may be

Table 6.3 Characteristics of Unemployment Insurance Programs: Latin America and the Caribbean

Country	Vesting period	Benefit duration	Benefit level
Argentina	Six months of contributions in the three years before unemployment; for temporary workers, 90 days in the 12 months before unemployment	Benefit paid for four months if the insured has 12–23 months of contributions; for eight months with 24–35 months; for 12 months with 36 months or more	Fifty percent of the insured's best wage in the six months before unemployment
Bahamas, The	Forty weeks of paid contributions, including at least 26 weeks of paid or credited contributions in the year before unemployment began or in any contribution year since 2003	Benefit paid after a two-week waiting period for up to 13 weeks	Fifty percent of the insured's average covered weekly earnings
Brazil	Six months of contributions	Benefit paid for three to five months, depending on the insured's duration of coverage	Eighty percent of average earnings is paid with average earnings up to R$767.60; plus 50% of earnings between R$767.61 and R$1,279.46
Colombia	Less than 20 days		One monthly wage for each year of employment; reduced benefit paid for less than a year of employment
Ecuador	24 months	Lump sum	
Uruguay	Six of last 12 months; rural workers 12 of last 24 months; irregularly paid 250 days in last 24 months		Fifty percent of salary or 12 days of earnings
Venezuela, RB	12 of last 24 months	Sixty percent of salary for up to five months	Sixty percent of salary

Source: Compiled from information in the International Social Security Association Observatory.

reported as having income from unemployment benefits but also having income from a new job.[5]

Nearly all LAC countries have severance pay regulations, and all of these cover redundancy. About half of dismissals are for other reasons. Benefits for those with five years of service range from a low of five weeks of pay in Belize, Grenada, and Suriname to 21 or more weeks in Argentina, Chile, the Dominican Republic, Ecuador, El Salvador, Guatemala, Honduras, Mexico, and Uruguay (Holzmann et al. 2012). This places the LAC region in the midrange internationally. The LAC countries have fewer requirements for administrative procedures associated with firing (e.g., the need to notify or seek approval from a third party) than most other regions (Pages, Pierre, and Scarpetta 2009).

Table 6.4 Characteristics of Unemployment Insurance Savings Account Programs: Latin America and the Caribbean

Country (year of introduction)	Coverage	Contributions	Eligibility requirements	Unemployment benefits	Other benefits	Social insurance	Funds management
Argentina (1975)	Construction workers	Employers: 12% of one month's wages for a year, then 8%	Proof of dismissal	Balance on separation	n.a.	No	Banking institutions
Brazil (1989)	Dependent workers not covered elsewhere	Employers: 8% of one month's wages	Contingent on type of separation	Balance on separation	Partial withdrawal allowed for housing or health expenses	No/other programs	Government
Chile (2002)	Dependent workers	Employees: 0.6% of one month's wages Employers: 2.4% of one month's wages Government contributions	Minimum of 12 contributions	One month's wages/year (up to five months) Decreasing benefits with minimum and maximum	n.a.	Minimum benefits guaranteed with the solidarity fund (up to two withdrawals every five years)	Recognized financial institutions (exclusive dedication)
Colombia (1990)	Dependent workers	Employers: 9.3% of one month's wages	Proof of dismissal	Balance on separation	Partial withdrawal allowed; funds can be used to guarantee some house loans	No/other programs	Recognized financial institutions (exclusive dedication)
Ecuador (mixed 2001)	Dependent workers	Employer: one month's wages/ year to individual accounts (monthly contribution)	Involuntary unemployment Minimum 48 deposits + one year of tenure	Balance on separation up to three times the average monthly wage in the previous year	n.a.	No/other programs	Recognized financial institutions (exclusive dedication)

table continues next page

Table 6.4 Characteristics of Unemployment Insurance Savings Account Programs: Latin America and the Caribbean (continued)

Country (year of introduction)	Coverage	Contributions	Eligibility requirements	Unemployment benefits	Other benefits	Social insurance	Funds management
Panama (1972)	Dependent workers	Employer: one week's wages/year + 5% compensation Employee: voluntary	Additional compensation contingent on type of separation	Balance on separation	Partial withdrawal allowed for housing, education, or health expenses	No/risk pooling within firms	Collective trust fund with approved financial institution
Peru (1991)	Private workers not covered elsewhere	Employer: two deposits of half of one month's wages	Proof of dismissal	Balance on separation	Fifty percent withdrawal allowed; additional withdrawal occasionally authorized	No	Banking institutions
Venezuela, RB (1997)	Dependent workers	Employer: five days' wages/ month Increases with tenure Maximum 30 days' wages/year	Three months' tenure	Balance on separation	n.a.	No/other programs	Recognized financial institutions/ employer

Source: Ferrer and Ridell 2012, table 7.1.

Note: n.a. = not applicable.

Figure 6.5 Percentage of Population Receiving Unemployment Benefits, by Selected Country and Deciles of Income Distribution: Latin America and the Caribbean, Selected Years

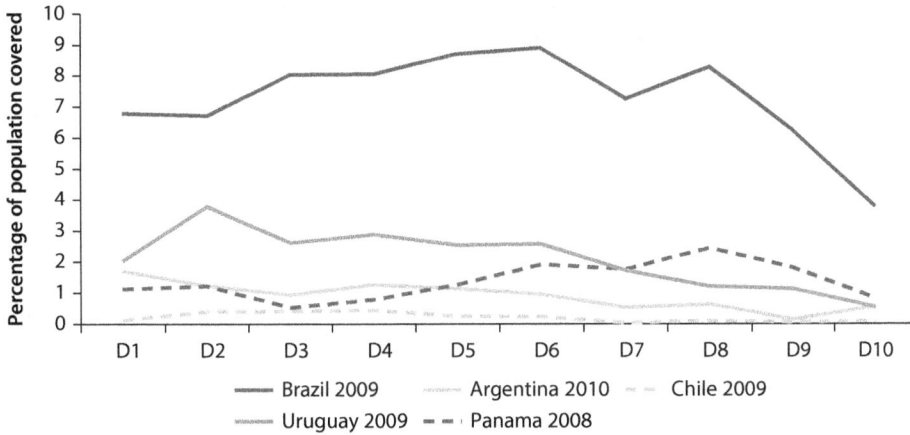

Source: Cerutti et al. 2014.

What Happened during the Financial Crisis

The countries hardest hit by the crisis were not well covered by UI or UISA. Of the 14 countries that fell into recession, only three (Brazil, Chile, and República Bolivariana de Venezuela) had UI programs; the remainder (Antigua and Barbuda, Costa Rica, Dominica, El Salvador, Honduras, Jamaica, Mexico, Nicaragua, Paraguay, St. Lucia, and St. Vincent and the Grenadines) did not. However, seven of the eight countries with UI and UISA programs sustained growth decelerations of over 6 percent. With a growth deceleration, the formal labor market would be expected to tighten. This was borne out in declines in net salaried employment in all countries (see chapter 2 for a disaggregated analysis), although whether the plunge crossed the threshold to negative net job creation varied. In Brazil, net job creation stayed minimally positive even in the worst quarters, whereas it moved in a negative direction in other countries.

In the LAC region, Chile saw the largest increase in its unemployment rate (3.5 percentage points), and it made the most changes to the rules of its unemployment program. The emergence of the global financial crisis prompted the Bachelet administration to fast-track reforms already in the works. The January 2009 reform allowed fixed-term workers to access the solidarity fund; relaxed the eligibility requirement for the solidarity fund by transforming it from a continuous contribution requirement (12 months) to a minimum density requirement (12 of the previous 24 months, with the last three continuous and with the same employer); raised the minimum and maximum solidarity fund benefits; changed the payment structure under the individual account; and allowed two additional payments during periods of high unemployment—that is, when the national unemployment rate is 1 percentage point higher than the four-year rolling average. The number of beneficiaries increased from about 10,000 per month by the end of 2008 to about 30,000 per month by the end of 2010, with an increase in the replacement rate as well. For example, fixed-contract workers previously would have been ineligible, but after the changes they would have an average replacement rate of about 35 percent (Bernstein, Fajnzylber, and Gana 2012). However, even this structural increase was insufficient. The share of unemployed covered by the UISA system, which had grown to about 22 percent in 2007, fell to about 18 percent in 2009 (Robalino, Newhouse, and Rother 2014).

Uruguay completed a permanent reform of its unemployment insurance system in 2008, just before the crisis, that facilitated benefits for affected workers. In this context, perhaps the most important change was an extension of benefits from six to eight months if the country is experiencing a recession, a trigger not in fact met. Workers aged 50 and older were eligible for benefits for 12 rather than six months. The benefit formula was revised, moving from a flat 50 percent of wages to an initially higher level to provide more adequate income support and then replacement rates decline each month to encourage a job search. The reform also introduced mandatory training for those receiving benefits for *causal de despido* (causal dismissal) for the second half of their benefit period. As a result of these changes, the share of unemployed covered by unemployment insurance rose from 13 percent in 2007 to 16 percent in 2008 and was 20 percent in early 2009 (Casanova 2009b).

Brazil temporarily extended by two months the duration of benefits for workers laid off in the months of December 2008 and January 2009 from jobs in the "most affected sectors," which were determined at the state level. This measure was confined to a single short period of the recession—one quarter of negative growth. It did not result in a greater average duration of benefits in 2009 for the year as a whole—the average spell of unemployment for formal employees was 3.9 months in both 2008 and 2009, although in the first quarter of 2009 the number of claimants increased by 22 percent and then fell for the remainder of 2009, by the fourth quarter to baseline rates (OECD 2010, 139). Approximately 217,000 workers benefitted from this provision, at a cost of 0.013 percent of GDP (Berg 2009). The total number of unemployed workers was 7–8 million (Robalino, Newhouse, and Rother 2014). Spending on UI increased by a bit more than trend, reaching 0.5 percent of GDP in 2009.

The Bahamas introduced a temporary financial measure under the National Insurance Scheme to pay up to 13 weeks of benefits at a rate just under minimum wage, US$200 a week (Ndahi 2009). In effect, this measure raised benefits for some—according to the 2004 rules, benefits were 50 percent of median weekly pay but capped at US$250 a week—and overrode the minimum contribution requirements (normally employment in 13 of the 26 weeks prior to dismissal and 40 lifetime contributions).

Mexico did not have a national unemployment insurance program, but the Distrito Federal initiated an unemployment insurance program in the fall of 2008 for city residents working for six months or more for firms in the city. It is unusual for unemployment insurance to be organized at the municipal level—pooling at the national or state level is the norm—but because Mexico City's population is so large (about 9 million people in the city proper) it actually provides a bigger risk pool than available in a number of small countries or U.S. states. The program, however, has not yet achieved significant coverage, reaching about 60,000 unemployed workers in each of 2008 and 2009 (Secretaria de Trabajo y Fomento al Empleo n.d.).

Some countries that did not muster full unemployment insurance modified their social insurance laws to provide some support to workers. Costa Rica extended the grace period from three to six months for health insurance coverage after loss of employment (ILO/World Bank 2012; World Bank 2010b). El Salvador allowed workers to maintain social security coverage for six months after being fired, a provision grasped by only 8,000 workers. The Dominican Republic allowed unemployed workers who had earned less than RD$1,000 a month (about US$285) to keep their health insurance for one year. Similarly, the Instituto Mexicano del Seguro Social (IMSS, Mexican Institute of Social Security) extended health insurance coverage for up to six months for dismissed workers and their families (Freije-Rodriguez and Murrugarra 2009). Mexico then went even further, allowing unemployed workers affiliated with IMSS to withdraw one month's income from their pension plans (Freije-Rodriguez, Lopez-Acevedo, and Rodriguez-Oreggia 2011). And at least two other countries, Antigua and Barbuda and El Salvador, proposed but did not implement UI programs.

Spending on unemployment benefits increased in all six countries with unemployment benefits in our database by about 0.1 percent of GDP. In addition to Brazil, Chile, Ecuador, and Uruguay, changes were inconsequential in Colombia, which is not surprising because it had both positive growth and only a small deceleration, and they were small as well in Argentina.

Statistics on the number of workers benefitting from severance pay are not maintained on a regular basis, and so we cannot see how they evolved in the crisis. We do not know of any changes in severance pay legislation because of or timed with the crisis (Murillo, Ronconi, and Schrank 2011).

Around the World
The LAC countries' coverage of unemployment, while much lower than that of Western Europe, is on a par with that of Eastern Europe according to benchmarking by Vroman and Brusentev (2009)—see table 6.5. They report that globally 27 of the 30 richest countries have unemployment insurance programs, but none of the poorest 30. In the OECD-20, recipiency rates are 63 percent, and replacement rates are 38 percent. Therefore, workers receive compensation for about a quarter of income lost from unemployment. In South America, the recipiency rates are 22 percent, or just on a par with those countries in the former Soviet Union and Central and Eastern Europe. Benefit rates in South America are on the high end of the spectrum, with replacement rates averaging 48 percent. Combining the coverage and replacement rates, recipients of UI in

Table 6.5 Earnings Loss Replacement, by Major Region, Countries with Unemployment Compensation Programs

Region	Total unemployment (millions)	UC beneficiaries (millions)	UC beneficiaries as % of unemployment	Replace-ment rate (%)	UC generosity
	(1)	(2)	(2)/(1) = (3)	(4)	(3) × (4) = (5)
OECD-20	22.3	14.2	63	38	0.24
Central and Eastern Europe	5.0	1.0	20	29	0.06
Former Soviet Union	7.7	1.7	22	15	0.03
East and South Asia	13.7	5.6	41	18	0.07
North Africa and Middle East	7.9	0.3	3	49	0.02
Sub-Saharan Africa	4.2	0.1	2	23	0.01
South America	11.4	2.4	22	48	0.10
Central America and the Caribbean	—	—	—	—	—
Total	72.3	25.2	35	33	0.12

Source: Vroman and Brusentsev 2009.
Note: In South America, 2.4 million of the 11.4 million unemployed workers receive unemployment benefits, or 22 percent. On average, those benefits replace 48 percent of their wages. Thus of total wages lost, unemployment benefits compensate for 10 percent; — = not available.

South America receive 10 percent of income lost to unemployment, or less than half the rate of the OECD-20 but higher than in other regions.

The LAC region's expansion of its UI programs during the crisis was in keeping with world experience. Many countries extended the duration and level of benefits, especially those in Eastern Europe (Isik-Demelik 2012; Robalino, Newhouse, and Rother 2014).

"Short-Work" or Part-Time Unemployment Schemes
Program Logic
Short-term work programs are intended to preserve jobs at firms experiencing temporarily low demand. They encourage work sharing, while also providing income support for workers whose hours are reduced because of a shortened workweek or temporary layoffs. Typically, the government grants a wage subsidy to the firm or pays partial unemployment benefits or other compensation directly to workers. Firms can thus pay less than the wage agreement in force and typically lower social security contributions as well in exchange for limits on the number of workers dismissed. To the extent that retaining workers protects the investments of households and firms in job-specific human capital that will be of value when a short downturn passes and firms return to profitability, job retention subsidies can have economic as well as social protection value. However, they can delay a restructuring of industries, firms, and jobs when needed. It can be difficult to distinguish the long-term viable firms and industries at the beginning of a downturn and to know how many workers they would fire in the

absence of the scheme's support. Thus such schemes may subsidize the employment of workers who would have been retained or who would be dismissed even after recovery of demand, which will reduce these schemes' cost-effectiveness. Schemes therefore try to balance eligibility requirements and subsidy values to encourage sufficient but not excessive take-up.

What Happened during the Financial Crisis

Publicly supported short-term work schemes to keep people in jobs were used in response to the global financial crisis in just a few countries in the LAC region. In Argentina and Uruguay, the scale was significant; in Mexico less so.

Argentina's Programa de Recuperación Productiva (REPRO, Productive Recovery Program) emerged from the convertibility crisis at the beginning of the decade. It then operated at a low level until 2008 when it was called into play to respond to the global financial crisis. The number of participating workers jumped from about 14,000 in 2007, to 23,000 in 2008, to 85,000 in 2009 (Bertranou and Mazorra 2009), and to 144,000 in 2010, before falling back slightly to 114,000 in 2011 (ILO 2011). These figures can be compared with the negative net creation of salaried jobs of just over 100,000 in the fourth quarter of 2009. The program provided income support of Arg$600 (about US$150) per month for workers who might otherwise have been laid off in qualifying firms. Companies could deduct this government-paid subsidy from the salary needed to comply with collective bargaining agreements. Moreover, companies paid social security contributions only on the portion of wages they paid. In return, enterprises promised to refrain from layoffs. To qualify for participation, firms had to show that they were profitable before the crisis and that they had solid prospects for recovery. Trucco and Tussi (2010) estimate that in 2009 about 80 percent of participating firms were in the tradable sectors; that 96 percent of participating firms were small and medium enterprises but that 8 in 10 participating workers were working in firms of 50 or more employees; and that with an average length of subsidy receipt of 8.5 months, the average cost per dismissal averted was US$951.

Uruguay issued an executive decree in July 2009 allowing workers whose workweek had been reduced by one or two days for up to a year to receive partial unemployment benefits. To qualify, firms had to show a drop in sales of at least 15 percent relative to the average of the same quarter in the previous two years. At the time of the decree, the program was expected to cover 4,000 workers. From February to June 2009, 37 percent of those claiming unemployment benefits (about 10,000 workers) were in this "suspended" category (Casanova 2009a).

Mexico set up a temporary job preservation program in 2008. It provided subsidies of Mex$110 per day (about US$8.23 according to the September 2008 exchange rate) for up to three-quarters of the workers in participating firms, for up to a total of Mex$5,100 per worker (US$382). Firms had to be in a narrowly defined set of industries (i.e., automotive, spare parts, electronics, and electronic appliance capital goods and suppliers thereof) that had been in existence for 12 months, that were in good standing with tax and social security payments and rules, and that had reached an agreement with workers on temporary reductions in wages or hours in exchange for job preservation. The program had a slow start-up, and it simplified its requirements three times, eventually reaching about 200,000 workers in 224 firms by September 2009 (Galhardi 2009). By contrast, net salaried job destruction in Mexico reached nearly half a million the following quarter.

Around the World

Work-sharing schemes were adopted in three-quarters of OECD countries. The countries with existing programs—France, Germany, Italy, and Japan—were able to generate high take-up for the schemes, about 2 percent of the workforce in France and 3 percent in Germany, Italy, and Japan. Germany's Kurzarbeit scheme is perhaps the most well-known of such programs. It covered nearly 1.5 million workers in May 2009, and is credited with keeping Germany's unemployment rate to half of what it otherwise would have been. For qualifying firms and workers, firms paid for hours worked and for a reduced portion of social security contributions. The employment agency paid workers for hours not worked at the replacement rate for unemployment benefits—for example, 60 percent of wages (OECD 2010; Brown and Koettl 2012).

Labor-Intensive Public Works Programs
Program Logic

Labor-intensive public works programs can be an effective alternative form of income support for the unemployed in countries where unemployment insurance is not available or for workers who are not eligible for it. The principle is simple and well known: pay low wages for relatively difficult full-time work, thereby serving as a "self-targeting" mechanism so that only people who really need support apply to work. Labor may be used in activities that yield social benefits, such as providing key infrastructure, community assets, or community services. Programs vary in how much emphasis they put on the investment value of the work and how much they regard the work requirement primarily as a feature that ensures self-targeting. Although such a program is conceptually and effectively a good substitute for unemployment insurance for the poor without access to social insurance, the global track record on public works reveals the challenges. Perhaps most important, such a program can be both expensive and administratively difficult (after all, it requires arranging useful work for large segments of the population). Ensuring that a list of shovel-ready projects and the required materials are on hand so that work can start quickly takes time and good organizational capacity. Thus the programs tend to be small relative to the niche of social policy needing to be filled (Grosh et al. 2008; Baez, Del Carpio, and Ngyen 2010; Subbarao et al. 2012).

Public Works Programs in the LAC Region

Latin America has a long record of public works programs. Chile's Programa de Empleo Mínimo (PEM, Minimum Employment Program) and Programa de Ocupación para Jefes de Hogar (POJH, Program for Jobs for Heads of Household) from the early 1980s are perhaps the largest in modern history, absorbing up to 13 percent of the labor force (Reinecke 2005). Argentina's Trabajar (To Work) program in 1998 and then Jefes y Jefas de Hogar in 2001 are more recent initiatives, and they demonstrate some of the difficulties of such programs. Trabajar was a modest program, peaking at 200,000 workers in October 1997 and able to enforce the work requirement rigorously and show good value for the work done as well as excellent targeting among the workers (World Bank 2000). Jefes y Jefas was much larger, peaking at about 2 million workers and still reasonably targeted, but it was much less able to enforce the work requirement or ensure the value of the work done. In 2004 only 55 percent of participants were working 20 hours or more a week or were in training. By 2008, that figure was a mere 19 percent (World Bank 2010a, table A2.1). Peru's A Trabajar Urbano (Urban to Work) program was launched as a contemporary of Argentina's Trabajar program, but it shrank rather than going out of existence as the economy improved. It was relatively small, peaking at 0.14 percent of GDP in 2002 and covering 0.5 percent of the urban population in 2003. It had a number of good-practice features such as labor intensity of 60 percent and good selection mechanisms for works and community involvement in their supervision, but the wage was relatively high, which made targeting problematic (Chacaltana 2009; Marini and Seguin 2012). Other temporary public works programs have come in and out of existence or ebbed and flowed in size—in Brazil, Bolivia, Colombia, and Mexico, for example, and, through their social funds, in Nicaragua and Panama. In general, all of these programs have been much smaller than the older Chilean and Argentinean programs.

What Happened during the Financial Crisis

From 2008 to 2010, Mexico scaled up its Programa de Empleo Temporal (PET, Program for Temporary Employment) as one of several labor market measures. PET was introduced as a response to the 1995 "Tequila" crisis, achieving significant scale in 1999 and 2000 and peaking at a million temporary jobs. The program was then sharply scaled back, providing by 2007 only a fifth that number of jobs. With the onset of the global financial crisis, PET was scaled up, covering 285,000 beneficiaries in 2008, 682,000 in 2009, and 894,000 in 2010 (OECD 2011; World Bank 2011d; CONEVAL n.d.). The total number of shifts per worker allowed was lowered from 176 to 132 in 2010, but the averages were less than that, 33 shifts per worker on average in 2008, intensifying to 53 per worker in 2009 and then falling to 44 per worker in 2010. PET targeted poor rural areas until 2010, when the rules were changed to allow coverage in urban areas and some targeting based on areas of high unemployment. A minimum of 65 percent of the budget must be used for wages, no more than 28 percent for materials and equipment, and no more than 7 percent for administration. Designed in this way, it conforms reasonably well with standard best practices. However, the program has not been able to concentrate works during the agricultural slack seasons; indeed, work has often peaked during the agricultural peak season. No comprehensive evaluation of PET has been conducted recently, but Scott (2009) shows that even though PET's targeting has deteriorated over the decade, in 2006 it was still one of the best-targeted programs in Mexico. The wage paid is just under the official minimum wage. An average rural household relying only on a single minimum wage would fall well short of the extreme poverty line and in the bottom 4 percent of the income distribution.

During the global financial crisis, other countries also counted on public works programs founded during past crises. In 2008 and 2009, Uruguay Trabaja was able to provide between 3,100 and 3,600 people, mostly women, with temporary part-time employment and some related benefits, including counseling, dental care, and a small amount of training (World Bank 2009b; Ministerio de Desarrollo Social, Uruguay 2012). The program is geared toward the long-term unemployed and socially vulnerable, and works are organized by civil society organizations. Peru's A Trabajar Urbana was reshaped into a national program, Construyendo Peru, in 2007, and a training arm was added. It did, however, act procyclically, increasing coverage in 2007 and 2008 when the economy was growing strongly and then seeing its 2009 budget cut to a third of its 2008 budget. To soften the impact of this budget cut on the program's ability to provide income support, program authorities shifted the concentration of activities to those higher in labor intensity and suspended training (Jaramillo, Baanante, and Sanz 2009).

Chile increased funding for its direct employment programs under Programa de Contingencia Contra el Desempleo (Contingency Program for Unemployment). This program was set up under the Fiscal Responsibility Law in 2006. It is activated when the national quarterly unemployment rate exceeds the prior five-year average, or 10 percent. There is also a provision for local triggering of the contingency. In February and March 2009, the program was triggered because the national unemployment rate exceeded the five-year average, and in April–July because the 10 percent threshold was met (ILO 2009). The largest direct employment program is Programa de Inversión en la Comunidad (Community Investment Program), which provides employment for unemployed heads of household aged 18–65 for three- to four-month periods. The employment is usually half-time at 50 percent of the minimum wage and with a pension contribution. The beneficiaries have to be registered with the Ficha de Protección Social, but they are not subject to a maximum cut-off score. The works carried out are proposed and supervised by the regional governments. Employment peaked in 2010 at 30,000 workers, or nearly double the 2007 level of 17,000, and continued to rise as the crisis abated, reaching 22,000 in 2012 (DIPRES 2012). In 2010 the program provided income support to as many workers as the UISA program.

El Salvador's Programa de Apoyo Temporal al Ingreso (PATI, Temporary Income Support Program) was launched as a response to the 2009 economic crisis. The program requires service in labor-intensive community activities and offers income support and training, especially to youth aged 16–24 and female heads of households living in poor urban areas affected by violence. Most PATI community activities are related to social and community services (e.g., child care, sports and youth activities, improvement of public spaces) and do not involve any substantive infrastructure activities. Training activities are designed to increase the employability of PATI participants in the labor market. They receive stipends of

US$100 per month for six months in exchange for six hours of work per day. This monthly grant is well below the minimum wage (US$173 as of January 2009) and the urban poverty line (US$165.70 in August 2009)—see World Bank (2009c). The program was intended to serve 60,000 youth over a three-year period, but after a small pilot in 2009 it was running at about 20,000 participants per cycle by the end of 2011. This is a significant size in relation to the program's target population. Every year, about 30,000 young Salvadorans enter the labor market for the first time and encounter scarce opportunities. Of these new entrants, about 4,000 are not able to find a job, and the majority who do find jobs end up in informal low-productivity activities (World Bank 2009c; FISDL 2011).

Intrigued by the type of support public works can offer and aware of the role they can play in crises, several other countries are testing such schemes. In 2010 the Dominican Republic launched a pilot public works program that may become important in the future but was too small and too late to have an effect in the downturn (World Bank 2010c). Similarly, Paraguay designed a pilot temporary employment program, Ñamba'apo Paraguay, for launch in 2010 (Ministerio de Justicia y Trabajo, Paraguay 2011), but Paraguay's Congress did not appropriate the funds to really get it off the ground. Colombia has put in place a temporary work program for the victims of a recent natural disaster (*ola invernal*) and is developing a mechanism for quickly scaling up and down a temporary employment program for future crises.

Around the World

With respect to direct employment in public works programs, the LAC region's current crop of programs is generally typical of world experience; most adhere in their design to many if not all of the best-practice features and are plausibly implemented, but they are also tightly rationed and contribute only a small share to overall employment. The global exception in coverage—India's Mahatma Gandhi National Employment Guarantee Act—is the only public works program operating with a formal guarantee of employment and with a vast scale of implementation, having covered about 10 percent of the labor force in 2008 (Ministry of Rural Development and Government of India 2010). A few other programs are large—for example, South Africa's Expanded Public Works Programme reaches 3.4 percent of the labor force, Indonesia's covers 1.4 percent, and the Russian Federation covers 1.0 percent (OECD 2010). Most other programs cover much smaller shares. Robalino, Newhouse, and Rother (2014) report that the median number of beneficiaries in programs used in response to the 2008–09 crisis was 0.1 percent of the labor force.

Public Employment Services

In addition to income support for the unemployed, governments may provide assistance to workers so they can reenter the job market. Among active labor market policies with such a purpose, public employment services are usually evaluated as among the most cost-effective; they have positive effects on employment probabilities and wages and can be provided at a relatively low cost.

Moreover, they can be the final link in a service chain that ensures that training and wage subsidies actually result in employment (see, for example, Betcherman, Olivas, and Dar 2004; Almeida et al. 2012).

Program Logic

Public employment services are meant to provide employers and job seekers with information that leads to better job matches, resulting in higher productivity for the firm or higher wages for the employee than would have been possible without the intermediation services. Services may include some or all job listings, job search–related counseling, services to employers, and referrals of job seekers to training or other support programs. Services are sometimes provided on a for-profit basis by the private sector or by not-for-profit agencies contracted by government. Public sector involvement (in direct provision or financing) may be justified if the public services focus on clientele not usually served by the private for-profit sector or who would otherwise be likely to be unemployed, especially if they would be drawing publicly financed benefits—unemployment benefits, social assistance, disability support, or public pensions. To be effective, the programs must develop a critical mass of jobs and job seekers and must be able to connect the two at low cost. The development of adequate services for employers, especially for employers of target groups on public benefits, such as the long-term unemployed, youth, or the poor, is perhaps especially challenging (see box 6.3) (Betcherman et al. n.d.).

Box 6.3 Lessons from Impact Evaluations on Keys to Effective Employment Services

Program evaluations conclude that the key determinants of positive employment impacts of basic employment services include the following:

- A "work-first strategy" applied to the entire public employment service
- Close dialogue and cooperation with the community, and especially with employers
- Investment in staff skills, first of all for the field positions
- A performance management system with clear targets, performance indicators, and processes for monitoring performances
- High-quality, up-to-date information and knowledge about labor market conditions, including labor demand (a Web-based, high-quality job vacancy data bank should be the core instrument)
- A pronounced client focus and client adjustment approach throughout all activities
- High-quality information and communications technology support for all public employment services activities and functions, especially for client information and services
- Good infrastructure for providing employers and job seekers with labor market information to and for communication between those two groups of clients
- A proactive, systematic approach to follow up on the registered job vacancies and registered job seekers at public employment services.

Public Employment Services in the LAC Region

Public employment services are not well developed in most countries in the LAC region. Of the 10 countries in the social protection database, the highest spenders on the eve of the crisis were Mexico and Peru, dispensing up to 0.01 percent of GDP—a tiny fraction of the average for OECD countries. Earlier, Argentina had launched a campaign to develop significant employment services as of 2006 as part of the strategy to move beneficiaries out of the Jefes y Jefas de Hogar program and back to independent employment. In general, however, employment services in the LAC region are still struggling to develop to best-practice levels, especially in their outreach to poorer workers and to employers—see World Bank (2010a) regarding Argentina and OECD (2009) regarding Chile. For example, Honduras's Empleate employment service does a better job of capturing labor demand from large formal enterprises than from smaller ones, and consequently it serves mostly the population with a secondary or university education and is still limited in coverage (World Bank 2012b). El Salvador's program was serving about 11,000 people a year prior to the crisis, mostly young and mostly secondary school graduates (World Bank 2012a).

What Happened during the Financial Crisis

A few countries bolstered their public employment services in response to the crisis, but there is little evidence of the impact of these services or the characteristics of their clientele. Even after expansion, they remain quite small relative to flows in and out of employment. Argentina continued its program to build capacity, nearly doubling the number of offices by the end of 2009. The number of clients served was about 72,000 in 2009, but that was only about 5 percent of the number receiving unemployment insurance (Cerutti et al. 2014). Priority for unemployment services was given to former beneficiaries of the Programa Jefes y Jefas de Hogar Desocupados who chose to transfer into the time-bound Seguro de Capacitacion (Training and Employment Insurance), which was designed to improve their employability with job training and employment services. The difficulties in building such services, however, led to only a quarter of the participants receiving training and employment services; half left the program because of time limits, and only 20 percent left to accept formal employment (World Bank 2010a). Mexico temporarily scaled up its budget for employment services to extend hours and improve services. It also increased staffing by nearly 20 percent between 2007 and 2009 (OECD 2010). Its service delivery rose from 200,000 to 350,000 clients (Cerutti et al. 2014), which though small in relation to the labor market was found by Heredia (2012) to raise somewhat the probability of job seekers finding formal jobs and to raise the number of hours worked per week (though not hourly wages). El Salvador set in place plans to expand coverage of its employment services from 14 urban centers to 66 municipalities and raise the quality of service and build links to other ALMPs such as training and workfare. Chile proposed to improve the information system for the nascent electronic labor exchange, among other reforms, making it available online instead of requiring people to visit the local employment services offices to use it. Postcrisis, Chile is carrying through with improvements in its public employment services. In 2011 it tripled funding (to 0.002 percent of GDP), using the monies to improve services in lower-income municipalities, to train staff in more effective differentiation of services by client profile, and to provide vouchers for the use of private employment agencies (OECD 2009, 2012).

In addition to plain labor intermediation, several countries offered a more comprehensive approach for unemployed youth (see box 6.4). This was an attempt to address the particularly large impacts on employment for young workers.

Box 6.4 Addressing Youth Unemployment: Examples from Chile and Argentina

In recent years, both Chile and Argentina have launched programs to support youth employment. Each country is trying to reach disadvantaged youth and to promote formal employment and the completion of secondary school, but the programs differ in important ways.

About half of the fiscal stimulus that Chile enacted in response to the financial crisis funded active labor market programs, of which public works programs were the largest. In addition, in 2009 the government introduced a wage subsidy for young low-wage workers, which in practice functions as an in-work benefit. The subsidy can reach up to 20 percent of wage income for those workers with the lowest wages and is gradually withdrawn as wages rise. A third of the subsidy goes to the employer and two-thirds to the employee. Salaried or self-employed workers between 18 and 25 years of age who are members of families in the poorest 40 percent (as measured by the targeting instrument) and who earn no more than the equivalent of US$10,000 per year are eligible. According to data from the Ministry of Social Development, the program benefitted 130,000 youth in 2009 and 210,000 in 2010. Youth can continue receiving the benefit as long as they meet the eligibility requirements. The age limit can be extended by up to two years if the applicant is attending certified courses or has a child while they are eligible. On the other hand, the subsidy ends the last month the youth is 21 years old if he or she has not graduated from secondary school, but can be reinstated once the certificate is obtained. In order to receive the subsidy, the employer (including the self-employed) must be up to date on all tax, social security, and health payments. The program is managed by the public training institute (SENCE), and the subsidy is paid by the Social Security Institute.

The government of Argentina has taken another approach to support better employment outcomes for disadvantaged youth. The Programa Jovenes con Mas y Mejor Trabajo (Program for More and Better Work for Youth), in operation since 2008, scaled rapidly from 10,000 participants that year to 75,000 in 2009 and 120,000 in 2010. The program is managed by the Ministry of Labor and implemented through the network of municipal employment offices. The design of the program is both comprehensive and flexible. The target group is secondary school dropouts. After participating in an obligatory introductory orientation workshop, dropouts are linked to a range of services, including remedial education, training, other employment-related workshops (including job clubs and training in job searches), internships, and entrepreneurship opportunities. As of the beginning of 2013, nearly 600,000 young people had signed up for the program,

box continues next page

Box 6.4 Addressing Youth Unemployment: Examples from Chile and Argentina *(continued)*

of which about 350,000 completed the orientation workshop. Reflecting the priority given to completing secondary education, about 340,000 have participated in remedial education classes. Youth receive a stipend as long as they are participating in an eligible program activity, as well as "prizes" based on specific accomplishments. In part because of the scale of the program and the relative inexperience of the municipal employment offices, the program has faced some challenges in mobilizing sufficient services for its participants, particularly in the areas of training and internships. Nevertheless, data on the results to date are encouraging. So far, about a third of youth who have completed the program were able to secure formal employment within a year. A complementary comparison with a similar population in the household survey indicated that over the period 2009–10 the labor force insertion rate for program participants was about 50 percent higher than for those who did not participate (17.7 percent versus 11.6 percent).

Table 6.6 A Comparison of Density of Public Employment Services Offices: Latin America and the Caribbean and Other Selected Countries

LAC region		Comparator countries	
Country	Number of public employment services offices per 100,000 habitants	Country	Number of public employment services offices per 100,000 habitants
Brazil	0.6	Cyprus	0.78
Colombia	0.18	Mauritius	1.16
Dominican Republic	0.1	Portugal	1.17
El Salvador	0.11	Spain	1.9
Honduras	0.04	Thailand	0.13
Mexico	0.13	Tunisia	0.81
Nicaragua	0.16	Turkey	0.36
Panama	0.34		
Peru	0.14		
Venezuela, RB	0.1		

Source: Pages, Pierre, and Scarpetta 2009, table 7.2.

Around the World

Spending on public employment services in Latin America is low, and that is reflected in the lower density of services than in other emerging economies, especially those in Europe and Central Asia (see table 6.6). Moreover, many European countries give their employment services a more prominent role in social assistance than does Latin America, requiring social assistance recipients to register with public employment services and to accept the training or jobs provided by them, although this requirement is often not backed in substance with enough services to be effective. In the LAC region, this linkage is much less common, even though some assistance programs are beginning to seek ways to help households increase their earnings and become independent. Some of these programs, such as Chile's Solidario (Solidarity Program) and Colombia's Trabajemos Unidos (United

Understanding the Poverty Impact of the Global Financial Crisis in Latin America and the Caribbean
http://dx.doi.org/10.1596/978-1-4648-0241-6

We Work), include linkages to a customized set of services, including, as needed, employment and training. In the OECD countries, public employment services have played a key role in the recent trend toward activation policies. Greater emphasis is placed on one-to-one counseling and the preparation of action plans to obtain employment by clients. The services have also been at the forefront of the reform agenda in public sector management and results-based management.

Social Assistance

Social assistance covers a wide range of programs of different modalities and with somewhat different purposes, but all are meant to provide the poor or vulnerable with income support. It can include minimum income guarantees, conditional cash transfers, child allowances, social pensions, income support for the disabled, school lunches, and segues into fee waivers or price reductions for essential services such as health care, education, or utilities. Eligibility criteria and program rules can focus some programs on short-term assistance for those facing shocks; other programs may concentrate on longer-term support for the chronically poor; or there may be some combination of the two. Earlier, this chapter reported on the total expenditures of the full panoply of instruments. This section looks in more detail at those that account for most of the spending and policy action in the years around the time of the global financial crisis, especially CCTs, social pensions, other cash transfers, and school feeding. For each typology of programs, we briefly review the program logic, then look at the form these programs take in the LAC region, and finally describe the changes made in these programs at the time of the crisis. Although not all the changes were likely deliberate responses to the crisis, their occurrence at that specific point in time did help the population affected by the crisis.

Conditional Cash Transfers
Program Logic
Conditional cash transfer programs seek to break the intergenerational transmission of poverty by transferring cash to poor households on the condition that those households make prespecified investments in the human capital of their children. The cash transfer is intended to alleviate households' current poverty, and the conditions attached to it are intended to increase the human capital of the new generation, thereby improving their future prospects. These programs generally target the poor, mostly families with children. The targeting mechanisms include geographic targeting, household targeting, or a combination of the two. The "conditions" that accompany the transfers generally require that these households use basic preventive health care and ensure school attendance. However, programs vary widely in how thoroughly and frequently they monitor compliance with the conditions and in the size of the penalties for noncompliance. That said, the large body of evidence produced by evaluations reveals that these programs target poverty effectively, raise household consumption, increase the quantity and improve the quality of food consumed, increase

school enrollment and the use of selected health services, and in many cases reduce child labor but not adult labor (Fiszbein et al. 2009; World Bank 2011b).

CCTs in the LAC Region

CCTs have become the flagship social assistance programs in the LAC countries, covering 110 million people (more than 20 percent of the population of the region). In 2010, 17 countries in the region had at least one such program (table 6.7), and since 2000 their spending has increased substantially, especially in the countries where they are national flagship programs such as Brazil, Colombia, Ecuador, and Mexico (figure 6.6). Reforms to the child allowance programs in Argentina, Chile, and Uruguay have made these programs the least weakly conditioned as well and have extended them to cover the informal sector, accompanied by large increases in tax-financed expenditures on social assistance for mostly poor children.[6]

Table 6.7 Beneficiaries of Conditional Cash Transfer Programs: Latin America and the Caribbean, 2010

Country	Program	Spending (% of GDP) in 2010	Total number of beneficiary households in 2010	Number of beneficiary individuals in 2010	% of population
Argentina	Asignaciones Familiares por Hijo	0.56	1,872,173	3,527,527	9
Bolivia	Bono Juancito Pinto	–	–	1,625,123	17
Bolivia	Bono Juana Azurduy	–	130,337	638,652	7
Brazil	Bolsa Familia	0.39	12,778,220	52,390,702	27
Colombia	Familias en Accion	0.35	2,598,566	11,693,547	26
Costa Rica	Avancemos	–	46,304	185,214	4
Dominican Republic	Solidaridad	–	764,913	2,103,429	21
Ecuador	Bono de Desarrollo Humano	0.80	1,220,463	6,379,532	47
El Salvador	Comunidades Solidarias	0.09	105,900	508,320	–
Guatemala	Mi Familia Progresa	–	591,570	3,253,635	24
Honduras	Bono 10,000	0.16	81,911	409,555	6
Honduras[a]	PRAF	–	132,158	926,070	13
Jamaica[a]	PATH	–	–	360,000	13
Mexico	Oportunidades	0.48	5,560,540	27,246,646	26
Panama (2008 data)	Red de Oportunidades	–	70,599	398,807	12
Paraguay[b]	Tekopora	–	99,015	554,484	9
Peru	Juntos	0.14	471,511	2,593,311	9
Trinidad and Tobago[c]	TCCTP	–	–	32,650	3
Uruguay	Asignaciones Familiares	0.39	100,660	420,128	12

Sources: CEPAL database and Cerutti et al. 2014.
a. Planned coverage.
b. Includes the Ñopytyvo and Propaís II programs.
c. 2009 data on beneficiaries.
Note: – = not available.

Figure 6.6 Spending on Conditional Cash Transfers: Latin America and the Caribbean, 2000–10

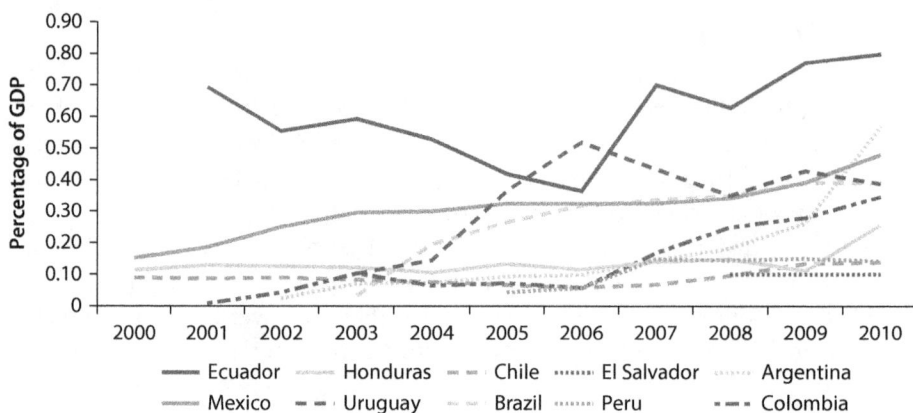

Source: Cerutti et al. 2014.

Figure 6.7 Coverage of Conditional Cash Transfer Programs, by Country and Quintiles of Pretransfer Income Distribution: Latin America and the Caribbean, 2008–10

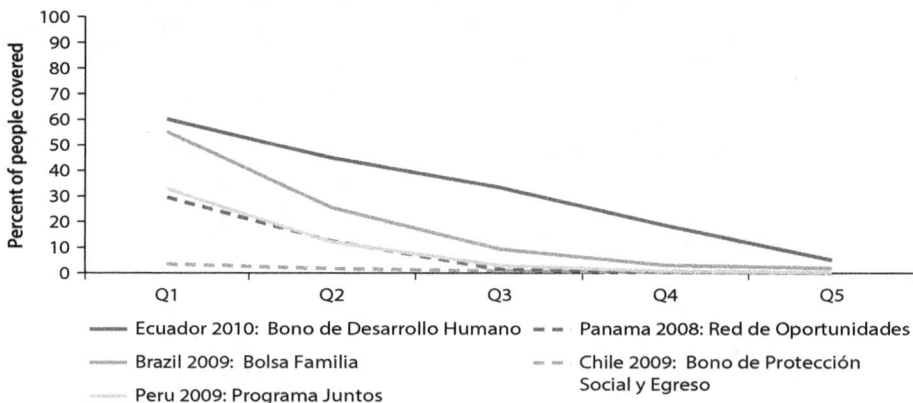

Source: Cerutti et al. 2014.

Program coverage varies substantially by country. In some countries, these programs cover a small percentage of the population, often living in specific areas. In others, programs have national coverage, and they reach a large percentage of the population (see table 6.7). The population coverage varies from under 10 percent of the populations of Bolivia, Costa Rica, Paraguay, and Peru, to about a quarter of those in Brazil, Colombia, and Mexico, and an even larger share in Guatemala and Ecuador. Not only do the programs have fairly high coverage, but their coverage is also highly progressive, with coverage rates among the poorest quintile multiples of what it is for the richest quintile (see figure 6.7), though still well short of all the poor.

Although CCTs are primarily intended to address long-term structural poverty, their prominence in the LAC countries' social protection systems have made them an important mechanism for protecting households from shocks. Part of their role stems from their origins—some programs began (and found momentum) in response to a crisis such as those in Mexico, Colombia, and the Dominican Republic. But the main reason that CCTs can be an important vehicle for crisis response is that these programs have already established an administrative capacity and a client relationship with a (sometimes large) share of the most vulnerable population to whom they provide regular income. Indeed, impact evaluations have shown improved child welfare outcomes, even in households facing shocks such as falling prices of coffee in Mexico (Gitter, Manley, and Barham 2011) or increasing food prices in El Salvador (de Brauw and Murrugarra 2011).

The targeting instruments of most CCT programs in the region (see table 6.8) were designed to address chronic poverty and thus are not as flexible as they would need to be to address transient poverty from a crisis. This approach has several aspects:

- Most programs use proxy means tests to judge welfare—measures that are designed to be relatively stable indicators of chronic poverty rather than to fluctuate with short-run income changes (the exception is Brazil's program, which uses a self-declared measure of income to determine eligibility).
- Some programs target only specific geographic areas (e.g., programs in El Salvador, Guatemala, Panama, Paraguay, and Peru), concentrated mostly or exclusively in rural areas. Furthermore, some CCT programs (e.g., Oportunidades in Mexico) operate only in locations deemed "supply ready," thereby excluding areas that lack health and education services. Depending on the coverage of the program and where the crisis hits, those hurt may be excluded from these programs—for example, in the financial crisis layoffs were expected in urban areas, which did not fit the rural focus of many of the CCTs.
- About half of programs accept new registrants only periodically rather than on an ongoing basis.
- Most programs target only families with children, whereas the crisis may affect families with different types of demographics.
- Most programs are budget-rationed rather than guaranteeing a place to all who meet the eligibility criteria. The programs are set up to allow households to benefit for multiple years, with recertification only every few years and in several cases on an ad hoc basis rather than for predetermined cycles.

What Happened during the Financial Crisis

During 2008 and 2009, the decade-long expansion of CCTs continued, with most countries for which data are available showing an increase in spending (figure 6.6). There was variation across countries, with Peru's expenditure for Juntos (Together) as a percentage of GDP increasing by just 3.8 percent, while El Salvador's funding for Comunidades Solidarias Rurales (Rural Community

Table 6.8 Targeting Rules, Conditional Cash Transfer Programs: Latin America and the Caribbean

Country	Name of program	Which targeting methods are used?				Which best describes the enrollment or registration process?		
		Categorical	Means test (verified or not)	Proxy means test	Geographic targeting	Open or ongoing—anyone can apply anytime	Periodic open season	Blend
Argentina	Asignacion Familiares por Hijo			x		x		
Bolivia	Bono Juancito Pinto	x				x		
Bolivia	Bono Juana Azurduy	x				x		
Brazil	Bolsa Familia		x			x		
Colombia	Familias en Accion			x	x			x
Costa Rica	Avancemos			x				
Dominican Republic	Solidaridad			x	x			x
Ecuador	Bono de Desarrollo Humano			x				
El Salvador	Comunidades Solidarias Rurales			x	x			
Guatemala	MiFaPro			x	x		x	
Honduras	Bono 10000			x	x		x	
Honduras	PRAF			x	x			
Jamaica	PATH			x		x		
Mexico	Oportunidades			x	x	x		
Panama	Red de Oportuniades			x	x		x	
Paraguay	Tekopora			x				
Peru	Juntos			x	x		x	
Trinidad and Tobago	TCCTP	x		x				
Uruguay	Asignaciones Familiares	x		x				

Source: Interviews with World Bank's task team leaders (TTLs).

Solidarity) increased by 75.6 percent. The three countries with large, well-established programs—Brazil, Colombia, and Mexico—increased spending by 11.8, 12.2, and 14.7 percent, respectively.

During the crisis, most countries in the region modified to some extent their existing programs or introduced new ones (table 6.9). Every country that had an existing CCT program expanded coverage or increased the generosity of benefits, in most instances to address the negative effect of the economic crisis. Three countries (Belize, Bolivia, and Honduras) introduced a new program. Ten out of the 20 programs increased the number of beneficiaries, five rolled out to new areas of the country, seven raised benefits, and three changed the benefit structure. Although some of these changes were planned and were not merely a reaction to the crisis, crises often create the political environment needed to change programs.

Many countries reached out to existing beneficiaries by increasing the level of benefits, the quickest of possible program responses. For example, in Brazil both the variable benefits (paid per child) and the basic benefit (for extremely poor families irrespective of the number of children) were raised by about 10 percent. In Mexico, benefits were increased on top of inflationary adjustments in 2008 (US$4.00) and in 2009 (US$10.00 a month). In the Dominican Republic, the benefit level was increased by 27.3 percent.

Increasing benefits is a fast and administratively inexpensive measure, but it is to the advantage of only the existing beneficiaries of a program. Expanding coverage can be administratively complex and may have implications for the long-term sustainability of the program. As we have seen, the coverage rates of the poorest quintiles are far from complete, and the people hit the hardest by a crisis may not be the ones that are already beneficiaries of a program. Does this mean that programs should expand in response to a crisis? The answer is less straightforward than one might think. The administrative capacity for new fieldwork for expanded coverage may not be in place or sufficient. Expansion may be particularly difficult in geographic areas previously not served. Moreover, expansion raises the question of whether the larger coverage should be permanent, and, if not, how it would be reduced. In fact, no country has scaled back expansion carried out during the crisis.

Some CCT programs took policy actions to expand enrollment. In 2009 the new Salvadoran administration maintained the CCT program, expanding it to poor urban areas and complementing the program with other interventions such as a cash transfer to the elderly living in the 100 poorest municipalities. Mexico modified its targeting system and introduced distinctions for urban and rural areas, which allowed more urban families to join the program. Although the number of beneficiary families remained constant at 5 million from 2004 to 2007, starting in 2008 the program expanded first by just 1 percent, then by 3 percent in 2009, and then by almost 12 percent, reaching 5.8 million families in 2010. Moreover, to address the problem of "supply readiness," Mexico greatly expanded its Programa de Asistenctia Alimentaria (PAL) to be able to enroll households who did not qualify for Oportunidades because of either location or family situation (Rangel 2009). The program was integrated with the program

Table 6.9 Changes in Conditional Cash Transfer Programs during the Global Financial Crisis: Latin America and the Caribbean, 2008–09

Country	Name of program	Change in spending (%)	Increased number of beneficiaries in areas already working	Rolled out in new areas of the country	Raised benefit level within existing structure	Changed benefit structure	Changed eligibility criteria	New program initiated in response to or after crisis
Argentina	Asignacion Universal por Hijo	–						x
Belize	Boost							x
Bolivia	Bono Juana Azurduy							x
Bolivia	Bono Juanito Pinto						x	
Brazil	Bolsa Familia	11.8	x		x			
Colombia	Familias en Accion	12.2	x					
Costa Rica	Avancemos		x					
Dominican Republic	Solidaridad		x		x			
Ecuador	Bono de Desarrollo Humano	22.9	x					
El Salvador	Comunidades Solidarias	75.6		x				
Guatemala	MiFaPro					x		
Honduras	Bono 10000	–		x				x
Jamaica	PATH	20	x		x			
Mexico	PAL		x	x				
Mexico	Oportunidades	14.70	x	x	x	x		
Panama	Red de Oportuniades				x			
Paraguay	Tekopora			x	x	x		
Peru	Juntos	3.8	x	x				
Trinidad and Tobago	TCCPP							
Uruguay	Asignaciones Familiares		x		x			

Source: World Bank data.

Note: Blank cells signify that no changes were made.

Programa de Apoyo Alimentario en Zonas de Atención Prioritaria (PAAZAP, Program for Food Assistance in Priority Areas), which was launched in 2008 with the objective of reaching the smallest and most dispersed areas of the countries not reached by PAL. In over two years, the integrated program went from being exclusively rural and small (125,000 families in 2008) to being slightly more urban and much larger (52 percent of its 825,000 beneficiary families lived in urban areas in 2010). In Colombia, Familias en Accion (Families in Action) increased its number of beneficiaries by almost 50 percent in 2009, from 1.8 million families (7.9 million people) in 2008 to 2.6 million families (11.6 million people) in 2009. The families prioritized for the expansion were the victims of fraudulent Ponzi schemes whom the government aimed to compensate. In Costa Rica, the program Avancemos (Let's Advance Together), established in 2006 with 8,000 beneficiaries, saw its number of beneficiaries rise from 118,000 in 2008 to 151,000 in 2009. In the Dominican Republic, the Solidaridad program underwent a big expansion in 2008 and almost doubled, from 1.2 million individuals in 2007 to 2.1 million in 2008. It has remained rather constant since. In Jamaica, the number of beneficiaries of PATH remained stable in 2008 and 2009 at about 355,000, but increased to 419,000 in 2010. In Ecuador, the coverage of the Bono de Desarrollo Humano (BDH, Human Development Grant) increased from 1 million to 1.2 million between 2008 and 2009. In Peru, the number of beneficiaries of Juntos climbed from 2.3 million in 2008 to 2.6 million in 2010. In Paraguay, the program Tekopora increased coverage significantly in 2009, from 14,000 families to over 80,000.

Brazil is the only LAC country that uses a means test for eligibility for its CCT, but because it was not operating as an entitlement program in 2008, its scale-up was not automatic. The government did take action to significantly scale up its program following the crisis, but it was not motivated primarily by the crisis. Rather, it sought to adjust to changes in the estimates of the potential target population. The threshold for eligibility was raised from R$120 to R$140 for moderate poverty and from R$60 to R$70 for extreme poverty, thereby bringing an additional 1.8 million families into the program and raising total enrollment from 10.6 million families in 2008 to 12.4 million in 2009. The cost of these measures and the increase in benefits are estimated at R$410 million, or approximately 0.014 percent of GDP, bringing the total cost of the program to R$11.8 billion or 0.4 percent of GDP (ILO/World Bank 2012).

In Guatemala, the government launched the conditional cash transfer program Mi Familia Progresa (MiFaPro, My Family Progresses) in early 2008. This program was an attempt to address the stagnation in the fight against extreme poverty between 2000 and 2006, low levels of public spending on social welfare programs, and the inefficiencies of the major existing programs in addressing the vulnerabilities of the poor. The program combined geographic and individual targeting and was scaled up very rapidly: by 2009 about 448,000 families (about 24 percent of the population) in the poorest areas of the country were benefitting from the program. At the end of 2009, the government introduced an additional nutrition benefit to increase the transfer to families with young children.

Belize and Honduras began new programs in response to the crisis, and Bolivia started programs just after but not closely linked to the crisis. Belize's BOOST program was launched in February 2011, and it now reaches 3,177 households (12.5 percent of all poor households). Although Honduras has had experience with subregional CCT programs since early 2000s, the national CCT program, Bono 10,000, started with 100,000 rural poor households in 2010, and now reaches 250,000 households (20 percent of the population) in both rural and urban areas.

The simulation from a macro-micro modeling framework for Mexico presented in chapter 5 demonstrates how a CCT program provides a government with an easy way to channel resources toward the poorest during a crisis. The simulations show the effects of, first, the expansion in coverage of the Oportunidades program by 750,000 households, assuming that the increase in coverage all came in the lower half of the income distribution and there is a proportionate incidence to the families already enrolled, and, second, an increase in benefits of Mex$120 per month for all recipients, old and new (figure 6.8). In the figure, the orange (middle) line shows the effect of the increase on the coverage, the blue (top) line the result of the combined policy change.

The expansion of Oportunidades significantly mitigated the impacts of the crisis for the poor. Without the policy response, the incomes of those in the 20th percentile of the distribution would have fallen by just over 8 percent; after the change the fall was about 5 percent. For those in the 10th percentile, the effect was even larger—their incomes fell not 8 percent but by about 3 percent.[7] Chapter 3 noted that income fell at the bottom end of the income distribution in Argentina, Brazil, Costa Rica, El Salvador, and Paraguay as well, and so the ability to support some of the households who can least tolerate a reduction in income is useful.

Figure 6.8 Simulated Effects of Increased Coverage and Benefits for Oportunidades Program, Mexico

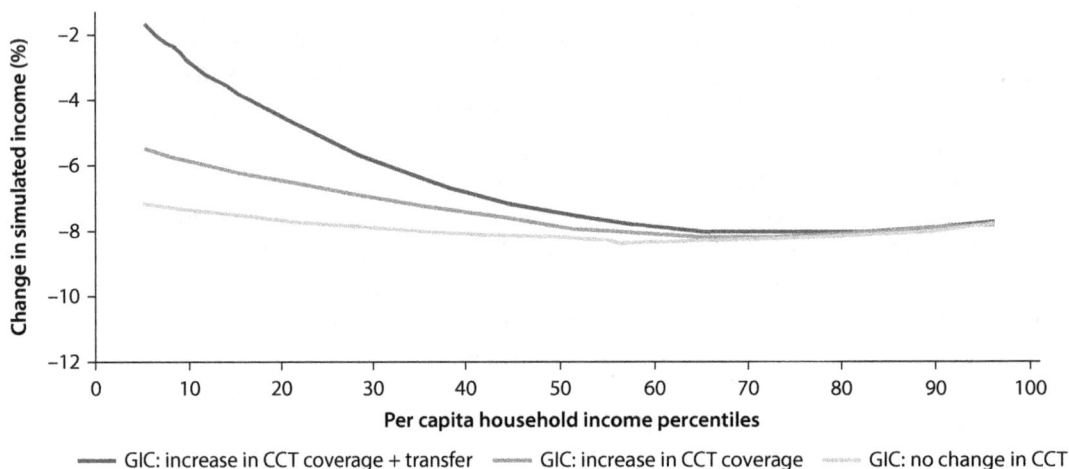

Sources: Chapter 5 of this study and simulations based on La Encuesta Nacional de Ingresos y Gastos de los Hogares (ENIGH, National Household Income and Expenditure Survey).

There are, however, limits to the mitigation that programs targeting poverty, especially the region's CCTs, can provide. First, because such programs target the poor, they help few households in the middle of the income distribution, although in Mexico it was the middle of the distribution that suffered the largest proportional income losses. In most countries, the CCT programs serve only families with children, and in some countries operate in only defined geographic areas, usually favoring rural areas where chronic poverty is highest. There are limits in the opposite direction as well. Both the coverage and benefit level of Oportunidades were relatively large even before the crisis.[8] To scale them up too far would have been imprudent because the program must play a balanced role in social policy and avoid overwhelming disincentives to labor. Starting from lower baseline coverage and benefits, several other countries had more room to scale up their CCTs (largely for their role in long-run social protection), but they sped up in an attempt to assist in the moment of crisis.

Around the World

Few non-LAC countries scaled up their conditional cash transfer programs in response to the crisis, but the Philippines was a notable exception. In February 2008, its 4Ps program was a small localized pilot serving 6,000 households. In response to the financial crisis, the government decided to accelerate program expansion and scaled up to over 321,000 beneficiary households by the beginning of 2009. The program areas selected by early 2009 covered 148 municipalities. By July 2009, the program had expanded again to cover an additional 700,000 households in about 100 municipalities with a poverty incidence of 60 percent or higher. By May 2012, the program had further expanded to cover approximately 3 million households (World Bank 2012c).

Social Pensions

Program Logic

Social pensions are intended to provide a measure of income support where contributory pension systems have incomplete coverage. The programs are financed from general tax revenues rather than labor taxes, and benefits are not linked to earnings. Some have only age requirements; some also target poverty. Social pension schemes are at the intersection between both contributory social insurance and social assistance. They are best designed when they segue well to both of these parts of the larger social protection system.

Social Pensions in the LAC Region

Social pensions are a branch of transfer policy that has grown significantly in recent years in Latin America. Eleven of the 18 programs existing in the region began after 2000, and seven of them since 2006 (see table 6.10). Some countries such as Brazil and Argentina established the right to a minimum income transfer (commonly called a pension) at a certain age for individuals not receiving any other form of formal pension, and in some cases with additional eligibility conditions. Other countries such as El Salvador, Peru, and Mexico established old-age

Understanding the Poverty Impact of the Global Financial Crisis in Latin America and the Caribbean
http://dx.doi.org/10.1596/978-1-4648-0241-6

Table 6.10 Noncontributory Pensions: Latin America and the Caribbean

Country	Program	Spending (% of GDP) in 2010	Number of beneficiary individuals in 2010	Year started	% of population
Argentina	Programa Pensiones no Contributivas	0.03	1,056,347	1948	2.6
Bolivia	Renta Dignidad	–	765,917	2008	7.9
Brazil	BPC	0.28	3,401,541	1996	0.0
Brazil	Previdencia Rural	1.36	5,494,908	1993	0.0
Chile	Pensión Básica Solidaria	0.34	1,011,095	2008	5.9
Colombia	SP programs for the elderly	0.08	593,448	2003	0.0
Costa Rica	Regime no Contributivo	–	88,164	1974	2.0
Ecuador	Pension Asistencial	0.28	502,828	2006	3.7
El Salvador (2011)	Nuestros Mayores Derechos	–	19,534	2011	0.3
Mexico	Programa 70+	0.10	2,105,306	2006	2.0
Mexico	Oportunidades Adulto Mayor	–	80,000	–	0.1
Mexico	Programa 70+ DF	–	464,998	2001	5.3
Panama	100 a los 70	–	81,773	2009	2.4
Paraguay	Pension Alimentaria Adultos Mayores Indígenas	–	–	2011	–
Peru	Pension Minima	–	3,742	2001	0.0
Peru (2011)	Pension 65	–	25,902	2011	0.1
Trinidad and Tobago	Senior Citizen Pension	–	73,110	–	5.6
Uruguay	Pension no contributiva a la vejez y por invalidez	0.50	82,890	1919	2.5

Sources: CEPAL social pension database (http://dds.cepal.org/bdps/) and Murrugarra (2011).
Note: Brazil's Benefício de Prestação Continuada (BPC, Continuous Benefit) includes transfers to both the elderly and the disabled. Chile's Pensión Solidaria Basica (BSP, Basic Solidarity Pension) replaces the old PASIS program; – = not available.

income support programs targeting the elderly poor living in the localities where a CCT is currently operating, so that these programs are implemented using the existing delivery network of a poverty-targeting program. In Jamaica, the elderly (60 years and older) who do not receive a pension can be beneficiaries of the CCT called PATH.

Few household surveys collect information on participation in these programs, but information is available for three countries: Brazil, Chile, and Mexico. Figure 6.9 shows that in Chile more than half of the 65 and over population in the poorest two deciles was covered by the Pensión Básica Solidaria (PBS, Basic Solidarity Pension) and the Aporte Previsional Solidario (APS, Solidarity Contribution) in 2009 (Cerutti et al. 2014). In Brazil, coverage is much more limited, but this may be explained by the fact that the BPC is just one of the many programs benefitting the elderly and is limited to urban areas (in rural areas the elderly benefit from rural pensions, which have the same level of benefits but are not means-tested). Because the elderly are still a low share of the population in Brazil, overall coverage of the population by social pension programs is low (see figure 6.10).

Figure 6.9 Coverage of Social Pension Programs, by Country and Quintiles of Pretransfer Income Distribution among Households with Elderly Adults: Brazil, Chile, and Mexico, 2009 and 2010

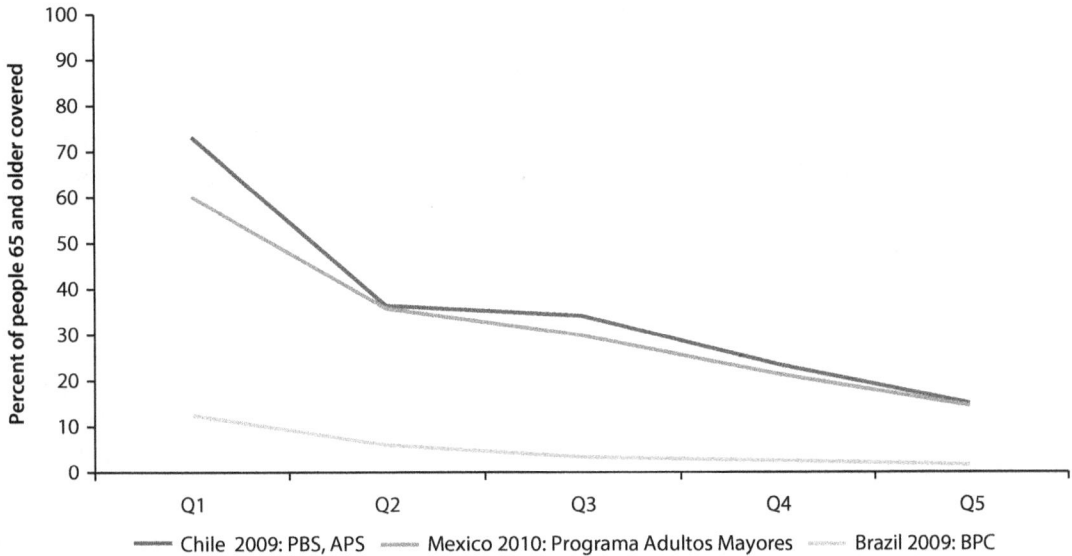

Source: Cerutti et al. 2014.
Note: BPC = Benefício de Prestação Continuada (Continuous Benefit); PBS = Pensión Básica Solidaria (Basic Solidarity Pension); APS = Aporte Previsional Solidario (Solidarity Contribution).

Figure 6.10 Coverage of Social Pension Programs, by Country and Quintiles of Pretransfer Income Distribution among All Households: Brazil, Chile, and Mexico, 2009 and 2010

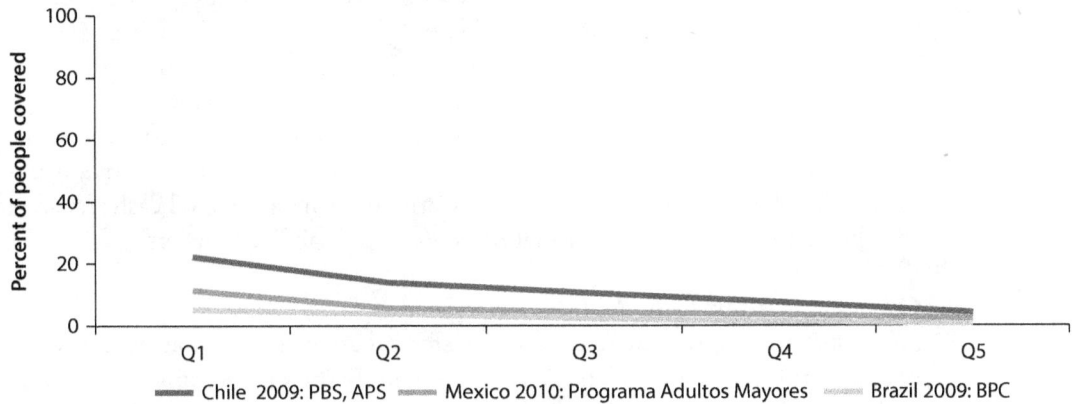

Source: Cerutti et al. 2014.
Note: BPC = Benefício de Prestação Continuada (Continuous Benefit); PBS = Pensión Básica Solidaria (Basic Solidarity Pension); APS = Aporte Previsional Solidario (Solidarity Contribution).

What Happened during the Financial Crisis

Between 2008 and 2010, there were notable expansions of social pensions in nine countries.[9] They were not necessarily motivated by the crisis, but nonetheless they provided income support during a difficult time. For example, in 2009 the new Salvadoran administration complemented the CCT program with another intervention, the Pensión Básica Universal-Adulto Mayor (Basic Universal Pension for the Elderly), a cash transfer to those over the age of 70 living in the same poorest 32 municipalities covered by the CCT. These individuals receive a pension transfer of US$50 a month provided they do not receive any other pensions. More than 7,000 elderly benefitted from the transfer during 2009. Similarly, Panama established its program in 2009, and in Bolivia Renta Dignidad (Income for Dignity) replaced the existing Bonosol program. In 2008 Chile introduced an old-age Pensión Básica Solidaria (Basic Solidarity Pension—PBS Vejez) to replace two previous programs, PASIS and PMG. It aimed to support all persons over the age of 65 who received no other pension and were deemed to be in the poorest half of the population according to their poverty score. Beginning in July 2008, this benefit rolled out gradually, starting with a benefit of US$105 per month and reaching the poorest 40 percent of the population. By July 2009, the amount had risen to US$132 per month, and coverage targeted the poorest 45 percent of the population. The coverage target rose to 50 percent by September 2009, 55 percent by July 2010, and 60 percent as of July 2011, a year ahead of the planned schedule.

Other Cash Transfers
Program Logic

In the social protection toolkit, unconditional cash transfers (UCTs) span a wide variety of purposes and designs. Among the most common are minimum income guarantee programs for the poor, which are common in Europe and various other developed countries; child allowances to provide income supplements to households with higher dependency ratios, also most common in Europe; transfers to the elderly or disabled to (partially) substitute for earnings—a program growing everywhere; and often a variety of sector-linked benefits such as housing or utility subsidies and fee waivers for school, uniforms, or textbooks. The list is diverse, and yet in the LAC region many of these programs were not used by governments as part of the crisis response. Thus we provide here a very selective treatment of UCT programs, focusing on the Caribbean's means-tested cash transfers and the increasingly common social pensions and disability transfers.

Other Cash Transfers in the LAC Region

Some sort of poverty-targeted cash transfer program is common in the small island Caribbean states such as Antigua and Barbuda, Dominica, Grenada, St. Kitts and Nevis, St. Lucia, and St. Vincent and the Grenadines.[10] They command the largest expenditure among the numerous social assistance programs in all the countries for which information is available, though spending varies from 0.15 percent of GDP in St. Kitts and Nevis to 1 percent of GDP in St. Vincent and the Grenadines. The programs usually operate with an informal means test, and so in theory would find it easy to respond to a crisis-induced upsurge in need. However, the targeting and monitoring systems of these programs are very poorly developed, and there is little information on their impacts or evolution over time (World Bank 2009a, 2009d, 2009e, 2009f, 2011a; Williams et al. 2013).

Several countries are building programs of income support for the disabled. In Argentina, a noncontributory disability pension was initiated in 1997, and the expenditure was equivalent to 0.032 percent of GDP. This program then grew significantly, with the number of beneficiaries rising from 75,000 in 1997 to 576,000 in 2010. Meanwhile, the expenditure increased tenfold, from 0.032 percent of GDP in 1997 to 0.35 percent in 2010. In Brazil, the disability pension launched in 1996 had a similar evolution, with spending rising from 0.02 percent of GDP in 1996 to 0.32 percent in 2010. The number of beneficiaries rose from 346,000 in 1996 to 1.9 million in 2010. In Ecuador, the disability pension program that began in 2006 with an expenditure of 0.002 percent of GDP and 5,000 beneficiaries grew to 65,000 beneficiaries in 2010, at a cost of 0.036 percent of GDP. Meanwhile, a transfer for children with disabilities that began on a very small scale in 2008 with just 1,500 beneficiaries increased tenfold to reach 18,000 beneficiaries and 0.007 percent of GDP in 2010.

What Happened during the Financial Crisis

A few clearly crisis-related changes were made in UCT programs during the global financial crisis. In March 2009, the government of Chile paid a one-time bonus to poor families so they could cope with the effects of the crisis.[11] The measure benefitted 1.7 million families with a transfer of Ch$40,000 (approximately US$66). Of this 1.7 million, 100,000 were beneficiaries of Chile Solidario who did not receive family allowances; 600,000 received the Subsidio Unico Familiar (Unique Family Subsidy); and 1 million were families receiving family allowances in the private or public sector and who had annual incomes of less than CH$400,000 (approximately US$660). This benefit was distributed again in March 2010 following the earthquake, but it was then discontinued. In the Dominican Republic, the government put in place two targeted subsidies, the Bonogas-household and the Bonogas-driver,[12] to address the problem of rising oil prices. The program for households provided over 800,000 poor households with a monthly subsidy of RD$228 (US$7). The amount was based on the average amount of gas consumed by the poor. About the same time, in November 2009 the government of the Dominican Republic began to implement a means-tested electricity subsidy, Bonoluz, whose roll-out was much slower. During the first year of implementation, it reached only some 150,000 families.

Noncontributory programs for the disabled also saw increases in spending and beneficiaries in several countries around the time of the crisis. Argentina's program increased spending from 0.17 percent of GDP in 2008 to 0.28 percent in 2009, and the number of beneficiaries increased from 297,000 to 453,000. In 2008 Chile instituted the Pensión Básica Solidaria de Invalidez (Disability Basic Solidarity Pension), and spending doubled from 2008 to 2009—that is, from 0.08 percent of GDP to 0.18 percent. Ecuador created the program Ecuador Sin Barreras (Ecuador without Barriers)[13] in 2008, Misión Solidaria "Manuela Espejo" (Solidarity Mission "Manuela Espejo")[14] in 2009, and the Bono Joaquin Gallegos Lara (Joaquin Gallegos Lara Benefit) in 2010.[15] Within three years, overall spending on disability programs in Ecuador increased from

0.01 percent of GDP in 2008 to 0.08 in 2010. In Brazil, spending on the already generous noncontributory programs for the disabled increased by only 10 percent, to 0.31 percent of GDP.

In addition to the program-specific direct policy actions to increase benefits, the benefit rates of many programs were raised because they are tied to the minimum wage, which increased substantially in a number of countries in 2009. The benefit levels for both social pensions and other social benefits such as funeral or maternity grants, disability benefits, unemployment insurance, and wages on public works jobs are frequently but not ubiquitously tied to the minimum wage. Real minimum wages in the LAC region were raised a positive amount in 2008–09 in three-quarters of the countries, with five countries increasing by 10 percent or more (Argentina, El Salvador, Honduras, Nicaragua, and Uruguay). Mexico, Panama, Paraguay, and Peru, which were among the countries with largest decelerations, and Mexico and República Bolivariana de Venezuela, which were among those with most negative growth, allowed minimum wages to erode slightly, presumably to take the pressure off employment.

Around the World

Compared with the OECD or Eastern Europe, the LAC countries have few (and they are underdeveloped) minimum income guarantees or last-resort social assistance programs to provide temporary income support to those suffering shocks. Although such programs are seemingly well suited to the problem and are a policy option that is increasingly being considered in the LAC region (e.g., Chile's Ingreso Etico and Brazil's Brazil Cariñoso), Eastern Europe's experience was that in fact they played a smaller role in the crisis response (or a less automatic one) than it was initially assumed they would. In most countries, the natural course was for unemployment insurance, which generally assists families across the income spectrum and pays higher benefits, to be the first line of response. Families would then turn to the last-resort programs only after unemployment benefits expired. In several countries, eligibility thresholds for the minimum income guarantee program had been allowed to erode in both relative and real terms during the high-growth years preceding the crisis, and so the programs were very small, covering in some cases only the poorest 3–5 percent of the population. Moreover, the commonly used guaranteed minimum income design implied that raising the eligibility threshold would provide the existing beneficiaries with higher benefits, which would lessen the freedom of policy makers trying to provide social protection when fiscal space was at its tightest. And some of the programs were financed locally rather than nationally, which made the fiscal space problem all the more problematic as local revenues fell because the deficit rules for subnational entities were strict (Isik-Demelik 2012).

School Feeding
Program Logic
In social protection concepts, school feeding programs are akin to conditional cash transfers, providing a benefit for children who attend school. The growing

body of impact evaluation literature points to the positive effects of school lunch programs on school enrollment and daily attendance, with most of the evidence provided by low-income countries and the lower-income settings within them (Adelman, Gilligan, and Lehrer 2008).

School Feeding Programs in the LAC Region
In Latin America, school feeding is very much a part of government social policies, although it has received fewer headlines because its place in social policy is somewhat more established and constant than that of many other programs. Moreover, where school days are longer than a few hours, as is more common in middle-income countries, students would naturally need to eat in the middle of the day, and thus school feeding is more of an educational logistics issue than a social protection one. Coverage is high, both in terms of the number of countries with programs and in terms of the share of households covered. According to map 6.3, school feeding is of higher density in the LAC region than in any of the other developing regions. Figure 6.11 indicates that the overall coverage of children is quite high, indeed nearing saturation for the poor, in several countries in the region (the figure shows coverage rates for all countries in which household surveys provide information on program participation). To the degree that not all children are covered, the targeting is progressive, an outcome often achieved by focusing resources first on schools in poorer areas and on lower grades. However, because the cost per child is much lower than for CCTs or child allowances, the total expenditures in Brazil, Colombia, and Honduras are lower for school feeding programs than for the cash transfers, but on a par or higher than in Peru and El Salvador, where the cash transfer programs are relatively small.

What Happened during the Financial Crisis
In some of LAC's lower-income countries, scaling up school feeding was a policy response to the food price increases of 2008 and continued once the financial crisis hit. For example, in Nicaragua an increase in school feeding was the main social protection response, whereas in Haiti it was one of several. Prior to 2008, both countries' school feeding programs did not saturate needy areas and thus had room to scale up. Moreover, neither country had a significant poverty-targeting cash transfer program to use as an alternative means of transferring income support to poor families. In Nicaragua, a grant from the Global Food Crisis Response Program in January 2009 allowed the country to supplement its Programa Integral de Nutricion Escolar (PINE, Integral Program for School Nutrition) to purchase food for about 263,000 additional children in 51 poor municipalities for 133 school days. PINE is geographically targeted and has more progressive incidence than most of Nicaragua's social programs. About a third of households in the bottom decile are covered by PINE, compared with less than a tenth of households in the top decile. Simple before-and-after comparisons suggest quite good impacts: the retention rates in targeted municipalities evolved from 84.8 percent in 2008, to 96 percent in 2009, to 98.6 percent in 2010. The attendance rates in targeted municipalities evolved from 78.8 percent in 2008,

Understanding the Poverty Impact of the Global Financial Crisis in Latin America and the Caribbean
http://dx.doi.org/10.1596/978-1-4648-0241-6

Map 6.3 School Feeding: Country Programs, 2006–08

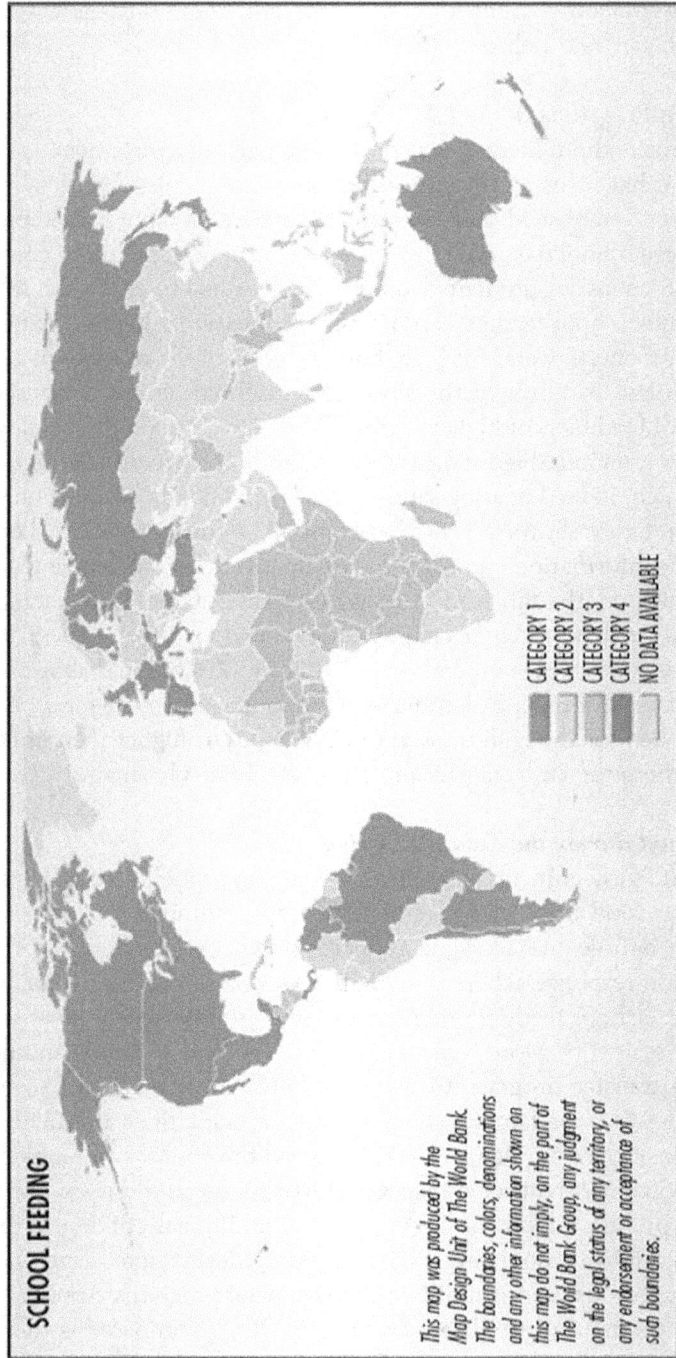

SCHOOL FEEDING

This map was produced by the
Map Design Unit of The World Bank.
The boundaries, colors, denominations
and any other information shown on
this map do not imply, on the part of
The World Bank Group, any judgment
on the legal status of any territory, or
any endorsement or acceptance of
such boundaries.

APRIL 2009

IBRD 36834

CATEGORY 1
CATEGORY 2
CATEGORY 3
CATEGORY 4
NO DATA AVAILABLE

Source: Partnership for Child Development 2008, in Bundy et al. 2009.
Note: Category 1: countries where school feeding is available in most schools, sometimes or always; category 2: countries where school feeding is available in some way and on some scale; category 3: countries where school feeding is available primarily in the most food-insecure regions; category 4: countries where there is no school feeding.

Figure 6.11 Coverage of School Feeding Programs, by Country and Quintile of Pretransfer Income Distribution: Latin America and the Caribbean, 2008–10

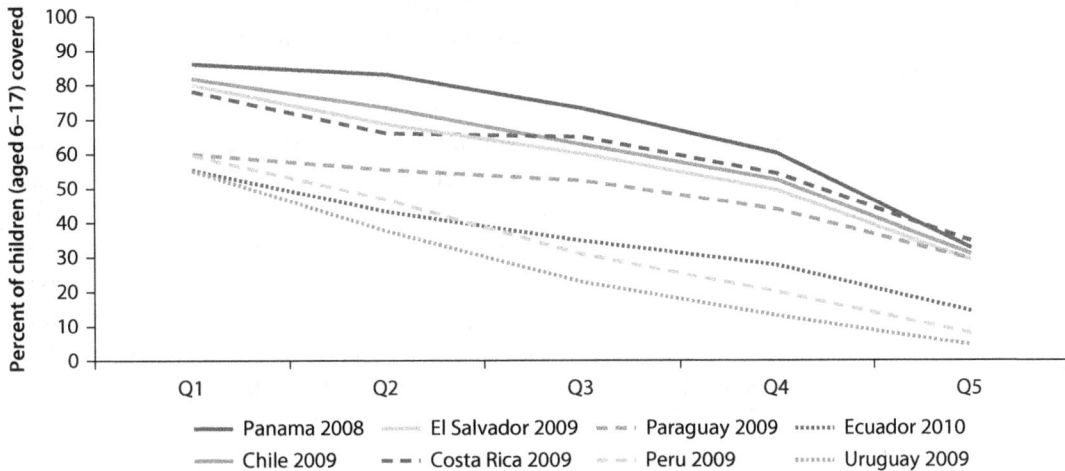

Source: Cerutti et al. 2014.

to 83 percent in 2009, to 80.8 percent in 2010 (World Bank 2011c). These results show that the potential of school feeding programs is limited by size and budget to scale up to good effect. There are, however, some lessons with respect to program mechanics—the operation requires that agreements be signed between agencies and that food be procured on a large scale. Both of these took longer than initially expected and are a reminder that even the scale-up of a working school feeding program is not achievable with the stroke of a pen.

Around the World

Globally, the scale-up of school feeding programs was a common policy response among poor countries when food prices rose precipitously in 2008. A number of low-income countries had school feeding programs but not cash transfer programs, or they felt more able to start one, drawing on the cadre of teachers and parents already involved in the school system. In Africa, for example, school feeding was a vehicle of response in 23 countries (World Bank 2008).

Reflections

How Does It All Add Up?

An active social protection policy both before and during the global financial crisis helped to protect some but not all of those affected by the crisis. In contrast to prior crises, many more countries had social assistance programs that already reached millions of people, and many of the programs were expanded or modified around the time of crisis in ways that helped to mitigate its effects. In several countries, those at the bottom of the income distribution suffered moderate losses in earned income. For them, cash transfers provided at least stability and often an increase in the nonearned income, thereby helping in a nontrivial, though partial, way to offset declines in labor incomes among those who could least afford them. While far from perfect and very uneven across countries, this ability to support the poor during a crisis was a radical improvement over the efforts of decades past.

Indeed, the LAC region went into the crisis well-endowed with CCTs and other programs geared toward the chronic poor. And even though they were not set up for a crisis response, the region did use them. The programs were not designed to respond automatically to shocks, but in many countries they underwent changes around the time of crisis, either explicitly in response to the crisis or because of the fortunate timing of policy developments already under way. Benefits could be increased relatively quickly. Increases in coverage were more difficult to arrange logistically and thus slower to implement. Moreover, they were accomplished with the same poverty-targeting methods designed for the chronic poor. Thus they helped improve coverage among them, but may not have adequately captured the new poor.

Because the pain of the crisis was felt more through reductions in wages than open unemployment, with the biggest reductions among the poorest, the existing poverty-targeting social assistance programs were more useful policy instruments than might have been expected. At the outset of the global financial crisis, there was not a strong presumption that the income losses from it would be concentrated among the poor. There was concern about income losses across the spectrum of welfare and about open unemployment. As descriptive statistics and modeling of counterfactuals in earlier chapters show, much of the pain of the crisis was spread across many workers who continued to work but earned less. In Mexico, for example, an estimated 42 million people earned about 8 percent less, and about 750,000 workers lost their jobs. Thus the ability to supplement the incomes of households that were earning the least at the outset and could ill-afford to suffer the income drop was a very big part of an adequate crisis response. And the simulation results suggest that the expansion of Oportunidades was very effective, halving the income loss among the poorest quintile.

Despite the many attempts to expand or create labor market programs during the crisis, these efforts remained small relative to the need in most countries and absent in others. Today, UI and UISA programs are still missing in Mexico and in most of Central America and the Caribbean. Even where such programs exist, they provide benefits to a minority of the unemployed. "Short-work" schemes were used in only a few countries, and they were small. Public works jobs as a substitute for UI or UISA were used as well in only a handful of countries, and they were generally small relative to need. Employment services were generally nascent, although the crisis boosted interest in some countries.

The joint effect of program responses on households' reported incomes could only be calculated for four countries, and they show a wide range of efficacy (see figure 6.12). In Ecuador, the increased receipt of public transfers offset declines in labor income for those in the poorest two deciles. In Mexico, increases in public transfers were able to offset less than a third of the loss of labor income for

Figure 6.12 Growth Incidence Curve, by Four Income Sources: Ecuador, El Salvador, Mexico, and Uruguay, 2008–09

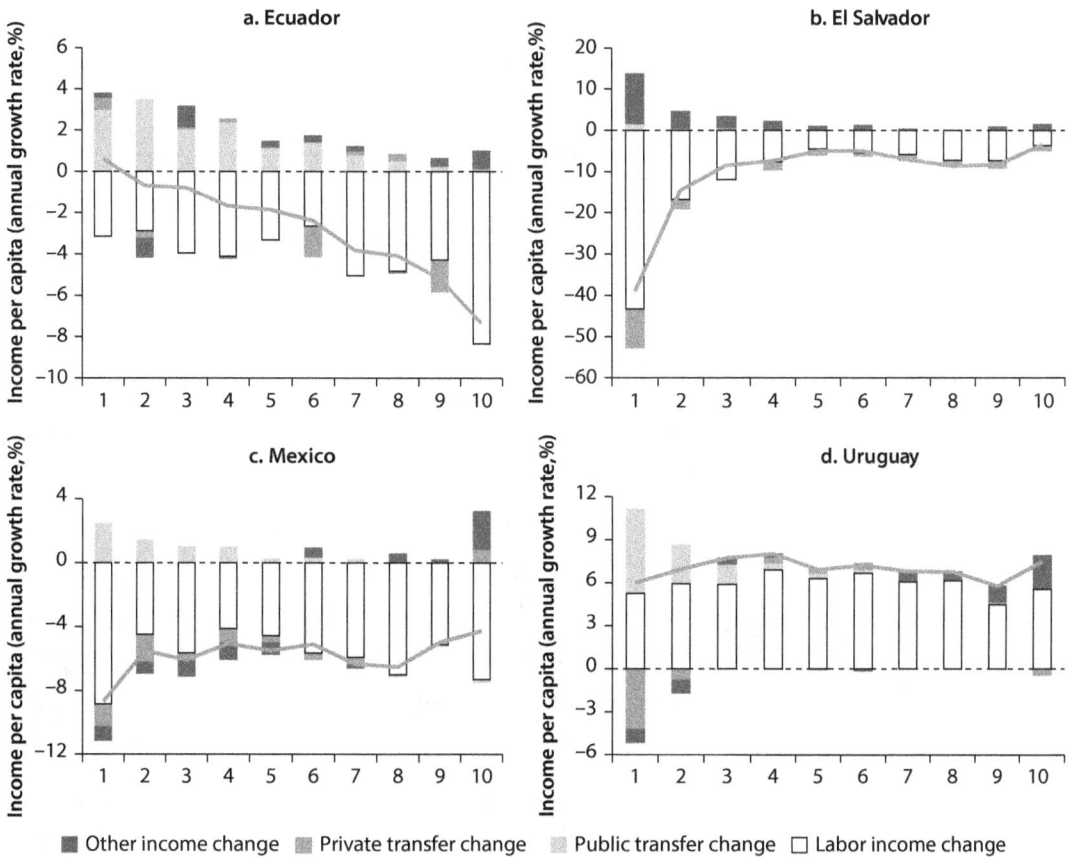

a. Ecuador

b. El Salvador

c. Mexico

d. Uruguay

■ Other income change   ▨ Private transfer change   ░ Public transfer change   ☐ Labor income change

Sources: SEDLAC harmonized data sets and ENIGH, 2008 and 2010.

the poorest two deciles. In El Salvador, the offset offered by the small increases in public transfers was trivial against the much larger income losses by the poorest two deciles. In Uruguay, labor incomes rose, but public assistance increased as well and was well targeted to the poorest two deciles. It more than offset reductions in private transfers and other income.

The increases in expenditures on social assistance and labor programs in 2008 and 2009 were not well correlated with the changes in poverty during the crisis. Table 6.11 compares the size of the shock with the size of the response by presenting the changes in the poverty gap over 2008 and 2009 as a percentage of GDP for the 13 countries traced in chapter 3 and the changes in expenditure on social assistance and labor market programs for the countries for which we have data. Argentina, Brazil, and Chile show large increases in spending and declining poverty. Conversely, where poverty rose, spending was rarely increased enough to fill the increased gap.

Understanding the Poverty Impact of the Global Financial Crisis in Latin America and the Caribbean
http://dx.doi.org/10.1596/978-1-4648-0241-6

Table 6.11 Changes in the Poverty Gap and Social Assistance Spending in Selected Countries as a Percentage of GDP: Latin America and the Caribbean, 2008 and 2009
Percentage points

	PG, moderate			PG, extreme			Change in social assistance and UI/UISA/ public works spending		
	2008	*2009*	*Change*	*2008*	*2009*	*Change*	*2008*	*2009*	*Change*
Argentina	0.572	0.553	−0.019	0.357	0.346	−0.012	1.060	1.443	0.383
Brazil	1.909	1.799	−0.111	1.193	1.124	−0.069	2.653	2.949	0.296
Chile	0.419	0.405	−0.014	0.262	0.253	−0.009	1.371	2.305	0.934
Colombia	2.935	2.709	−0.226	1.834	1.693	−0.141	0.925	0.975	0.050
Costa Rica	0.611	0.691	0.080	0.382	0.432	0.050	—	—	—
Dominican Republic	3.225	2.925	−0.300	2.016	1.828	−0.188	—	—	—
Ecuador	2.287	2.803	0.516	1.429	1.752	0.323	1.508	1.767	0.259
El Salvador	3.930	4.787	0.857	2.456	2.992	0.536	0.446	0.596	0.150
Honduras	9.504	9.022	−0.482	5.940	5.639	−0.301	0.399	0.369	−0.030
Mexico	1.306	1.497	0.192	0.816	0.936	0.120	0.593	0.730	0.137
Paraguay	3.695	3.836	0.141	2.309	2.397	0.088	—	—	—
Peru	2.885	2.670	−0.215	1.803	1.669	−0.134	0.474	0.467	0.007
Uruguay	1.385	1.183	−0.201	0.865	0.740	−0.126	1.124	1.374	0.249

Sources: Poverty gaps: see note; spending data: Cerutti et al. 2014.
Note: The values of the PGs as a share of GDP are calculated based on the PGs presented in chapter 3. They are then multiplied by the corresponding international poverty line (either US$4.00 or $2.50) converted to local currency using the purchasing power parity (PPP) index; multiplied by 365 to convert from an annual figure; multiplied by the number of poor (e.g., the headcount times the population); divided by GDP in local currency units (LCUs); — = not available.

Impact evaluations of policy responses to the crisis are not possible in most cases, and so inferences must rely on the degree to which design and implementation seem to comply with good practices. Across such a large swath of programming, there will, of course, be variation, and it is difficult to assemble in a literature review a good sense of the on-the-ground quality of implementation. It is possible to say that the programming responses described in this chapter largely incorporated many if not all the sensible design features. A number of the programs were built on a solid institutional basis, and indeed many of the CCT programs had strong prior records of operational processes and impacts on household welfare. The UI programs have had fewer evaluations, but they had been operating on similar scales for a number of years and so should not have met undue challenges of operational process. A minority of the programs reviewed were new and so faced the inevitable start-up challenges, or met with significant capacity constraints, but even these may act as a base for future program development.

Where Does the Region Go from Here?

The detailed micro modeling in chapter 5 showed that crisis-induced unemployment represents a complex puzzle for social policy analysts. During the global financial crisis, households with unemployed workers suffered significant income losses, enough to prompt some to urge a social policy response. The macro-micro modeling for Mexico suggested that income losses were significant for job losers—on the order of 24 percent for those households with skilled workers who lost their jobs and 37 percent for those with unskilled workers—enough to tumble them down the income distribution. The simulations also suggest that two-thirds of losses were concentrated among those with more years of education and who were younger. Job losses were spread across the income distribution, but they peaked in the sixth decile for unskilled workers and the eighth decile for skilled workers.

No single program will solve the full problem of income support for the unemployed, but a carefully devised set of programs may begin to weave a safety net that can lessen the shocks to some if not all households:

- Unemployment insurance can support those in the formal sector. In Mexico, the crisis propagated in significant part through the manufactured tradable sector, which is relatively formal, although the coverage of unemployment insurance will always be limited by the extent of the informal sector, which, overall, constituted 50 percent of the Mexican workforce in 2008.
- UISAs have the potential, though not a strong track record, of voluntarily including workers from the informal sector. Affiliating workers in the middle or top of the income spectrum and among the more educated may be somewhat easier than affiliating the poorer or less educated workers. In Mexico, it was possibly easier to affiliate groups that were hit the hardest by the crisis.
- Employment in labor-intensive public works jobs is another option for income support for the unemployed. This approach has a track record of assisting those at the lower end of the earning and skills spectrum, often informal workers—the people least likely to benefit from UI or UISA, making public works a good complement to UI and UISA programs.

The crisis outlined vividly the differences in the programs addressing chronic poverty, promoting human capital accumulation, and geared toward providing equality of opportunity versus risk management. The CCTs, designed to provide equality of opportunity, could not (and were not meant to) fully match the needs in the crisis. Those who lost jobs may not have been poor before the crisis and thus would not have been affiliated with a chronic poverty reduction program. Even if the job loss reduced their income so that they then qualified for the poverty-targeting programs, they would have lost a full wage earner's contribution to welfare, which may have been all their income. Thus the benefit level of existing CCTs that are designed to top up earned income may not have been sufficient for even a minimum consumption basket, much less to maintain the prior standard of living. Similarly, for the larger number of people who maintained employment but lost wages, only a portion were poor enough, or had children of the right ages, or lived in the areas of the countries covered to be assisted by the program. And where the CCT programs were expanded for the crisis, it is not clear whether they should or will return to their prior shape or size. In some cases, governments used the prompt of the crisis to create or expand programs that were missing or too small, even when viewed through the lens of long-run policy in a stable or growing economy. However, some of the programs have become quite large, and questions have arisen about whether they have become too large. Crisis-related expansion intensifies those questions.

Without diminishing the focus on equality of opportunity that makes so much sense in a region with such historic and marked inequality, some of the changes that are being discussed in the design of some elements of the CCT programs would enable them to be better able to respond in crisis. First, operating programs nationally, with funding levels that correspond to the number of families deemed eligible by the chosen poverty criteria, is obviously a fundamental issue to support in both stable and crisis times. A second step would be to provide income to all families that meet the poverty criteria irrespective of the presence of children—a few countries have already taken this step. This would enable these programs to serve a fuller social assistance or last-resort role. On-demand enrollment is an important element to ensure that new families or families affected by a negative shock (whether idiosyncratic or systemic) can access the programs. On demand implies either guaranteed funding (e.g., an entitlement rather than rationed budget) or a fairly regular flow of exits through recertification or children aging out of benefits. It also implies a stable local administrative apparatus, something found in some but not all CCT programs presently. Some programs might move toward quantifying income within or, instead of using proxy means tests, toward making the entrance criteria more sensitive to short-term changes in welfare. This will be more feasible in more formal economies, and the information technology revolution is easing constraints on means testing by making it more feasible to cross-check more kinds of records.

The LAC region is beginning to and should press ahead in expanding coverage and improving the performance of cost-effective active labor market programs. These programs can improve productivity and equity and have a place in both long-run and crisis agendas. Public employment services are gaining momentum, supported by the evaluation evidence that they can be cost-effective and serve a region-wide goal of moving households from CCTs into greater independence. Youth-focused programs have been rising on the policy agenda secularly because of chronically high youth unemployment rates, demographic change swelling the youth cohort in some countries, and concern that idleness can contribute to more negative social behavior. Because youth unemployment rates rose even more than other employment rates during the crisis, and because youth training and placement programs tend to have higher impacts than other training programs, these programs would seem particularly appropriate for priority among active labor market policies for future development.

Improvements in income support for the unemployed via expansion of UI, UISA, and public works programs are also warranted. UI and UISA programs will not be a cure-all—they will suffer from incomplete coverage because of informality—but even the partial coverage of sensible programs is better than none. Partial coverage would assist a portion of the population directly, reducing the welfare and human capital costs of a crisis, and it is an instrument that complements the others, providing significant replacement income to population strata not reached through tightly targeted poverty programs. More extensive use of public works programs is also an obvious complement. There is ample experience in the world and a good deal in the LAC region to show that the programs can be helpful in rounding out the policy package. Both UI, UISA, and public works programs can be highly countercyclical, reducing their fiscal burden automatically when the crisis eases in a way that social assistance programming does not. Moreover, UI and UISA can be largely self-financing over the medium run. Indirectly, more extensive and successful programs for income support for the unemployed may reduce political pressure to load onto CCT programs the burden of dealing with labor shocks. This would allow the CCTs and other social assistance programs to focus on their core mission of mitigating chronic poverty and fostering equality of opportunity. It is important, especially in countries where social assistance programming is reaching high levels of coverage and benefits, to contain pressures for further expansion, and especially to handle roles for which CCT programs are poorly suited.

Benefits may arise from strengthening the coherence and linkages within the different parts of the social protection system. At the highest level, this will involve thinking about the mix of policies to better balance the coverage among groups and risks—for example, addressing chronic poverty and inequality versus the shorter-term risks to income (both cyclical and idiosyncratic), or, within the risk of unemployment, the relative roles of severance pay, UI, UISA, and public works. On a lower level, this will entail better linkage of income support and active labor market policies. The region is increasingly experimenting with such linkages as a way to provide a ladder out of poverty. The linkages can also be important in balancing income support with potential labor disincentives. For many years, governments managed labor disincentives by providing stingy benefits, and mostly to groups not expected to work such as children, the elderly, or the disabled. Activation or graduation policies, if successful, could make it feasible to provide more adequate income support and to working families as well.

These improvements in social protection will be sought within a tighter fiscal situation than the one that underlay the big secular increase in the first part of the 2000s. Growth was unusually rapid during the period, which created space for additional fiscal expenditure. Much more moderate growth is forecasted for coming years, and because of the need to reduce crisis-related deficits and debt, money for social protection will be harder to find. Thus the social protection agenda is not just about improving coverage, but increasing impact and cost-effectiveness.

A final reflection is that better data are needed to guide policy. The household survey data in most countries do not allow for frequent, reliable estimates of the coverage or distribution of benefits from many, even flagship, social protection programs. Spending on social protection programs is spread throughout the budgets of many agencies across government and not aggregated automatically or regularly. Thus it is difficult for policy makers or their advisers to have a comprehensive view of efforts or the trade-offs among them. Nor are administrative data

Understanding the Poverty Impact of the Global Financial Crisis in Latin America and the Caribbean
http://dx.doi.org/10.1596/978-1-4648-0241-6

on processes such as applications for social assistance or social insurance collected or reported in ways that proxy changes in welfare at the household level. All of these systems need to be built. Such efforts will garner few headlines, but they are essential for more effective public expenditure in defense of social welfare.

Notes

1. The 10 countries are Argentina, Brazil, Chile, Colombia, Ecuador, El Salvador, Honduras, Mexico, Peru, and Uruguay.

2. Several countries also have significant energy subsidies that are not included in the totals reported here. The average for the region is 0.6 percent of GDP; Bolivia and Ecuador spent about 5 percent of GDP on subsidies in 2011 (IMF n.d.).

3. http://www.oecd-ilibrary.org/.

4. Labor training or retraining may also be pertinent, but our information base does not allow us to distinguish well enough between the bulk of training carried out for those employed and as part of ongoing policy with changes in programs and programming meant especially for those who lost work because of the crisis.

5. The income measure refers to the last month; the receipt of unemployment benefits refers to any period in the preceding year.

6. Child allowances in the LAC region began as part of the contributory social insurance systems with the attendant limitations on coverage, but Argentina, Chile, and Uruguay put in place significant tax-funded noncontributory programs to complement coverage. Bono de Desarrollo Humano, founded in 1981, is the longest running. It is proxy means-tested, with the eligibility threshold set to include children from the poorest 40 percent of the population. Because of budget rationing, however, the program was not fully funded as an entitlement program until 2007, when coverage increased by about 50 percent, from 950,000 beneficiaries in 2007 to 1.4 million by the end of 2009. In 2009 Argentina expanded its program of child benefits to include the children of workers in the informal economy and of unemployed persons. The new Asignación Universal por Hijo (AUH, Universal Child Allowance) is tax-financed rather than contributory and complements the Asignaciones Familiares Contributivas (AFC, Contributory Family Allowance) that has developed since the 1950s. It benefits almost 5.4 million people, and the number of family allowance beneficiaries is expected to rise from 6.7 million to 11.3 million, the cost of which will represent approximately 1.5 percent of GDP (Rofman and Oliveri 2010). In Uruguay, two family allowance schemes had coexisted: one for salaried workers in the formal economy (reformed in 1980) and one for households with lower incomes, regardless of the type of employment (introduced in 1999 and modified in 2004). In 2008 the latter was replaced by the Nuevo Régimen de Asignaciones Familiares (NRAF, New Family Allowances Scheme). Coverage increased by 78 percent between 1999 and 2008 (Bertranou and Maurizio 2011). Some of these programs are "weakly" conditioned—for example, Argentina stipulates that 10 percent of its benefits depend on the use of education services, and Chile requires health visits for children younger than six years and school enrollment for older children, but it does not monitor attendance.

7. In fact, Mexican policy provided even more of a response, with the expansion of the PAL program by an additional 550,000 households in 2009–10 (from 129,803 in 2008 to 677,207 in 2010). The benefits are harmonized with Oportunidades's basic nutritional and health supports, but do not include the education-based benefits.

8. Transfers for the very poor decile accounted for about 40 percent of recipient household income in 2008. In 2010, as households' autonomous incomes fell and transfers rose, the share was closer to 50 percent—levels high enough to cause concern about labor market incentives.

9. According to Rofman, Apella, and Vezza (2013), these countries were Bolivia, Brazil, Chile, Peru, and Uruguay in 2008; El Salvador and Panama in 2009; and Paraguay and Trinidad and Tobago in 2010.

10. Belize, Jamaica and Trinidad and Tobago had programs in this tradition as well, but they have reformed them, replacing informal means tests with more systematically administered proxy means tests and adding conditionalities.

11. http://www.bcn.cl/de-que-se-habla/bono-solidario-marzo-2009.

12. Social Cabinet, November 2011.

13. Ecuador's overarching program to offer support to people with disabilities.

14. The Solidarity Mission "Manuela Espejo" program has provided disabled people with technical aides (wheelchairs, walkers, canes, anti-bedsore mattresses, visual aids, and kits) since July 2009.

15. The Joaquin Gallegos Lara Benefit provides US$240 a month through a caregiver to a person with a severe disability or a catastrophic illness and to children under age 14 living with HIV/AIDS.

References

Adelman, S. W., D. O. Gilligan, and K. Lehrer. 2008. "How Effective Are Food for Education Programs? A Critical Assessment of the Evidence from Developing Countries." *Food Policy Review* (9).

Almedia, Rita, Juliana Arbelaez, Maddalena Honorati, Arvo Kuddo, Tanja Lohmann, Mirey Ovadiya, Lucian Pop, Maria Laura Sanchez Puerta, and Michael Weber. 2012. "Improving Access to Jobs and Earnings Opportunities." Social Protection Discussion Paper 1204, World Bank, Washington, DC.

Baez, J., X. Del Carpio, and T. Nguyen. 2010. "A Synthesis of Impact Evaluations of Public Works Projects." Memo, World Bank, Washington, DC.

Berg, J. 2009. "Brasil: El seguro de desempleo." Global Job Crisis Observatory, International Labour Organization, Geneva.

Bernstein, S., E. Fajnzylber, and P. Gana. 2012. "The New Chilean Unemployment Insurance System: Combining Individual Accounts and Redistribution in an Emerging Economy." In *Reforming Severance Pay: An International Perspective*, edited by R. Holzmann and M. Vodopivec. Washington, DC: World Bank.

Bertranou, F., and R. Maurizio. 2011. "The Role of Labour Market and Social Protection in Reducing Inequality and Eradicating Poverty in Latin America." International Labour Organization, Universidad Nacional de General Sarmiento.

Bertranou, F., and X. Mazorra. 2009. "Argentina: Preventing of Lay-offs and Retaining Workers in Employment." Notes on the Crisis, International Labour Organization, Geneva.

Betcherman, G., K. Olivas, and A. Dar. 2004. "Impacts of Active Labor Market Programs: New Evidence from Evaluations with Particular Attention to Developing and Transition Countries." Social Protection Discussion Paper 0402, World Bank, Washington, DC.

Betcherman, G., G. Ragnar, T. Jones, C. Raif, and J. Benus. n.d. "Policy Note on Turkey's Active Labor Market Programs." World Bank, Washington, DC.

Brown, A. J. G., and J. Koettl. 2012. "Active Labor Market Programs: Employment Gain or Fiscal Drain?" Discussion Paper 6880, Institute for the Study of Labor (IZA), Bonn.

Bundy, D., C. Burbano, M. Grosh, A. Gelli, M. Jukes, and L. Drake. 2009. *Rethinking School Feeding: Social Safety Nets, Child Development, and the Education Sector.* Washington, DC: World Bank.

Casanova, F. 2009a. "Uruguay: Programme for Job Preservation by Reducing Working Hours, Combined with Training." Notes on the Crisis, International Labour Organization, Geneva.

———. 2009b. "Uruguay: Recent Reforms to Unemployment Insurance." Notes on the Crisis, International Labour Organization, Geneva.

CEPAL (Comité de Economia y Política de América Latina). 2010. "La Reaccion de los gobiernos de las Américas frente a la crisis internacional: una presentación sentética de las medidas de política anunciadas hasta el 31 de diciembre de 2009." División de Desarrollo Económico, CEPAL, Santiago.

Cerutti, P., A. Fruttero, M. Grosh, S. Kostenbaum, M. L. Oliveri, C. Rodriguez-Alas, and V. Strokova. 2014. *Social Assistance and Labor Market Programs in Latin America: Methodology and Key Findings from the Social Protection Database.* Social Protection and Labor Discussion Paper Series. Washington, DC: World Bank.

Chacaltana, J. 2009. "Mercados de trabajo y califacaciones: Diganóstico y políticas." Peru Country Office, World Bank, Lima.

CONEVAL (Consejo Nacional de Evaluacion de la Politica de Desarrollo Social). n.d. "Programa de Empleo Temporal (PET): Informe de Evaluacion Especifica de Desempeno 2009–10." Mexico.

de Brauw, A., and E. Murrugarra. 2011. *How CCTs Help Sustain Human Capital during Crises: Evidence from Red Solidaria in El Salvador during the Food Price Crisis.* World Bank, Washington, DC.

de Ferranti, David, Guillermo E. Perry, Indermit S. Gill, Luis Serven, Francisco H. G. Ferreira, Nadeem Ilahi, William F. Maloney, and Martin Rama. 2000. *Securing Our Future in a Global Economy.* Washington, DC: World Bank.

DIPRES (Direccion de Presupuesto). 2012. "Programas de Empleo Con Apoyo Fiscal, Evolucion 2007–2012." Gobierno de Chile, Santiago.

Ferrer, A. M., and C. Ridell. 2012. "Unemployment Insurance Savings Accounts in Latin America: Overview and Assessment." In *Reforming Severance Pay: An International Perspective,* edited by R. Holzmann and M. Vodopivec. World Bank, Washington, DC.

FISDL (Fondo de Inversion Social para el Desarrollo Local). 2011. "Programa Temporal de Apoyo al Ingreso." Powerpoint presentation, World Bank, Washington, DC, November 21.

Fiszbein, A., N. R. Schady, F. H. G. Ferreira, M. E. Grosh, N. Keleher, P. Olinto, and E. Skoufias. 2009. "Conditional Cash Transfers: Reducing Present and Future Poverty." Policy Research Report, World Bank, Washington, DC.

Freije-Rodriguez, S., G. Lopez-Acevedo, and E. Rodriguez-Oreggia. 2011. "Effects of the 2008–09 Economic Crisis on Labor Markets in Mexico." Policy Research Working Paper 5840, World Bank, Washington, DC.

Freije-Rodriguez, S., and E. Murrugarra. 2009. "Labor Markets and the Crisis in Latin America and the Caribbean (A Preliminary Review for Selected Countries)." Social Protection and Poverty and Gender Units, Latin America and the Caribbean Region, World Bank, Washington, DC.

Galhardi, R. 2009. "Mexico: Job Preservation Programme." Notes on the Crisis, International Labour Organization, Geneva.

Gitter, S. R., J. Manley, and B. Barham. 2011. "The Coffee Crisis, Early Childhood Development, and Conditional Cash Transfers." Working Paper Series IDB-WP-245, Inter-American Development Bank, Washington, DC.

Grosh, M., C. del Ninno, E. Tesliuc, and A. Ouerghi. 2008. *For Protection and Promotion: The Design and Implementation of Effective Safety Nets.* Washington, DC: World Bank.

Heredia, B. 2012. "Active Labor Market Policies in Mexico 2000–2011: Assessment and Recommendations." Human Development Department, World Bank, Washington, DC.

Holzmann, R., Y. Pouget, M. Vodopivec, and M. Weber. 2012. "Severance Pay Programs around the World: History, Rationale, Status and Reform." In *Reforming Severance Pay: An International Perspective*, edited by Robert Holzmann and Milan Vodopivec. Washington, DC: World Bank.

Holzmann, R., and M. Vodopivec. 2012. *Reforming Severance Pay: An International Perspective.* Washington, DC: World Bank.

ILO (International Labour Organization). 2009. "Chile: Fiscal Policy and Employment: The Contingency Programme against Unemployment." Notes on the Crisis, ILO, Geneva.

————. 2010. "Mexico: Employment Policies to Assist Vulnerable Groups and the Recently Unemployed." G-20 Country Policy Brief, G-20 Meeting of Labour and Employment Ministers. Paris, September 26–27.

————. 2011. "Argentina: Policy Initiatives to Boost Formal Employment Growth." G-20 Country Policy Brief, G-20 Meeting of Labour and Employment Ministers, Paris, September 26–27.

ILO/World Bank. 2012. *Inventory of Policy Responses to the Financial and Economic Crisis.* Joint Synthesis Report, World Bank, Washington, DC.

IMF (International Monetary Fund). n.d. *Recent Developments in Fuel Pricing and Fiscal Implications: Inputs for G-20 Energy and Commodity Markets Working Group.* Washington, DC.

Isik-Demelik, A. 2012. "Do Social Benefits Respond to Crises? Evidence from Europe and Central Asia during the Global Financial Crisis." Social Protection and Labor Discussion Paper 1219, World Bank, Washington, DC.

Jaramillo, M., J. Baanante, and T. Sanz. 2009. "Informe Final Presupuesto Evaluado, Construyendo a Perú." Ministerio de Economia y Finanzas, Lima.

Jaramillo, M., and J. Saavedra. 2005. "Severance Pay Programs in Latin America." *Empirica* 32: 275–307.

Kuddo, A. 2012. "Public Employment Services and Activation Policies." Social Protection Discussion Paper 1215, World Bank, Washington, DC.

Marini, A., and E. Seguin. 2012. "Hacia una red de protección social más efectiva y coherente en el Perú." In *Perú en el umbral de una nueva era Lecciones y desafíos para consolidar el crecimiento económico y un desarrollo más incluyente*, edited by S. G. Goldmark, C. F. Jaramillo, and C. Silva-Jáuregui. Lima: World Bank.

Ministerio de Desarrollo Social de Uruguay. 2012. *Evaluación, Seguimiento y Monitoreo de Programas y Políticas Sociales*. Montevideo.

Ministerio de Justicia y Trabajo, Paraguay. 2011. "ÑAMBA'APO PARAGUAY Programa de Empleo Temporal." Memo, Asuncion.

Ministry of Rural Development and Government of India. 2010. *Mahatma Gandhi National Rural Employment Guarantee Act 2005*. Delhi.

Murillo, M. V., L. Ronconi, and A. Schrank. 2011. "Latin American Labor Reforms: Evaluating Risk and Security." *Labor Reforms*.

Murrugarra, E. 2011. "Aging, Poverty and Social Protection in Colombia: Evidence and Policy Options." Social Protection, Latin America and the Caribbean, World Bank, Washington, DC.

Ndahi, H. 2009. "The Bahamas National Training Programme." Notes on the Crisis, International Labour Organization, Geneva.

OECD (Organisation for Economic Co-operation and Development). 2009. "Towards More Equal Job Opportunities." In *OECD Reviews of Labour Market and Social Policies*. Chile: OECD.

———. 2010. "Moving Beyond the Jobs Crisis." In *Employment Outlook 2010: Moving Beyond the Jobs Crisis*. Paris: OECD.

———. 2011. "Employment Policies to Assist Vulnerable Groups and the Recently Unemployed." G-20 Meeting of Labour and Employment Ministers, Paris, September 26–27.

———. 2012. "Reducing Poverty in Chile: Cash Transfers and Better Jobs." In *OECD Economic Surveys: Chile 2012*. Paris: OECD.

Pages, C., G. Pierre, and S. Scarpetta. 2009. *Job Creation in Latin America: Recent Trends and Policy Challenges*. Washington, DC: World Bank.

Rangel, F. G. 2009. "Programa de Apoyo Alimentario 2009: Evaluaciones, Resultados y Presupuesto 2010." Centro de Estudio para el Desarrollo Rural Sustentable y la Soberania Alimentaria, Mexico.

Reinecke, G. 2005. "Income Protection through Direct Employment Programmes: Recent Concepts and Examples from Latin America." *International Social Security Review* (58): 2–3.

Reyes, G., J. C. von Ours, and M. Vodopivec. 2012. "Reemployment Incentives under the Chilean Hybrid Unemployment Benefit Program." In *Reforming Severance Pay: An International Perspective*, edited by R. Holzmann and M. Vodopivec. Washington, DC: World Bank.

Robalino, D., D. Newhouse, and F. Rother. 2014. "Labor and Social Protection Policies during the Crisis and Recovery." In *Labor Markets in Developing Countries during the Great Recession: Impacts and Policy Responses*, edited by A. Banerji, D. Newhouse, D. Robalino, and P. Paci. Washington, DC: World Bank.

Rofman, R., I. Apella, and E. Vezza. 2013. *Más Allá de las Pensiones Contributivas en America Latina: Expandiendo la Protección de Ingresos de los Adultos Mayores*. Washington, DC: World Bank.

Rofman, R., and M. L. Oliveri. 2010. "Las Políticas de Protección social y su impacto en la distribución del Ingreso en Argentina." *Serie de Documentos de Trabajo sobre Políticas Sociales* 6, Human Development Department, Latin America and the Caribbean Region, World Bank, Washington, DC.

————. 2012. "La Cobertura de los Sistemas Provisionales en América Latina: Conceptos e Indicadores." *Serie de Documentos de Trabajo sobre Políticas Sociales* 7, Human Development Department, Latin America and the Caribbean Region, World Bank, Washington, DC.

Scott, J. 2009. "Mexico's Programa de Empleo Temporal: Evaluation and Agenda for Reform." Centro de Investigacion y Docencia Economicas, Mexico.

Secretaria de Trabajo y Fomento al Empleo. n.d. "Aniversario Programa Seguro de Desempleo del Distrito Federal." Ciudad de Mexico.

SHCP (Secretaria de Hacienda y Credito Publico). 2010. *Weekly Report.* SHCP, Mexico City, March 22–26.

Subbarao, K., C. del Ninno, C. Andrews, and C. Rodríguez-Alas. 2012. "Public Works Programs as a Safety Net: Design, Evidence and Implementation." World Bank, Washington, DC.

Trucco, P., and D. Tussie. 2010. "Learning from Past Battles in Argentina? The Role of REPRO in the Prevention of Crisis-Induced Layoffs." Latin American Trade Network.

Vodopevic, M. 2004. *Income Support Systems for the Unemployed: Issues and Option.* Washington, DC: World Bank.

Vroman, W., and V. Brusentsev. 2009. "Unemployment Compensation in a Worldwide Recession." Urban Institute, Washington, DC.

Williams, A., T. Cheston, A. Coudouel, and L. Subran. 2013. "Tailoring Social Protection to Small Island Developing States: Lessons Learned from the Caribbean." Social Protection and Labor Discussion Paper 1301, World Bank, Washington, DC.

World Bank. 2000. *Implementation Completion Report: Argentina: Second Social Protection Project.* Report 19553, World Bank, Washington, DC.

————. 2008. *Double Jeopardy: Responding to High Food and Fuel Prices.* Paper presented to the G8 Hokkaido-Toyako Summit, Washington, DC, July 7–9.

————. 2009a. *Grenada Safety Net Assessment.* Social Protection and Labour, Latin America and the Caribbean Region, World Bank, Washington, DC.

————. 2009b. "Programa Uruguay Trabaja Plan de Equidad." Conference paper, November.

————. 2009c. *Project Appraisal Document for El Salvador: Income Support and Employability Project.* Report 50885-SV, Washington, DC.

————. 2009d. *St. Kitts Safety Net Assessment.* Social Protection and Labour, Latin America and the Caribbean Region, World Bank, Washington, DC.

————. 2009e. *St. Lucia Safety Net Assessment.* Social Protection and Labour, Latin America and the Caribbean Region, World Bank, Washington, DC.

————. 2009f. *St. Vincent and the Grenadines Safety Net Assessment.* Social Protection and Labour, Latin America and the Caribbean Region, World Bank, Washington, DC.

————. 2010a. *Heads of Household Transition Project: Implementation Completion and Results Report.* Report ICR00001395, Washington, DC.

————. 2010b. *Opening the Door to Good Quality Jobs: The Role of Human Capital Investment and Social Protection Policies for Costa Rica.* Report No. 54925-CR, Report for Human Development Department, Latin America and the Caribbean Region, Washington, DC.

———. 2010c. *Restructuring Paper on a Proposed Project Restructuring of Dominican Republic Youth Development Project Loan.* Report 53981-DO, Report for Human Development Department, Latin America and the Caribbean Region, Washington, DC.

———. 2011a. *Antigua and Barbuda.* Social Protection Assessment, Social Protection and Labour, Latin America and the Caribbean Region, Washington, DC.

———. 2011b. *Evidence and Lessons Learned from Impact Evaluations on Social Safety Nets.* Independent Evaluation Group, Washington, DC.

———. 2011c. *Nicaragua: Implementation Completion Report, Trust Fund Grant (TF093698) for Emergency Food Price Response Project.* Report ICR00001826, Washington, DC.

———. 2011d. "Temporary Employment Programs: International Evidence and Mexico's Experience during the 2009–2010 Crisis (PART I)." Memo, Poverty, Gender and Equity Group, Latin America and the Caribbean Region, Washington, DC.

———. 2012a. *Opening the Doors to Good Quality Jobs: The Role of Human Capital Investment and Social Protection Policies for El Salvador.* Report for Human Development Department, Latin America and the Caribbean Region, Washington, DC.

———. 2012b. *Opening the Door to Good Quality Jobs: The Role of Human Capital Investment and Social Protection Policies for Honduras.* Report for Human Development Department, Latin America and the Caribbean Region, Washington, DC.

———. 2012c. *Philippines' Conditional Cash Transfer Program Impact Evaluation 2012: Findings from the Randomized Control Trials.* Manila.

Zhang, Y., N. Thelen, and A. Rao. 2010. "Social Protection in Fiscal Stimulus Packages: Some Evidence." A United Nations Development Programme/Office of Development Studies Working Paper.

Environmental Benefits Statement

The World Bank Group is committed to reducing its environmental footprint. In support of this commitment, the Publishing and Knowledge Division leverages electronic publishing options and print-on-demand technology, which is located in regional hubs worldwide. Together, these initiatives enable print runs to be lowered and shipping distances decreased, resulting in reduced paper consumption, chemical use, greenhouse gas emissions, and waste.

The Publishing and Knowledge Division follows the recommended standards for paper use set by the Green Press Initiative. Whenever possible, books are printed on 50 percent to 100 percent postconsumer recycled paper, and at least 50 percent of the fiber in our book paper is either unbleached or bleached using Totally Chlorine Free (TCF), Processed Chlorine Free (PCF), or Enhanced Elemental Chlorine Free (EECF) processes.

More information about the Bank's environmental philosophy can be found at http://crinfo.worldbank.org/wbcrinfo/node/4.

green press
INITIATIVE

www.ingramcontent.com/pod-product-compliance
Lightning Source LLC
Chambersburg PA
CBHW080415270326
41929CB00018B/3030